SAINTS AND SINNERS

SAINTS AND SINNERS

Why Some Countries Grow Rich, and Others Don't

Ali Mahmood

HarperCollins *Publishers* India

First published in India in 2013 by
HarperCollins *Publishers* India

Copyright © Ali Mahmood 2013

ISBN: 978-93-5029-405-5

2 4 6 8 10 9 7 5 3 1

Ali Mahmood asserts the moral right to be identified as
the author of this work.

The views and opinions expressed in this book are the author's own
and the facts are as reported by him, and the publishers are not in any way
liable for the same.

HarperCollins *Publishers*
A-53, Sector 57, Noida, Uttar Pradesh 201301, India
77-85 Fulham Palace Road, London W6 8JB, United Kingdom
Hazelton Lanes, 55 Avenue Road, Suite 2900, Toronto, Ontario M5R 3L2
and 1995 Markham Road, Scarborough, Ontario M1B 5M8, Canada
25 Ryde Road, Pymble, Sydney, NSW 2073, Australia
31 View Road, Glenfield, Auckland 10, New Zealand
10 East 53rd Street, New York NY 10022, USA

Typeset in 13/16 Linden Hill Regular at
SÜRYA

Printed and bound at
Thomson Press (India) Ltd

To Shaukat and Billo

With thanks to Ali, Ghalib, Yahia and Zia—
good friends in bad times

Contents

Introduction   1

SECTION ONE: CONFLICT

1. North Africa, Egypt and Algeria   13
2. Liberia and Sierra Leone: Lords of War   18
3. Angola: Oil Versus Diamonds   23
4. Ethiopia and Eritrea: A Very Long War   26
5. Israel: Hero or Villian?   32
6. Iraq: Saddam's Three Wars   39
7. The Yugoslav Wars: Europe's Own Horror Story   51
8. South Asia: A Nuclear Conflict Zone   60

SECTION TWO: CORRUPTION

9. Corruption in Iraq: Saddam, America and Democracy   91
10. Russia: The Kremlin, the Oligarchs and the Mafia   101
11. Saints and Sinners in Africa   122
12. Suharto: The Twenty-billion Dollar man   135
13. China Gets Tough on Crooks   140
14. India: Everybody Steals, Nobody Gets Caught   147

SECTION THREE: DEMOCRACY

15. Islamic Democracy   177

SECTION FOUR: FOUR SKETCHES OF DEMOCRACY

16. South Africa: Mandela and After   191
17. Iran: Ayatollahs in Command   200
18. Thailand: The King, Thaksin and General Prem   212
19. India: The World's Biggest Democracy   224

SECTION FIVE: SUPERPOWERS DO MATTER

SECTION SIX: GROWING RICH

20. Singapore: No Corruption, No Democracy   259
21. South Korea: General Park and the Chaebols   268
22. China: A Cat That Catches the Mice   281
23. Dubai: Hoping for a Comeback   301
24. Israel: Successful Socialism, Successful Capitalism   315
25. Botswana's Diamonds: A Blessing, Not a Curse   327
26. Malaysia Does It 'My Way'   335
27. India: A Story of Accidents   351
28. Pakistan: Failed or Failing?   365
    Conclusion: Leaders Make the Difference   382
    A Note on Sources   392
    Bibliography   393
    Websites Accessed   401
    Index   421

Introduction

When Gunnar Myrdal wrote his *Asian Drama: An Enquiry into the Poverty of Nations* in 1968, shaking off the shackles of poverty seemed an almost impossible task. Since then many countries that were formerly poor have grown relatively rich. Rising standards of living and growing economies have resulted both from good governance and from natural resource wealth, particularly oil.

But why have some countries prospered while the others have been left behind? This book looks at the key factors that have enabled some countries to grow rich while others remain poor. The two most deadly traps for developing countries are conflict and corruption. Countries that fall victim to conflict are unlikely to see prosperity and growth—the only exception to this has been Israel, where exceptional growth has taken place in the midst of never-ending conflict. After conflict, corruption has been the most important cause of failure in developing nations. But where peace, stability and clean government are essential to growth and prosperity, democracy is not. Opinion is divided as to whether democracy helps or hinders development, but there is no denying that some of the most

1

successful states across the world have not been democratic—
but then, neither were those countries that suffered great
disasters under greedy and wicked dictators. A very important
factor is the relationship with superpowers—in our time,
basically the US. The US can make you or break you, not just
by war but also because of its overwhelming economic power.
There are many reasons for spectacular success—two that
readily spring to mind are oil and diamonds; but even fabulous
natural resource wealth is not enough. The essentials for success
in creating prosperity are good governance and leadership—
and very often they are the two sides of the same coin.

This book basically looks at the struggles of developing
nations in Asia and Africa—why some have made a mess at the
cost of great human suffering, and how some have reduced or
even eradicated poverty; it covers current affairs, recent history,
political economy and development. Perhaps, because I come
from a poor country, Pakistan, I wanted to know what road
could lead a poor country out of poverty, out of misery. In 1972,
I spent a year in jail, much of it in solitary confinement; my
morning discipline was reading Gunnar Myrdal's book. Since
that time, I have continued looking for the answer to that
question.

This book is aimed at three types of readers; first,
professionals who are concerned with the region, including
administrators, bankers, politicians and others who need to
understand poverty, development and the likelihood of moving
from one to the other; second, students who want to understand
the story of success and failure in the region; and third, those
who are just curious about the world they live in, and have the

time to read a simple book about it. The book targets the young who are eager to know. The decision to write *Saints and Sinners* was made one evening when a young girl who worked as an anchor on my TV channel came to my apartment and asked me about a painting there, 'Who is this man?' I replied it was Mao Zedong. 'Who is he?' she asked. I told her he was Chairman Mao, the historic leader of China. To my astonishment, she had never heard of him, despite the fact that she was active in the media, and was a presenter of a daily chat show. She was an avid reader of the local newspapers, but the chairman had long slipped from their front pages. To be fair to the girl, she was equally amazed by my ignorance when she talked of Tupac Shakur.

My opinions have been fashioned by books; I have never been a keen reader of newspapers and agree with the statement of Thomas Jefferson that 'If you don't read the newspapers you are uninformed. If you do read the paper, you are misinformed.' Many books have thrilled me; an equal number have bored me. But some books have been crucial to the way I look at the world—this small list would include William Blum's *Rogue State: A Guide to the World's Only Superpower*, Joseph Stiglitz's *Globalization and Its Discontents*, Paul Collier's *The Bottom Billion* and Ha-Joon Chang's *Kicking Away the Ladder*. The Internet, also, has been an indispensible tool for research.

The first section of the book deals with conflict. After an introduction on how conflict damages countries, a series of short chapters deal with conflict in the following countries:

- North Africa
- Liberia and Sierra Leone

- Angola
- Ethiopia and Eretria
- Israel and Palestine
- Iraq and Iran
- Russia and Yugoslavia
- South Asia: India and Pakistan

The main areas of conflict that are covered here relate to Africa, the Middle East and South Asia. This does not mean that Southeast and Far East Asia were conflict free; on the contrary, they too experienced disastrous wars. Japan not only experienced defeat in the Second World War, but also with the tragedies of Hiroshima and Nagasaki, is the only country to have suffered the massive destruction of nuclear bombing. Both Korea and Vietnam were split in two by war, and Korea still remains a divided nation with the communist North facing off a very capitalist South. But these conflicts and wars have now receded into the past, and these nations having suffered the worst of war have learned from their experience and value peace. Even China has avoided war in its confrontations with Taiwan. The Yugoslav Wars, strictly speaking, relate to Europe and not Asia, but have been included to show that even civilized Europeans are capable of depravity, and have had to suffer from religious conflict between Christian Serbs and Muslim Bosnians. Many of these countries have not been able to recover from the wounds, with Angola being an example of a war-ravaged nation which recovered well, particularly because of the abundance of oil. Angola has been one of the stars of growth—matching China for the last decade. Israel is the only country that has prospered through and perhaps because of war, proving the exception to the rule that war usually is unmitigated disaster.

The next section deals with corruption. Despite the overwhelming empirical evidence against corruption, many continue to argue that the damage it causes is limited; some even claim that it can be beneficial! Perhaps this is because corruption has a massive constituency of those that are corrupt, and those who earn their livelihood through corruption. The reality, however, is that after conflict, corruption is the greatest barrier to growth and the greatest enemy of human happiness. One leader who recognized this was Lee Kuan Yew who created a corruption-free government, making Singapore 'the best run government in the world'. Botswana is another example of a country that succeeds by clean governance. It is no coincidence that the Transparency International list shows successful countries as the least corrupt and unsuccessful countries as the most corrupt. The section on corruption illustrates how it effects and obstructs development. Economic activity is slowed down, efficiency falls, the rule of law is weakened as the courts fail to deliver justice, while the police prey on the populace.

Short chapters describe the tragic destruction that corruption has caused in some of the worst-hit countries—Iraq, Russia, Nigeria and Indonesia. We also look at the two giants: India, where everyone steals but no one gets caught, and China, where extreme measures have been taken to stop corruption.

Section 3 deals with democracy. The contribution of democracy to development is still highly debated. Many of the most successful leaders of developing countries have been autocrats rather than democrats; but nevertheless, the US seems to be concerned with imposing democracy on developing countries, leading to the comment 'Be careful, or America will punish you with democracy.' The advocates of democracy point to the many disastrous examples of dictators to support their views, but democracy in poor countries has not always produced good and able leaders. Aristotle was undoubtedly right when he said 2,000 years ago that 'It is better for a city to be governed by good men than by good laws.' The problem is how to get good men. Winston Churchill summed the problem up with his comment: 'The best argument against democracy is a five-minute conversation with the average voter.'

The section on democracy includes a chapter on Islamic democracy which looks at the Muslim countries of Pakistan, Mali, Indonesia, Turkey and Malaysia, and concludes that there is no fundamental contradiction between Islam and democracy, though it cannot be denied that many Islamic countries are not democratic. Democracy has many variations, country to country; we look at four countries: South Africa, Iran, Thailand and India.

No country can prosper if it earns the enmity of a superpower, and today there is only one superpower, the United States. Section 4 looks at the US in the context of its effect on the developing world. The US military has played an active role in ensuring US interests, whether political, as in the Cold War against communism, or economic, to protect the free flow of oil and the special role of the dollar as the world's reserve currency. The American consumer has provided the market for export growth for all the economic miracles, whether based on sale of oil, manufactures or IT services. And dollar diplomacy is even more important than gunboat diplomacy in controlling a difficult world. Even after the great financial crash that has shaken America with bankruptcies, foreclosures and unemployment, the US military and the dollar retain their significance around the globe.

After a long journey through disaster zones and trouble spots, Section 5 brings us to countries that have succeeded in eliminating poverty and creating wealth through good governance. These success stories have much in common: determination and commitment, good, sometimes great leaders, political stability enabling a long-term vision, good governance, good institutions, good policies, education, skills and discipline, exports, capital, investment and savings, and a constructive population policy. They have also tried to stay clear of conflict, corruption and superpower dissatisfaction. The majority have not followed the democratic path. The section looks at eight countries that have succeeded and one that has not. The success stories are Singapore, Korea, Malaysia, China, India, Israel, Botswana and Dubai in the UAE. The country that has not succeeded is Pakistan. It is perhaps unfair to show India as a success and Pakistan as a failure, when many of their economic performance figures are not too far apart; but Pakistan is seen to be in a downward cycle whereas India is seen to be taking off in a trajectory of fast growth. There are two Indias, the India where hundreds of millions live in poverty and misery, and the new India of Bangalore and Hyderabad, the India of IT, software and off-shoring, which though it employs only a few million people, has nevertheless lifted the country from despair to hope.

The final chapter is on leaders—the 'good men' that Aristotle emphasizes as the most important ingredient in the success of nations. Many of these leaders have ruled their countries for decades as they pursued the policies of growth: Lee in Singapore, China's great leaders Mao and Deng, India's Nehru, South Korea's Park, Malaysia's Mahathir, the UAE's Sheikh Zayed, Dubai's Sheikh Rashid and Sheikh Mohammad, and the Botswana leaders Seretse Khama and Ketumile Masire; the great Nelson Mandela ruled for only five years but in that short time forever changed South Africa, while Mohandas Karamchand Gandhi never ruled for even a day but left his mark on history. Leaders do matter. It is these rare and exceptional men that change the destiny of nations and achieve the impossible.

Section One

CONFLICT

True peace is not merely the absence of tension; it is the presence of justice.

—Martin Luther King

Conflict is the outcome of man's inhumanity to man and is the most important cause of human suffering. It kills, maims and renders homeless; it prevents growth, disrupts economies, perpetuates poverty, illiteracy and disease, and destroys nations.

The Second World War was the last great contest between evenly matched Great Powers. The war marked the end of the British Empire, and two new contenders, the US and the USSR, emerged to replace Britain, the dying imperial power. Stalin had moved with great speed to re-establish the Russian empire in East Europe and Central Asia; a warning shot needed to be fired to show him the danger in challenging the United States. Two shots were fired—in Hiroshima and Nagasaki.

The war had ended, but a new war had started, the war against communism—a 'Cold War'—that spread to every part of the world over the next half-century. A war of attrition, where the protagonists, America and Russia, engaged in proxy wars in country after country in the Third World. The collapse of the USSR in 1991 ended the Cold War, and the nature of combat went through one more evolutionary change as the War on Communism was replaced by the War on Terrorism. The US now engaged in a series of 'small wars' with unequal states, and in confrontation short of war. After 9/11 these culminated in wars against Iraq and Afghanistan.

William Blum in his amazing book *Rogue State: A Guide to the World's Only Superpower* has exposed America as a 'rogue state': 'Between 1945 and 2005 the United States has attempted to overthrow more than 50 foreign governments and to crush more than 30 populist-nationalist movements struggling against intolerable regimes. In the process the US has caused the end of life for several million people and condemned many millions more to a life of agony and despair.'

Today, conflict between nations has been overshadowed by conflict within nations—between the haves and have-nots, whether in the form of class conflict, ethnic conflict or religious conflict. Destabilization and conflict are on the increase as desperately impoverished majorities grow resentful of the conspicuous consumption of the super-rich, who are often drawn from privileged ethnic minorities.

The growing cost of defence, to prevent conflict between and within states, spirals, while the cost of actual conflict is even higher. Security of life and property is destroyed as the nation decays from within with the erosion of the rule of law. Foreign investment is the first to disappear, but this is quickly followed by the flight of domestic capital; as money exits to safer havens, so do people as the brain drain gathers momentum; corruption increases and what is left of state funds is diverted from health and education to security and defence; the economy collapses. Conflict, once started, endures, lasting decades before some form of normalcy can be restored. The stories in this chapter, of conflict in Africa, the Middle East, the countries of former Yugoslavia and South Asia, show the impact of war on poor countries trying in vain to develop.

1

North Africa, Egypt and Algeria

Events are not a matter of chance.
—Gamal Abdel Naseer, who plotted his revolution
for a decade, but carried it through in an hour

EGYPT

In Egypt, the young revolutionary Nasser had removed the fat and debauched King Farouk and sent him into exile. Nasser wanted the Suez Canal, and Britain was determined to deny it to him, resulting in war—a short war, because the US cautioned and restrained the British, who backed down and resigned themselves to the loss.

The departure of the colonial powers created a new elite who advocated nationalism and democracy, often tinged with socialism; but soon Islam emerged as the most powerful ideology. The Muslim Brotherhood was started in Egypt by Hasan al Banna in 1928 and though not initially violent, was moved towards militancy by the Zionist colonization of the British Mandate of Palestine, and the birth of Israel. In 1948, a member of the Brotherhood assassinated Egyptian prime minister Mahmoud an-Nukrashi Pasha, and three months later the police killed al-Banna and arrested 4,000 members of the organization. The Brotherhood went underground. A few years later, in 1954, the Brotherhood attempted to assassinate Nasser as he was making a speech in Alexandria; once again the authorities arrested numerous members and banned the organization. The new face of the Islamic movement in Egypt was Sayyid Qutb who urged jihad against both Western democracy and Soviet communism, and even against other Muslim regimes whom he accused of trying to appease the Great Powers. Qutb was arrested, tortured and sent to prison where he wrote his manifesto, 'Milestones', in which he declared that both liberal democracy and socialism had failed, and it was now Islam's turn. On Qutb's release from prison in 1964, he conspired to assassinate Nasser; the plot was discovered; Qutb was arrested and executed, becoming, in the process, the godfather of al Qaeda.

When Nasser died in 1970 he was succeeded by Anwar Sadat, who legalized the Brotherhood and tried to win over the support of the Islamists. Sadat was assassinated in 1981 after signing a peace treaty with Israel. It gained him the Nobel Peace Prize but cost him his life. The assassin, a young officer, who killed Sadat during a military parade, proudly declared, 'I am Khalid Islambuli! I have killed Pharaoh! And I do not fear death!' The new leaders of the Brotherhood were even more committed to jihad, and would later become big names in the fundamentalist terror that later swept the world—Ayman al Zawahiri, who went on to become Osama's lieutenant, and the blind cleric Omar Abdel-Rahman, who was involved in the 1993 World Trade Center bombing. But Egypt's internal conflict and its assassinations were a mere sideshow to Egypt's external conflict with Israel which resulted in five wars, culminating in the Mubarak dictatorship supported by large handouts of American aid.

ALGERIA: OIL, CONFLICT AND ISLAM

Algeria has been a major victim of conflict and violence. After independence in 1962, the army controlled the state with a one-party dictatorship. While every state had an army, in Algeria the army had a state. The 1970s saw good times with per capita income rising from $370 to $830, and employment doubling; a welfare system provided free health care and education, and food costs were subsidized. But by the 1980s the economy faltered under the combined strain of falling oil revenues and a surging population, which grew from ten million in 1962 to eighteen million in 1980; mounting foreign debt led to rising debt service costs which soon equalled export earnings; an inefficient bureaucracy, mismanaged state-owned enterprises and escalating unemployment added to the problem. The good times were over. The ruling party, the National Liberation Front or FLN, started to lose momentum, as generals and their partners focused on the serious business of making money.

The Islamic socialism of the ruling FLN was increasingly challenged by the undiluted Islamic fervour of the Front Islamique du Salat (FIS); as government services deteriorated, Islamic networks filled the gap. The students and the unemployed led riots over consumer shortages and rising prices which the army ruthlessly crushed, killing 500, after which President Benjedid introduced reforms, ending the one-party system that had prevailed for twenty-six years. The hard-line FIS swept the local elections.

A young Algerian explained his position, 'You have only four options: you can remain unemployed and celibate because there are no jobs and no apartments; you can work in the black market and risk being arrested; you can try to emigrate to France to sweep the streets of Paris; or you can join the FIS and vote for Islam.' The new leaders were Abassi Madani and his deputy, Sheikh Belhadj, a firebrand who stated: 'Democracy is a stranger in the House of God; there is no democracy in Islam.' The army was alarmed, and feared that once in power, the Islamists would never leave; it would be 'one man, one vote, one time'. In the first round of the national elections the FIS dominated, winning 188 out of 231 seats; the Berbers came second and the FNL trailed the field with only sixteen seats. The generals cancelled the election, staged a coup, and moved aggressively to crush the FIS. Madani and Belhadj were arrested and were not released for the next twelve years.

When violence erupted, the generals declared a state of emergency, made mass arrests and banned the FIS. The new president, Mohamed Boudiaf, a respected freedom fighter, tried to clamp down on the FIS and the corruption of the ruling elite and put an end to the exploitation of Islam for partisan politics. But within six months he was assassinated by his bodyguard. From 1992 till 2002 Algeria was racked by violence and civil war, in the course of which over 100,000 Algerians lost their lives. Several Islamic guerrilla groups participated in the orgy of killing, but the most violent that came to dominate the uprising was the extremist Groupe Islamique Armee (GIA). The GIA targeted prominent persons and foreigners alike using terror tactics with their slogan, 'No dialogue, no reconciliation, no truce'; with the breakdown of law and order, extortion, protection mafias and smuggling became rampant.

Abdelaziz Bouteflika, the new president, tried without great success, to reach a reconciliation with the Islamists, offering amnesty to fighters. The peace initiative stalled, while the low-level insurgency continued, since it seemed that violence suited both sides; the military used violence to justify the state of emergency which protected the system of corruption and patronage with oil revenues reaching $10 billion a year; the Islamists too had learned to profit from the war economy. Caught in the crossfire, the people of Algeria suffered. By 2005 President Bouteflika managed to bring the violence substantially under control with his Charter for Peace and Reconciliation and was again re-elected in 2009.

Today, though Algeria has significant oil revenues, the economy has remained stagnant, a legacy of the lost decade of conflict.

2

Liberia and Sierra Leone: Lords of War

Short sleeve or long sleeve?
    —A soldier, before chopping off the arm of a man

The Hague trial of Charles Taylor, former president of Liberia, for crimes against humanity was the closing chapter of the bloody civil wars in Liberia and Sierra Leone, as he denied all charges from murder to rape, sexual slavery, and the use of child soldiers. Taylor was dramatically portrayed in the Hollywood movie *The Lord of War* and was part of the strange story of Liberia, which was founded as a colony in 1847 by freed American slaves who wished to immigrate to Africa. These freed slaves, the Americo-Liberians, ruled through the True Whig party for a hundred years—a term that has been unparalleled in modern party politics. Proud of their American heritage, they adopted a lifestyle reminiscent of the South American, with pillared mansions, top hats and tails, a flag copied from the American flag and the dollar as legal currency; the capital was named Monrovia after James Monroe, the fifth president of the United States. This strange elite looked down on the locals and in turn reduced some of them to the rank of slaves, as they monopolized power and wealth. William Tolbert, the last of the line, earned a substantial personal fortune with the support of his brother, the finance minister, and his son-in-law, the minister of defence.

One night in 1980, master sergeant Samuel Doe climbed over the palace gate with a small band of soldiers, and killed Tolbert and his defenders. They announced a coup, and executed ministers and officials in an impromptu ceremony where thousands of the gleeful public cheered as the officials were strung up and shot. Doe, with his trendy suits and Afro hairstyle, aligned with America and severed diplomatic relations with the USSR, running an ethnically based dictatorship that ignored public opinion and election results. As Doe's government grew increasingly corrupt and repressive, he banned political opposition, murdered opponents and favoured his own ethnic group, the Krahn, an indigenous tribe, leading to civil war with Charles Taylor's rebel army, the National Patriotic Front of Liberia (NPFL). This was the First Liberian Civil War which put Charles Taylor in power; it was followed by the Second Liberian Civil War which finally removed Taylor from power. Together this period of civil war lasting almost fifteen years resulted in the deaths of 200,000 people out of a total population of under four million, and the displacement of almost half the population, resulting in almost two million refugees. The civil war also destroyed the Liberian economy leading to the impoverishment of the Liberian people. Most businesses were destroyed or heavily damaged; foreign investors left and the United Nations banned timber and diamond exports from Liberia. The capital remained without electricity and running water for months; corruption became rampant, and unemployment and illiteracy were endemic. Samuel Doe was captured by the rebels, tortured and killed; his naked body was dragged through the streets in a wheelbarrow as an example. A videotape of his torture became a bestseller, showing the guerrilla leader, Prince Johnson, sipping a Budweiser while Doe's ear was cut off.

Taylor needed money to buy arms to fuel his insurgency. Liberia's neighbour to the north, Sierra Leone, had diamonds. It was the struggle for diamonds that was the motive for the violence; it was the money from the sale of the diamonds that would pay for weapons, and for the war; to get his hands on the diamonds, Taylor backed and armed the rebel forces in Sierra Leone, the RUF (the Revolutionary United Front) under the leadership of Foday Sankoh. The Sierra Leone Civil War which began in 1991 resulted in the death of thousands and the displacement of more than two million people (over one-third of the population) over eleven years. The RUF abducted thousands of boys and girls who were turned into soldiers and prostitutes, through a brutalization process that often forced them to kill their own parents. High on drugs and alcohol, this terrible army mutilated men, women and children, amputating arms and legs with machetes, and leaving a legacy of 20,000 amputees, victims of their atrocities. Mutilation of hands, feet, breasts, buttocks, lips, ears, noses and genitalia were common, and the victims were given inhuman choices—rape your sister or lose an arm! Men were forced to sit with their children to watch their wives being raped by gangs of soldiers. Women were degraded, enslaved, mutilated, raped, sodomized and forced to live in the wild as 'soldiers' wives'. A particularly violent group known as The West Side Boys or West Side Niggaz, was influenced by American gangsta rap music and Tupac Shakur. High on marijuana and heroin, they would participate in torturing their own parents, and would wear women's wigs and clothing to accentuate their depravity, under leaders with names such as Brigadier Bomb Blast and Brigadier Papa. They hit media fame after kidnapping a group of British soldiers. Cannibalism was rife, and videos of the teenage soldiers were circulated as they cut out hearts and other organs from victims and ate them raw; this was done in open streets before international reporters, as the young cannibals explained how good they tasted.

Sierra Leone served as the background for the 2006 Hollywood movie *Blood Diamond*, starring Leonard Di Caprio. A country rich in diamonds and other minerals, years of civil war reduced it to the poorest nation in the world. Diamond revenues fell from hundreds of millions of dollars to a mere $10 million. The flow of diamonds which had enabled former president Siaka Stevens to amass a personal fortune of $500 million in his seventeen years of corrupt rule, and which had enabled warlord Charles Taylor to wreak havoc across nations in Africa's west coast, was reduced to a trickle and even that bypassed the people and only affected them by the tragedy that it caused.

Today, peace has been restored and Liberia, Sierra Leone and Guinea are trying to rebuild their societies, but it will be a long, uphill journey to recover from massive disaster, and for years to come the scars and lost limbs will serve as a sad reminder of the lost decade.

3

Angola: Oil Versus Diamonds

Formula for success: Rise early, work hard, strike oil.

—J. Paul Getty

Angola has substantial oil wealth, and by 2008 was producing two million barrels a day (bpd), giving it an income per capita higher than China, India, Pakistan or Indonesia. Its economy was growing at 16 per cent per annum, a rate double than that of the miracle economy, China. But Angola has emerged from a violent history of twenty-five years of civil war that tore apart the country, displaced over two million people and wasted over $40 billion of the country's wealth in a futile struggle. Angolan history is a story of superpower rivalry, of conflict over diamonds and oil, and the long hard war between two men—the urbane and secretive president, Jose Eduardo Dos

Santos, and the charismatic guerrilla fighter, Jonas Malheiro Savimbi, who spoke seven languages fluently, was well read in politics and philosophy and was a respected guerrilla fighter schooled in classic Maoist strategy of warfare. In 1992 an abortive election was attempted by the government, in which a common slogan among disillusioned Angolans was 'UNITA kills, MPLA steals'. This intense power struggle between the UNITA and the MPLA, which started in 1975, ended in the death of Savimbi in a battle with government troops, assisted by foreign mercenaries. Savimbi sustained fifteen machine-gun bullets to his head, throat, upper body and legs before he died; his successor died from wounds received in combat ten days later; six weeks after, a ceasefire was signed.

The long Angolan civil war was a superpower conflict, a resource war, a war of corruption and greed. Since independence in 1975, Angola had been ruled by the Movimento Popular de Liberacao de Angola (MPLA) which had led the war for independence against the colonial regime of the Portuguese. In 1979 Jose Eduardo dos Santos became president, leading a Marxist regime which was backed by the USSR and Cuba; the rebels were led by Savimbi and his National Union for the Total Independence of Angola (UNITA) anti-communist group which was supported by the United States and South Africa; both sides were adequately supplied with armaments by their superpower sponsors.

Angola is a country rich in oil and diamonds; the MPLA government controlled the oil, the UNITA rebels controlled the diamonds, securing $2 billion from diamond sales between 1992 and 1998. Initially, UNITA gained ground due to

Savimbi's military skills, taking over more than half the territory of Angola, but over the years as the UNITA revenues from diamonds fell, and the MPLA revenues from oil rose, the tide turned.

After the ceasefire, the Angolan recovery has moved fast to rebuild the country and the economy, and in 2009, Angola took over the prestigious OPEC presidency. Today, Angola is an important supplier of oil to China, and also to America, but the majority of its people still live below the poverty line as oil has bypassed them and mainly benefits the elite in power. Half of the country's food needs are imported, a sad testimony to the ravages of civil war in a state that had once been self-sufficient in food production. Angola's two million barrels of oil production and ten million carats of diamond production are still plagued by mismanagement and corruption. In 2005 Transparancy International rated Angola one of the ten most corrupt countries in the world. Angola remains a coastal enclave economy where the oil industry employs a mere 10,000 people with the majority of the population living on subsistence agriculture disconnected from the affluent and privileged.

Angola is a striking example of a potentially rich country devastated by conflict, corruption, superpower politics and mismanagement, but also how fast a country can recover once these destructive factors are removed.

4

Ethiopia and Eritrea: A Very Long War

If you see oppression of the poor, and justice and righteousness trampled in a country, do not be astounded.

—King Solomon

The thirty-year war between Ethiopia and Eritrea was Africa's longest war—a war which was supported, armed and financed by America and Russia, a sub-war in the Cold War between the two superpowers. It is the story of three remarkable people—Emperor Haile Selassie who ruled Ethiopia for sixty years, the dour Marxist Mengistu, and the heroic Eritrean rebel leader Isaias Afewerki.

Ethiopia is an ancient empire, and its emperor, Haile Selassie, claimed descent from the Biblical figures Solomon and Sheba. The sultry Sheba decided to travel to meet Solomon, whose reputation for brilliance had reached her. Solomon already had 400 wives and 600 concubines, but he too was fascinated by his visitor, and prepared a special banquet for her, in which he fed her 'meats with salt, fish with peppers and drinks laced with vinegar'; after dinner he suggested they sleep together, an offer that she was happy to accept with the proviso that he was not to take her by force, since she was keen to preserve her virgin status. Solomon agreed but asked for reciprocity—that she swore not to take anything of his by force. After a few hours' sleep, Sheba woke with a raging thirst due to the salt, peppers and vinegar of her diet, but Solomon stopped her and negotiated, trading water for sex which resulted in the birth of the Ethiopian dynasty, once more reinforcing his reputation for exceptional wisdom.

Emperor Haile Selassie was the last in this line, and ruled for almost sixty years exercising total power from 1916 to 1974, giving daily and detailed orders to his ministers and officials, as he walked the palace grounds with his pet lions, until he finally grew old and quite senile; in a state banquet for President Mobutu, he asked his aide, 'Who is that man opposite me?'

The last emperor finally met his end in a dungeon, where he was killed and then buried in concrete under a lavatory. His nine princesses, daughters and granddaughters, were also imprisoned, abused, their hair shorn and finally killed. For over a year, before he was put to death, the emperor was interrogated about his Swiss bank accounts: 'Where is your fortune?' the interrogators asked; 'I have no hidden fortune,' he had answered; the interrogators persisted, suggesting that he must have made some provision for his retirement, to which the emperor haughtily replied, 'For an emperor, there is no retirement.'

The emperor's successor was the dour introverted Marxist rebel Mengistu Haile Mariam, a member of the Derg, the committee of mid-ranking army officers that took power initially in the name of the emperor. Mengistu first came into the limelight when he argued forcefully for the execution of Selassie's notables and finally established his monopoly of power. Mengistu presided over, and to a large extent contributed to, one of the twentieth century's greatest famines which hit international headlines with Bob Geldof and his Live Aid concerts. While the West pumped in money and food to alleviate the effects of the famine, Mengistu continued to use starvation as a weapon of war by denying food supplies to the rebels in his Tigrean province and the insurgent Eritreans determined to break free from Ethiopia. Over 1,000,000 died and countless others were displaced as refugees fleeing to adjacent countries, or as part of Mengistu's resettlement schemes to clear war zones of potential hostiles. Finally, Mengistu fled into exile to Zimbabwe (then under President Robert Mugabe), leaving behind a country devastated by war and a people impoverished by his disastrous policies.

The sole survivor of the three is Isaias Afewerki, hero of the thirty-year war for independence and dictator of the state of Eritrea, who has ruled the country since its secession from Ethiopia in 1991, without elections or democracy. Whether hero or villain, Afewerki is no ordinary man. For three decades he led his rebel army through an impossible war to victory in a David-and-Goliath struggle against a strong professional army backed by immense support of a superpower. Living in mountains and caves on a shoestring budget he maintained the morale of his troops in their heroic struggle and by superior military strategy won battle after battle. Since independence he has been an autocratic ruler who tolerates no dissent, no free media, and no elections. The country remains desperately poor with a per capita income of $600 per annum in 2012, and is dependent on food aid from abroad.

Why did this war last thirty years? Why did it receive such heavy backing in arms and money from the superpowers? What were the objectives of those involved?

- The Ethiopians, living in a landlocked country, wanted access to the sea.
- The Eritreans wanted independence.
- The Americans wanted the Kagnew communications base in Asmara.
- The Russians wanted to expand their Marxist base in the Horn of Africa.

How did it all start? After the Second World War, the British dismantled the Italian empire in Africa, plundered the assets that the Italians had bequeathed to Eritrea, and passed the question of what to do with it to the United Nations, who imposed a federation formula as a compromise between Ethiopia's desire to incorporate Eritrea as part of a greater Ethiopia, and Eritrea's desire for complete independence.

The UN underwrote the arrangement and left Haile Selassie to honourably implement the terms. But the emperor was, by nature, committed to empire, and pushed forward with policies to dominate the smaller Eritrean nation—a ban on political parties, extension of the Ethiopian laws to cover Eritrea, and discrimination against the Muslim population led to resentment which escalated when Ethiopia tried to impose their language as well on the Eritreans. The Eritreans repeatedly tried to approach the UN, who had put together the federation compromise, but the UN maintained a stony silence. This led to a guerrilla resistance and, finally, war.

The UN reluctance to fulfil their obligations to Eritrea was due to a desire to appease the United States, who had committed support to Ethiopia, and who had an important stake in Asmara, the Eritrean capital which now fell under Ethiopia. A strange accident of geography had made Asmara the best place in the world to send and receive radio signals; in the age before transmitting stations were replaced by satellites, this made Asmara a most important resource for America. The US spy station in Asmara had a reach that covered half the world, leading to the comment of a state department official that 'The benefits from Asmara can be obtained from no other location. Therefore US rights in Eritrea should not be compromised.' In 1953 the US and Ethiopia signed a twenty-five-year agreement for the Asmara base, and American pressure made sure that the UN would default on its commitments. The UN was an old hand at the compromises that 'realpolitik' demanded, and had showed its cruel pragmatism in the Congo Crisis of 1961 which had led to the murder of its first legally elected prime minister, Patrice Lumumba, in the events in Western Sahara in the 1980s (when there were as many as 20,000 deaths in the Western Sahara

War—1975 to 1991—between Polisario Front and Morocco) and in the genocide of over 80,000 Tutsis in Rwanda in 1994. While the UN played dumb, the US Secretary of State John Foster Dulles was more forthright, 'From the point of view of justice, the opinions of the Eritrean people must receive consideration. Nevertheless, the strategic interest of the United States makes it necessary that the country has to be linked to Ethiopia.'

America wanted the Kagnew base; Ethiopia wanted the Eritrean coastline; a deal was struck and America gave Ethiopia the arms and support it needed to keep Eritrea under control. America gave Ethiopia a modern army. But it was not enough, and the guerrilla war dragged on. The emperor was removed, then killed, and the new Marxist regime of Mengistu settled in. The passing years decreased the importance of the Kagnew transmitting station; satellites were the new technology, and America started to lose interest in Ethiopia and its Marxist regime, opening the door for the Russian entry into the region. The Russians provided billions of dollars of armaments and support to Mengistu, making his army the strongest in Africa.

Neither famine, nor deprivation, nor the overwhelming force of Ethiopia's army, nor their own lack of funds could persuade the guerrilla army to recognize reality as they fought on; finally the impossible happened, and they won. The state of Eritrea was born, and Mengistu fled into exile leaving Ethiopia $6 billion in debt to her Russian allies after a war that had killed thousands, had displaced one-third of the Eritrean population and had seen the growth of a generation that had never known peace. A small nation of guerrilla fighters had defeated an empire.

5

Israel: Hero or Villian?

All of the land of Israel is ours.

—Yitzhak Shamir,
former prime minister of Israel

Over the last half-century, oil and war have defined the Middle East, home to both Israel and Saddam Hussein. Napoleon once said, 'History is a myth agreed upon.' Theodor Herzl, the founder of Zionism, spoke of 'a people without a land, looking for a land without a people', but as Shimon Peres, president and twice elected prime minister of Israel, aptly pointed out, Herzl did not seem to be aware of the presence of an Arab population in Palestine. With the creation of the State of Israel, five million Jews found a home, even as four million Palestinian refugees lost theirs.

For fifty years, the heroic struggle of the Israelis has been eulogized. 'They arrived in a desolate, sparsely populated region and drained the swamps, irrigated the desert, grew crops and built cities. They introduced libraries, hospitals, art galleries, universities . . . and the concept of individual rights.' Though swamped in a sea of hostile Muslim neighbour states, they emerged victorious in a series of wars as a reincarnation of David struggling against a massive Goliath. The myth of Israel's magical fighting prowess endured through the War of Independence, the Suez War, the Six Day War, the War of Attrition, the Yom Kippur War, the War in Lebanon and against the Palestinian Intifadas.

Not only did the Israelis excel at war, they also showed their formidable skills in building a highly successful modern economy. Where most nations have suffered in war, the Israelis prospered. Even Great Britain, the superpower of its time, had emerged from the war with Germany with its economy shattered and its empire doomed. Israel, on the other hand, has seen its per capita income rise to $30,000 per annum in 2010, challenging the wealthy nations of Europe through unending war and conflict—a shining success story when compared with the miserable $1,500 per capita income of its Muslim adversary, Palestine. The Israelis welcomed homeless Jews from all over the world. The only outcasts, denied a home, were the original Palestinians, who now lived in miserable camps in the West Bank, in Gaza, in Jordan and other countries of the Middle East. For them, the right to return was forever denied.

The secret behind Israel's amazing success was America. By 2008, America had provided over $100 billion of direct aid to Israel, half of which was military aid. In addition, the US had provided indirect support, which the *Washington Report on*

Middle East Affairs had estimated as 'the costs to the American Taxpayers of the Israeli-Palestinian conflict: $3 trillion'. The officially published figure of $3 billion a year for US aid to Israel, though sufficient to keep Israel on the top of the list of aid beneficiaries, is merely the tip of the iceberg. American support has included economic sanctions on Iran, Iraq, Libya and Syria and has led to an Arab oil embargo and impacted oil prices. America has also supported the development of the Israeli arms industry, which today is the ninth biggest arms exporter in the world, earning over $4 billion a year. America also used its influence to reduce Muslim hostility to Israel. Anwar El Sadat was persuaded to sign a peace treaty for which a grateful America continues to reward Egypt, which remains the second biggest recipient of US aid. American influence may also be working behind the scenes to ensure that the high level of protests by the oil-rich Arab states are not matched by an equally high level of financial support to those fighting for the cause of Islam. But Iran has a will of its own and continues to support the Hezbollah, whose charismatic leader Hassan Nasrullah has emerged as the new people's hero in the Middle East. Like so many other regional conflicts, power politics lurks behind the scenes, directing events.

The common explanation of the American commitment to Israel is the power of the Jewish lobby in the US; but this is not convincing. The establishment in America would not have been duped into blindly following a course that cost hundreds of billions of dollars, that entailed indirect costs of perhaps trillions of dollars, that led to half a century of instability and warfare, that alienated the Muslims—a quarter of the world's people—

that resulted in 9/11 and the War on Terror, that could endanger oil supplies and certainly affected oil prices, unless there was a clear and important US interest. War and instability were the US goals in the region, through which the oil-rich monarchies could be controlled and manipulated, and because of which US arms sales to the region could prosper and grow. The Middle East, home to a relatively small part of the world's population, is involved in almost one-fifth of the world's trade in armaments. Abu Dhabi, with half-a-million citizens, is the biggest buyer in the region, and the third biggest importer in the world. Conflict continues as long as enough people profit from it; the arms trade is a profitable business and oil is even more profitable.

The Palestinians did not profit from the half-century of conflict. By 2009, 60 per cent of Palestinians lived in poverty; a third of the labour force was unemployed, and those that were lucky enough to have found work were paid only 70 per cent of what they had earned a decade before. Ninety per cent of external trade is with Israel and the current account deficit is 80 per cent. Their wretched economy stands in glaring contrast to the booming Israeli economy with its high-tech and software, its diamond trade and arms industry, its export of agricultural products and a tourist industry with 3.45 million visitors a year. Strong US support continues and it has already waived $42 billion in old loans even as it commits another $30 billion in aid to Israel over the coming decade. Meanwhile, Israel has requested America for another $20 billion-worth of military hardware.

More painful than the material hardship were the atrocities

and humiliation that became the everyday experience of the Palestinians. The world watched and condemned the massacres of Sabra and Shatila, when the Israeli defence force surrounded and closed the refugee camps outside Beirut as they encouraged Phalangist paramilitary forces to kill, rape and plunder through a forty-eight-hour rampage. The world listened as one soldier asked his commander, 'What do we do with the women and children?' and received the heartless answer, 'You know what to do with them.' The UN passed a resolution condemning the massacre as 'an act of genocide' but all Western democracies abstained from voting. The resolution was filed away with the hundreds of other ineffective resolutions in which the US and Israel had voted against the rest of the world. No matter how the votes fell, the US had its way, oblivious to the words of its Declaration of Independence which enjoined them to pay 'a decent respect to the opinions of mankind'. Whereas the US and Europe raised no protest over the massacre at Sabra and Shatila, condemnation was voiced from one unexpected source: the Kahan committee, constituted by the Israeli parliament to investigate the incident, published its findings that Israel was indirectly responsible and Ariel Sharon bore personal responsibility for the atrocities. As a result of the report, Sharon was forced to resign as defence minister.

After half a century of conflict, the faces and the issues have changed. Where the original struggle had questioned the existence of the Israeli state, today the negotiation is about the creation of the Palestinian state. Although hard statements are issued by Hamas that it will never recognize the right of Israel to exist as a Jewish state, and will never make peace with the country, it is understood that this is only a posturing as part of a hard-line negotiating process. Though the current prime minister, Benjamin Netanyahu, has given harsh preconditions to the dialogue for a Palestinian state, it would seem that demilitarization to the extent of 'No army, no control of its own air space' is a hard-ball opening position which may soften under American persuasion. In an atmosphere of total mistrust, the key issues to an acceptable state for the Palestinians are the Israeli settlements and Jerusalem. Jerusalem, home to the Dome of the Rock, the al Aqsa Mosque and the Temple Mount/ Haram al-Sharif, will remain a permanent disputed area. The Separation Wall remains a provocation that has been condemned worldwide and declared illegal by the International Court of Justice, which used strong language in its 2004 ruling that 'the construction of the wall being built by Israel, the occupying power, in the Occupied Palestinian Territory, including in and around East Jerusalem, and its associated regime are contrary to international law'. It is also undisputed that the wall eats well into the territory of the West Bank. The right to return for the Palestinian refugees is also recognized as a lost cause. Israel is adamant that right or wrong, they will not be allowed back. President Obama of the US is only recognizing necessity when he says, 'they must relinquish the right to return'.

After the 1967 war, the Israelis occupied the Sinai peninsula, the Gaza Strip, the Golan Heights, the West Bank and East Jerusalem, starting a fresh influx of Israeli settlers. The settlement process involved the takeover of private Palestinian lands, and was declared illegal by the United Nations, the

Amnesty International and the European Union. After the peace treaty with Egypt, Israel withdrew its settlers from Sinai and the Gaza Strip, but the number of settlers in East Jerusalem and the West Bank increased, till they numbered almost half a million. Theodor Meron, the legal advisor to the Israeli Foreign Ministry, gave his confidential opinion to the Israeli government that the civilian settlements in the administered territories were illegal; US presidents Jimmy Carter and Barack Obama, however, have made public statements to the contrary. Even Tzipi Livni, chairwoman of the Kadima Party in Israel, vowed to dismantle them, but the settlements have expanded with Netanyahu's support. The Jerusalem issue is even more explosive due to the heavy religious considerations. Religious history and important religious sites prevent either party from withdrawing and it is unlikely that any agreement will be reached by the adversaries on this issue.

Recent polls have shown that 73 per cent of Palestinians and 60 per cent of Israelis say that the chances of establishment of an independent Palestinian state in the next five years is low or, rather, non-existent. The continuation of conflict is clearly detrimental to the interests of the Palestinians whose quality of life continues to fall; it is also clearly beneficial to the Israelis, whose quality of life continues to grow. It can also be safely assumed that continuation of the conflict also suits the United States, since it continues spending billions of dollars in support of Israel, which fuels the resistance to compromise and peace.

6

Iraq: Saddam's Three Wars

My name is Saddam Hussein. I am the president of Iraq and I want to negotiate.

—Saddam Hussein, on his capture by US troops from his spider-hole hideout

Saddam Hussein led Iraq into and through three wars, the Iran–Iraq War, the Gulf War and the Iraq War. Saddam was a monster created, supported and finally destroyed by the United States. Saddam worked for the Central Intelligence Agency (CIA) before he became politically prominent; his handler was an Iraqi dentist. At the age of twenty-two, Saddam was involved in a botched attempt to assassinate Abd al-Karim Qasim, the prime minister of Iraq. He fled and was moved to Egypt by the CIA, which supported him financially. Qasim decided to withdraw from the anti-Soviet Baghdad Pact (1955) signed with the US and UK, and started to buy arms from the USSR. In 1963 he was killed in a coup, and Saddam returned and took charge of the Ba'ath Party's secret intelligence apparatus, remaining close to the CIA as he presided over the mass killings of communists. A US state official when asked about the legality of the killings, replied, 'We were frankly glad to be rid of them. Did they get a fair trial? You have to be kidding. This was serious business.'

In 1979, Saddam visited Amman, where he met three CIA agents to discuss his plans to invade Iran. In 1980 Saddam declared war on Iran. Ayatollah Khomeini's Islamic revolution had soured Iran's relations with America, whom he branded 'The Great Satan'. The US had lost the affections of the Iranian people when the CIA toppled the popular government of Prime Minister Mohammad Mosaddegh and installed the Shah, who developed into a ruthless tyrant with his secret police force, Savak, trained by the CIA. Savak brutalized Iran through the widespread and inhuman use of torture, suppressing all political opposition in the country, but America stuck to the Shah right till the end, earning the hatred of the Iranian people. The US strongly opposed the Khomeini regime, and certainly hoped that the war with Iraq would weaken if not destroy it. The US actively supported Saddam's war effort by supplying the Iraqis with billions of dollars of credit and by providing military intelligence and advice.

The war lasted eight years with a million casualties, and finally ended without either side gaining an inch of territory. During this period Iraq received $35 billion in support from the West, and over $40 billion from the oil-rich Arab Gulf states. The US also supplied chemical weapons to Saddam who used them freely against Iran, leading to 100,000 Irani victims of chemical attacks. He also used them on his own people, the Kurds, who had been demanding autonomy, in 1987–88, in a series of bombings culminating with the Halabja massacre of 16 March 1988. Saddam's cousin, 'Chemical Ali', was in charge of this inhuman campaign, and twenty years later he was convicted and sentenced to be hanged for these crimes. The cost of the war exceeded $1.2 trillion ($600 billion each for Iraq and Iran), economic development was stalled and oil exports disrupted. Iraq, an oil-rich nation, became massively indebted and went bankrupt. Where Iraq suffered the greater financial loss, Iran suffered higher human casualties, substituting soldiers' lives for lack of money. Ten-year-old boys were sent to die as martyrs, many without weapons, on missions to detonate mines and draw fire. The boys carried plastic keys, which they were told would guarantee them entry into heaven if they died in battle. Too many died. The Iraqi guards described the young prisoners taken: 'When we capture them, they cry for their mothers.'

Meanwhile America honoured Saddam, who was made an honorary citizen of Detroit. The US helped in building Saddam's army into the most powerful army in the Middle East outside Israel. They supplied chemical and biological agents and technology to Iraq, knowing that these weapons were being used against Iran and against the Kurds in Iraq. When Iraq used cyanide, mustard gas and nerve agents in the war, the US blocked the UN censure of Iraq's use of chemical weapons.

The Iraq–Iran War (1980–88) pitted soldier against soldier in bloody trench warfare in the last of the old-style wars. The Gulf War of 1991 was the first of the new-style, high-tech wars, watched avidly on CNN around the world. The Iran war was long, lasting eight years; the Gulf War was short, lasting ten months from the invasion of Kuwait till the ceasefire, with actual fighting between the Allied Forces and Saddam's army lasting only six weeks, an inappropriately brief period for 'The Mother of All Battles'. The US and the Arabs, who had been Saddam's greatest supporters in the Iran War, were now his enemies, resentful of the vast reserves of oil and money he now controlled as conqueror of Kuwait. The cause of the war was money—or rather, the lack of money in the empty coffers of an Iraq bankrupted by eight years of war. When Kuwait demanded loan repayment from Iraq, Saddam countered with allegations that Kuwait was stealing Iraqi oil from the disputed Rumailia oil field. When the US ambassador to Iraq, April Galespie, told Saddam that his dispute with Kuwait did not affect the United States, he took this as a signal that he was free to attack Kuwait.

The Iraqi hunger for Kuwait was not new. In 1939, King Ghazi of Iraq had prepared to conquer Kuwait, but was forced to abandon his plans due to an unforeseen car accident which killed him. Prime Minister Qasim, in 1961, had threatened to invade Kuwait; in 1973 brief hostilities and skirmishes had taken place when the Iraqis had occupied a border post and claimed territory before they were persuaded by the Saudis to step back.

The US assembled half-a-million troops as it prepared for

Operation Desert Storm. The preparation took months, the bombardment from the air that followed took forty days, the ground offensive that completed the kill was over in 100 hours. But though Saddam was beaten, he was not removed, and the next twelve years saw bombing and economic sanctions that resulted in a breakdown of society and forced hardship on the entire population, and the death of perhaps a million children. In the war and its aftermath 177 million pounds of bombs were used to blast Iraq. The prevailing attitude was captured by William Blum, in his explosive best-seller *Rogue State*, where he quotes a US soldier: 'We own their airspace . . . We dictate the way they live and talk. And that's what's great about America right now. It's a good thing, especially when there's a lot of oil out there we need.'

The Gulf War saw the widespread use by America of depleted uranium (DU). Scientists doing research in the US were proudly shown his prize trophy by a young boy—a nine-legged frog he had found in a contaminated stream. So far, there have not been any nine-legged babies born in Iraq, but the high level of deformed births has led new mothers to drop the question, is it a boy or a girl. Instead they ask, 'Is it normal?' Even US war veterans returning from the Gulf have spoken against birth defects caused by depleted uranium poisoning; the danger of the use of depleted uranium in the war was highlighted by a British radiation expert, Chris Busby, who believes that this constitutes a danger to the whole world, since the radioactive particles are carried across continents by the winds and their radioactivity persists for over four billion years and can cause cancers such as leukaemia and brain damage, kidney failure and extreme birth defects—killing millions for centuries to come, a crime against humanity which may rank with the worst atrocities of all time. When the noted journalist John Pilger encountered children killed by DU, he wrote, 'The children's skin had folded back, like parchment, revealing veins and burned flesh that seeped blood, while the eyes, intact, stared straight ahead. I vomited.' In the three-week period of conflict in Iraq during 2003, the US had used over 1,000 tons of depleted uranium munitions.

In 1991, while the Americans were content to smash Iraq's army and recover Kuwait, they did not want to finish the job and remove Saddam. Instead, President Bush announced on Voice of America, 'There is another way for the bloodshed to stop: and that is for the Iraqi military and the Iraqi people to take matters into their own hands and force Saddam Hussein, the dictator, to step aside.' The Kurds in the north and the Shias in the south, encouraged by the American president, went into open rebellion. When Saddam countered with violent repression, they turned to America for support, but were disappointed as President Bush explained, 'I made clear from the very beginning that it was not an objective of the coalition or the United States to overthrow Saddam Hussein.' Thousands were killed and millions driven from their homes as Saddam re-established control. After the military onslaught Saddam punished the Kurds with a blockade, denying them food, finance, fuel and electricity. He started an Arabization campaign bordering on genocide to end the Kurd claim to Kirkuk oil, leading the Kurds to comment, 'For others, Kirkuk's importance is that it lies on a sea of oil. For us it is important because it lies in a sea of our blood.' In the south, the Shia uprising was crushed and the Shias were punished; prominent Shia leaders were executed or assassinated. The war may have been lost, the army beaten, but Saddam was back in control. For twelve years the people of Iraq suffered from the combined effects of repression by the regime and sanctions imposed by America, spreading poverty and despair in a crumbling nation.

In 2003, the world was shocked as the United States once again declared war against Iraq. Whereas America's role in the Gulf War had been appreciated, her starting the Iraq War was not. Important countries made their distaste clear. Europe's response provoked America to differentiate 'old' Europe from the 'new'; France distanced herself from the US war policy leading the Americans to rename French fries as 'victory fries'. Even within the United States, opposition to the war was voiced. Barack Obama, America's president-to-be, was eloquent and firm as he spoke out against the coming war which Bush, Cheney and Rumsfeld were preparing, on 2 October 2002:

> I don't oppose all wars. What I am opposed to is a dumb war. What I am opposed to is a rash war. What I am opposed to is the cynical attempt by Richard Perle and Paul Wolfowitz and other armchair, weekend warriors in this Administration to shove their own ideological agendas down our throats, irrespective of the costs in lives lost and in hardships borne.
>
> What I am opposed to is the attempt by political hacks like Karl Rove to distract us from a rise in the uninsured, a rise in the poverty rate, a drop in the median income—to

distract us from corporate scandals and a stock market that has just gone through the worst month since the Great Depression. That's what I am opposed to. A dumb war. A rash war. A war not based on reason but on passion, not on principle but on politics.

Now let me be clear—I suffer no illusions about Saddam Hussein. He is a brutal man. A ruthless man. A man who butchers his own people to secure his own power . . . He's a bad guy. The world and the Iraqi people would be better off without him. But I also know that Saddam poses no imminent and direct threat to the United States, or to [its] neighbors, that the Iraqi economy is in shambles, that the Iraqi military is a fraction of its former self, and that in concert with the international community he can be contained until, in the way of all petty dictators, he falls away into the dustbin of history.

I know that even a successful war against Iraq will require a US occupation of undetermined length, at undetermined cost, with undetermined consequences . . . I'm opposed to dumb wars.

You want a fight, President Bush? Let's finish the fight with Bin Laden and al Qaeda . . .

You want a fight, President Bush? Let's fight to make sure our so-called allies in the Middle East, the Saudis and the Egyptians, stop oppressing their own people, and suppressing dissent, and tolerating corruption and inequality, and mismanaging their economies so that their youth grow up without education, without prospects, without hope, the ready recruits of terrorist cells.

You want a fight, President Bush? Let's fight to wean ourselves off Middle East oil, through an energy policy that doesn't simply serve the interests of Exxon and Mobil.

Those are the battles we need to fight. Those are the battles we willingly join. The battles against ignorance and intolerance. Corruption and greed. Poverty and despair.

But in 2003 America went to war. Almost a century before, at the time of the British invasion of Iraq, Lt Gen. Sir Stanley Maude had stated: 'We have come here not as conquerors but as liberators to free you from generations of tyranny.' The Iraqis were not convinced. This time it was the Americans who had come as liberators; again, the Iraqis were still not convinced.

- Bush announced that he had gone to war to protect the world from Iraq's weapons of mass destruction; but no weapons were found.
- Bush announced that he had gone to war in retaliation for 9/11; but Saddam, wicked as he was, had no part to play in 9/11.
- Bush announced that he had gone to war because Saddam was supporting al Qaeda; but it was common knowledge that Saddam hated al Qaeda.
- Bush condemned Saddam for gassing the Kurds, but it was America that had supplied the gas.

Why then did America go to war? How did America conduct the war? And what has been achieved by the war? As in so many other wars, money and economic advantage were the prime movers. Honoré de Balzac once said that behind every great fortune lies a great crime; it seems that behind every great war lies a great amount of money to be made. The oil man in Dick Cheney, vice-president under Bush, was disturbed that while US oil was excluded by US sanctions from participating in the huge business opportunities of Iraq and Iran. New players such as China and India were expanding their stakes in the absence of American competition. With rising prices and burgeoning demand, this was not acceptable. Since Iran seemed a no-go area for the near future, America had to find a way to get back into Iraq. War was the way.

The second motive was financial. The US Federal Reserve's greatest nightmare is that the Organization of the Petroleum Exporting Countries (OPEC) would switch its international transactions from a dollar standard to a euro standard. In 2001, Venezuela floated the idea of switching to the euro as their oil currency standard; less than a year later a coup, generally believed to have been US sponsored, removed President Hugo Chávez, but to the surprise of all, in two days he was back. Iraq made the switch from dollar to euro in November 2002. On 20 March 2003 America went to war against Iraq.

When Iraq made the switch in 2002, the exchange rate was 0.80 to a dollar; within the year the dollar depreciated against the euro. Saddam also converted Iraq's $10 billion reserve fund at the UN into euros. Later Iran joined the exodus, followed by North Korea, and then China, Venezuela, some other OPEC nations, and then Russia followed the trend. An OPEC switch to the euro would lead to a flushing out of dollars and their replacement with euros. The dollar would crash; foreign funds would stream out of US stocks and bonds, resulting in a run on banks. The US economy is intimately tied to the dollar's role as a reserve currency; it dominates other countries through its currency, leading to the comment: 'World trade is now a game in which the US produces dollars and the rest of the world produces things that dollars can buy.'

How did America conduct the war? Brutally. John Pilger, the award-winning journalist, questioned a marine who told him, 'We had a great day; we killed a lot of people. We dropped a few civilians, but what do you do? There were women standing near an Iraqi soldier when we opened fire; one of them fell; I'm sorry, but the chick was in the way.' The horror of the war was summed up in two words: Abu Ghraib. The Abu Ghraib prison in Iraq saw shameful and inhuman incidents of torture, sodomy and homicide inflicted by the US military on prisoners of war. Two years later, when seven American soldiers were convicted for torture, photographs emerged of hooded prisoners being forced to masturbate naked in front of their captors, a naked man covered in excrement forced to pose for the camera, of ruthless beatings and other acts of torture and humiliation. Forced penetration with dogs, women forced to expose their breasts at gunpoint, and forced homosexual acts were common. *The New York Times* described incidents such as

- urinating on detainees;
- jumping on a detainee's broken leg so that it would not heal thereafter;
- pouring phosphoric acid on detainees;
- sodomizing detainees with a baton;
- tying ropes to detainee's legs or penises and dragging them across the floor;
- sexual abuse and rape of young girls.

Donald Rumsfeld, the Secretary of Defense, apologized: 'I offer my deepest apology. It was un-American. And it was not consistent with the values of our nation.' Other senators condemned: 'The American public needs to understand we're talking about rape and murder here. It was pretty disgusting, not what you'd expect from Americans.'

The end of the dictator did not mean the birth of a secure democracy. Internal violence escalated, dividing the nation into three separate groups of Kurds, Shia and Sunni, as resistance to the American occupation continued. Government and society broke down leaving life unsafe and burdened with disruption of social services, electricity, water, hospitals. The Shia–Kurd alliance dominated and the influence of Iran grew. Was it worth it? When US Secretary of State Madeleine Albright was asked the same question, with the country shattered and half-a-million children dead as a result of the war, she took a moment to consider before making her famous reply, 'Yes, it was worth it.'

7

The Yugoslav Wars: Europe's Own Horror Story

They don't have to rape anybody. Serbian women adore my 'Tigers'.
—Arkan

Josip Broz Tito, the hero of Yugoslav resistance in the Second World War, was a guerrilla fighter, who ruled for thirty-five years till his death in 1980. He broke with Stalin and built a successful economy in a state of 'unity and brotherhood' in which no one questioned 'Who is a Serb? Who is a Croat? Who is a Muslim? We were all one people'. When Tito died, Yugoslavia died, and the new 'strongman', Slobodan Milosevic, rose to power. Where Tito loved women, with a string of wives and mistresses floating through his presidential mansions,

Milosevic loved only his wife, Mira, his college sweetheart. Where Tito built Yugoslavia into a successful state, Milosevic tore it apart with his Serb nationalism and ethnic wars, as he ruled first Serbia and then Yugoslavia between the years 1989 and 2000.

In 1962 Milosevic celebrated his twenty-first birthday; in the same year his father committed suicide. Ten years later his mother committed suicide. He presided over, or caused, the worst wars that Europe has seen after the Second World War, which resulted in over 300,000 dead, 2.5 million refugees and a genocide that shocked Europe. He died in prison, under trial for crimes against humanity, and was buried, at his request, under a tree where he had in 1958 experienced his first kiss with Mira. After he was buried, a group of vampire hunters raided the grave and drove a three-foot wooden stake through his heart to prevent him from 'returning from the dead'.

Carla Del Ponte, the chief prosecutor in the case against Milosevic, made her public statement following his death: 'I deeply regret the death of Slobodan Milosevic. It deprives the victims of the justice they need and deserve. In the indictment which was judicially confirmed in 2001, Milosevic was accused of sixty-six counts of genocide, crimes against humanity and war crimes committed in Croatia, Bosnia and Herzegovina and Kosovo between 1991 and 1999. These crimes affected hundreds of thousands of victims throughout the former Yugoslavia. The prosecution case contains sufficient evidence capable of supporting a conviction on all sixty-six counts.' She also stated that the most senior perpetrators, General Ratko Mladic and Radovan Karadzic, were still at large; Zoran

Dindic, the man who had the courage to bring Milosevic to trial in the Hague, had been murdered in Belgrade three years earlier.

Yugoslavia comprised six republics and two provinces with a population of twenty million of which the eight million Serbs constituted the largest ethnic group, with the five million Croats and the four million Bosnians as the smaller nationalities. The Serbs also dominated the Yugoslav People's Army (JNA), one of the strongest armies in Europe, capable of fielding a force of one million soldiers in war. Milosevic based his political rise on Serb nationalism as he hit the headlines in a Kosovo rally of Serb protestors who were being beaten by the police, with his cry, 'No one shall have the right to beat you any more.' Milosevic then started supporting Serb minorities in non-Serb states such as Croatia and Bosnia to rebel against the majority governments.

Alarmed by the growing aggression of Serb nationalism, non-Serb republics voted for independence in a series of referendums in Slovenia, Croatia and Bosnia; this in turn led to a full-fledged war with the Serbs. These wars included the war in Slovenia (1991), the Croatian war of independence (1991–95), the Bosnian war (1992–95), the Kosovo war (1996–99), the Southern Serbia conflict (2000–01), the Macedonian conflict (2001), and NATO bombings of 1995–96 and 1999. The Serbs were moved to war by Milosevic's ambitions for a 'Greater Serbia'. The wars lasted ten years and terminated in settlements reached under pressure of NATO bombing and US mediation; they reduced much of former Yugoslavia to poverty and the combination of war, bad governance and mafia criminality resulted in collapse of GDP levels which are still below the 1970 levels (6 per cent growth till the end of the 1970s took per capita income to $2,000 before the economy collapsed). Borders were redefined, but there were no winners.

The Yugoslav wars were exceptionally brutal, and showed that even Europe was capable of atrocity and crimes against humanity. The Srebrenica massacre which took place in July 1995 was particularly shocking, since the UN had declared Srebrenica the first of the 'safe areas' and 400 armed Dutch peacekeepers were present at the time. The massacre was commanded by General Ratko Mladic and was defined as genocide by the International Criminal Tribunal for the former Yugoslavia, whose presiding judge Theodor Meron (the same Meron who had advised the Israeli government on the illegality of Israel's settlements in the West Bank and the Gaza Strip) stated at his address at the Potocari Memorial Cemetery, the Hague, on 23 June 2004: 'By seeking to eliminate a part of the Bosnian Muslims, the Bosnian Serb forces committed genocide. They targeted for extinction the 40,000 Bosnian Muslims living in Srebrenica, a group which was emblematic of the Bosnian Muslims in general. They stripped all the male Muslim prisoners, military and civilian, elderly and young, of their personal belongings and identification, and deliberately and methodically killed them solely on the basis of their identity.' The International Court of Justice further ruled that Serbia had violated the obligation to prevent genocide. Twenty years after the brutal campaign of ethnic cleansing in Bosnia, General Ratko Mladic finally went on trial, defiantly challenging 'Tell me what I've done wrong?' In Srebrenica, 8,000 Muslim men were lined up and shot, their bodies dumped in mass graves, women raped, and homes looted. The UN may have designated Srebrenica as the first 'safe area', but it did not prove very safe.

But General Ratko was a mere moderate when compared with the mass murderer Zeljko Raznatovic, aka 'Arkan and his Tigers', who became an internationally recognized warlord after Western newspapers published Ron Haviv's photograph of Arkan standing with a tiger cub in his hand, in front of a tank covered by his masked paratroopers. Arkan, the son of a senior Yugoslav airforce officer, started his career of crime as a juvenile delinquent snatching purses, and grew into a bank robber, police agent, businessman, paramilitary leader, politician and mafia boss. Ron Haviv, the photographer who met and photographed him, described him thus: 'He was charming, extremely smart and deceptively evil. Egotistical, baby-faced, and he considered himself the saviour of the Serbian people. He was a likeable guy, except that he was a pathological killer. He liked pretty women.' Arkan was wanted in six European countries for robbery, and for murder in Germany. He shot his way out of a Swedish court, escaped from prison in Belgium and lived in London for two years, giving him a fluency in the English language. Another Serbian mafia mobster, Goran Vukovic, commented, 'Of all of us, Arkan robbed the most banks. He walked into them almost like they were self-service stores—banks were his specialty as well as escapes from prison.'

Arkan built a marble mansion, which became one of Belgrade's unofficial landmarks, took over the Red Star football club, and married the rock diva Svetlana 'Ceca'. His wedding gift to the lovely Ceca became an object of some embarrassment when they were interviewed on Belgrade's Pink Television; a viewer phoned in to compliment her on her gold and diamond necklace, and correctly described an inscription on it; 'How did you know?' the TV show's host asked, as the duo shifted uncomfortably on the plush sofa; 'Because Arkan stole it from me in Bjelina,' came the reply. Arkan's coffers received a steady flow of valuables stolen from Muslims. Arkan and his Tigers were linked by the war crimes tribunal at the Hague to the Vukovar hospital massacre, in which hundreds of patients, mainly Croats, were taken to a deserted field and executed.

Arkan developed a fine expertise in the art of ethnic cleansing. His Tigers would arrive at a town or village and would brutally mutilate and kill the men, in the thousands; the women would be publicly raped by gangs of his soldiers in front of their families to cause maximum humiliation; children too were not spared. Ron Haviv describes a scene:

> They dragged the husband out of the house first, across the street from the mosque. The local butcher. The soldiers were telling me not to take photographs. Then the wife was dragged out. She was screaming—shots rang out and the husband went down. The wife reached down and took his hand in hers, then they shot her and she went down. Then they dragged out the sister-in-law. I walked back towards some other soldiers who had just taken a kid on the lawn of the mosque. He broke free and tried to escape but couldn't— there was a wall. They shot him in the back. Over the road they shot the butcher's sister-in-law before the order came to move to another part of town.

The Tigers continued this raping, beating, torturing and killing as they swept into unsuspecting towns and villages. The thousands of women who were raped by the gangs of Serb soldiers, Muslim girls and Kosovar Albanian women, were then kept in concentration camps while their pregnancies matured, to ensure healthy births of the new 'Serb' babies. Men who survived execution starved in the concentration camps, living skeletons waiting to die. A Bosnian delegation to the UN said that 200,000 people were killed, 12,000 of them children; up to 50,000 women were raped and 2.2 million were forced to flee their homes. This was genocide at its worst. Rumour that Arkan and his Tigers were coming was sufficient to cause a total community to flee in panic: one town with a population of 33,000 had 16,000 Muslims and Croats; a week later the numbers were reduced to 100 Croats and 300 Muslims—the town had been 'ethnically cleansed' by experts.

Richard Holbrooke of the US foreign office once asked Slobodan Milosevic why he didn't do something about Arkan. 'I am afraid of him,' replied the leader, but finally someone who was not afraid of him walked into the Intercontinental Hotel and assassinated him, a bullet through the eye, in full public view. It is rumoured that the assassination was ordered by Milosevic, who was concerned about Arkan giving evidence against him in the Hague trial; most suspect that just as the Yugoslav state had built up Arkan, only the state would have been powerful enough to tear him down.

If Arkan was a mafia capo, Milosevic was the don—patient, calculating and ruthless. He had already shown that even his friends must fear him; raised to power by his university friend

Ivan Stambolic, he turned against him forcing Stambolic's resignation as president of Serbia and then replacing him. In 2000 the former Serbian president was kidnapped; three years later his body was found and Milosevic was charged with ordering the murder. In 2006 the Supreme Court of Serbia ruled that Milosevic had ordered the murder of Stambolic. Killing his friends and massacring his enemies, Milosevic has been compared to Adolf Hitler, and Bill Clinton described his actions thus:

> He sought to expand his power by inciting religious and ethnic hatred in the cause of Greater Serbia, by demonizing and dehumanizing people, especially the Bosnian and Kosovar Muslims ... He unleashed wars in Bosnia and Croatia, creating two million refugees and leaving a quarter of a million people dead ... He stripped Kosovo of its constitutional self-government, and began harassing and oppressing its people.

But in one respect Milosevic was very different from Hitler—whereas Hitler had no interest in wealth, Milosevic was one of the great kleptocrats, reputed to have earned a billion-dollar fortune through his criminal activities while in power. He stole state assets and supported mafia criminals, including his son Marko, who ran a major cigarette smuggling syndicate and other illegal ventures with the support of the state; black market currency deals and special concessions created more illegal profits for his family. Much of his fortune was transferred to accounts in Russia, China, Switzerland, Cyprus, Lebanon and South Africa; authorities subsequently froze seventy million pounds sterling in the Swiss accounts alone. Milosevic is believed to have used the state airline JAT to fly suitcases of cash abroad. But what he stole was insignificant in comparison with what he destroyed. He financed the war by printing more and more currency notes leading to the world's highest hyperinflation; the result was bankruptcy and criminalization of the state and the destruction of a nation and its people.

8

South Asia: A Nuclear Conflict Zone

An eye for an eye only ends up making the whole world blind.
—Mahatma Gandhi

The year 1947 saw the joy of independence from British rule. It also saw the pain of a bloody partition that tore apart the subcontinent with the displacement of over ten million people and more than a million killed. India and Pakistan have fought three wars, and never-ending skirmishes over Kashmir, and India has fought one war with China. East and West Pakistan fought a civil war against each other which resulted in the break-up of Pakistan and the birth of Bangladesh; Pakistan has lived through decades of war and conflict in its Federally Administered Tribal Areas (FATA) on its border with Afghanistan and in the disputed lands of Kashmir. In addition to wars with each other, these countries have suffered from a series of internal conflicts, that have destabilized their societies and bled their economies.

Assassinations of leaders have been frequent. India has lost three of its national leaders to assassination: Mahatma Gandhi killed by a Hindu extremist, Indira Gandhi by a Sikh, and Rajiv Gandhi by a Tamil. Four of Pakistan's national leaders have been assassinated: Prime Ministers Liaquat Ali Khan, Zulfiqar Ali Bhutto, President Zia-ul-Haq and Benazir Bhutto. Provincial governors have also not been spared: Nawab Akbar Bugti in Baluchistan, Hayat Sherpao and Fazle Haq in the North West Frontier Province and Salman Taseer in the Punjab. Bangladesh has also seen three national leaders assassinated: Sheikh Mujibur Rahman, founder president of the nation, Prime Minister Mansoor Ali and President Ziaur Rahman. Nepal saw the bloody murder of King Birendra together with his queen and nine of his family members by the crown prince. At the southern tip, Sri Lanka has seen decades of bloody war with the Tamil Tigers who have killed many ministers and one president, Ranasingha Premadasa; in addition, the socialist prime minister Solomon Bandaranaike was assassinated by a Buddhist monk.

The subcontinent has a population in excess of one-and-a-half billion—about a quarter of the world's people—and is home to two antagonistic nuclear powers, India and Pakistan. Whereas other regions, such as Southeast Asia, are emerging from conflict, the subcontinent is sinking further into instability and today poses perhaps the greatest threat to world peace.

PAKISTAN: AVOIDING PEACE

The Pakistan that was born in 1947 did not last twenty-five years. The Punjabi elite alienated other ethnic groups who felt that they were being unfairly treated and at first demanded autonomy, and later independence. When the Bangladesh Awami League emerged as the largest party in the 1971 elections, the West Pakistani regime declared war rather than concede power; India supported the Bengalis, the Pakistani army was defeated; 90,000 prisoners of war were taken and Bangladesh broke away from Pakistan. The deprived smaller nationalities, Baloch and Sindhi, continued to struggle against Punjabi domination, and within Sind language riots erupted in clashes between the Sindhi sons of the soil and the Muhajir refugees from India. Jihad, the battle cry of fundamentalist Islam, was taken up first against the Russians by the Mujahedeen, then against the Afghan establishment by the Taliban, and finally against the Pakistani establishment by the Pakistani Taliban. Islamic jihad with its suicide bombers disrupted life throughout Pakistan. Meanwhile, the Baloch nationalists escalated their struggle for a country of their own.

In Iraq, America had created a Frankenstein in Saddam Hussein, whom she later had to destroy; in Afghanistan, in her proxy war with the USSR, she gave birth to Islamic jihad. The fundamentalist fighters, given huge supplies of money and armaments, had developed battle experience and a taste for war. When the Russians departed, they looked for a new enemy. War was easy to start but difficult to stop; the fighters had no other skills and had grown comfortable with the economy of war with its easy money. The madrassas churned out legions of would-be martyrs, eager to join the battle. Pakistan's ISI had hoped to fulfil its objectives through these legions of Islam, to gain strategic depth in Afghanistan, and to liberate Kashmir. They did not expect the blowback that followed, the destabilization within Pakistan, the Red Mosque siege in Islamabad in July 2007, the sectarian killings, the kidnappings and general deterioration of security, and the flight of capital and professionals to safer shores. What had started as a game had grown into a very serious problem. Pakistan was coming apart.

The militant groups fell into five main categories:

- The al Qaeda focusing on its war with America and its international agenda, but ever ready to attack the Pakistani regime.
- The ousted Taliban of Mullah Omar, struggling to win back Afghanistan from the Karzai regime.
- The Pakistani Taliban fighting to destabilize Pakistan in their war against the pro-US Pakistani regime and the US troops.
- The freedom fighters waging their guerrilla war to liberate Kashmir and to attack their enemy India.
- The sectarian groups who killed Shias and other minority sects in Pakistan whom they defined as Enemies of Islam.

Together they destabilized Afghanistan, Kashmir, Pakistan and parts of India. Their story has already run through more than three decades between 1979 and 2012, and there is no end in sight. Military insurgency is fed by a steady supply of weapons, money and dedicated soldiers, all of which were and still are readily available to the Islamic jihad.

For President Zia-ul-Haq it was an easy call; he was himself a devout Muslim. America needed his help against Russia. Muslims both within Pakistan and worldwide opposed godless communism, and the opportunity presented by Afghanistan offered him a legitimacy that he badly needed after his controversial and unpopular execution of Bhutto. America supplied the weapons, and together with Saudi Arabia committed and delivered on the money; fighters were drawn from inspired Muslims who came in from all corners of the Muslim world, and from the madrassas, the religious schools that proliferated faster than McDonalds' franchises boosted by Saudi financial support. The handling and control of the jihad against the Russians was entrusted to the ISI, the Inter Services Intelligence, the largest 'intelligence' service of the Pakistani army, which also acted as the pipeline for all the money that was provided to support the struggle.

For as long as the Russian war continued, Pakistan could do no wrong in the eyes of America; when President Zia spurned the American offer of $400 million as 'peanuts', the offer was raised to a more acceptable figure, as the US poured in the money and support dramatically depicted in the Hollywood movie *Charlie Wilson's War*. Even Pakistan's nuclear programme under A.Q. Khan was quietly accepted, with the US president signing off on Pakistan's compliance year after year, to allow the continued disbursement of US aid to Pakistan. It was a good time for all, ending in a jubilant celebration of victory, with the Afghans proudly claiming 'We have defeated the Russian empire. We are invincible.'

On 17 August 1988, six months before the Russians

withdrew from Afghanistan, President Zia, together with most of his top commanders, was killed in a mysterious plane crash. Though the US investigators claimed the crash was caused by a mechanical problem, common to many C-130 aircraft, the Pakistani investigators suspected foul play. Theories abounded of the CIA or Russia's KGB plotting an assassination, and 'exploding mangoes'. General Hamid Gul, the ISI chief, suggested that the US might be responsible; Ijaz-ul-Haq, General Zia's son, said that he was '101 per cent sure' that Murtaza Bhutto was involved; the *Sunday Times* said that the pilot had boasted to a confidante, 'The day Zia flies with me, that will be his last flight.' The crash of the C-130 ended the era of the 'Pakistani billionaire generals', but the era of the 'billionaire Afghan warlords' was just beginning.

The events of 9/11 that resulted in the destruction of the World Trade Center twin towers in New York opened a new chapter in the Afghan wars. The Taliban regime had played host to Osama bin Laden and his al Qaeda, and were reluctant to hand him over. In the war with Russia the Afghans had been America's ally; in the war of revenge that followed 9/11 the Afghans were America's enemy. President Musharraf was given an ultimatum—either you are with us or you are against us. Musharraf told the Americans: 'I am with you'; he also told the jihadists: 'I am with you'—a delicate balancing act that he maintained for as long as he retained power. He could not walk away from American money, but neither could he walk away from the Taliban and the jihadist groups who were important ISI assets. The Americans called his behaviour 'hypocrisy'; Musharraf would have preferred Mao's term to describe his relationship with Chiang Kai-shek during the Japanese invasion: 'Dual Policy'. Musharraf continued his clandestine support for the Islamic fighters in both Afghanistan and Kashmir, and when forced by the US to stop supporting terrorists, he drew a fine distinction between 'terrorists' and 'freedom fighters'. America preferred its own definition of the word: 'A terrorist is someone who has a bomb, but doesn't have an air force'!

The extremist groups grew to more than twenty in number, but some were more prominent than others. The Lashkar-e-Taiba (LeT), a Wahabi group, was founded by Hafiz Saeed in 1990. Close to the ISI, it acted mainly in Kashmir, and maintained a low profile in Pakistan. Recognized as one of the most ferocious groups, it enforced a discipline that encouraged beards and ankle-length shalwars, and forbade films, TV and music. One of their more famous ventures was the attack on the Red Fort in Delhi. The LeT explained their peaceful coexistence with the government in Pakistan: 'Our main objective is to carry on jihad against non-Muslims. Islam does not allow waging jihad against Muslims.' Between 10,000 and 30,000 fighters were trained in their camps.

Jaish-e-Mohammed (JeM) was formed by Masood Azhar who was freed from an Indian prison in the Indian Airlines hijacking settlement (1999); JeM quickly built up its reputation in a series of spectacular attacks in Kashmir, including their raid on the Kashmir state assembly. They then launched a dramatic commando-style attack on the Indian Parliament in Delhi for which they claimed responsibility but later backtracked. When President Musharraf banned the group, they turned their venom against targets within Pakistan, first Christians and Shias, and then Musharraf himself, whom they tried to assassinate.

The Sipah-e-Sahaba (SSP) of Haq Nawaz Jhangvi operated on a one-point anti-Shia agenda, and its breakaway party, Lashkar-e-Jhangvi (LeJ), led by Riaz Basra, exerted tremendous pressure on the Pakistani government to have Shias declared non-Muslims. Terror attacks and suicide bombings escalated in what many saw as a proxy war between Saudi Arabia and Iran on Pakistani soil. The government watched in frustration, as judges were unable or unwilling to try cases on arrested terrorists due to death threats. Terrorist leaders who were arrested mysteriously escaped due to sympathizers within the government ranks. Finally, the Punjab government under Shahbaz Sharif started 'extrajudicial killings' as the only way to deal with the terror, and in response the extremists planned assassinations of the Sharif brothers, Nawaz and Shahbaz. Numerous assassination attempts were made against Musharraf and even against his prime minister, Shaukat Aziz. The ISI saw their pet cub grow into an uncontrollable tiger now ready to turn against its handlers.

The first phase of conflict saw the Americans, the Pakistanis and the Islamist fighters all on the same side, against the Russians. In the second phase, after 9/11, the US fought against the Taliban, with Musharraf playing both sides. The third phase started in 2009 with the breakdown of the Swat Valley peace deal in which the Zardari government offered Sharia law to the Tehreek-e-Nafaz-e-Shariat-e-Mohammadi (TNSM) in exchange for a cessation of hostilities. When headlines

announced 'Defiant Taliban forces advance to within 60 miles
of Islamabad', the panic buttons were pressed, as confused
Pakistanis asked, 'Where is our army?' and nervous Americans
questioned, 'Are their nukes safe?' The army high command
now had to take a stand. Where previous escalation of violence
and a general breakdown of law and order had not been enough
to focus the army, where the attacks on five-star hotels in
Karachi, Peshawar and Islamabad had not provided decisive
provocation, the advance on Islamabad followed by the attack
on the military headquarters, GHQ, on 10 October 2009,
forced firm resolve for the first time on the army high command.
The pretence was over; war had begun in earnest; a war in
which one side must win and one side must lose. The Pakistanis
finally saw the war as their own, with the US, despite their
embarrassing drone attacks, a firm ally. Baitullah Masud of the
Tehrik-i-Taliban Pakistan (TTP) had been a formidable
guerrilla leader. His successor, Hakimullah Masud, was
more rash and made serious mistakes; his random bombs which
killed Pakistani civilians en masse alienated Pakistanis
from his Taliban, and even more disastrously, the high-profile
attack on the GHQ made the Pakistani army his implacable
enemy.

The war that has started in earnest is unlikely to end soon.
The $7.5 billion that America has promised in aid may prove
to be 'peanuts' when compared to the economic losses that
Pakistan will suffer from the conflict. Pakistan may survive as
a nation, but will it follow countries such as Uganda—a
prosperous African country with a per capita income of $949
in 1980 before it was reduced by five years of civil strife to a

mere $31? Will the Pakistani rupee, which has fallen from a rate of 60 to a rate of 95 to a dollar, accelerate the country's slide into the hyperinflation that was witnessed in other conflict zones such as Yugoslavia, Iraq and Iran, wiping out the savings of the entire middle class, as famine racks the poor? More than a century ago, Lord Curzon, the viceroy of British India, wrote: 'No patchwork scheme will settle the Waziristan problem. Not until the military steamroller has passed over the country from end to end will there be peace. I do not want to be the person to start the machine.'

While the extremists and the Pakistani army battle it out in the North West Frontier Province, the joker in the pack is Baluchistan, a vast province covering almost half the area of Pakistan with a very small population of less than eight million Baloch. When ruling India, the British had evolved a formula for dealing with the people that inhabit the Pakistan of today: 'Rule a Punjabi, crush a Sindhi, buy a Pathan and respect a Baloch.' Over the last fifty years the Punjab and its army which have replaced British rule have followed a different policy for Baluchistan, a policy which relies less on respect and more on repression and war. The result has been a series of Baloch uprisings, a strong Baloch national movement and four legendary leaders, Mir Ghaus Bakhsh Bizenjo, Nawab Khair Bakhsh Marri, Nawab Akbar Bugti and Sardar Ataullah Mengal.

Baluchistan has been blessed—or cursed—with significant natural resources, with a large strategically located landmass, a thousand-mile coastline, oil and gas, copper and gold, iron, zinc, coal and uranium. The Baloch have suffered through a prolonged conflict with Islamabad over these resources. The new port at Gwadar has aggravated the situation, increasing Baloch resentment over the fresh wave of Punjabi settlers and the takeover of large tracts of land by the army.

The war has escalated after the assassination of Nawab Akbar Bugti, whose grandson Baramdagh Bugti now leads the Baloch Republican Army, which along with the Baloch Liberation Army and the Baloch Liberation Front represents the hawks in the Baloch nationalist movement. The hawks demand independence, but now even mainstream political parties such as Akhtar Mengal's Baluchistan National Party are not far behind, with demands not just for powers over legislation, finance and natural resources but for the right to their own paramilitary force, along the lines of the Peshmergas of the Kurds.

The Baloch have long complained that Islamabad has always exploited Baluchistan, taking its gas, oil and minerals, but giving nothing back; they also point to the illiteracy rate of 80 per cent and the disappearance of 8,000 Baloch activists as examples of Islamabad's unfair treatment. Protests are voiced about the 'Yellow Water' of Chagai, contaminated by the nuclear tests, which causes cancer and blindness. Strident Baloch leaders warn: 'Pakistan should learn a lesson from Yugoslavia and Indonesia. This country is heading towards Balkanization.' The lack of security scares away investment and raises questions about the viability of a trans-Baluchistan gas pipeline from Iran, but this does not disturb the Baloch separatists who say they are happy if foreign investors stay away—'When we are independent, we will bring our own investors.'

Conventional military strategy has always advised against multiple fronts in wars and conflict. Pakistan's strategy has been the opposite. The Taliban civil war in the north-west, the Baloch uprising in the west, the Kashmir struggle in the north, and hostility with India simmering on their eastern border, all drain the exchequer, enhance instability, scare away capital and investment, and lead to serious deterioration of law and order. Meanwhile, unrestrained population growth, which is expected to reach 300 million by mid-century; failure of the education system, which has been bypassed by the information economy; a deteriorating industrial sector unable to compete with China and the Far Eastern tiger economies; an energy economy dependent on expensive oil imports; rampant corruption and a cavalier approach to governance and nation building have increased the incidence of poverty to 70 per cent of the people, who struggle against inflation and rising prices to feed their families on income levels that are just not enough. The elites enjoy a life of luxury and privilege, and the rulers with unlimited wealth and power grow ever more distant from their subjects. Pakistan can no longer avoid change.

THE MAHATMA'S INDIA

Over the last fifty years India has fought one war with China, and three-and-a-half wars with Pakistan (Kargil being the 'half'). After the turn of the century, diplomatic breakthroughs have improved areas of the Indo-Chinese relationship, but the Indo-Pak hostility seems to be getting worse. Indian disputes with China started under British rule, when Sir Henry McMahon expanded the British Empire by defining the border as 'The McMahon Line'; the Chinese have never accepted the Line.

In 1950 China conquered Tibet, claiming it as an integral part of China; this further aggravated hostility, with seemingly implacable disputes over Tibet, Sikkim, Aksai Chin (Jammu and Kashmir) and Arunachal Pradesh. Disputes led to war in 1962—a short and fast war, in which China defeated and overran the Indian positions. But then, victorious China unilaterally withdrew its army back to its pre-war positions behind the McMahon Line. China remains in occupation of 38,000 sq. km of Aksai Chin, and in 1987 India created the new state of 'Arunachal Pradesh' in the 90,000 sq. km of territory south of the McMahon Line, an area that China continues to claim as its own.

Though the two giants still claim large tracts of territory along their 3,500 kilometre Himalayan border, the situation has remained largely peaceful since the 1962 border war, and diplomatic initiatives have overtaken military offensives. India has recognized Tibet as an integral part of China, and China has accepted Sikkim as part of India, leaving Arunachal Pradesh as the key unresolved border concern. The new focus is on trade and cooperation. The Chinese and Indian state oil companies have formed joint ventures in bidding for overseas oil projects, and trade between the two countries exceeded $50 billion by 2008. India and China still have a long way to go before their relationship becomes comfortable, but at least they understand how important it is to eliminate conflict, and have seriously embarked on the journey.

Indians saw Jinnah's creation of Pakistan as the dismemberment of their country. In Pakistani eyes, India took its revenge for the break-up of India during Partition in 1971 when its army defeated the Pakistani troops in East Pakistan and helped create the breakaway state of Bangladesh. But it was Kashmir which became the heart of the conflict between the two nations.

As things appeared from the Pakistani perspective, at the time of Partition, three princely states posed a problem, Junagadh, Hyderabad and Kashmir. Junagadh was a Hindu majority area with a Muslim ruler who wanted to join Pakistan; a plebiscite was held and the state voted to join India. Hyderabad was also a Hindu majority state with a Muslim ruler; the Nizam, reputed at that time to be the wealthiest man in the world, wanted independence for Hyderabad, but India sent in its army and forced the accession to India. Kashmir, on the other hand, was a Muslim majority state with a Hindu ruler, who wanted his state to remain independent. Pakistan holds that the Muslim majority preferred to join it. After the Pashtuns from the North West Frontier Province invaded Kashmir, the maharaja fled to Delhi seeking Indian support, which was given in exchange of signing the agreement for accession to India, resulting in the First Kashmir War (1947–48). UN mediation helped in ending the war with the establishment of the Line of Control dividing Kashmir into an Indian part, Jammu and Kashmir, and a Pakistani part, Azad Kashmir and the Northern Areas. The UN resolution also called for a plebiscite in which the people of Kashmir would decide which course they preferred, but the plebiscite was never held, leaving an outstanding bone of contention between the warring neighbours.

The Indo-Pak War of 1965 was once again over the Kashmir

issue. Pakistan sent guerrilla forces into Indian Kashmir to stir up a rebellion; India retaliated by launching a full-scale attack on Pakistan, and after the largest tank battle since World War II, a UN-mandated ceasefire ended the war; President Ayub Khan of Pakistan and Prime Minister Lal Bahadur Shastri of India met at Tashkent and agreed to the withdrawal of their troops to the pre-war positions.

After 1989, armed insurgency against Indian rule broke out in Kashmir as Islamic jihad fighters who had learned their lessons in guerrilla warfare in Afghanistan against Russia became active. They demanded independence from India, or union with Pakistan. India, in turn, accused Pakistan of sponsoring cross-border terrorism.

In 1998, India and Pakistan conducted nuclear tests, demonstrating their nuclear capability. The following year they battled in Kargil, once more over the Kashmir issue. In 2001, Pakistan-based terrorist groups led a devastating attack on the Kashmir assembly building in Srinagar, followed a couple of months later by an attack on the Indian Parliament in Delhi. Cross-border terrorism continued, attacks becoming ever more dramatic, and in November 2008, the spectacular Mumbai attacks were shown on TV screens around the world as the landmark Taj Hotel became the scene of a dramatic shootout with black smoke billowing over the burning city. This was Mumbai's own 9/11.

The one war between India and Pakistan that was not directly related to the Kashmir issue was the war of 1971. The Bengalis had a long-standing grievance against unfair treatment by West Pakistan, and in the elections conducted by General

Yahya, their Awami League emerged with a massive majority. Instead of passing power to Mujibur Rahman, the Bengali leader, the Pakistani army moved in with a crackdown resulting in over a million deaths amidst accusations of genocide. An estimated ten million Bengalis fled to India. The Indian army intervened and after two weeks of intense fighting, the Pakistani forces surrendered and 90,000 prisoners of war were taken.

Half a century of hostility has bled the economies of both India and Pakistan, and development has suffered. The massive outlay on both nuclear and conventional defence expenditures has left too little money to support education, health and infrastructure requirements. Pakistan, the smaller nation, has suffered the most, as defence spending and debt servicing have consumed the lion's share of yearly budgets.

Religion has been the driving factor of much of India's internal conflict, with outbursts of violence against Muslims, Sikhs and even Christians. The rise of an aggressive Hindu communalism has threatened India's image as a secular, democratic state in which the rule of law prevails. The BJP, the RSS, the Shiv Sena and the Jana Sangh are all partners in the rise of Hindutva, the creed of the Hindu extremists, whose ideology has been clearly spelled out in the authoritative history by D.R. Goyal, *Rashtriya Swayamsevak Sangh*: 'Non-Hindus, particularly Muslims and Christians, have been enemies of everything Hindu and are therefore to be treated as threats. Hindus must develop the capacity for massive retaliation, and offence is the best defence.' Bal Thackeray, the founder president of the Shiv Sena, started his life as a cartoonist, then went on to be known as 'the Emperor of the Hindu Heart' as he lead the aggressive Hindu populist movement.

Anti-Christian violence had increased when the Hindu nationalist BJP came to power in 1998. Hindu extremists burnt churches and Bibles, destroyed or defiled Christian schools, colleges and cemeteries, forced the reconversion of Christians to Hinduism by threats of physical violence, raped nuns and murdered priests. Gujarat, Maharashtra, Uttar Pradesh, Madhya Pradesh and Delhi have all suffered anti-Christian violence under BJP rule. The terrible story of Graham Staines, an Australian Christian missionary who was burnt to death in the state of Orissa, along with his two little sons, Timothy and Philip, shocked the world. In 2008, Prime Minister Manmohan Singh strongly condemned this violence against Christians as a matter of great 'national shame', and Pope Benedict XVI criticizing the violence called upon Hindus to remember Gandhi and his advocacy of non-violence. Perhaps the gentle Pope forgot that Gandhi himself was killed by Hindu extremists, who were not too impressed with Gandhi's philosophy.

In the 1970s the Akali Dal had emerged as the power in Punjab politics; it promoted Sikh nationalism. To counter the independent-minded leadership of the Akali Dal, Sanjay Gandhi and Zail Singh, his home minister, started to build up an obscure preacher named Jarnail Singh Bhindranwale. But this charismatic maverick quickly grew out of control and started to defy his former sponsors in Delhi. Civil disorder increased in Punjab, and in 1978 a sub-sect of the Sikhs was attacked in the Golden Temple at Amritsar. The return to power of Congress in Punjab led to an upsurge of Sikh militancy and demands for an independent Sikh republic of Khalistan. A reign of terror was unleashed in the Punjab with accusations that Pakistan was supporting the insurgents. As violence grew, Bhindranwale was arrested amidst a shootout which killed twelve of his supporters, but was later released, further enhancing his stature. Finally, Indira Gandhi sent in the army to flush out Bhindranwale and his militant supporters who had entrenched themselves in the Golden Temple, the Sikh holy of holies. 'Operation Blue Star' routed the insurgents, with thousands being killed including Bhindranwale, whose body was found in the basement.

But that was not the end of it. The operation was seen as a violation of the Golden Temple, and in 1984 it led to the assassination of Indira Gandhi by two of her Sikh guards. That same night retaliation started with the targeted killing of Sikhs by angry Hindu mobs, and the destruction of their homes. Over a thousand Sikhs were killed in Delhi alone; shops were looted, women were raped, and atrocities were committed as the violence spread to other cities. Some among the ruling Congress party were seen by many as having encouraged the violence as the police stood by and watched, while the army was kept on the sidelines. Only in Calcutta was it different, where the communist chief minister Jyoti Basu moved quickly to control the mobs and to protect the Sikhs, showing what could be done if there was political will. After the bloodletting was over, normalcy was restored. Today, India's prime minister, Manmohan Singh, is a Sikh.

The Babri Masjid was named after Babur, the first Mughal emperor, who conquered the north of India in the early sixteenth century. The Hindus claimed that it had been erected on the site of a temple, and in 1984 started a campaign for its demolition, which culminated, on 6 December 1992, in the destruction of the mosque by a frenzied mob of 150,000 people.

The assault on the Babri Masjid in Ayodhya (Uttar Pradesh) was initiated by a 6,000-mile march led by L.K. Advani, the hard-line BJP leader, who proceeded through India whipping up Hindu emotions. When they reached Delhi, the Congress government did not stop the procession, and the marchers continued onwards, ignoring the law and threatening those who stood in their way. Narasimha Rao, the prime minister, sat quiet, not willing to stand against majority Hindu sentiment, and only moved to dismiss the state government in Uttar Pradesh after the mosque had been destroyed. Hysteria led to a rampage of killing, burning and looting across north and west India. Mumbai was the scene of the worst violence, with many deaths and thousands dislocated, as Muslims sought shelter in Muslim areas, and Hindus in Hindu areas. Finally, the army was called in and peace was restored; but it was not to last.

This incident moved Hindu–Muslim tension and violence to new heights. On 12 March 1993 thirteen bomb explosions shocked Mumbai, killing 250 and wounding another 700 people. The bombs that shook Mumbai were cited as revenge by the Dubai-based mafia don, Dawood Ibrahim, with alleged support from Pakistan. Almost a decade later, in 2002, tragedy ensued when a coach of a train returning with pilgrims from Ayodhya, the Babri Masjid site, was engulfed in fire. Fifty-eight pilgrims died in the blaze. It was seen as a deliberate act of arson. The retaliation that followed lead to the deaths of thousands of Muslims and accusations of genocide. The local administration in Gujarat was blamed for colluding in the massacre. The Hindu nationalist chief minister of Gujarat, Narendra Modi, continues to be blamed by many for encouraging the pogrom, justifying it on the grounds of the burning of the railway coach at Godhra. But nevertheless, in the elections that followed, Modi was re-elected as chief minister with a two-thirds majority in the state assembly.

The rise in communal tensions was mirrored by a rise in the fortunes of the BJP, the Hindu nationalist party, whose delegates in Parliament rose dramatically as a result of the communal issue:

- 1984: 2 members
- 1989: 86 members
- 1991: 120 members
- 1996: 161 members
- 1998: 182 members

Finally, in 1999, the BJP formed the government at the centre with Atal Bihari Vajpayee as prime minister.

India retains its international image as a secular, non-violent democracy with a tradition of the rule of law. The killing worked both ways; in Hindu-majority parts of India it was the Muslims who suffered, but in Kashmir, where the Muslims dominated, it was the Hindu Pandits who were the victims of Muslim extremists. The last fifteen years have seen the Pandit population in Kashmir reduced from a quarter million to hardly a few thousand. The horrors of Partition occurred over half a century ago, but its legacy endures, as Indians question

Pakistan's role in Kashmir, in the Sikh uprising of the 1980s, and in the dramatic terrorist attacks in Delhi and Mumbai. Meanwhile, the Pakistan establishment accuses Delhi of supporting Baloch insurgents and even the Pakistani Taliban in their war against Islamabad.

In 2006, Manmohan Singh described the Naxalites as the greatest threat to the security of India. Since then the movement has grown. Also known as 'Maoists', they now operate in 195 out of India's 604 districts spread across sixteen states, and their influence extends over nearly 92,000 sq. km in an area known as the 'Red Corridor' through Jharkhand, Chhattisgarh, Madhya Pradesh, Bihar, Andhra Pradesh, West Bengal and Orissa. The movement started in a village called Naxalbari in West Bengal and, inspired by Chairman Mao, has championed the rights of the downtrodden, the lower castes, landless labourers, poor peasants and the tribals. The Naxalites believe in class war and violence directed against the state and its agents, the police, landlords and district administrators, which have resulted in over 6,000 deaths in the last few years. Discontent and disillusionment have drawn the downtrodden to the movement which now has up to 50,000 supporters and 10,000 guerrilla fighters. Availability of finance is plentiful, and computer discs seized by the police from one of the leaders show that in 2007 the group raised over $200 million from illegal taxation and 'protection money' collected from areas under their control.

The government has, in turn, set up 'Cobra', a special action force to combat the insurgents. Death and capture have led to frequent change of the guerrilla high command. The rebels oppose the corruption in the political system and campaign to win the hearts of the oppressed by welfare work and meting out instant justice by punishing oppressors. The movement poses a grave threat to the integrity of the country and is a constant drain on the economy, but its solution does not seem to lie in the naked use of brute force, which has so far proved ineffectual. The government has now put together its anti-Naxal plan which includes a $1.5 billion package for development works in the affected areas.

The 'Seven Sisters' are known around the world as the giant oil companies that dominated the twentieth century; but India too has its own seven sisters—the seven states of north-east India: Assam, Nagaland, Tripura, Meghalaya, Manipur, Mizoram and Arunachal Pradesh. Their ethnic and linguistic difference from the rest of India has been the cause of much conflict. Assam at the time of Partition included Nagaland, Mizoram and Meghalaya, and historically was not part of India until the British Raj annexed the territory and included it in British India; Arunachal Pradesh was also outside India until the border was redrawn to include this territory, as was Sikkim. Manipur and Tripura were princely states with their own rulers. All these territories felt alien to mainland India; their 'doves' demanded autonomy or states of their own, their 'hawks' demanded complete independence, and they were prepared to fight for it. With a total population of less than forty million, and controlling only twenty-five out of the 543 seats in the lower house of the Indian Parliament, the Lok Sabha, this isolated and remote area continued decades of insurgency and conflict with Delhi.

The first to raise their demands were the Nagas, who went to Delhi shortly after Partition to plead their case; when told that they could have autonomy but not independence they even met Mahatma Gandhi, who told them, 'Personally, I believe you all belong to me, to India. But if you say you don't, no one can force you.' But forced they were, as Nehru himself admitted—'We have not succeeded in winning the people of these areas. In fact, they have been drifting away.' Almost reluctantly, Nehru responded to the insurgency in Assam by sending in the army: 'There is no doubt that an armed revolt has to be met by force, but our whole past and present outlook is based on force by itself being no remedy. We have repeated this in regard to the greater problems of the world. Much more must we remember this when dealing with our own countrymen who have to be won over and not merely suppressed.'

The Assam struggle was led by the United Liberation Front of Assam, ULFA, who stressed that theirs was not a secessionist movement but a struggle for liberation from the clutches of India's illegal occupation. They claimed that Assam had never been a part of India at any time in their history, and that they had suffered economic exploitation and persecution at the hands of India. India, on the other hand, banned the ULFA as a terrorist organization, and accused it of having links to Pakistan's ISI. The ULFA has assassinated prominent figures, such as the brother of Lord Swraj Paul, a prominent Indian businessman settled in the UK; it has also fought a war of economic sabotage, bombing oil pipelines, trains and government buildings, and raises substantial finance from robbing banks, selling 'protection', and extorting money from businessmen, bureaucrats and politicians. The Indian army has in turn responded ruthlessly. India has accused China of sponsoring these movements but has never been able to provide concrete evidence. The region remains underdeveloped, despite a substantial natural resource base, and waits for stability and peace before a serious take off of the economy can be launched.

The south has also seen violence in the Tamil conflict. India has provided arms and money to insurgents on both sides, and has also sent in its own Indian Peace Keeping Force (IPKF), which was greatly resented. The thirty-two-month presence of the IPKF in Sri Lanka was unsuccessful, resulting in the deaths of 1,100 Indian soldiers and over 5,000 Sri Lankans, and costing India an estimated twenty billion rupees. It also led to the assassination of Rajiv Gandhi. The Tamil insurgency ended in 2009 when the Tamil Tigers admitted defeat and their leader Vellupillai Prabhakaran was killed.

India's post-Partition history has seen hostility and war against neighbouring states of China and Pakistan, religious conflict against the Muslims and Sikhs, and a rise in Hindu militancy. It is also facing threat by the Naxalite militants. But through it all, India has successfully maintained its position in the community of nations as a democratic, secular state committed to Mahatma Gandhi's principles of non-violence and peace.

Section Two

CORRUPTION

I either want less corruption or more chance to participate in it.

—Anonymous

Corruption and conflict are the mother and father of failed states. They result in poverty, misery and human suffering. Corruption is the result of greed, and plagues too many poor countries; but even within these states there are beneficiaries and victims of corruption. Broadly speaking, the rulers and elites are the beneficiaries, and their lives are enriched by the fruits of corruption. Many politicians and senior public officials in the poorest countries are corrupt and themselves rank among the super rich of the world. The middle class is both a beneficiary and victim of corruption; a large number of government employees earn more from bribes than from their salaries, and many earn their livelihood as brokers, agents and facilitators, working as intermediaries in the networks of bribery. Businessmen who bribe plead the Doctrine of Necessity:

85

'If I do not pay a success fee for any contract I sign with government organizations, big or small, I will be out of business very quickly.'

The poor are the victims of corruption; nobody bribes them, and for every need they are harassed by corrupt bribe seekers—pay to get a job, pay to keep a job, pay the police whether to file a complaint or merely to protect oneself from the police, pay for access to education or health, pay for fair judicial process, pay for water, electricity and other services. In poor countries the poor starve to pay.

Corruption can be divided into two categories: 'grand corruption' and 'petty corruption'. It is grand corruption that grabs headlines:

Suharto (President of Indonesia, 1967–98) $15–35 billion

Marcos (President of the Philippines, 1972–86) $5–10 billion

Mobutu (President of Zaire, 1965–97) $5 billion

Abacha (President of Nigeria, 1993–98) $2–5 billion

Milosevic (President of Serbia/Yugoslavia, 1993–98) $1 billion

Suharto, Marcos, Mobutu, Abacha and Milosevic are the last generation big five, but new billionaire presidents are emerging year after year. Transparency International (TI) dedicates itself to fighting corruption, which it describes as 'the misuse of entrusted power for private gain'. The TI 2011 corruption index lists Somalia, Myanmar, North Korea, Afghanistan, Uzbekistan, Turkmenistan, Iraq, Haiti and Sudan among the most corrupt countries. Switzerland is listed as one of the least corrupt countries; but Switzerland, the banking capital of the world, is where the stolen money ends up. The US, Japan, the UK and the rich European countries such as Germany and France come high on the list of corruption-free countries, but are also high on the list of TI's Bribe Payers Index. Kellogg, Brown & Root, a Halliburton subsidiary, pleaded guilty to massive bribery to secure $6 billion in contracts, and agreed to pay $402 million in fines, of which Halliburton, the parent company, agreed to pay $302 million. US investigations traced $150 million in bribes paid to Nigerian officials and deposited in Swiss banks. The Nigerian minister of justice, Michael Kase Aondoakaa, said that the money was part of the $180 million given in bribes by Halliburton to Nigerian officials. Perhaps if Halliburton was a country it would come high on the list of the most corrupt. In December 2008, Siemens, the engineering conglomerate, agreed to settle corruption probes in the US and Germany by a payment of $1.3 billion in fines and penalties. Siemens was under attack for violations of the Corrupt Practices Act by repeated payment of bribes to secure contracts around the world.

The least corrupt nations are happy to help the rich rulers of poor nations rob their people. They look after the stolen money, almost all of which ends up in Switzerland and other safe havens in rich countries. Companies from the 'clean' countries provide the stolen money through bribes paid in project contracts, purchases of military equipment and commodities, and allocations of favourable concessions for extraction of natural resources such as oil. The 'black' money is then invested in assets in the West through a very 'private' banking system. The elite in rich and poor countries enjoy a partnership which promotes and protects profits, whether from drug mafias or from big business deals with corrupt leaders in poor countries.

Petty corruption, though less dramatic, is even more important in the everyday activities of people in developing nations. It frustrates, harasses, oppresses and makes life difficult and often unbearable. The most intrusive areas of corruption are the police, the courts, the tax and land registry departments, customs, state electricity companies, education and health sectors, and all regulatory authorities where executive discretion can be bought and sold. Petty corruption falls heaviest on those who can least afford to pay, and is a major cause of misery. If you do not get governance right, it is the poor who suffer.

Corruption is more than a moral issue; it is an economic issue. It is the most important factor in restricting and preventing growth in the economy, in keeping a nation poor, and in perpetuating human suffering.

- Corruption deters investment
- Corruption reduces capital availability
- Corruption wastes funds available to the government
- Corruption distorts the economy
- Corruption widens the gap between the rich and the poor
- Corruption increases flight of capital
- Corruption increases brain drain
- Corruption replaces meritocracy with patronage
- Corruption reduces national savings
- Corruption increases unemployment
- Corruption increases illiteracy, and degrades education
- Corruption degrades the quality of national manpower
- Corruption weakens government's delivery of goods and services to the people
- Corruption destroys democracy

These are some of the consequences of corruption. Unfortunately, the crucial importance of fighting and defeating corruption is not fully appreciated. Avoidance of corruption is not enough. Fighting corruption is the key responsibility of leadership in both rich and poor countries; but fighting corruption is not easy: when you fight corruption, it fights back. It is only through effectively containing corruption that we can hope to build sustainable and growing economies. The cancer of corruption is illustrated by stories from Iraq, Russia, Africa, Southeast Asia, China and India.

9

Corruption in Iraq: Saddam, America and Democracy

I think we Americans, of all people, understand the importance of
a good, legal constitutional framework as the basis of political life.
—Paul Bremer,
former US administrator in post-war Iraq

Over three decades—Iraq, the cradle of civilization, a wealthy oil state, a nation that enjoyed widespread prosperity—was reduced to poverty by conflict and corruption. The extraordinary story of Iraq involved the creation and destruction of Saddam Hussein by the US, a series of wars, the invasion and occupation of the country, the breakdown of society by violence and terrorism, and the reduction of the

Iraqi people to a life of poverty, insecurity and hopelessness.

The rule of the dictator Saddam ousted the rule of law; Saddam did whatever he wished, and took whatever he wanted. Initially, his corruption was that of a typical Third World dictator.

But after sanctions were imposed on Iraq by the UN in 1995, the Oil-for-Food programme (OFF) expanded Saddam's corruption to new heights, not just in Iraq, but on the international stage. OFF was designed to limit Saddam's control over Iraqi oil revenues. Under the programme, revenues from sale of Iraqi oil were placed in an account controlled by the UN and Iraq could spend the money only for permitted purchases such as food and medicine. But the programme allowed Saddam to sell his oil to buyers of his choice at prices he determined, a loophole that he exploited to create a gala of graft, theft and fraud. Between $60 billion and $100 billion were transacted under the OFF programme, and Saddam is said to have taken up to $10 billion in kickbacks and share of profits from his chosen buyers who were given oil vouchers at concessionary prices. But even more amazing than the bribes Saddam took from the OFF programme were the bribes he gave to powerful political players on the world stage. In 2004, the Iraqi daily Al-Mada published a list of 270 recipients of concessionary Iraqi oil, which included companies, individuals, associations and political parties. The gift of 'free' money to these recipients allowed Saddam to buy support for his policies from around the world.

The Al-Mada list shows Russia as the largest beneficiary of Saddam's largesse. Russia received 1.366 billion barrels. Major beneficiaries included the Liberal Democratic Party of Vladimir Zhirinovsky, the Russian Communist Party, Vladimir Putin's Peace and Unity Party, the National Democratic Party, the Russian Orthodox Church and the Russian Association for Solidarity with Iraq. Major companies that were given concessionary oil included Lukoil, Gazprom, Russneft, Soyuzneftgaz, Sidanco and Yukos. In addition, the son of the former Russian ambassador to Iraq, a former prime minister of the USSR, and the director of the Russian president's office received large allocations.

The Middle East was also well covered by Saddam's influence-buying spree.

- In Egypt, Khalid, the son of the former president Nasser, Imad Al-Galda, a member of parliament from Mubarak's National Democratic Party, and prominent editors of Egyptian newspapers
- In Libya, Prime Minister Shukri Ghanem
- In Palestine, Abu Al-Abbas and Abdullah Al-Hourani of the Palestine Liberation Organization (PLO)
- In Syria, the sons of the Syrian defence minister, and prominent media owners
- In Lebanon, the son of the Lebanese president Émile Lahoud
- In Jordan, Mashhour Haditha, the former chief of staff, and other prominent persons

In Europe, scandals broke out over the Labour MP George Galloway's payments in Britain, and the French payments which were linked to Chirac, and included a former minister of interior. Switzerland, Spain and Italy were not out of it either. Prominent political parties that were given Iraqi oil quotas included the Left Party and the Socialist Party in Yugoslavia, the Romanian Labour Party, the Bulgarian Socialist Party, the Slovakian Communist Party, the Party of the Hungarian Interest, the Ukraine Social Democratic Party and the Belarus Liberal Party.

Asia and Africa were also covered by Saddam:

- The Indian Congress party
- Indonesian president Megawati
- And companies and individuals in Sudan, Yemen, Cyprus, Turkey, Vietnam, Bangladesh, Malaysia, Pakistan, United Arab Emirates, Morocco, Algeria, Tunisia, Panama, Thailand, Chad, China, Nigeria, Kenya, Bahrain, the Philippines and Saudi Arabia.

Saddam bought political influence in the world in the style of the great powers, the US and USSR. Saddam was spectacular in the bribes he took, but was more than spectacular in the bribes he gave.

The final twist in the tale was when the UN sought to investigate the OFF payments, but were handicapped by a 'coincidence' that Nobel Peace Prize recipient and UN Secretary General Kofi Annan's son, Kojo, was employed by the Swiss inspection company Cotecna (which later achieved further notoriety in the Benazir Bhutto/Asif Zardari corruption scandal in Pakistan). Cotecna received the inspection contract from the UN. So Kofi Annan appointed a high-powered panel (including the American economist Paul Volcker) to investigate; the panel needed a resolution from the UN Security Council before they could start. Unfortunately, Russia, Great Britain and France, all permanent members of the council, were beneficiaries of the OFF largesse—the resolution was never passed.

But Saddam was merely a preamble to the corruption that followed with the American occupation of Iraq. The Coalition Provisional Authority (CPA) of the US and its allies has been labelled the most corrupt administration in history, surpassing the widespread fraud of the UN OFF programme. The CPA spent or wasted $20 billion belonging to the Iraqi people— squandered, stolen, given away, or simply lost. The three policies that made the CPA style of government unique were:

- Payment in cash;
- No metering of oil exports;
- No-bid contracts to American companies.

Philip Giraldi, a former CIA officer, vividly describes the 'payments in cash' scene in his article in the *American Conservative* (October 2005). The world watched in amazement the uncontrolled plunder of Iraqi oil wealth by its American conquerors.

- In fifteen months the CPA distributed $15 billion in complete disregard of the principles of accountability— most of the payments were in cash.
- 363 tons of $100 bills were flown across from the US, in plastic-wrapped 'cashpaks' of $1.6 million each.
- Unaccounted money was moved by helicopters and trucks, often disappearing en route. In one notorious incident

$1.5 billion in cash was delivered to an unknown courier in the Kurdish territories, never to be seen again.

- In the last month of CPA rule $5 billion was hurriedly shipped from New York in a desperate last-minute spending spree.
- Theft, fraud and crony contracts consumed billions of dollars; bills for soldiers' meals were paid for three times the number of meals actually served; trucks purchased without spare parts were abandoned or destroyed rather than repaired; one company contracted to move $82,000 worth fuel from Kuwait to Iraq demanded $27 million for the job!

The combination of a cash payments system with a decision not to properly record revenue ensured that accountability was weak at best, and non-existent in too many instances. Governments do not normally run their finances in this way, and the resulting corruption was inevitable. Giraldi criticizes the pattern of contract award for its cronyism, where massive no-bid contracts were awarded to companies with close ties to the US administration:

Halliburton, Vice-president Dick Cheney's former company, was awarded a no-bid contract with a value close to $10 billion. In June 2005 Pentagon contracting officer Bunny Greenhouse told a congressional committee that the agreement was the 'most blatant and improper contracting abuse' that she had ever witnessed, a frank assessment that subsequently earned her a demotion.

Criminal investigations were opened by the US Justice Department and continued through to 2009.

Scandals abounded. The US contractor Custer Battles was awarded a multimillion dollar no-bid contract for the security of the Baghdad airport, despite the fact that it had no previous experience in the field. They were also entrusted with providing security for the exchange of Iraqi currency, where allegedly much of the currency 'replaced' by Custer Battles has never been accounted for. CACI International, another US contractor, was involved in the Abu Ghraib prison interrogations, which have shocked the world with the brutal torture videos that later came to light.

The greatest scandals revolved around Halliburton and its subsidiary KBR, which had up to $18 billion in contracts including the $7 billion no-bid 'Restore Iraq Oil' award. The ties with Vice-president Cheney raised hard questions of conflict of interest, and Rumsfeld's office is alleged to have taken control of every aspect of the oil infrastructure contract. The company reached a low in 2005 with the cover-up of the gang rape of its employee Jamie Leigh Jones by other KBR employees on 28 July 2005. Jones was drugged, raped and confined in a security container without food, water or medical treatment. Because of contract restrictions Jones was barred from suing her employer.

The corruption bonanza continued under the interim government of Ayad Allawi. Ministries where corruption seemed most rampant were Interior, Defence, Trade, Health, Oil, Education, Water Resources, Finance, Electricity and Labour. Aiham Al Sammarae, an American/Iraqi businessman who became Minister of Electricity, was convicted for corruption and jailed; but in dramatic movie style, he was twice busted out of jail, first by US contractors, who overpowered Iraqi police and rushed him from the courtroom to the US embassy but later returned him, and the second time by soldiers of Blackwater, America's mercenary army. He was returned to the US, and is living in his million-dollar home in Chicago. When asked in Chicago if he feared arrest, he replied, 'Well, I will be so surprised if that happens in the States. Did I do anything wrong in the United States? No. Did I pay my taxes, every penny, every year? Yes.'

The most spectacular case of corruption during the interim government was the Defence Ministry scandal. The minister, Hazem Shaalan, formerly a small businessman in Britain, and his chief procurement officer, Zaid Cattan, a former Polish/Iraqi salesman from Europe, were behind the disappearance of almost all their procurement budget of $1.3 billion. Together, they awarded eighty-nine contracts, all paid in full via cash transfers in advance, before any work was done and without any bank guarantees or other security. Judge Radhi al Radhi, head of the Commission on Public Integrity, expressed his opinion that 'more than half of the $1.3 billion had been stolen'. Both Shaalan and Cattan were convicted in absentia, and are now living comfortably abroad. When tapes were played in which Cattan stated that he would deposit 'forty-five million' into the minister's private account, Cattan countered, 'I did not say dollars, I only said I would deposit forty-five million'. The interviewer replied, 'Well, you're going to give him 45 million of something.' 'Yes,' Cattan acknowledged, 'but I don't remember what.'

But insatiable greed soon turned mere corruption into violence and killing, as individuals and gangs fought for the loot. Dale Stoffel, a small-time American arms dealer, was awarded contracts for the refurbishment of Russian tanks in Iraq. As in other deals, middlemen were imposed. When Stoffel was unable to collect payments owed to his company, he complained to the Pentagon and to Congress that the Defence Ministry was ripping him off; he then returned to Iraq to try to collect his money; in December 2004 his BMW SUV was found riddled with bullets, and the bodies of Stoffel and his associate Joseph Wempel were recovered from a morgue. Killing, kidnapping and torture became the new rules of the game. Money was there to be taken; a senior interior ministry official flew to Beirut in a helicopter accompanied by $10 million in newly printed Iraqi dinars; he has yet to return!

Responsibility for dealing with the corruption was entrusted to the Commission for Public Integrity (CPI) whose head judge, Radhi al Radhi, launched a crusade to battle the corrupt regardless of their power or influence. 'The cost of corruption that my commission has uncovered so far across all the ministries in Iraq has been estimated to be as high as $18 billion,' he said. But the obstacles put in his way included violence, intimidation and personal attacks. Thirty-one employees in his department were killed, including twelve of their family members, one of whom was left dangling from a meat hook; his own relatives were targeted, and a missile was fired at his house. But al Radhi persevered; he obtained arrest warrants for the former defence minister and his top aides, all of whom fled the country; he launched investigations against twenty current and former ministers and alienated the political establishment which tried to fire him, and had to move with bodyguards to protect himself against death threats. Al Radhi's CPI resembled 'the Untouchables' of Chicago's Capone era. But his crusade was brought to a close by Prime Minister Nouri Al Maliki who issued a memo prohibiting investigations of current or former high-level Iraqi officials without the permission of the prime minister himself. Al Radhi was pushed out of his job by Al Maliki, and forced to flee Iraq. Seeking asylum in the US, he moved his family to Washington DC, where he lives in a small apartment with donated furniture being supported by American friends.

On 3 May 2009, *The New York Times* announced: 'Gunfight breaks out as Iraqi soldiers try to arrest trade officials.' The trade ministry was responsible for the $5 billion food programme, and warrants had been issued against nine officials including two of the brothers of the minister Falah Al Sudani on charges of importing food unfit for human consumption, theft of food stocks, theft of $39 million from ministry funds, and obstruction of justice. Kickbacks and fraud were alleged. *The NY Times* said that PM Al Maliki had vowed to crack down on corruption which was crippling progress in Iraq, but political pressure and blackmail hindered any serious efforts. It was estimated that by 2006 as much as $4 billion a year was being lost to corruption. In a dramatic sequel to the shootout at the ministry, the aircraft on which the minister was flying to Dubai was ordered back and the minister was arrested.

As criminals grew rich, Iraq was reduced from affluence to poverty, as a once prosperous people were crushed by unemployment, starvation and a breakdown in governance.

10

Russia: The Kremlin, the Oligarchs and the Mafia

Laws exist to protect the rich and punish the poor.
—Russian proverb

Little thieves are hanged, but great ones escape.
—Russian proverb

Russia, riddled with corruption and repression, was a failing state when Mikhail Gorbachev took power. He tried to change the system with his policies of Glasnost and Perestroika, but the resistance from the communist elite led to the end of the USSR, the Russian empire, and the end of the Gorbachev regime. Boris Yeltsin was the new man. He had the strength to force change, to overcome all resistance, and to build the new 'democratic and capitalist' Russia. In his massive makeover of a nation he was assisted by his team of 'reformers' led by Gaidar and Chubais. Yeltsin was not interested in amassing personal wealth, and the reformers were unusually honest men, but together they created the most corrupt society of the modern world. Yeltsin's decade was a decade of corruption, mafia, looting of the assets of the state, lawlessness, the new Russian businessmen, and finally the oligarchs. It was also the decade of destitution, poverty and hardship for the majority of the Russian people. For the change Yeltsin brought, he was loved; for the suffering he forced on the Russians, he was hated. When he died, Yeltsin was described as 'The man Russia loved. Once.'

The new private sector started with stealing the products of the state enterprises. This theft included 'trading' in these products—buying them at absurdly low or subsidized prices and selling them at market prices, but delaying or denying payment of the sale proceeds to the state companies. The Russian rouble was collapsing, with daily loss of value as inflation spiralled. The rouble under communism was worth $2; by 1995, $1 was equal to 5,000 roubles. By delaying payment, money could be placed in short-term trades of foreign currency or commodities with immense profits. Trade, finance and licencing spawned corruption as cliques of bureaucrats, red managers of state-owned enterprises and the new businessmen conspired to steal the assets of the state. This road led big and small alike to the cornucopia of capitalism. Boris Berezovsky, the future oligarch and cabinet member, started with his association with Vladimir Kadannikov, the director of Autovaz, the state-owned plant that produced Lada cars, and manufactured more cars than any other factory in the world. Together they ensured that Berezovsky cornered delivery of Lada cars at knock-down prices to resell to the market at a huge profit, at the expense of the state. Licencing for the export of natural resources of the state at discounted prices was another huge racket that led to the creation of substantial wealth, and not a few fortunes. Vladimir Putin himself was involved in scandal in 1991 when working at the St Petersburg mayor's office, where he was responsible for licencing of commodity exports in exchange for vital food imports. A commission investigating Putin recommended he be sacked for his role in giving licences for underpriced exports of non-ferrous metals in exchange for $93 million of food imports that never arrived.

Once sufficient seed capital had been collected through theft and trade, the more ambitious businessmen and their cronies in the bureaucracy moved on to finance—joint stock companies and banks. Where there were rules they were ignored; it was not about providing service but about ripping off other people's money. Once again Berezovsky was at the forefront with his All-Russia Automobile Alliance (AVVA) scheme which drew millions from naïve investors who gave him their money for a plant to produce a 'people's car'. The investors lost and Berezovsky grew richer. Banking raised the players to new levels in using other people's money in the get rich free-for-all. The money was used as 'venture capital' by the new bankers. The leaders were those that cornered the big blocks of state funds. Vladimir Guzinsky, later to become the media oligarch due to his close relationship with Yuri Luzhkov, the Moscow mayor, secured Moscow's operating capital, sizeable cash deposits on which to build his 'banking' activities. Berezovsky got the Aeroflot Russian Airlines accounts due to his close relationship with Yeltsin's son-in-law Valery Okulov, who ran Aeroflot, and with whom Berezovsky had a history of shady dealings. Vladimir Potanin, with his strong connections to the establishment, secured the juicy customs account. One of Russia's largest private banks, Inkombank, was taken over by Mafia chief Semion Mogilevich, known as the red mafia 'boss of bosses'. Mogilevich, also known as 'the Brainy Don', has an advanced degree in economics; his illicit businesses are alleged to include arms dealing, contract killing, drug trafficking, money laundering, oil smuggling, prostitution and securities fraud. Mogilevich lived for several years in Israel, and is believed to be a Jew, as are many other of the oligarchs, including Khodorkovsky, at one time the richest of them but now in jail in Russia, and Abramovich, perhaps now the richest, living in England. The list of Jewish oligarchs includes Vekselberg, Friedman, Ivanishvili, Abramov, Nevzlin and Berezovsky, all of whom have been prominent in the *Forbes* list of billionaires.

The Russian mafia spread its tentacles over Russia and across the world. With links to the Russian security services and to the government, it permeated the economy. Many private businessmen—according to some accounts 80 per cent of the business community—were forced to pay protection money to survive, and the mafia involvement covered up to 40 per cent of the economy. The red mafia was recognized as the most powerful mafia in the world, surpassing the Sicilian or Colombian, and was undoubtedly the most vicious. Among the best known were the Dolgoprudnenskaya and the Solntsevskaya families. St Petersburg was home to the Tambon syndicate, and even Chechnya had the Obshina, its own mafia family. The mafia was deeply involved in the massive arms trade in weaponry stolen from the military of the former USSR. In a famous case, a member of the red mafia known as 'Tarzan', living in Miami, sold six Soviet military helicopters to a Colombian drug lord, and was apprehended trying to sell a $100 million submarine to the Colombian to take his smuggling operation to new heights. The mafia was used both by the private sector and by the state security services for contract killing and intimidation.

The next step in the evolution of the Russian economy was privatization. Every building, every factory, every resource, every asset was owned by the state. Chubais decided that everything must be privatized immediately—it was now or never—before vested interests could obstruct and prevent this from happening. Privatization proceeded in three steps:

- Spontaneous privatization (1988–91)
- Voucher privatization (1992–94)
- Loans for shares (1995–97)

Opposition came from the Communist Party, but the strongest resistance came from the 'red directors', the managers of the state-owned enterprises. The red directors had grown used to treating their enterprises as their own property; they were not going to let the 'new Russians', the would-be buyers of their companies, take them over. Without bringing the red directors on board, privatization was impossible, so Chubais devised

'sweeteners' to seduce them. Finally, the concessions included
passing 51 per cent of the voting shares at a nominal price to the
directors and workers; in practice this meant that the red
directors got almost all of the giveaway. The red directors
became the new capitalist elite. They stole from the workers,
they stole from the minority shareholders, they stole from their
companies. But all this was condoned by the reformers, as
'corruption for the sake of democracy'.

The takeover battles fought over ZNGG, a small exploration
and drilling company, and United Energy Systems, UES, the
world's biggest power company, demonstrate the struggle for
corporate control that was taking place throughout Russia.
ZNGG was privatized, and the new owners with 54 per cent
of the equity installed a new manager. But Oleg Kudrin, the
old-style, hard-drinking red director, refused to let them in.
The locals, under the influence of Kudrin, refused the
newcomers transport, accommodation, and even landing rights
for their helicopters. Kudrin refused to register the shares of
the new owners, denying their ownership rights. So the new
owners sought redress in court and won, but Kudrin refused
to recognize the court decision. Finally, the new owners took
over by force, but Kudrin's team barricaded themselves in a
part of the building and ran rival control, threatening the
newcomers with a shootout. A stalemate developed until power
brokers in Moscow made a deal. In the meantime, Kudrin had
practically bankrupted the company with unauthorized stock
market speculation. When the new owners finally established
control, the company owed 42 billion roubles in back taxes
and was in turn owed a huge amount by the government.

Commenting on the debt, the new director said, 'It's a strange sort of debt which can get larger or smaller all by itself. Yeltsin says one thing, or signs some decree in Moscow, and the debt changes.'

UES, the national electricity company, was old-style, and its managers were old-style. A young banker with modern views, Boris Brevnov, was sent to clean up UES and bring it into the new economy. UES was described as the world's worst managed electricity utility; total chaos in management had led to blackouts throughout Russia. But when Brevnov arrived, he was resisted by the red director, Anatoly Dyakov, a former Soviet minister. Their views on running a company were worlds apart; the red managers would offer their visitors cognac; Brevnov offered bottled water! As Brevnov took charge, he discovered that Dyakov was siphoning off a significant part of the company revenues into offshore bank accounts. But under an antiquated legal system this was not illegal. The corruption had spread to the regions where corrupt station managers were bleeding the operations. Brevnov stopped much of the leakage and the value of the UES shares doubled in the first eight months of 1997.

The main thing was to create a capitalist system; it did not matter who the capitalists were, or how they behaved. To create support for his privatization in the face of determined resistance from the communists and the red directors, Chubais announced that 'vouchers' would be given to all Russians. Each voucher, with a face value of 10,000 roubles, was given free to each citizen, which he could use to buy shares in any privatized company. This ensured that the public demanded more privatization. Chubais needed to convert the red managers to privatization; to overcome their resistance he facilitated their takeover of the enterprises as new owners at practically no cost. The red managers used ruthless tactics to get control of the vouchers; in many cases they stopped paying salaries to their workers, forcing them to sell their vouchers at a minimal cost in order to survive. Forgery, fraud and blatant theft became prevalent.

It was the 'loan for shares' scheme that led to the most outrageous robbery of state assets, and enabled the new millionaires to become real billionaires. Under this scheme, the businessmen lent money to the government secured by the collateral of shares in major state companies that controlled oil and nickel, and when, as expected, the state was unable to pay off the loans, they bought the shares at absurdly low prices. Why did the state give away billions of dollars in what could be seen as an extraordinary scam? The reason was to secure the political and financial support of the new oligarchs who were created through the scheme, and to hit the vast and growing power and wealth of the red directors. Two of the companies, Lukoil and Surgutneftegaz, were sold to their red directors. A handful of other companies were sold to the new oligarchs and their partners. Sidanko, the Siberian oil company, was sold to Potanin, a powerful oligarch who had been an originator of the loans for shares scheme; he bought 51 per cent of the shares for $130 million, and two years later sold 10 per cent to British Petroleum for over $500 million! Potanin also bought Norilisk Nickel, a twenty-five billion dollar company, for $170 million, in a rigged auction in which all three companies that were allowed to bid were owned by him. Mikhail Khodorkovsky took the oil company Yukos, buying almost 80 per cent of the company for less than $300 million. In less than a decade the company was valued in excess of $25 billion. The sale of the companies were signed, but completion of the process was delayed till after the presidential elections, committing the new owners to get Yeltsin re-elected before they could walk away with their prize. In this way, Yeltsin was able to secure the colossal funding and press support he needed for his re-election.

Russia's most important company in the energy sector is Gazprom, the most profitable company in the world (2011 profits of $44.495 billion), sitting on 30 per cent of the world's gas reserve, employing close to half a million people, and constituting 10 per cent of Russia's GDP. It has given Russia one prime minister in Viktor Chernomyrdin, and one president, Dmitry Medvedev. In 1989 Chernomyrdin had privatized Gazprom, selling 15 per cent of its shares to management and employees at a nominal price. Chernomyrdin and his second in command, Vyakhirev, became billionaires in the process, but that was not enough for them. Gazprom provided the major slush fund for the government, and Chernomyrdin gave significant financial support to 130 political candidates for elections. By 1992, when Chernomyrdin became prime minister, his 1 per cent of the company was estimated to be worth between $1 and $7 billion, and he himself was labelled 'the Chief Mafioso in the country'. The CIA found that it cost a German business executive a $1 million bribe to get a meeting with Chernomyrdin. *The Times* wrote, 'The post-Communist reform process was now exposed as a vast organized crime racket from which a handful of Zionist billionaires gouged hundreds of billions of dollars . . . This netted Chernomyrdin a personal fortune of at least $5 billion.'

Gazprom has a history of paying high prices for supplies and contracts, and of using intermediaries at very high commission rates. Itera, a company working out of Florida, was used for several years as an intermediary in sales to Ukraine, and an estimated $7 billion was siphoned off through it. In 2000 Gazprom sold off assets worth $6 billion for $300 million. In one project, Gazprom gave Itera a stake worth $850 million for a vague promise to invest in the future; Itera also received a 35 per cent share of the lucrative Belarus gas market worth $500 million annually. The Russian press has reported that Chernomyrdin and Vyakhirev were behind Itera, and enriched their families through it. When Boris Federov, an investor and a former minister of finance, criticized the company's leadership, he was threatened with jail. He received visits from the mafia, and his dog was poisoned. In 2001 Itera was replaced by a new intermediary, Eural Transgas, with links to the mafia boss Mogilevich. Eural was later replaced by a new company, Rosukrenergo, which made enormous profits, buying Gazprom gas for $2.27 per million cubic feet and reselling it for $5.55.

Gazprom has also been accused of strong-arm tactics, blowing up pipelines in Russia to claim *force majeure* making it unable to take delivery of Turkmenistan gas which had been contracted at prices above the current market price. Leakage and theft from Gazprom has been estimated at up to $4 billion annually. Putin has moved fast to replace Chernomyrdin's mafia with his own, and according to Belkovsky, a Russian political analyst, Putin through offshore trusts now owns 4.5 per cent of Gazprom.

While privatization was being rushed through by Chubais, Moscow, under its strong boss, Mayor Luzhkov, was not willing to go along with the national policy. Luzhkov was an efficient, practical, old-style boss, who had his own ideas about how Moscow was to be run. Luzhkov's model would be Moscow Inc., where he would decide who would get what. Luzhkov declared war on Chubais: 'From now on you are my ideological enemy, and I am going to fight you.' Luzhkov had no respect for Chubais' new captains of industry, whom he criticized as people who knew nothing about running factories. They put their money in Swiss bank accounts and bought expensive houses abroad, or yachts and other expensive toys, and had no feeling for their country or the suffering of poor Russians, he felt. Luzhkov said that Chubais had privatized Russia 'the way a drunkard sells off all his possessions in the street in order to buy booze'. Prime Minister Chernomyrdin sided with Chubais, but Yeltsin, who had not forgotten Luzhkov's support against a rebellious parliament, sided with Luzhkov, who then ran Moscow as his own personal empire.

In Moscow pandemic corruption spawned violence and mafia-driven protection rackets. Crime syndicates were woven into the city administration. The American partner in the Radisson Hotel, Paul Tatum, was gunned down and killed on 3 November 1996; he had been embroiled in disagreements with Umar Dzhabrailov, the representative of Moscow City,

his partner in the hotel. Umar was rumoured to be part of the
Chechen mafia in Moscow. Luzhkov was a boss whom nobody
could challenge. When Gaidar, the leader of the economic
reformers, spoke out against corruption in Moscow, Luzhkov
sued him and won. Moscow was a city famous for its 'telephone
justice', in which a secret phone call would tell the judge how
the case was to be decided. But Muscovites felt that Luzhkov's
'corruption' was a small price to pay for the efficiency of his
administration. One commentator explained the massive
popularity of the mayor and his resounding election victories:
'Perhaps Luzhkov is on the take, but he is getting this place
[Moscow] into shape. So why should I waste my time on him?
Others do nothing but steal.'

Luzhkov created his own clan which included his oligarchs.
His wife, Yelena Baturina, became the richest woman in Russia
with a personal fortune that *Forbes* put at $4 billion. Her
construction company regularly secured a substantial chunk of
contracts in Moscow, and she hit the headlines in London when
it was reported that she had bought Witanhurst, a ninety-
room mansion, the largest house in London after Buckingham
Palace. The second leg of Luzhkov's financial support structure
was Vladimir Yevtushenkov, who was, after Luzhkov's wife,
the closest person to the mayor, and had been best man at his
wedding. Yevtushenkov's company Systema was a shadowy
corporation which grew by 600 per cent in two years between
1994 and 1996. Systema took over the Moscow
telecommunications company in an insider deal, at a price of
$136 million, of which $100 million could be provided in
equipment—a mere fraction of the $2 billion market

capitalization of the company. Systema quickly built a conglomerate that included banking, insurance, real estate, telecom and cellular phone companies. In 2005, the Russian *Forbes* showed Yevtushenko as number six on their billionaires list, with a fortune of $5.1 billion. But despite having the richest wife and the richest best man, both new billionaires under his rule, Luzhkov retained the respect of Muscovites for his positive contribution to Russia's most important city, and for a while was considered a possible presidential candidate before the rise of Putin.

Yeltsin himself was targeted in the high-profile Mabetex scandal. The Swiss construction company had been awarded contracts for refurbishing the Kremlin, and also for restoring the White House, Russia's parliament, after it had been badly damaged by tanks when Yeltsin in late 1993 attacked the House and the rebellious members in the 'Second October Revolution' which cemented his victory over the communists and a hostile parliament. Evidence came to light that Mabetex had provided credit cards to Yeltsin's daughters, and had also made $1 million available to the president on a foreign visit. Using these credit cards his daughters had spent $600,000 on lavish purchases in a short time. The Mabetex case acquired greater prominence with the dramatic exposure on television of the Prosecutor General Yuri Skuratov in bed with two naked prostitutes; Skuratov denied the allegations saying the pictures were doctored, but was later forced to resign his post. The matter involved the Presidential Property Management Department, a massive body which controlled an estimated $600 billion worth of property, and in which Putin was the second in command. Putin's work in dealing with the matter earned him recognition and respect from Yeltsin. Yeltsin used the property department to hand out gifts, such as dachas, to people he wanted to reward. The head of the department, Pavel Borodin, also fell victim to corruption charges.

The amounts involved in the Mabetex scandal were small in the general scale of corruption prevalent in Russia, but they hit at the president himself. It seems that more than Yeltsin it was his daughters who were attracted to easy money. Both his daughters were close to the oligarch Berezovsky, who came under investigation for his relationship with the husband of Elena, the Aeroflot chief, in shady deals involving the airline. Tatiana, who was important in the unofficial Kremlin power structure, was linked to the Fimaco scandal. This involved the flow of $50 billion of state funds through a Jersey company, Fimaco, formed with $1,000 capital. It was alleged that $235 million had been passed on to Tatiana's offshore bank accounts. Skuratov had been instrumental in the expose. The Fimaco case was not the only financial scandal involving offshore banking and money laundering.

The privileged group around Yeltsin came to be known as 'The Family'. The family included Yeltsin's friend and tennis coach who was favoured with a billion-dollar duty-free cigarette business through his National Sports Fund. While The Family enjoyed the international high life of yachts, mansions and parties, the people of Russia starved, suffered and died under hyperinflation, joblessness and mafia violence. Yeltsin had lost the love of the people, but nevertheless, was reconfirmed as president in 1996 through an unholy deal with the oligarchs. Four years later when he passed on power to Putin, another deal was evident. Twelve days after Putin was sworn in as interim president, on the last day of December, he signed his first decree granting Yeltsin, the members of his family and those living with him legal immunity from arrest, searches of house or person or questioning for the rest of their lives.

The new man was very different from the old. Where Yeltsin was big, Putin was small. Yeltsin was warm and emotional, Putin was cold and reserved. Yeltsin was an alcohol addict, Putin was a disciplined karate fan. Yeltsin's enemies were forgiven, Putin's died. Duma Deputy Galina Starovoitova, the prominent pro-democracy Kremlin critic, was murdered in her apartment building in St Petersburg. Critics of the Moscow bombs which led to war in Chechnya died with amazing frequency—reporters Igor Domnikov, Sergey Novikov, Iskandar Khatloni, Sergey Ivanov and Adam Tepsurgayev— were murdered. Sergei Yushenkov, vice-chairman of the commission formed to investigate charges that Putin's KGB had planted the apartment bombs, was gunned down; other members of the commission died or were beaten up or jailed; Yuri Shchekochikhin died of suspected thallium poisoning; Nikolai Girenko, a prominent human rights defender, was shot dead in his home in St Petersburg; Paul Klebnikov, editor of the Russian edition of *Forbes* magazine, was shot and killed in Moscow; Victor Yushchenko, the anti-Russia candidate for the presidency of Ukraine, was poisoned, but miraculously survived; Andrei Kozlov, the first deputy chairman of Russia's Central Bank, who campaigned against money laundering, was shot and killed in Moscow; Anna Politkovskaya, the internationally renowned journalist and writer who wrote *Putin's Russia*, was shot and killed at her home in Moscow; Alexander Litvinenko, KGB defector and author of the book *Blowing up Russia*, which accuses the Kremlin of masterminding the Moscow apartment bombings, died of thallium poisoning in London; Daniel McGrory, senior correspondent of *The Times* (London), was found dead in his apartment shortly after his interview for Dateline NBC which aired a report on the killing of Litvinenko, who the British authorities believed to have been murdered in a state-sponsored assassination. With Putin in the Kremlin, Russia changed.

Putin understood Russia's form of capitalism. In St Petersburg he had been in charge of the new economy, and controlled licences permitting export of state-owned resources in exchange for food imports; he had also been in charge of the state's interests in the lucrative casino business; both these sectors of the St Petersburg economy involved profits and scandals, and the casino business had linkages to the mafia. In 1992 Putin was investigated and recommendations were made that he be dismissed. Putin moved on to Moscow, where he was placed as second in command in the Kremlin Property Management Department, which controlled $600 billion worth of assets. Here again, financial scandals abounded, and brought down Putin's boss, Borodin.

But Putin moved on and up. In quick steps he moved from head of the Russian Secret Service, to prime minister to president. Putin moved fast as president; he knew what he wanted, he understood Russian business and Russian politics, and he was 'connected', with a strong manpower reserve from the secret service operatives and his St Petersburg associates. His focus was the media, the oligarchs, and the oil and gas sector. The media barons Berezovsky and Guzinsky were ousted, their media assets taken over, and the oligarchs themselves were driven into exile. This was followed by repression and murder of reporters, editors and writers, till the media was fully terrorized and tamed. In the first few months of his presidency, Putin removed the gas barons at Gazprom, who had already become billionaires, and replaced them with his own men—Dmitry Medvedev, who later became Putin's president, and Alexey Miller, the new CEO. Next to go was Khodorkovsky, the richest of the Yeltsin oligarchs. His oil company, Yukos, was hit with huge tax claims and was taken over, while Khodorkovsky himself was thrown into jail. The days of Yeltsin's 'Family' were over; it was now the time of 'the Friends of Putin'.

Stanislav Belkovsky, the director of the National Strategic Institute, a Moscow think tank, in an interview with the German newspaper *Die Welt*, spoke about Putin's hidden wealth. Belkovsky claims that after eight years in power, Putin has secretly accumulated more than $40 billion, making him Russia's, and Europe's, richest man. According to Belkovsky, Putin effectively controls 37 per cent of the shares of Surgutneftegaz, Russia's third biggest oil producer, worth $20 billion; 4.5 per cent of Gazprom, and at least 75 per cent of Gunvor, a mysterious Swiss-based oil trader, fronted by the reclusive Timchenko, who has been linked to Putin, and which posted profits of $8 billion in 2007. But whether the ultimate beneficiary is Putin or 'his friends', such as Timchenko, Sechin, or Mikhail and Yuri Kovalchuk, there is no denying that exceptional and easy money has been made in the oil and gas sector. The relationships are clearly sensitive, leading *The Sunday Times* of 1 March 2009 to apologize: 'In our article last week we stated wrongly that Gennady Timchenko is a close friend of Vladimir Putin and is a former KGB agent. The true position is that though Mr Timchenko and Mr Putin do know one another, the relationship is more one of casual acquaintanceship than of friendship, or of the two men being close friends.'

Gazprom, the 'government's wallet', was the centre of Putin's focus. Assets were bought, assets were sold; money was made both ways. Between 2001 and 2007 Gazprom spent $44 billion in buying non-gas assets. The purchase of the oil company Sibneft from Abramovich, a 'Friend of Putin's', at a high price of $13 billion, raised questions. But as fast as Gazprom bought companies at inflated prices, it sold off its own assets at discounted prices as asset stripping to the value of $60 billion took place. Gazprom insurance subsidiary Sogaz, its pension fund, Gazfond, and its mass media interest, Gazprom-Media Holdings, fell into the hands of Rossiya Bank, whose largest shareholder was Yuri Kovalchuk, Putin's close friend. The Gazpro-Media shares were sold for $166 million; two years later they were valued at $7.5 billion. Sogaz was sold for $120 million. The real value was estimated at more than ten times the purchase price and the son of Putin's cousin was a 12 per cent partner in the deal. After sale, the premium income of the insurance company rose from $500 million to

$1.5 billion as other state-owned companies, including the railways, were ordered to insure with it. Sibur, Russia's largest petrochemical company, was under sale to its former chairman, Goldovsky, who was arrested from the reception of Alexey Miller, the Gazprom CEO, and later fled. Putin warned Miller, 'Be careful. One day you may yawn a little too widely and lose more than Sibur.' Soon after that, 40 billion roubles of Sibur debt was written off by Gazprom, and the company was sold at a ridiculously low price to a favoured buyer. The most significant transaction was the 'shuffling' of the shares of Gazprom itself, which were bought and sold till finally 6.4 per cent of the equity, having a value of about $20 billion, 'slipped off the table'. Belkovsky alleges that 4.5 per cent has been passed into Putin's hidden ownership.

Trading in oil and gas also gave a flood of fast and easy money to favoured companies. Gunvor, the mysterious Swiss company, has become the third biggest oil trader in the world; its chairman, Timchenko, has made the *Forbes* list of richest billionaires. Intermediaries in Gazprom sales have earned fortunes. Itera earned hundreds of millions of dollars till it was replaced by Eural Transgas, which fell into disfavour due to alleged links to organized crime and was replaced by a new company, Rosurenergo. Like its predecessors, this new company makes enormous profits on each trade. Gazprom also embarked on a multibillion dollar pipeline construction spree, the feasibility of which was questioned. Gazprom construction rates at $3 million per kilometre were double the world average rates of $1.5 million.

But sophisticated manipulation of the economy to create fast and easy profits was not restricted to the oil and gas sector alone. In the automobile business, duties were increased on foreign cars and the import of second-hand cars to give a boost to Avtovaz and Gaz, the companies of Chemezov, and the oligarch Deripaska. The minister of communications, Leonid Reiman, a 'close friend' from the KGB, was named by an arbitration court in Zurich as the real owner of telecom assets worth $6 billion which had been supported by beneficial privatizations and licences. In another press exposure, Oleg Shvartsman, an obscure businessman, claimed he was managing $1.6 billion on behalf of a group of secret service officers; he claimed that the officials had 'earned' the money in 'velvet privatizations', the process under which companies were sold off to selected businessmen at extraordinarily low prices. Russia's deputy finance minister, Sergei Storchak, was arrested and charged with embezzling $43 million, despite the protest of his boss, the finance minister, who argued that Storchak was innocent. A senior government prosecutor alleged that corrupt officials were skimming over $120 billion a year.

Despite the immense corruption that had put Russia at 143 on the Transparency International list of corrupt countries in 2011, Putin's popularity with the Russian people remained high, due to the strong economy and rising standards of living caused by the oil bonanza and high prices of the commodities that Russia exported to the world. Nemtsov, a prominent opposition leader who had been a deputy prime minister under Yeltsin, put it succinctly: 'Putin made an invisible contract with the Russian people by which they tolerate corruption, mismanagement, crime and constraints on the mass media so long as they have buying power and continue to live better than they did in the Yeltsin era. But if the economy falters that contract could be broken. They might then demand accountability. Reforms only happen when the money runs out'. (From *Putin: The Results* by Boris Nemtsov and Vladimir Milov.)

After the worldwide finance crisis, the Russian economy nosedived. Falling oil prices and falling international demand resulted in one million Russians losing their jobs; the stock market lost 75 per cent of its value, almost double the 40 per cent loss of the American market. The rouble fell drastically against the dollar. But by late 2011 the economy bounded back with growth supported by energy exports, both of oil and gas. Not even corruption and mismanagement could counter Russia's natural advantages, for despite all Russia remained the world's largest country, with the world's largest gas reserves, and in 2011 the country also overtook the kingdom of Saudi Arabia as the world's biggest oil producer.

11

Saints and Sinners
in Africa

Clearly I would be lying if I said I do not have a bank account in Europe; I do. I would be lying if I said I do not have considerable money in my account; I do. Yes I do have a fair amount of money. However, I would estimate it to total less than fifty million dollars. What is that for twenty-two years as head of state in such a big country.

—Mobutu Sese Seko,
former president of Zaire

There are things we can learn from you.

—Richard Nixon to Mobutu

Africa, a continent of vast natural wealth, remains the home of the most poor and downtrodden people on the planet. Corrupt leaders and their partners in crime have robbed Africa of at least $140 billion, and perhaps as much as $300 billion since independence. Corruption is the major cause of the extreme poverty and suffering that has been the destiny of this sad continent.

In an endless list of those who have looted Africa, two names stand out for the scale of their theft: General Sani Abacha of Nigeria and President Mobutu of Zaire, who between them stole $10 billion from their countries. Their theft was made possible by the collusion of Western companies which provided much of the money in the form of bribes, and the Western banking system that received the stolen money and protected it.

Year after year Transparency International has shown many African states as among the most corrupt in the world; of the fourteen most corrupt states in TI's 2011 Corruption Perception Index, eight are African: Angola, Chad, the Democratic Republic of Congo, Libya, Burundi, Equatorial Guinea, Sudan and Somalia. It is no coincidence that these are also on the UN list of the world's poorest nations. Other African states that figure high on both lists (most corrupt and most poor) include Guinea, Zimbabwe, Guinea-Bissau, Cote d'Ivoire, Central African Republic, and Uganda. Like chicken and egg, corruption and poverty go together.

NIGERIA: OIL WEALTH MEANS MORE TO STEAL

One state that has been very corrupt since its independence is Nigeria. Nigeria, with significant oil wealth, is not a poor nation. Nigerians, however, are a poor people, with 70 per cent of Nigerians living on less than a dollar a day, deprived of basic needs such as health, education, sanitation, clean water, and, for much of the day, electricity. A culture of corruption has proliferated over the years. The Gowon military regime was inefficient and corrupt and was deposed by a military coup in 1974. The army chose Murtala Muhammad, who was a brigadier in the army and a national hero, but he was assassinated in 1976 and General Obasanjo ruled for the next three years. From 1979 to 1983 Shehu Shagari, an elected president, struggled with a recession economy hit by falling oil prices, till he too was removed by a military coup. A succession of military rulers followed: Generals Buhari, Babangida, Abacha and Abubakar, justifying their takeover as an assault on corruption, but each proving more corrupt than his predecessor. Abacha built a multibillion dollar fortune from corruption, and after his death Nigeria recovered more than a billion dollars from his estate, but in 2008 the three generals Buhari, Babangida and Abubakar astounded the world by defending Abacha, claiming that the Abacha corruption charges were 'unfounded and baseless'!

Abacha is recognized as one of the most corrupt heads of state of modern times, and estimates of the money he stole run to $6 billion. His main focus was Nigeria's booming oil industry. He received kickbacks for awarding exploration licences on favourable terms to foreign oil companies, and bribes from oilfield supply companies for drilling, pipeline contracts and petrochemicals. He took commissions from trading companies allotted oil quotas from Nigeria, siphoned off more than $2 billion from state-owned refineries, and when they were unable to provide refined oil products, earned massive commissions on import of deficit products. When his son's company, Delta Prospectors Ltd, reached full production in its barite mining operation, imports were banned, giving Delta a monopoly in supplying the oil industry.

The Lebanese Chagoury family was deeply involved in business with Abacha. The press reported that 'when Gilbert Chagoury flies into Abuja he is treated like a head of state. He arrives in private jets and is whisked off from the tarmac without all the customs, immigration and security hassles to the presidential villa'. The Chagoury family took up diverse businesses in Nigeria, including contracts to buy Nigerian oil, to supply fertilizer and build major projects. The lucrative oil trade was conducted through London oil trading firms Arcadia and Addax, and the Swiss-based company Glencore, controlled by Marc Rich, the notorious oil trader, who had fled US arrest warrants for tax evasion. These firms became Nigeria's main trading partners during the Abacha era.

Abacha's most important business partner was Halliburton and its subsidiary, KBR. The subsidiary hit the headlines when its CEO, Jack Stanley, pleaded guilty to charges of having paid bribes of $180 million in Nigeria, to secure a $6 billion contract. Stanley named Abacha, and also confessed that he had kept for himself several million dollars of the bribe money in offshore bank accounts. Future president Obasango, a founding member of Transparency International, was also named. The US courts sentenced Stanley to seven years imprisonment, and fined the company $500 million.

Abacha did not live the ostentatious international high life favoured by other corrupt dictators, with mansions and chateaux all over the world. He was not excited by conspicuous consumption, desiring only to amass extraordinary wealth. He lived a reclusive life seldom leaving the presidential villa where he conducted his business and did his deals. His one passion, prostitutes, finally killed him. After stuffing himself with Viagra, he indulged in a marathon session with a number of hookers who were summoned to the villa. He ended his life on the floor of the presidency, foaming at the mouth. After his death Nigeria pursued the stolen money both in the country and offshore. By 2009 almost $2 billion had been recovered, $750 million by voluntary surrender by the family who were allowed in a settlement to keep $200 million, N570 million from Switzerland, $350 million from Jersey and $150 million from the UK. The Citibank private banker who handled the Abacha account in Mayfair, London, when asked if the bank had fulfilled its due diligence obligations to ensure that the deposited funds were legitimate in view of the lack of proportion between President Abacha's salary and the deposits made, replied that they were informed of profitable contracts. An example of 'a profitable contract' was the contract for supply of children's vaccines where the state paid $111 million to buy vaccines which the Abacha company had purchased for $23 million, leaving a very comfortable profit of $88 million—an inhuman crime which clearly did not disturb the conscience of the banker. The comment of the British Banking Association was: 'Suspicion is a state of mind. Sometimes they get it wrong.' Abacha died leaving an estate worth between $3 and $6 billion including 500 properties.

After a brief interlude under General Abubakar, General Obasanjo was elected and ruled for eight years. Obasanjo was a man of dignity and stature, and had been a successful president before. He declared a campaign against corruption. Obasanjo has always declared himself to be honest, despite the fact that questions circulated how a military man who retired with savings of N20,000 could become so immensely wealthy despite a full-time political involvement as president for eight years. Rumours have circulated about his Obasanjo Farms, his N200 million investment in Transcorp, his N40 million investment in Bells University and his presidential library. But Obasanjo has always protested his innocence, and defies any investigation to produce evidence of corruption against him. His most embarrassing scandal emerged from the divorce proceedings of his son, Gbenga, and wife, Mojisola, when Gbenga accused his wife of a sexual relationship with his father. In his affidavit, filed in court, Gbenga said that Mojisola secured favours and contracts from her father-in-law in return for sex. He claimed, 'The lurid sexual relationship with her own father and his father, General Obasanjo, gave him great pain and psychological trauma'. But despite scandals, allegations and accumulation of wealth, Obasanjo seems to have emerged reasonably unscathed, and is respected widely both in Nigeria and internationally.

Obasanjo led a campaign against corruption, which he blamed for most of Nigeria's governance problems, and in 2003 appointed fearless crime-buster Nuhu Ribadu as head of the Economic and Financial Crimes Commission (EFCC), the Nigerian anti-corruption agency. Obasanjo gave full support to Ribadu, who was empowered, promoted and reappointed for a second term as EFCC head in 2007. In 2005, two years after the commission's establishment, the World Bank and the World Economic Forum's governance survey listed Nigeria as one of the twenty-one most improved nations in the world. Ribadu worked with missionary zeal and brought corrupt politicians, previously deemed untouchable, to court in handcuffs; he initiated thousands of cases and secured 270 convictions including nine state governors, the president of the senate, members of parliament and even his own boss, the inspector general of police, from whom $150 million was recovered.

In December 2007 the EFCC charged former Delta State governor James Ibori, one of the country's wealthiest politicians, who had netted $700 million from his activities, with 103 counts of corruption; $15 million in cash which he had paid to bribe Ribadu, and which Ribadu gave in to the state as evidence, was used against Ibori. Ribadu also went for the infamous '419 scams', the international email frauds that operated out of Nigeria and were cheating people around the world of $1 billion a year. The EFCC seized cash and property of $750 million from these fraudulent mafias.

Ribadu's war on corruption earned him many enemies and even assassination attempts; but as Ribadu himself used to say, 'If you fight corruption, it fights back.' On 15 April 2008, Nuhu Ribadu received the World Bank Jit Gill Memorial Award for Outstanding Public Service for having led a courageous anti-corruption drive in Nigeria. On 4 August 2008, the Police Service Commission in Nigeria announced the demotion of Ribadu from assistant inspector general of police to deputy commissioner of police. Two weeks after the arrest of the powerful state governor, Ribadu was ordered to resign and join a 're-education' course. After surviving a second assassination attempt, Ribadu left Nigeria for the UK. In an interview with *The Washington Post*, when Ribadu was asked what came of his investigation of the powerful state governor who had tried to bribe him, Ribadu replied that he was no longer in jail, 'he is a huge person in politics. He is the biggest one in the ruling party. He just bought a new jet'! Ribadu had tried to take on the system, the corruption mafia entrenched in high places; like Judge Radhi of the Iraqi Commission on Public Integrity, he was moved into exile after failed assassination attempts.

ZAIRE'S MOBUTU: 'A LEADER OF VISION'

Zaire (the Democratic Republic of the Congo) under Mobutu is a vivid illustration of a nation destroyed by greed and corruption. Mobutu Sese Seko, the son of a cook and a hotel maid, became president and ruled Zaire for over thirty years, amassing a personal fortune rumoured to be over $5 billion. Mobutu ruled by the naked use of terror and money, backed by CIA support; presidents from Kennedy to Nixon to Reagan all showered him with appreciation and praise. Reagan called Mobutu 'a voice of good sense and good will'; Nixon described him as a leader of stability and vision, and George H.W. Bush, as CIA director, said that he had appreciation and respect for Mobutu's 'dedication to fairness and reason'. Meanwhile, in Zaire itself, Mobutu was described as a kleptomaniac and a

Zairian Caligula. He was endorsed in a series of elections
where he was the only candidate for president. The Democratic
Republic of the Congo was rich in copper, cobalt, diamonds
and other natural resources when Mobutu took power. By the
time he was removed, Zaire was bankrupt, its currency
worthless, unemployment running at 80 per cent, its
administration paralysed. Mobutu replaced the 'rule of law'
with the rule of fear and patronage. Starting with a series of
public executions to make it clear that dissent would not be
tolerated, he used killing and torture as tools of control.
Journalist and writer Michela Wrong describes the extent and
horror of his brutality in her book *In the Footsteps of Mr Kurtz*.

Mobutu's fortune came from CIA payments—calculated at
$150 million during the first few years—nationalization and
appropriation of foreign companies, and simple looting of the
treasury, which Mobutu treated as his personal property to do
with as he pleased. Of the 2,000 foreign companies that were
taken over without compensation, the best were retained by
Mobutu for himself and his family; other 'plums' were given to
his favourites. An estimated $250 million a year was plundered
from the state-owned mining company Gecamines, and in 1988
$400 million disappeared from Zaire's foreign bank accounts.
Consignments of state-owned cobalt, copper and diamonds
were stolen by Mobutu from the state, and payments received
from their sales abroad went directly to personal accounts.
While Mobutu enjoyed a lifestyle of conspicuous consumption,
Zairians starved, were unemployed, or earning salaries whose
values were totally eroded by hyperinflation. The rule of law
died; the rule of the gun took over. Money became the key to

politics; one observer commented: 'It's like a mafia—all Zairian politicians are poor. For survival they have to engage in politics; to earn a living they have to remain on the side of power.'

When money ran short for payoffs, Mobutu simply ordered that more money be printed—the result was hyperinflation of 5,000–10,000 per cent a year. Money was worthless as value endlessly eroded, and a monthly wage could hardly support a family for a week. In 1993, five 'new zaires' could buy one British pound; in 1997, when Mobutu was removed, it took 200,000 new zaires to buy one pound. It is no coincidence that Iraq, Russia, Zimbabwe and Zaire, countries plagued by extraordinary corruption, were also the scenes of uncontrolled hyperinflation, showing once more the destructive effect on national economies when the greed of elites takes over.

As he bankrupted his country, and as his people starved, Mobutu expanded his palace at Gbadolite, his 'Versailles' in the jungle; the runway at Gbadolite airport was lengthened to accommodate his Concorde jet. Like the kings of France, Mobutu wanted his dynasty, but his plans were frustrated by the death of his son from AIDS.

NOT ALL AFRICAN LEADERS ARE CROOKS

The list of corrupt African dictators who have enriched themselves while destroying their countries is long; it includes Eyadama in Togo, Omer Bongo in Gabon, Obiang Nguema in Equatorial Guinea, and many many more. But there have also been heroes and countries that have fought corruption. Nasser in the north of Africa and Mandela in the south were both incorruptible as they struggled to build their countries; and countries such as Botswana and Ghana show that all African states are not prepared to tolerate corruption.

At independence in 1957, the Ghana that Kwame Nkrumah inherited was one of Africa's richest states; by the time he was removed, Ghana was bankrupt. Ghana sank into a culture of corruption and decay, a hopeless mess. With the emergence of Jerry Rawlings, a new hope was born. A passionate nationalist of exceptional integrity, the young flight lieutenant failed in his first coup attempt; he was imprisoned and sentenced to death. Before he could be executed, his admirers, other young officers, sprung him from jail, and by 1979 he took the country in his first successful coup. He had only two objectives: to 'clean house' and to restore democracy. 'Cleaning the house' was Rawlings' determined first step to eradicate corruption; in a dramatic move he executed three former heads of state, all generals; he also executed five other senior generals who were also reputed to be corrupt. Without any delay he held national elections, peacefully handed power to the victors and withdrew from government. But the cleansing had changed nothing. By 1982 he was back, this time to stay and to put things right.

Rawlings, whose initials 'J.J.' earned him the nickname of 'Junior Jesus', worked with integrity and dedication to bring Ghana back from the brink. His period in office showed significant achievements in the restoration of democracy, the promotion of education, improvement in housing supply, the spreading of the benefits of electricity throughout Ghana, the reformation and improvement of agriculture, and the delivery of clean water to the people, resulting in the eradication of guinea worm infestation caused by unclean drinking water.

He also played no small part in getting Kofi Annan, a Ghanaian, elected secretary general of the United Nations. Ghana under Rawlings saw the birth of a new era of prosperity and democracy. When he had served his two terms as president, Rawlings stepped down, allowing the vice-president John Atta-Mills to contest. Mills lost, the opposition won; an era was over, as Rawlings gave Ghana his greatest gift—the smooth and peaceful transfer of power, so rare an event in Africa. A sad but telling story of his integrity is when his wife needed an important operation in Switzerland, Rawlings did not have the money to pay, but managed to borrow from a friend. Humiliation followed humiliation, as even the driver of the Ghana ambassador's car was forbidden from using the embassy vehicle to take Mrs Rawlings from the hospital to her hotel after the operation; the driver, in protest, used his own small personal car showing his respect for the ex-president.

The 2009 elections reversed fortunes and gave victory back to Rawlings' protegee John Atta-Mills—a happy swan song for a beautiful man, who had served and ruled with emotion, passion and dedication, leaving us his simple words of wisdom: 'When something is going wrong and you don't stop it, after a time you don't see it any more.' Leaders of coups always justify army rule as a crusade against corruption and corrupt politicians, but then show great reluctance to leave office as they accumulate offshore fortunes through their own corruption. Rawlings risked his life to take power, but voluntarily stepped down twice, having fought corruption, and leaving office as poor as he had come.

Botswana is a country with a territory larger than France

and a population smaller than Kuwait. It has the lowest corruption in Africa and is noted for its clean government; it has enjoyed the highest level of economic growth in the world, for years surpassing that of the tiger economies of the Far East. It is also a successful democracy. Botswana seems to be an enviable success, but it is not. Botswana has had the highest incidence of AIDS in the world, which in 2002 had reached almost 40 per cent of the adult population; Botswana has fought the disease with its usual efficiency, and has brought it down to below 30 per cent of the adult population. But with an average life expectancy of below thirty, Botswana despite its remarkable economic and political success is not a success story.

12

Suharto: The Twenty-billion Dollar Man

You know, what you regard as corruption in your part of the world, we regard as family values.

—General Suharto

The countries of Southeast Asia show the strong link between corruption and economic performance. Myanmar, formerly Burma, is the poorest country in the region, and is regularly at the bottom of the Transparency International Corruption Perception Index; Singapore, whose economy is one of the world's outstanding success stories, has exceptional governance, free of corruption. Japan and Hong Kong also combine clean governance with strong and successful economies. Whereas Indonesia and the Philippines, two countries where corruption is prevalent, have remained relatively poor countries with poor economic performance. The list includes, in descending order, Taiwan at 32nd (most clean), South Korea at 43rd, Malaysia at 60th, China at 75th and Thailand at 80th. The economic performance of these countries seems to mirror their corruption ratings, offering strong proof that clean countries become rich whereas corrupt countries become poor. The example of China is particularly interesting—whether compared with Russia, the other ex-communist country, or with India, the other billion-population country. Of the three countries, China's economic growth is the highest, and its level of corruption the lowest—surely this is not a coincidence.

Big money plays an important role in Thai politics, with newspapers full of juicy stories of the goings on between businessmen and politicians. Allegations of corruption have been a major cause of the collapse of governments in Thailand, and the major parties are backed, if not owned, by big business interests. Election costs are exorbitant and political players must make large sums of money, or at least enrich their financial backers, if they are to stay in the game. The Sophonpanich family of Bangkok Bank and the Tejaphaibul family of Bangkok Metropolitan Bank have stood behind national parties, and the telecommunications billionaire Thaksin Shinawatra has himself served as prime minister. Banharn Silpa-archa, another businessman who rose to the job of prime minister, collapsed under accusations of corruption and nepotism.

In the Philippines, Ferdinand Marcos and his friends gave new meaning to the term 'crony capitalism' as he plundered the state, stealing vast sums, and his wife frequently drew funds from the central bank to pay for her foreign shopping trips. Imelda's shoe collection became a major scandal as newspaper gossip columns contrasted it with the poverty of the Philippine people. Marcos is estimated to have plundered between five to ten billion dollars from the Philippines during his presidency, and perhaps provided the inspiration to Suharto in Indonesia who raked in a sum of between fifteen and twenty-five billion dollars for his family, the greatest political haul of modern times.

The scale of Suharto's corruption is unparalleled. Business conglomerates were assembled for his three sons, his three daughters, two grandchildren, his half-brother, and a handful of other relatives. The total Suharto family business empire has been valued at $25 billion before he fell from power. The money-making strategies included sweetheart deals with Pertamina, the state-owned oil company, borrowing hundreds of millions of dollars from banks with no intention to repay, giving licences, concessions and monopoly privileges, as well as the creation of new and ingenious scams. In all, the Suharto family accumulated significant stakes in more than 1,250 companies in Indonesia. The eldest daughter, 'Tutut', acquired stakes in 111 companies, including toll roads, mining, flour milling, television, banks; she held 14 per cent share in Indonesia's largest private bank, Bank Central Asia. Tutut's husband had another fifteen companies of his own. The second daughter, Titiek, was involved with seventy companies, several in the financial services sector including stockbroking and banking, but she also invested in shopping centres and cement production. The youngest daughter, Mamiek, built up interests in mobile telecommunication, land reclamation and aircraft leasing. Her husband had his own separate business interests in chemicals. The eldest son, Sigit, had interests in 115 companies, many in big infrastructure projects and heavy industry, and also owned 16 per cent of the Bank Central Asia Group. Bambang, the second son, controlled the Bimantra Group, the largest of the Suharto conglomerates, with interests in 327 companies in Indonesia in addition to large overseas holdings. Tommy, the youngest son, had stakes in 127 companies in Indonesia including the car industry, petrochemicals and airlines. Other Suharto family members who also demonstrated their business genius were half-brother Probosutedjo with 119 companies, cousin Sudwikatmono with 288 companies, and grandson Ari.

Some of the Suharto family deals were embarrassing. After buying the Lamborghini car company in Italy, Tommy decided to build an Indonesian 'national car'—the Timor; getting exemption from import duty and sales tax, which gave him a 30–50 per cent edge on the market, he imported fully assembled Kia cars from Korea, renamed them 'Timor' in Indonesia, and marketed them as the Indonesian 'national car'. Tommy's clove monopoly, named BPPC, earned annual profits of $100 million by forcing farmers to sell cloves at $3.50 a kilogram to his consortium which they resold to cigarette manufacturers at $6. A study revealed that the BPPC had cost the farmers more than $750 million in five years and had crippled the clove industry. Grandson Ari's shoes for schoolchildren scam was planned to net him $80 million a year; the scheme was simple— all schoolchildren must buy and wear Ari shoes, which he bought from manufacturers and marked up by 40 per cent. There was an uproar of protest that the grandson of the president was seeking to fleece poor families and the scheme had to be abandoned. Ari was a fan of Richard Branson and his Virgin brand, and came up with his own brand, 'Sexy', to sell Sexy clothes, Sexy soft drinks and Sexy beer in Sexy cafés. As the Suhartos enjoyed the fruits of office, basking in America's praise of Suharto as 'our kind of guy', human rights in Indonesia suffered, and 80 per cent of the population struggled to survive on less than $1 per day, while brutal repression was perpetrated in East Timor, which finally seceded from the country in 2002. The economy collapsed in the Asian financial crisis of 1997 as the currency lost 85 per cent of its value against the dollar, and the Indonesian economic 'miracle' disappeared, proving to have been no more than a mirage. Suharto resigned with his last days being beset with health problems. When he died he was buried with full state honours, showing that crime does pay, provided it is on a big enough scale.

13

China Gets Tough on Crooks

Laws are useless when men are pure, unenforceable when men are corrupt.

—Chinese proverb

In 2011, Transparency International put China at seventy-fifth place in its list—significantly better than India at 95th place, Pakistan at 134th, and Nigeria and Russia at 143rd. China differs from other countries in that it recognizes the dangers of corruption, is determined to do something about it, and actually punishes offenders. Compare the amnesties given to corrupt politicians in Pakistan with the death sentences regularly handed out to prominent offenders in China, including Liu Jinbao, the former president of the Bank of China, Mu Suixin, the mayor of Shenyang, together with his deputy (for corrupt land deals), Zheng Ziaoyu, a top drug administrator who was executed (for taking bribes to approve substandard medicines), and Liu Zhihua, former vice-mayor of Beijing who was sentenced to death for taking $1 million in bribes. Even the high-placed Vice-admiral Wang Shouye, a close friend of President Jiang Zemin, was given a suspended death sentence for taking $20 million in bribes. Wang was brought down by one of his mistresses when he refused to acknowledge their son. When his two homes were searched, 52 million yuan were found in his refrigerator and microwave, and another $2.5 million in his washing machine. Wang was a favourite of Jiang who had showered him with honours, giving him the title of 'outstanding cadre'. Wang, in return, looked after Jiang's 'friend', Song Zuying, the pretty little singer whose song and dance troupe fell under the navy.

China's ruling elite attained power through a process that is very different from other countries. Though patronage and networking certainly play their part in the elevation of party members. The Organization Department of the Chinese Communist Party (CCP) is unique in the professionalism of its approach to the selection of leaders. A detailed and complete investigation into the history of the selected candidate looks carefully into his character, his performance in previous postings, the opinions of those he has worked with, both subordinates and superiors, and prepares a dossier which is then circulated to those who have to decide on promotion to higher office. The grooming process takes decades, and any leader who makes it to the top—to the Standing Committee of the Politburo—is put through a screening process that leaves little to chance. Candidates with character flaws are quickly weeded out. This selection process is much more thorough than the selection of top-level executives in even the most professional of multinational companies. As a result, those who get to the top tend to be very serious political leaders who deserve empowerment. Leaders at the top in China are comparatively clean and corruption scandals at the level of the Politburo are rare. But further down the organization, particularly in the provinces, corruption becomes a much more common phenomenon, in an environment where socialist ideology has become redundant, religion irrelevant, and where the new get-rich-quick culture lures party commissars and bureaucrats into shady alliances with the new capitalists.

Corruption was not an issue in Mao's time, and even in the early days of Deng's transition economy, it was not a matter of concern. But by the time Jiang Zemin came to power, the new capitalism had created too many opportunities for powerful party bosses to enrich themselves and their supporters, and corruption spread like a cancer through the party in the provinces. The party was in a vulnerable position after the Tiananmen Square incident (1989), and public resentment was high against mafia-style party bosses who were abusing their authority, leading Jiang to initiate a widespread clampdown. Between 1988 and 1993 the Central Commission for Discipline Inspection disciplined over 700,000 party members, and expelled 150,000. This war on corruption by the central high command continued under Hu Jintao, and disciplinary action was taken against more than 100,000 party members yearly. President Hu and Prime Minister Wen have warned that corruption threatened the credibility and legitimacy of Communist Party rule and vowed to stamp it out. In 2005 the party committee investigated more than 147,000 corruption cases, and more than 10,000 officials were convicted. Punishments were severe, with frequent death sentences. Unlike other Third World countries where a blind eye is turned to corruption and leaders refrain from taking aggressive action against past offenders in the belief that future governments will be equally generous in forgiving misdemeanours of their governments, both Jiang's third generation leadership and Hu's fourth generation were serious in their determination to stop corruption.

Land speculation and the connivance of city officials with big business have caused widespread resentment and protests; award of contracts by public entities to private business, fraud and bad debts in the banking sector, general theft of state funds, tax evasion and customs fraud have been major areas of misuse of power. A report by the Ministry of Commerce estimated that 4,000 officials have fled overseas in recent years with roughly $50 billion in embezzled money. In 2005 alone, the National Audit Office found that $35 billion in state funds was misappropriated. A report from the Carnegie Endowment for International Peace claimed that corruption costs China more every year than it spends on education, and is one of the most serious threats to the country's stability. In 2003 corruption cost the Chinese economy a staggering $86 billion. In the provinces, kickbacks, bribes or simple theft has 'transformed entire regions into local mafia states'.

The three high-profile corruption convictions that hit the

top echelons of the party were the cases against Chen Xitong (Mayor of Beijing and Politburo member), Cheng Kejie (former vice-chairman of the Standing Committee of the National People's Congress) and Chen Liangyu (Shanghai party boss).

Chen Xitong was a powerful regional chief who ran Beijing as his own private empire and was a member of the powerful Politburo. He was close to Deng Xiaoping, and was once seen as a possible successor to Deng. As mayor of Beijing, he supported the use of force against the Tiananmen protestors and was responsible for the declaration of martial law in Beijing which led to the killings. Chen, a rival to Jiang, was targeted by the Shanghai clique members Zeng Qinghong and Jia Qinglin who orchestrated his downfall in 1995. Chen was sentenced to sixteen years imprisonment and his son was also imprisoned; Chen's vice-mayor committed suicide.

The highest official to receive the death penalty, since the founding of the People's Republic of China in 1949, was Cheng Kejie who was vice-chairman of the Standing Committee of the National People's Congress (NPC). Cheng, who was the former chairman of the Guangxi Zhuang Autonomous Region in South China, had used his powers to take forty-one million yuan in bribes when serving in Guangxi, in partnership with his mistress Li Ping. The money was deposited in offshore banks and was recovered after Cheng's crimes were exposed. Li Ping gave devastating testimony against him in the trial, apparently turning against her lover who had promised to divorce his wife and marry her. The severe punishment against Cheng displayed the determination of the CPC Central Committee to clamp down on corruption; the party leadership stressed that opposing corruption is a serious political struggle which is decisive to the fate of the party and the nation.

In 2006 President Hu was positioning himself for the seventeenth Party Congress to be held in 2007, in which he would consolidate his power. Jiang, now a retired elder who had given up his formal positions, still retained substantial influence through the Shanghai clique, a group of top-level party bosses from his home turf. When Jiang moved to Beijing, he took with him Zeng Qinghong, the wily strategist, as his key advisor. Shanghai was left in the control of Chen Liangyu, the strong party secretary whose political machine controlled the Shanghai economy, including the priceless real estate holdings of the city, and who was a member of the twenty-four-man national Politburo. Under the Chinese system, regions and major cities are independent of control from Beijing, and Chen and his team wielded immense local power. Furthermore, with the umbrella of protection from their patron, Jiang, they were considered untouchable. But in September 2006, Hu struck; Chen was detained, along with several others of his gang, and was sentenced to eighteen years imprisonment for financial fraud, abuse of power, and accepting bribes. After his downfall, many stories emerged of his misconduct over the years, including subsidized sales of city land to his brother at one-tenth of the market price, and of his numerous affairs.

The war against corruption continued unabated in China, bringing down many other regional bosses. The former mayor of Shenzhen was implicated, as was Liu Zhihua, vice-mayor of Beijing, who was in charge of projects for the Beijing Olympic Games till he was fired in June 2006. He received a suspended death sentence for bribes in return for doling out contracts, loans and other favours for money. The court said the bribes were pocketed by Liu and his mistress Wang Jianrui. Liu was not a one-woman man; he was reputed to have several mistresses, one of whom, Zhang Yike, videotaped them having sex. When they had a fall-out, she sent the hour-long tape to party officials.

All party bosses who are tempted to stray should be warned: don't think it can last forever; even the most powerful can fall. Another sad lesson which can be drawn from the tragic romances of Admiral Wang, Cheng Kejie, Xu Zong-Heng, Liu Zhenhua and so many other fallen bosses is that 'hell hath no fury like a woman scorned'.

14

India: Everybody Steals, Nobody Gets Caught

Corruption has become a low risk and high reward activity.
—Atal Bihari Vajpayee

The independence of India was seen as the triumph of morality over the brute force of empire. Gandhi symbolized moral power and provided an inspiration for world leaders such as Martin Luther King, Jr, and Nelson Mandela. His influence endured during the early years of Nehru and Shashtri, but then India changed. Indira Gandhi was convicted of electoral corruption and Narasimha Rao was found guilty in a bribery scandal, although sympathetic superior courts later reversed the charges. Transparency International has found India the least corrupt of the South Asian nations, though South Asia, together with Africa and Central Asia, ranks among the most corrupt regions of the world. In 2011, the TI index showed India at 95th place, as compared with Sri Lanka at 86th, Nepal at 154th, Pakistan at 134th, and Bangladesh at 120th. Afghanistan and Myanmar fared even worse, tying at the 180th place out of 183 nations.

The major Indian corruption scandals and the stories of the most notorious politicians illustrate Indian values and attitudes, where cunning and fraud are admired and seldom get punished, and where even those who receive temporary convictions retain their power allegiances and public following. The courts often pronounce offenders guilty, only to reverse their judgements, so that finally almost all emerge unscathed. In the long list of politicians against whom major allegations of corruption have been made, certain names stand out—Mayawati, Jayalalitha, Lalu Prasad Yadav, Mulayam Singh Yadav, Sharad Pawar, Suresh Kalmadi, Andimuthu Raja, Madhu Koda, Karunanidhi and B.S. Yeddyurappa—but whispers continue about many others in power who cannot be safely criticized, and rumours abound of those who have relinquished power as very rich men with no real explanation of the source of their wealth.

In 1971 Indira's Congress won the elections amidst opposition outcry that there had been large-scale electoral fraud. Raj Narain, who had been defeated by Indira Gandhi, filed cases of fraud and on 12 June 1975 the Allahabad High Court found the prime minister guilty, surprisingly not of the serious charges like bribery and election malpractice levelled against her but of minor, inconsequential crimes like the misuse of government machinery in her campaign, declared her election null and void, unseated her and banned her from contesting elections for the next six years. Fourteen days later, on 26 June

1975, a State of Emergency was declared. Elections were postponed and top opposition leaders were arrested, including J.P. Narayan, Morarji Desai, Charan Singh, Jivatram Kripalani, Atal Bihari Vajpayee, Lal Krishna Advani and Raj Narain. In January 1977 Indira called fresh elections and in March, the Emergency ended. In the elections the Congress was badly defeated by the Janata Party which scored a simple majority; Indira and her son Sanjay both lost their seats as did most of their loyal followers.

Trivial charges of electoral corruption, which *The Times* compared to 'a traffic ticket', changed the history of India. Significantly, despite the orders of the high court, Indira refused to resign and insisted that the conviction did not affect her position, saying: 'There is a lot of talk about our government not being clean, but from our experience the situation was very much worse when the opposition parties were forming government.' The Congress would return to power in 1980 but the rising trouble in Punjab made it an unsettled time. In 1984 Indira Gandhi was assassinated by her own bodyguards, who were taking revenge for Operation Blue Star to oust militants from the Golden Temple in Amritsar in June that year.

Her son, Rajiv, replaced her, winning convincingly with a strong sympathy vote in 1985, and then moved towards modernizing the economy. In 1985 Rajiv could do no wrong; by the time of the 1989 elections, Rajiv could do nothing right—his clean young image had been destroyed by the Bofors scandal. In 1986 the Indian government had awarded a $1.4 billion contract to the Swedish armaments company Bofors for the supply of 400 howitzers. A year later Swedish radio claimed that Bofors had paid bribes to top Indian politicians to secure the deal. Despite Rajiv's attempts to cool the debate, the scandal escalated and in 1989 electoral defeat of the Congress party removed Rajiv from power. The new prime minister was V.P. Singh, India's Mr Clean. The mood of the times was honest government, and the slow process of the law on the Bofors case started. Banks in Switzerland and then Britain froze accounts. After a decade, in 1999, the CBI filed its first chargesheet naming the Italian Quattrocchi and Defence Secretary S.K. Bhatnagar, among others. Rajiv Gandhi's name figured as 'an accused not sent for trial' since he had been assassinated at a political rally, in 1991. Quattrocchi was arrested in Malaysia then released; the Hinduja brothers, prominent as England's super rich, were charged. Defence Secretary Bhatnagar and Win Chadha, another accused, died of health problems in 2001, and the momentum of the litigation started to fade. In 2004 the Delhi High Court cleared Rajiv Gandhi of involvement in the Bofors kickback scandal, the Hindujas were also cleared, and the freeze was lifted on close to $5 million in Quattrocchi accounts.

As Rajiv's power crumbled, three leaders jockeyed in the wings to take over as prime minister—V.P. Singh, Chandra Shekhar and Narasimha Rao. But in the shadows, a certain figure started to play a strange part in the political drama that was unfolding. Chandraswami was India's own Rasputin, a tantric 'godman' who emerged on the world stage as a spiritual guide to the rich and famous, moving in the company of arms dealer Adnan Khashoggi, actress Elizabeth Taylor and the Sultan of Brunei. In India Chandraswami had an elite following which included two prime ministers, Narasimha Rao and Chandra Shekhar, chief minister of Bihar, Lalu Prasad Yadav, and Governor Romesh Bhandari. Chandraswami was eager to see Rao win the prime ministership, which would give him unfettered personal power, but they were threatened by the growing stature of V.P. Singh, whose 'Mr Clean' reputation appealed to the mood of post-Bofors India. The conspiracy to smear V.P. Singh was labelled the 'St Kitts forgery Scandal'. Rao and his godman were accused of forging documents showing that Ajeya Singh, the son of V.P. Singh, had opened an account in a St Kitts bank in 1989, and had deposited $21 million in it, on behalf of his father. Rao was formally charged in 1996 after his term as PM expired but was soon acquitted along with Chandraswami and his sidekick 'Mamaji'. Rao and Chandraswami were again charged in the paper pulp scandal that exploded when an offshore Indian businessman, Lakhubhai Pathak, alleged cheating and corruption; but again they were acquitted.

Another corruption scandal of Rao's politics was the JMM scandal, in which it was alleged that Rao, through a representative, offered millions of rupees to members of the regional party Jharkhand Mukti Morcha (JMM) to vote for him during the 1993 no-confidence motion against the prime minister. Shailendra Mahato, one of the members who had accepted the bribe, turned approver. The CBI special court said that four JMM MPs were paid Rs 5 million each and the bribe money was deposited in the Punjab National Bank in New Delhi. Rao and his colleague, Buta Singh, were convicted and sentenced to three years' rigorous imprisonment. They were granted bail, appealed against the conviction and were cleared of all charges in 2002 by the appellate court on grounds of lack of credibility of the approver's testimony.

Rao is called the Father of India's Economic Reforms. Inheriting a bankrupt and dysfunctional economy, he bypassed the many party aspirants for the post of finance minister and appointed Manmohan Singh, an honest and respected economist with no previous involvement in politics. The crisis of the early 1990s was averted as the rupee crashed, falling 90 per cent, from 17 to 32 against the dollar; the economic liberalization brought in foreign investment which grew from $132 million in 1992 to $5.3 billion in 1995, as India's growth rates skyrocketed. Rao's economic success despite his corruption scandals seemed to be contrary to the principle that corruption destroys economic growth, but a closer investigation shows that Rao cannot be accused of amassing wealth through corruption—both his major scandals, St Kitts and the JMM, did not involve corrupt money making on his part, although they were certainly examples of the shortcomings of the Indian democratic norms. The Pathak case was seen as unauthorized use of Rao's name by the manipulative Chandraswami gang.

The economic reforms which started the dismantling of the Licence Raj played an important part in reducing corruption in government, a process which has continued under the prime ministership of Manmohan Singh. But unfortunately, reducing corruption does not mean eliminating corruption. In August 2009 Buta Singh was in the news as police arrested his son Sweety Singh, caught taking Rs 10 million of a Rs 30 million bribe from a garbage collection contractor.

Gautam Buddha achieved enlightenment meditating under a giant Bodhi tree in Bihar. Bihar was the birthplace of Ashoka, one of India's greatest rulers who founded the Mauryan Empire, the centre of the Gupta Empire of India's Golden Age; the headquarters of Sher Shah Suri and the birthplace of Guru Gobind Singh. Bihar is also the home base of India's enigmatic political boss, Lalu Prasad Yadav. The state, with a population of 100 million before its bifurcation, was larger than most countries in the world. With almost 60 per cent of its inhabitants living below the poverty line, it was notorious as a dysfunctional, misgoverned state plagued by the highest level of corruption in India. In 2004, after fourteen years of Lalu's rule, *The Economist* had written: 'Bihar had become a byword for the worst of India, of widespread and inescapable poverty, of corrupt politicians indistinguishable from the mafia dons they patronize, and a caste-ridden social order that has retained the worst feudal cruelties.' The charismatic populist Lalu had ruled with his devil-may-care folksy humour ignoring normal middle-class values. A joke circulated about Lalu described the visit of a Japanese business delegation attracted by the potential of the state's mineral wealth. 'Give us mineral rights,' the Japanese said, 'and within six months Bihar will be like Japan.' 'That's nothing,' replied Lalu, 'Give me Japan, and in six weeks it will be like Bihar.'

After seven years of misrule, Lalu was forced to step down from chief ministership due to the 'Fodder Scam' involving the alleged embezzlement of almost $200 million from the state treasury. A local mafia of corrupt politicians, bureaucrats and businessmen had formed, which registered vast herds of non-existent livestock, or 'ghost cattle'. Money sanctioned in state budgets for feeding these ghost herds was stolen by this mafia. Surprisingly, the investigation was ordered by Lalu himself. Prosecuting Lalu was not easy. Not only did he wield immense power and popularity in the state, but even at the centre his support was crucial for the survival of the coalition government. Prosecution of Lalu began in earnest, and between 1997 and 2001 Lalu was jailed five times; in addition to the fodder cases, a disproportionate assets case was also filed against Lalu and his wife. Lalu commented that the fodder scam may have ended his prospects of one day becoming the prime minister of India. Lalu was down but not defeated; on resigning, he appointed his wife Rabri Devi, a traditional housewife with no political experience, as chief minister in his place. When outraged journalists criticized the appointment of his wife, Lalu retorted, 'Who do you want me to appoint? *Your* wife?' Lalu and his wife controlled the chief ministership for fifteen years between them.

In 2005 Lalu took over the railway ministry in Delhi. Indian Railways with 2.4 million employees is the largest commercial employer in the world, and had for decades been an unmitigated commercial disaster, losing billions. A government report in 2001 predicted bankruptcy by 2015 with annual losses reaching $12 billion (the whole budget of India, by comparison, is $128 billion). But to the surprise of all, Lalu's term as railways minister was shockingly successful as he has led one of the most spectacular corporate turnarounds in history, with the Railways raking in cash and posting surpluses in billions. In his 2008 speech in Parliament, while introducing the 2008–

09 Railways Budget, Lalu proudly stated: 'The cash surplus of the Railways rose steadily from Rs 9,000 crore in 2005 to Rs 14,000 crore in 2006, to Rs 20,000 crore in 2007 ... In 2007–08 we will create history once again by turning a cash surplus before dividend of Rs 25,000 crore ($ 6.25 billion). Our achievement, on the benchmark of net surplus before dividend, makes us better than most of the Fortune 500 companies in the world.' Respected management schools around the world, from Harvard to the Indian Institutes of Management, studied Lalu's leadership in managing the turnaround, although in 2009, his successor Mamata Banerjee disputed Lalu's numbers as being inflated.

During his chief ministership Lalu reinforced the principle that corruption destroys the economy of a state and perpetuates poverty. As railways minster Lalu illustrated the power of leadership and governance in creating wealth. Lalu emerges as both hero and villain!

Even more amazing than Lalu's story is the story of Bihar after Lalu. In 2005 Nitish Kumar, a clean-living electrical engineer-turned-politician, was elected chief minister for the second time. He had previously held office in 2000 for seven days till ousted by Lalu. Nitish Kumar turned Bihar around. In 2005, when he took office, Bihar was recognized as the most corrupt state in India; after six years of his administration, in 2011, Bihar was recognized as the least corrupt state in India, with the highest rate of growth. *The Times of India* reported: 'Bihar, which was synonymous with poverty, has emerged as the fastest growing state for the second year running, clocking a scorching 13.1 per cent growth in 2011–12.'

In just six years Bihar, the most wretched state in India, had become the star of the Indian economic scene—lowest corruption, highest rate of growth—a shining example of what could be achieved by one determined man!

Two ladies who have played the power game in Indian politics are Mayawati and Jayalalitha, both of whom have been accused of corruption. Jayalalitha is a former actress who was close to the prominent actor and former chief minister of Tamil Nadu, M.G. Ramachandran. After his death a struggle between his wife and Jayalalitha led to a temporary setback for their party, but then Jayalalitha took control and has served as chief minister three times with an important number of seats even at the national level. She has created her own personality cult, and there are stories of her adoring followers walking on burning coals or drawing her portrait with their blood as demonstrations of their loyalty. Her extravagance is legendary, with estimates of her expenditure on the wedding of her foster son running into millions of dollars. Charges of corruption lead to police raids on her home resulting in the seizure of 28 kg of jewellery, gold, diamonds and other precious stones, ninety-one wristwatches, forty-one air conditioners, 10,500 saris, and 750 pairs of shoes. Imelda Marcos had more pairs of shoes, but Jayalalitha many more outfits. The disproportionate assets case filed against her revealed a growth of her wealth from $0.5 million to $15 million over her five years (1991–96) in power. Several of her ministers were linked with her in the scams and scandals.

Mayawati, the Dalit leader, who represents India's most underprivileged community, was in 2007–08 one of the highest tax payers in India. Though she paid Rs 26.26 crore as income tax (more tax than Mukesh Ambani, India's richest businessman) the source of her income remained clouded. Her declared wealth increased fifty times, rising from Rs 10 million in 2003 to Rs 500 million in 2007. When filing her income tax return for the assessment year 2008–09, she estimated her income to be Rs 600 million and deposited advance tax of Rs 150 million. When investigators questioned the source of her wealth, Mayawati claimed donations from party workers. Her critics counter corruption, citing the sale of party tickets in elections, bribes for transfers of officials, and numerous scams such as the Taj Corridor scam, involving illegal construction around the Taj Mahal, famous as one of the great wonders of the world. Chargesheets have been prepared against her for having acquired 'disproportionate assets'. Despite her reputation for corruption, Mayawati has been elected four times as chief minister. In the 2002 state elections, people with alleged criminal records won 206 out of the 403 seats in the UP assembly, giving the local mafias a simple majority in the house. UP's population of 200 million would make it the world's fifth largest nation; its eighty seats in the Indian national parliament has ensured its political importance and UP has provided eight out of the fourteen prime ministers who have ruled India.

The list of scams and scandals is long. The 'Telgi scam' involved the printing of fake stamp paper on a huge scale, with monthly profits estimated at $40 million; guilty Congress party leaders confessed and were punished with thirteen years' imprisonment and a fine of $40 million. The 'Barak Missile' scandal involved military purchases from Israel for an amount in excess of $250 million. Bribes and kickbacks led to charges against the defence minister George Fernandes and the former navy chief. As a result, Fernandes resigned and several arrests took place. The 'Hawala Scandal' embarrassed some of the country's leading politicians on the exposure of a $18 million bribery scandal involving the Jain brothers, but the prosecution failed because the court ruled that hawala records were inadequate as evidence.

Even the squeaky clean Manmohan Singh came under fire in the 'cash for votes scandal' as the opposition demanded his resignation over allegations that the government was bribing MPs to survive a no-confidence motion when the Left withdrew its support over the Indo-US nuclear deal in 2008. As 2010 drew to a close, three scandals hit the Manmohan Singh government: Ashok Chavan, the Congress chief minister of the state of Maharashtra, was forced to resign over a housing scam. Another Congressman, Suresh Kalmadi, the chief organizer of the Commonwealth Games, had to step down due to kickback allegations.

The mother of all scams was the multi-billion dollar 2G spectrum scandal. Andimuthu Raja, the DMK telecommunications minister, awarded 122 new telecom licences in 2007–08 on a first-come first-served basis, instead of following the auction process. The unreasonably low prices at which the licences were sold—estimated at a loss of $40 billion to the exchequer—indicated massive bribery and kickbacks. The DMK was a partner of the Congress, and Manmohan Singh was slow to act against Raja, earning censure from the Supreme

Court. Raja was finally charged, arrested, jailed for fifteen months but then released on bail. The DMK, smeared by the scandal, was defeated in the 2011 elections as Jayalalitha returned to power winning 199 out of the 234 seats. The voters of Tamil Nadu, resentful of the corruption of Raja and the DMK, turned back to Jayalalitha in their hope for a clean government!

~

Corruption in authoritarian China differs from the nature of corruption in democratic India. The leadership in China sees corruption as a major threat to the legitimacy of the Communist Party, and encourages public protest to clamp down and punish the personal greed of bureaucrats and party officials at the provincial level.

In India, leaders recognize that corruption is a part of the democratic system, starting with overspending in elections, of which all politicians are equally guilty, and then leading to the horse-trading that cements coalitions at the national level. Candidates for Parliament must either make their own money to finance future elections, or must make alliances with businessmen or criminals to ensure election funding. Regional power bases are mafias where patronage and the disbursement of illegal favours ensure support. The days of ideological politics are long gone.

China and Russia, the two communist countries in transition from communism to capitalism, have also shown fundamental differences. In Russia, the destruction of the Communist Party and the savage privatization process led to the total criminalization of society and the takeover by mafia capitalism, a road which Chinese leaders have been keen to avoid.

Rich country politicians differ from those in poor countries; in rich countries many billionaires become leaders, in poor countries, many leaders, politicians and generals alike, become billionaires. In rich countries sex scandals outnumber corruption scandals—from Britain's defence secretary John Profumo's resignation over the beautiful call girl Christine Keeler, to the World Bank president Paul Wolfowitz's resignation after he raised his girlfriend's salary to a level higher than that of Secretary of State Condoleezza Rice's; Israeli President Moshe Katsav resigned after being accused of rape; even US presidents created headlines, with the famous relationships between Marilyn Monroe and the Kennedy brothers, and Bill Clinton's Monicagate defence statement, ' I did not have sexual relations with that woman.'

More recently, Italy's prime minister Silvio Berlusconi was tried for allegedly paying for sex with seventeen-year-old Moroccan belly dancer Karima el Mahroug (a.k.a. 'Ruby the heart stealer'). He denied the charges, joking, 'I'm seventy-four years old and even though I may be a bit of a rascal, thirty-three girls in two months seems to me to be too much, even for a thirty-year-old.' Other Berlusconi scandals included the eighteenth birthday party of Noemi Letizia, an aspiring TV actress, and 'bunga bunga parties' with titillating stories of striptease and erotic acts. He had also appointed Mara Carfagna (a former topless model) as 'Equal Opportunity' minister.

But there have also been incorruptible leaders who have

created and built nations, fought for human and moral values
and won the respect of history:

- Mahatma Gandhi, of whom Albert Einstein said,
  'Generations to come will scarce believe that such a one
  as this ever in flesh and blood walked upon this earth.'
- Muhammad Ali Jinnah, whose achievement is summarized
  by his biographer, Stanley Wolpert, 'Few individuals
  significantly alter the course of history. Fewer still modify
  the map of the world. Hardly anyone can be credited
  with creating a nation state. Mohammad Ali Jinnah did
  all three.'
- Nelson Mandela, one of the world's most revered
  statesmen, who led the struggle to replace the apartheid
  regime in South Africa with a multi-racial democracy.
  Jailed for twenty-seven years, he emerged to become the
  country's first black president.
- Mahathir Mohamad, Malaysia's man of history, who over
  twenty years in power raised living standards of the
  Malays and put Malaysia on the map as he sought change
  on a historic scale.
- Lee Kuan Yew, under whose over three-decade rule
  Singapore grew from being a developing country to one
  of the most developed nations in Asia.
- Mother Teresa, who described herself as 'By blood and
  origin I am an Albanian. My citizenship is Indian. I am a
  Catholic nun. As to my calling, I belong to the whole
  world. As to my heart, I belong entirely to the heart of
  Jesus.'

- Ayatollah Sistani, the low-profile top-ranking Grand Ayatollah in Iraq who rarely made political statements but rejected and scuttled the US plan for transfer of sovereignty to an unelected provisional government in 2004 with his remark 'We want free elections, not appointments.'
- Deng Xiaoping, the father of the Chinese economic miracle, who received Queen Elizabeth in October 1986 with the words 'Thank you for coming all this way to meet an old Chinese man.'
- And Mao Zedong, poet, philosopher, writer, guerrilla fighter, communist, revolutionary and leader, who smashed the old system and created the new, who educated and empowered the Chinese people and created the new China.

Leaders are, and always will be, controversial. Who were great? Who were false? Who should we honour, who should we condemn? Andrew Carnegie, at one time the richest man in America, stated his conclusion: 'The older I get, the less I listen to what people say and the more I look at what they do.'

Section Three

DEMOCRACY

Democracy is a device that ensures that we shall be governed no better than we deserve.

—George Bernard Shaw

Don't buy a single vote more than necessary. I'll be damned if I'm going to pay for a landslide.

—Joseph Kennedy

Freedom House, the independent democracy watchdog organization, has called the twentieth century 'Democracy's Century'. At the beginning of the century, universal adult suffrage did not exist in a single country across the world; by the end of the century 60 per cent of the world's population lived under democratically elected governments. Freedom House further categorizes countries as 'free, partly free and not free'. 'Partly free' are those countries that talk the talk, but don't really walk the walk. Democracy has fought for human rights and has reduced the incidence of oppression and torture. Today, the nightmare horror stories of the past have faded from public memory with the passing of time: the inhuman activities of secret services in authoritarian dictatorships, the Gulag Archipelago, the SAVAK under the Shah, the 'disappearances' in Argentina where victims of torture were chained like dogs in 'kennels', and where women prisoners were taken to city bars for the night to perform, or taken to 'picnics' as dates by their captors, sex slaves to be raped or tortured at will by sadist guards.

But democracy has not been universally accepted as the best way to achieve 'the greatest good of the greatest number'. It has been opposed on ideological grounds by communist states and by religious states; it has been rejected by military rulers as leading to corruption and instability; and it has been ignored by monarchies who look at 'democratic countries' and conclude that it doesn't work. For half a century perhaps the greatest obstacle to the spread of democracy was the role of America and the USSR, who supported dictatorships that promoted their interests. Many economists believed that democracy was detrimental to economic growth, and even revered institutions such as the World Bank and the Asian Development Bank argued that authoritarian governments were more successful than democracies in promoting growth in the early stages of development of a country, quoting the spectacular success of the East Asian miracle economies. Writers from Samuel Huntington to Fareed Zakaria, in books ranging from *Political Order in Changing Societies* to *The Future of Freedom*: *Illiberal Democracy at Home and Abroad*, recommend authoritarian government as the way to fast growth. The phenomenal success of the East Asian Tiger economies— Singapore, Hong Kong, Taiwan and South Korea—seemed to prove the validity of the theory. Humphrey Hawksley, the BBC commentator, in his book *Democracy Kills* poses the question: 'What's so good about having the vote?' His answer suggests that there is not much good.

Much evidence indicates that voting to appoint a government in the developing world can lead to war, disease and poverty. From Pakistan to Zimbabwe, from the Palestinian territories to the former Yugoslavia, from Georgia to Haiti, the holding of elections has produced high levels of corruption and violence. Tribal and religious divisions have become institutionalized into power blocs that have led to ethnic cleansing. Political parties rely on brute force and patronage. Parliaments represent not broad constituencies but vested interests and, amid much fanfare, constitutions are written but rarely upheld.

The respected Oxford economist Paul Collier who in 2008 won the Arthur Ross Book Award for 'the world's best book on international affairs' also concludes in his *The Bottom Billion* that democracy in the societies of the bottom billion has increased all kinds of political violence—assassinations, riots, guerrilla activity and civil war and establishes through extensive research that poor democracies with a per capita income below $2,700 are dangerous.

Those who defend democracy as the best road to development highlight the comparison of North with South Korea, of North with South Vietnam, and of East with West Germany. They admit that the Asian tigers were all dictatorships, but point out that so were the worst performing regimes, such as Burma, the Philippines under Marcos, and Cambodia. The fastest and the slowest growing economies were all dictatorships, in the middle lay the democracies, less exciting but also less disastrous. Halperin, Siegle and Weinstein in their book *The Democracy Advantage* put forward the case that democracy does a better job raising living standards in poor countries than does authoritarian government. They even try to explain that the China versus India story is not final proof of the superiority of authoritarian growth over democratic growth—despite the fact that over a twenty-year period, 1982–2002, China's per capita income quadrupled (from $189 to $940) whereas India's only doubled (from $239 to $496). They emphasize that China's take-off started in the 1970s whereas India seriously undertook economic reforms only in 1993, fifteen years later, and the final verdict will only emerge after mid-century. Even US Secretary of State Condoleezza Rice signalled a u-turn from America's Cold War policies that created dictators such as Pinochet in Chile, Marcos in the Philippines or Mobutu in Zaire, when she announced: 'For sixty years, my country, the United States, pursued stability at the expense of democracy in this region, here in the Middle East, and we achieved neither. Now we are taking a different course. We are supporting the democratic aspirations of all the people.'

The spread of democracy over the last few decades has been motivated by economic incentives. Central European countries that have emerged from the break-up of the USSR have been keen to join the European Union, which demands a culture of democracy as a condition of membership of the club. Financial support from the World Bank, IMF and other multilateral institutions now leans toward democratizing nations, so poor countries are under pressure to democratize. America's claim that its war in Iraq was to liberate the Iraqis led to the quip: 'Be nice to America or they will punish you with democracy'! But rich and powerful nations are free to choose their own preferred forms of government. The West's needs for China's money, Saudi oil and Russian gas overrides political ideology.

The journey from dictatorship to democracy is traversed by the long line of democratizing nations—those that pay lip service to democracy but have a long way to go before they can truthfully be called democratic. Taking slow steps forward and sometimes quick steps back, a democratizing nation can spend decades on the journey without ever getting there. For democracy is much more than periodic elections, more often than not bogus; democracy includes the rule of law, the checks and balances that result from the separation of powers, and the democratic institutions that are essential to real democracy. Electoral fraud is the norm and truly free and fair elections are few and far between. Electoral victory satisfies legitimacy requirements abroad, but is viewed with cynicism at home. Incumbents have the advantage, and access to an arsenal of dirty tricks with which to beat their opponents, though losing always remains a possibility, as Kaunda in Zambia, Mugabe in Zimbabwe and General Musharraf in Pakistan discovered. Intimidation of voters is common, as for example in Kenya under Moi. Strong candidates are frequently barred from the electoral process, whether by constitutional control as in Iran by the Council of Guardians, or by exile as in Pakistan under Musharraf where chief political leaders like Benazir, the Sharif brothers and Altaf Husain of the MQM all sat it out. The use of minority groups as scapegoats is a sure way of collecting votes, as has been shown by Mugabe attacking white interests in Zimbabwe, or the BJP criticizing Muslims in India. Bribery and the illegal use of big money in elections are universal and rules for limitation of electoral expenses are simply ignored. The electorate identifies itself along ethnic or religious lines, and votes accordingly regardless of the policies or performance of its leaders, as was most clearly demonstrated in the Iraqi elections after the last war, when Shias voted for Shias, Sunnis for Sunnis, and Kurds for Kurds. Finally, if all else fails, the ruling party can always miscount the votes to show an overwhelming majority.

Kofi Annan commented that good governance is perhaps the single-most important factor in eradicating poverty and promoting development. The rule of law is the most important aspect of good governance; it should ensure the existence of good laws, equality of all before the law, an independent judiciary and a police force committed to protection rather than extortion. The reality, however, is political interference and corruption—what in South Asia is called 'rishwat and saffarish'. Connections do matter, and money buys justice. The police are brutal and corrupt and act as predators, not protectors of the citizens. Access to justice is difficult, delivery of judicial services is weak, and lawlessness is rampant. The system fails to protect citizens from theft, violence and official abuse. The Russians have a proverb that laws exist only to protect the rich and punish the poor.

A world governance survey of developing countries conducted in 2000 by the United Nations University showed countries with relatively high-scoring justice systems included India, Jordan, Thailand, Chile, Mongolia and Tanzania; medium-scoring countries were China, Indonesia, Argentina, Peru and Bulgaria; the low-ranking ones were Pakistan, Russia, the Philippines, Kyrgyzstan and Togo; the lowest among them, with the worst system of justice, was Pakistan where complaints were voiced that 'judiciary is corrupt to the core and there is no such thing as justice in Pakistan'. Litigants suffered due to high costs and delays holding true the maxim 'justice delayed is justice denied'. The countries that fared the worst in regard to access to justice were Pakistan, the Philippines and Russia, where it was felt that money bought justice and only the rich had legal recourse whereas the poor had no rights at all. Due process was seen to be the weakest in Russia where the laws were still evolving, and in Pakistan where it was felt that evidence was routinely doctored by a totally corrupt police force. Independence of the judiciary was weakest in China, where the Communist Party dominated the judiciary and was itself above the law; corruption was widespread at the local levels, and connections were the key to successful litigation since equality before the law was non-existent. In many countries in Africa and South Asia, such as Afghanistan and Pakistan, elders, tribal chiefs and religious leaders played an important part in settling disputes and were preferred over courts which were seen as too expensive and did not inspire trust.

The philosopher and economist Adam Smith believed that 'a tolerable administration of justice, peace and low taxes is all that is necessary to carry a state to the highest degree of opulence'. Property rights and the enforceability of contracts induce savings and investment, and attract foreign capital. But twenty-first century states need more—they need institutions that promote good governance, an efficient bureaucracy, free media, professional armed forces, independent banking finance and private sector regulation, political parties and freedoms, and checks and balances of executive power with an unbiased anti-corruption authority. These institutions are needed to assist the judiciary and ensure a meaningful rule of law, for laws are not self-enforcing—how laws are enforced depends on who is enforcing them.

After the judiciary, the bureaucracy is the most important institution for good governance. Singapore owes much of its success to the quality of its bureaucrats, who were attracted by the million-dollar salaries offered by the state to ensure that the best brains chose government service over the private sector. But whereas Singapore follows the merit system, India follows the quota system, in which jobs are reserved for underprivileged groups, and class or caste, not merit, is the basis for a substantial number of government jobs. Iran's religious institutions encourage an 'old boy network' which gives preferences to clerics and many other countries sell off lucrative government positions to the highest bidders who then recover their 'investment' through bribery.

In most poor countries salaries are low, but the majority of civil servants make this up through corruption. Those countries who maintain clean and capable civil services are able to promote and implement good policies that improve delivery of services to their people and create growth in the economy. Good judges and good administrators will produce good governance. In the final analysis, performance is driven by the quality of people. As Aristotle observed 2,000 years ago, 'It is better for a city to be governed by a good man than by good laws.'

Democracy can be promoted or destroyed by the armed forces, who may have lost their monopoly of 'power that comes from the barrel of the gun' but still control a preponderance of gun power. In the last quarter of the twentieth century the coup d'état became the most common method of regime change in developing countries. Hundreds of coups succeeded, hundreds failed. Since 1945 there have been 357 successful coups; Bolivia holds the record for the most coups—192 since its independence in 1825. But in many other states there is the military-dominated government. Pakistan has been ruled by the military for almost half of its existence since 1947, and views differ on the contributions of the three generals who took power through coups, Ayub Khan, Zia-ul-Haq and Pervez Musharraf. Coups have been used to remove corrupt and incompetent rulers who were democratically elected, but coups have also been used by corrupt and selfish generals to stifle democracy and good governance.

Mega-army states (the US with its 1.5 millio army, China with 2.1 million, India with 1.3 million and Russia with over one million) have been surprisingly free of coups. But at the level below the mega-army states, countries with large armies of half a million and above have been dominated by the military—for instance, Turkey, Egypt, Iran, Iraq, Pakistan, Myanmar and Korea.

Military leaders have ranged from the respected to the ludicrous, from Kemal Ataturk, founder of the Turkish republic, to Idi Amin of Uganda. Large armies are expensive to maintain, and involve economic choice—not guns or butter, but guns or schools, guns or hospitals; but even at the cost of fewer schools and less hospitals, the cost of guns may be worth it if leading to more security and protection from foreign or even internal threats. Money is required to keep armies armed, but also to keep generals happy and loyal. But the supply of armaments requires more than money—it requires America; armies and their generals are today hooked on to America with a dependency that can be compared to a drug addict's bond with his 'supplier'.

Good governance cannot hide behind closed doors. It needs to be seen, to be exposed, to be transparent and to be accountable. Good governance is protected and promoted by access to information through newspapers, television and the Internet. The function of the media in society is to inform, but the objective of those who own the media is to make money. How much money a newspaper makes is determined by what it informs—a problem that is not new, for even Thomas Jefferson pointed out, 'If you don't read the newspapers you are uninformed. If you do read the paper, you are misinformed.' Napoleon said that he feared three newspapers more than 100,000 bayonets; but many of today's rulers who have power and intend to keep it make sure that the newspapers fear them—they control the media through the carrot and stick. The grant of revenue through government advertising, newsprint control and access to broadcasting frequency is the carrot; closure, jail and finally assassination are the stick. Russia under Putin has seen a rise in assassinations of journalists and writers, but in 2006, Iraq alone saw sixty-nine assassinations of journalists—almost as many as the rest of the world combined.

Television is becoming ever more important, and satellite broadcasting provides censor-free access to news channels; top channels such as CNN and BBC have been joined by *Al Jazeera* which offers 'the other point of view'. The importance of getting the other point of view was cynically expressed by Malcolm X, the Black Panther activist, 'If you're not careful, the newspapers will have you hating the people who are being oppressed, and loving the people who are doing the oppressing.' The new twenty-first century information source is the Internet, which allows independent views to be disseminated, and cannot be controlled by financial or physical intimidation. Independent media has created new heroes: Robert Fisk, John Pilger and finally Muntadhar al-Zaiydi, the Iraqi TV correspondent who achieved instant star status when he threw his shoe at President Bush, shouting 'This is a farewell kiss, dog.' But the latest and most exciting hero of the new media is Julian Assange of Wikileaks, which has exposed a goldmine of secret diplomacy and statecraft.

Economic institutions allow the private sector to work independently of the whims of those who hold political power. They give businessmen and professionals the confidence to invest their money within the country and to plan for the future. Governments in developing countries have traditionally held economic power in their own hands; they decide who gets a licence, who gets land, who gets credit; they also use state policy to make themselves and their cronies rich and politically secure, regardless of whether the policies are in the long-term interests of the people. Fiscal and monetary policy is handled with a ruthless disregard of economic fundamentals. An independent central bank can ensure a constructive approach to money supply, interest rates and inflation; independent private sector banks can ensure that loans are given on a commercial and not on a political basis. The 1991 economic reforms in India have shown the stimulus to the economy that resulted from the termination of the old-style 'Licence Raj'. Independent economic institutions link economic rewards to productive self-interest, so that productivity, efficiency and merit replace crony capitalism and corruption, and promote growth of the economy. The strengthening of economic institutions is of paramount importance for growth, and produces results whether the regime is authoritarian or democratic. How the rulers got to power is less important than how they use power. Policy and pragmatism, not ideology, is the key.

Western parliamentary democracy is based on the role of competitive political parties, with differing policy platforms, and a readiness to play by the 'rules of the game'; in these countries democracy has proved effective in maintaining a non-violent negotiation process to decide how the national cake will be divided and shared. In developing countries, however, the nature and role of political parties has been very different and quite often destructive. These countries lack a culture of democracy, and parties have been part of the problem rather than the solution. Instead of policy platforms, they have become ideological platforms for socialism, religion, ethnicity and class; the personality cult of the 'big man' or 'great leader' has been the raison d'être of many ruling parties in developing states. Ideology has more often than not been the excuse or justification for power, to be used or abused by ruthless political leaders.

Intolerance, hooliganism, anti-democratic attitude, unfair electoral practices and undemocratic leadership procedures have promoted the rise of hereditary parties and political dynasties—the Nehru–Gandhi dynasty in India, the Bhutto–Zardaris in Pakistan, and the growth of 'family politics' in the Middle Eastern republics of Egypt, Syria and Lebanon. The leader, not the party, is the fount of policy; debate or dissent is discouraged, and party discipline controls would-be critics, sometimes crudely, as in Zimbabwe under the ruling ZANU-PF. Inner-party democracy is discouraged by leaders who consider parties their personal or their family property. Powerful politicians keep their parties intentionally weak. The countries of the former USSR have shown that real democracy with democratic parties is unlikely to emerge when the culture of democracy, as understood by the West, just does not exist. In too many former communist new states, a partnership between the mafia, the former KGB and the old communist party creates a criminal elite in a criminalized state. In too many states the elite have used parties as a mere vote-catching machine which needs to be fed by patronage and corruption. More and more parties are being criminalized. In the 2002 elections in Uttar Pradesh, India, tainted candidates won 206 out of the 403 seats.

Huge sums are required to win elections, and candidates overspend the limits prescribed by the law. For many years the candidates of the ruling Liberal Democratic Party (LDP) in Japan, which ruled the country almost continuously for fifty-four years, spent ten times what the law allowed. In South Korea the law limited election expenses to $112,000 but candidates regularly spent between three to four million dollars; in India candidates spend ten to fifteen times the legal limit. Candidates regularly pay party leaders to buy nominations. In Thailand vote buying is the norm and parties are bribed to switch sides. Foreign funding of parties and leaders further complicates the issue—even Nelson Mandela's African National Congress (ANC) received tens of millions of dollars from Saudi Arabia, Indonesia, the UAE and Malaysia. The role of the CIA and the communist countries in funding parties that suit their purpose is common knowledge; the recent rise of cross-border financing by oil-rich Islamic states to promote their own preferred versions of Islam further complicates the Western democratic process.

Legislators who spend big to get elected then have to recover their expenditure. The result is corruption. The term 'corruption' implies a misuse of the system, but in developing democracies with their own special type of political parties, corruption is the system; parties in power have extorted payments from big business. In South Korea presidents Park Chung Hee and Roh Tae Woo ran 'foundations' financed by contributions by big business; companies that did not pay were denied access to credit and harassed by tax investigations. The consequence has been an erosion of public trust in political parties to such an extent that military intervention is often welcomed by a public disgusted with the corruption and mismanagement by parties, as in Pakistan when Musharraf took over from the politicians. But Musharraf's mistakes in turn led to his rejection, bringing back the politicians and Asif Zardari to power. It is unlikely that parties in most developing countries will in the near future change and adapt Western norms, and this will continue to hold democracy back from really contributing to development. With opinions so divided on democracy's value, perhaps the tipping point could be Winston Churchill's remark: 'The best argument against democracy is a five-minute conversation with the average voter.'

15

Islamic Democracy

True Islam permits neither elections not democracy.
—Maulana Sufi Mohammad

Democracy is Islam.
—Dr Syed Husain Pasha

A fifth of the world's population is Muslim, and they constitute the majority in about forty states. At this stage of their history, many of these states are less democratic than other parts of the world. Does this mean that Islam and democracy are incompatible? This question has been at the centre of a debate for centuries. Islam preaches equality and justice and has strong traditions of *shura* (consultation), *ijma* (consensus) and *ijtihad* (interpretation)—there is nothing in Islam that is fundamentally opposed to democracy, justice, freedom, equality or tolerance. It is true that many Muslim societies are undemocratic, but it is equally true that many Muslim societies are un-Islamic. It is true that Arab countries are among the least democratic, but most Muslims are not Arab, and neither are the largest Muslim nations—Indonesia, Pakistan, Bangladesh, Turkey and Iran. Intellectuals have cited figures ranging from the Persian philosopher Al-Farabi to the Urdu poet Mohammad Iqbal, from the Sudanese religious leader Hasan al Turabi to the Irani sociologist Ali Shariati, and Hasan al Banna and Sayyid Qutb of the Muslim Brotherhood to show that Islam and democracy are either compatible or incompatible; but the answer lies with the one billion Muslims of today who want both democracy and Islam.

PAKISTAN

Pakistan was formed as a new homeland for Muslims, just as Israel was created for Jews. Jinnah, the founder, was a democrat, and Bhutto, the other important political leader of Pakistan, was also committed to 'Islamic Democratic Socialism'. The military rulers who have dominated Pakistani politics were not the result of Islam's conflict with democracy, but were encouraged and supported by America to further the strategic purposes of the US. General Zia did promote Islamization in Pakistan, but it was his support of 'Charlie Wilson's War' against the Russians that made him indispensable to the US and kept him in power till he was assassinated. General Musharraf also became an important American ally in the post 9/11 war against the Taliban. Pakistan's long interludes of military dictatorship were US imposed or supported, and did not come about because Islam and democracy are incompatible.

The current rise of an Islamic alternative to Western parliamentary democracy is because of mass disillusionment with the experience of democracy in Islamic countries that has promoted and protected corrupt leaders and elites who have ruthlessly plundered the nation, ignoring the real issues of the masses—poverty, unemployment, illiteracy, corruption and exclusion. While traditional political parties have engaged in their elaborate dance for power, the religious parties have dug in their roots among the poor through the mosques and the madrassas.

The desperate and deteriorating situation of conflict and corruption in Pakistan seems to support economist Paul Collier's contention that democracy does not work in the poorest of countries; an authoritarian government has a better chance of saving a failed state. Pakistan's current democratic dilemma stems from the voiding of the National Reconciliation Ordinance (NRO), Musharraf's law which gave amnesty to politicians faced with corruption charges. The cancellation of the NRO leaves many key ministers and parliamentarians vulnerable to prosecution and arrest. Corruption cases are to be revived even against President Zardari, who claims immunity from prosecution for as long as he holds the office of president, as provided for by the constitution. Citizens smoulder in frustration—the drama is yet to be played out.

MALI

Mali is one of the poorest countries in the world; it is also predominantly Muslim. But Mali is recognized by Freedom House as a full-fledged free electoral democracy. For twenty-three years the former French colony suffered dictatorship. In 1991 General Toumani Tour deposed the dictator in a bloodless coup and within fourteen months steered the country to its first multi-party elections. He himself did not seek the presidency. The elected president served two terms, as allowed by the constitution, then stepped down in 2002. The popular General Tour then ran for president and won 64 per cent of the votes. Malians enjoy a full range of human rights under a democratic system free of illegal arrests, torture or 'disappearances'. However, corruption still weakens the state, and 64 per cent of the eleven million inhabitants are afflicted with poverty; an illiteracy rate above 50 per cent and a high population growth rate remain serious problems. Mali's economy depends on agriculture, and it is Africa's largest cotton producer, but only 50,000 of Mali's one million hectares of fertile land is cultivated. The country is desperately short of investment. The economy is badly affected by the US and EU cotton subsidies which condemn African cotton-growing countries to poverty. Over the last ten years the US government subsidies totalling $24 billion to American cotton farmers, despite WTO's ruling some of these subsidies illegal, have enabled the US to export cheaply, depressing prices and leaving farmers in poor countries unable to compete. Democracy and poverty do not make good bedfellows; voting does not fill the belly, and frustration grows as people lacking education, health care and safe drinking water ask, 'Is this democracy?' The danger to democracy in Mali is not Islam, but poverty.

INDONESIA

Indonesia with a population of 240 million is the largest Muslim nation, and after 1975 has been frequently cited as proof of the incompatibility of Islam with democracy. But the Suharto dictatorship that dominated Indonesia for over three decades was the only dictatorial interlude in the otherwise democratic government that this nation has experienced. In 2009 Freedom House categorized Indonesia as a fully functional electoral democracy. Sukarno, the nationalist liberator of Indonesia, was a democratic populist, but was seen as a danger by America because of his socialist leanings. The CIA played an important role in the massive slaughter of the half-a-million so-called communists in 1965 and in the Suharto takeover that followed. Sukarno and democracy's downfall was not a consequence of Islamization but of the breakdown of Sukarno's relationship with America with his famous remark, 'To hell with your aid!' The US then supported Suharto in building up the Indonesian economy. The 'Berkeley Mafia'—a group of American economists—provided the policy guidelines that brought in foreign capital to exploit the natural resource opportunities of the country which led to the growth of the economy, of corruption and of the Suharto family fortune.

But after the 1997 East Asian financial crisis, the Suharto system imploded and Indonesia reverted to electoral democracy. Suharto resigned in 1998, after which a succession of presidents followed: Habibie, Wahid, Megawati and Susilo Bambang Yudhoyono. Democracy was back in the saddle. In the 2004 elections which brought Yudhoyono to power, all the three leading candidates were moderates and favoured the continued separation of the state and the mosque. Though there have been incidents of Islamic violence such as the tragic bombing of a Bali nightclub by the terrorist group Jemaah Islamiyah, and riots against the resented Chinese minority that dominates business, Indonesia remains a moderate Islamic nation committed to the democratic process. Though it still suffers poverty, unemployment, corruption and inadequate infrastructure, the Yudhoyono presidency has seen substantial recovery with declining debt and growing foreign exchange reserves which now exceed $110 billion. Its stock market was one of the three best performers worldwide in 2006–07. Despite a series of disasters—tsunami, volcanic eruptions, a major earthquake and flooding—the per capita income now approaches $4,000. The world's largest Muslim nation seems quite comfortable with democracy.

TURKEY

Turkey, with a population of over seventy million and a per capita income of $13,000, is an important Muslim democracy. It was also the seat of the last Islamic caliphate and the capital of the Ottoman Empire, which after choosing the losing side in the First World War, was defeated by the Allied forces. But though the Sultan with his capital at Istanbul was defeated, one Turkish military commander refused to accept defeat— this was Ataturk who had distinguished himself at Gallipoli against the Allied forces, with his chilling appeal to his soldiers: 'Men, I am not ordering you to attack. I am ordering you to die.' Mustafa Kemal Ataturk resigned from the army and embarked on the War of Independence, for which he was sentenced to death by the regime in Istanbul. But neither the Sultan nor the Allied forces found Ataturk easy to defeat and he continued his struggle till 1923, when peace was restored with the Treaty of Lausanne in which the Republic of Turkey was declared with Ataturk as president.

He quickly moved to abolish the Sultanate, but the position of the Caliph, the spiritual leader of the community of Islam, was more difficult to attack. Nevertheless, the bold move was made, and the institution of the caliphate, which had endured for over a thousand years, was finally ended. Ataturk then proceeded with the modernization of Turkey according to his vision of a secular, Westernized country: 'We must liberate our concepts of justice, our laws and our legal institutions from the bonds which, even though they are incompatible with the needs of our century, still hold a tight grip on us.'

- Islam was de-established
- The Sufi orders were banned
- The ulema class was disbanded
- Islamic dress was forbidden
- The traditional Arabic alphabet was changed
- Religious education was sidelined and education was reformed
- Islamic law was replaced by European codes
- Government and religious affairs were separated (laicism)

Ataturk did not see these moves as attacks on Islam. Rather, he maintained, 'The religion of Islam will be elevated if it will cease to be a political instrument as has been the case in the past.' His determined approach could be seen in the new laws:

the Hat Law of 1925, and the Law Relating to Prohibited Garments in 1934. He was convinced that only by copying the principles and practices of the West could Turkey be moved out of the decaying values of past glory. Though Ataturk accepted the theory of democracy, by nature he was autocratic, and he had to fight the reactionary groups who resisted his reformation: the Shaikh Said Rebellion, the opposition movement within his own party (the Republic People's Party), and even a plot to assassinate him in 1926; nevertheless, he encouraged the formation of a new opposition party in 1930, the Liberal Republican Party. The new ideology of state was called 'Kamalism'.

From that time, the army and the judiciary have taken on the role of the guardians of the constitution. On three occasions the army has intervened by a coup, but each time it has gone back to the barracks once the danger has passed. In 1997 the military manoeuvred the removal of the Islamic-oriented prime minister Necmettin Erbakan. And as recently as 2007 the Turkish general of army staff published a stern memorandum on its website stating that certain groups were exploiting religious feelings for their sinister goals and warned that they would not stay neutral, but as guardians of the state's secular character would uncompromisingly defend the principal of secularism. This warning by the military was aimed at Prime Minister Recep Tayyip Erdogan, the Islamist leader of the ruling Justice and Development Party (the AKP) which makes no secret of its Islamic roots. In 2006 the president warned that 'Religious fundamentalism has reached alarming proportions. Turkey's only guarantee against this threat is its secular order.' The

AKP under Erdogan has a successful record of political stability, economic growth, democratic reforms and increasing linkages with the European Union, which Turkey wants to join, and Erdogan confirms that he fully accepts Turkey's secular system, saying, 'A political party cannot have a religion, only individuals can.' But it is well known that he is against Western new year celebrations, and against alcohol which he feels should be banned, and he has condemned swimsuit commercials as 'lustful exploitations'—all considered to be Islamist attitudes.

But it is interesting that any threat to democracy in Turkey, posed by the shadow of military or judicial intervention, is aimed at an Islam-leaning party which not only constitutes government but has won 341 out of the 550 parliamentary seats—a massive majority; in Turkey it is not Islam that is threatening democracy but, rather, the Turkish system of democracy that is threatening Islam.

MALAYSIA

Malaysia is a successful Muslim majority state with a history of elections and democracy in which the United Malay National Organization has dominated. The UNMO through its Barisan National coalition, which includes the minority Chinese and Indian parties—Malaysian Chinese Association (MCA) and Malaysian Indian Congress (MIC)—together with eleven other smaller parties, has ruled without a break. Malaysia is a dominant party state, though not a one-party state. Its most famous and controversial leader was Dr Mahathir bin Mohamad, prime minister from 1981 to 2003, who lead the emergence of Malaysia as a successful and wealthy nation whose economy grew at 10 per cent annually in a decade marked by political stability. Dr Mahathir is a highly respected leader credited with Malaysia's success, but his outspoken criticism of America and the West has provoked strong reactions. An example is his comparison of the 9/11 New York Trade Center deaths with the deaths of Afghans and Iraqis under US bombings: 'If innocent people who died in the attack on Afghanistan and those who have been dying from lack of food and medical care in Iraq are considered collaterals, are the 3,000 who died in New York, and the 200 in Bali also just collaterals whose deaths were necessary for operations to succeed?'

Despite his critics 'Dr M' is honoured as the visionary who nurtured an Asian tiger. Malaysian business was dominated by the Chinese ethnic minority, and the Malay 'sons of the soil' were economic underdogs; Mahathir's politics was for uplifting the poor Malays, and in 1969 he was forced out of UNMO for criticizing the leadership on this issue. While in the political wilderness Mahathir wrote his book *The Malay Dilemma* which was banned. Years later, when he took power, he implemented his policies to promote the 'bumiputras' by preferential treatment through quotas in education and jobs, and through enhanced business opportunities. Mahathir's policies were echoed in South Africa when Nelson Mandela inherited the post-apartheid economy with an impoverished and underprivileged black population.

Mahathir had an autocratic temperament, and he could be intolerant of dissent. He was accused of interfering with the judiciary's independence and in weakening democracy in

Malaysia. The conviction of his former deputy and designated successor, Anwar Ibrahim, for corruption and sodomy, received universal condemnation as abuse of power by Mahathir. The charges were believed to be false, and Sukma Dermawan, Anwar Ibrahim's brother who was forced to confess to having sex with Anwar, later retracted his confession saying he was tortured by the police who threatened to kill him and physically humiliated him, groping his genitals and subjecting him to other tortures. Other evidence also proved to be questionable, and the government's claim that the sex took place in a certain building had to be withdrawn when it was shown that the building did not exist at the time. The entire incident was deplorable, but coincidentally, Anwar represented Islamism in Malay politics; once again Islam was the victim rather than the antagonist of democracy.

A few years after the Anwar Ibrahim incident, Mahathir retired from prime ministership and later from the UMNO itself, but remained an active commentator on Malay politics. In the 2004 general elections, Abdullah Ahmad Badawi, Mahathir's designated successor, led the Barisan National (BN) to a landslide victory gaining control of 92 per cent of the seats in parliament, leading to born-again democrat Mahathir's comment, 'I believe that the country should have a strong government, but not too strong. A two-thirds majority like I enjoyed when I was prime minister is sufficient but a 90 per cent majority is too strong. We need an opposition to remind us if we are making mistakes. When you are not opposed you think everything you do is right.' Four years later, in the 2008 elections, the ruling party coalition fell to below a two-thirds majority for the first time since 1969. The opposition platform against crime, inflation and corruption won eighty-two seats as compared to the BN's 140 seats, and Anwar Ibrahim won his own seat with a strong majority. Abuse of democracy had put Anwar Ibrahim in jail, but democracy had once more put him back in parliament. But either way, the compatibility of Islam and democracy was not under question.

Freedom House admits that half the world's Muslim countries have functioning democracies, and are certainly democratizing states. But from a review of the politics of these states, it seems that Islam is not to blame but rather it is the legacy of colonialism that denied these countries the opportunity to evolve during the period that democracy spread in the West. In this respect colonized Muslim states were no different from colonized Christian states, or East Asian, South American and African states dominated by great power countries, or communist states dominated by authoritarian communist parties. Democracy grows best under conditions of freedom.

Section Four

FOUR SKETCHES OF DEMOCRACY

One-man-one-vote is a most difficult form of government.
Results can be erratic.

—Lee Kuan Yew

Democracy has many faces which differ from the conventional Western parliamentary model. A brief look at four emerging nations—South Africa, Iran, Thailand and India—shows how these countries, though all professing democracy, have very different concepts of what it means and how it is practised. South Africa is the story of the ANC's successful revolution against apartheid, whereas Iran is a regime that followed Khomeini's successful Islamic revolution; Thailand is a monarchy still struggling with democracy, and India *is* the world's biggest democracy. There is a surprising similarity between Iran and Thailand, both with populations of about seventy million, both of which were running similar per capita incomes of just below $10,000 till 2006, and both of which had a supra-democracy force, the Supreme Guide in Iran and the king in Thailand; both have experienced disorder with street demonstrations in Tehran protesting the last election of Ahmadinejad over Mir-Hossein Mousavi, and demonstrations in Bangkok of Thaksin's red shirts against the royalist yellow.

16

South Africa: Mandela and After

I have fought against white domination, and I have fought against black domination. I have cherished the ideal of a democratic and free society in which all persons live together in harmony and with equal opportunities. It is an ideal which I hoped to live for and to achieve. But if needs be, it is an ideal for which I am prepared to die.

—Nelson Mandela

India had Gandhi to lead her independence struggle, South Africa had Mandela. Gandhi and Mandela, the two saints of twentieth-century politics, gave immense moral authority to their parties, the Congress in India and the African National Congress in South Africa, both attaining unchallengeable statures in their post-independence politics. From 1994, when

Mandela became president, till today, the ANC has dominated South African politics. Sure of electoral victory, the ANC has ensured free and fair elections, respect for the opposition parties, freedom of media and the rule of law. In all this South Africa has been a model democracy. Mandela's achievement in reconciliation has outshone Gandhi's, who was unable to reconcile the hostile Hindu and Muslim factions and the bloodshed that led to Partition. Mandela's successful reconciliation of blacks and whites after the long atrocity of apartheid was the miracle of South Africa. After twenty-seven years of imprisonment, Mandela combined saintly forgiveness with astute strategy in recognizing that the armed struggle, which he himself had lead and suffered for, was unlikely to win. He also recognized that South Africa could not afford to antagonize and lose white capital and white professional skills. His greatness lay in his being able to contain emotion and to negotiate reconciliation with de Clerk, to hold together a rainbow nation. Together with Archbishop Tutu he put together the TRC, The Truth and Reconciliation Commission, to try to assuage the resentment of the vast majority who had suffered the atrocities of apartheid. The commission was empowered to grant amnesty to those who committed abuse during the apartheid era, as long as the crimes were politically motivated and there was full disclosure by the person seeking amnesty.

Mandela led by example; his dramatic gestures showed the extent to which he himself was prepared to forgive and forget: his remarkable lunch for Percy Yutar, the state prosecutor who tried for the death sentence for Mandela, and who publicly expressed his disappointment when Mandela was only jailed

for life, and his visit to the ninety-four-year old widow of
Prime Minister H.F. Verwoerd, the hard-line racist who
allowed the Sharpeville massacre (when on 21 March 1960 the
South African police opened fire on a crowd of black protestors
and killed sixty-nine) and banned the ANC as he proudly
boasted that he had never shaken the hand of any black man.
Mandela was more than merely politically savvy; he had a
grace that stemmed from exceptional generosity of heart, an
ability to love. His birthday gift to Helen Suzman, the white
leader of the Democratic Party for thirty-six years in
parliament, was pure Mandela. On Helen's ninetieth birthday
she received a surprise phone call from Mandela asking, 'Do
you have any of your oxtail stew on the simmer?' Mandela then
dropped in for lunch with the old politician with whom he had
had numerous disagreements, but for whose role in fighting for
black rights he had great admiration.

Mandela negotiated an end to apartheid, but this was only
his first gift to his nation. After becoming president, by his
magnanimity he steered the country away from conflict; by his
example of integrity he fought corruption; and by leaving office
after only one four-year term he set a tradition of orderly
succession. As the National Party moved to dismantle
apartheid, the threat of conflict loomed from two quarters:
first, it was assumed that an explosion of violence between
whites and blacks was inevitable, and it took all of Mandela's
skill, commitment and courage to bring the two communities
back together, and the promise of amnesty played a critical
part in the compromise; second, fighting between the Inkatha
Freedom Party of Chief Buthelezi and the ANC had been

carrying on since 1983 and would claim 25,000 lives before it was brought under control; between the time of Mandela's release in 1990 and his assumption of the presidency in 1994, 10,000 people were killed in political violence. Mandela won over both his antagonists, forming his Government of National Unity after the 1994 elections with a cabinet of twelve ANC representatives, six from the National Party and three from the Inkatha Freedom Party. Mandela's personal honesty raised the integrity of his nation. Certainly there was corruption, but much less than had been feared; by the time he left office, South Africa stood thirty-fourth on the Transparency International list, in the top 30 per cent of clean countries. Mandela's last gift to his country was voluntarily stepping down from power after just one four-year term. Where other rulers clung to power for decades, and aimed for thirty-year presidencies, Mandela set a precedent of self-control and orderly succession which is essential if democracy is to endure.

Mandela inherited a country on the brink of collapse and bankruptcy. The National Party had presided over an economy hammered by international sanctions and overspending on defence, burdened by debt and had seen practically no growth over their last decade in power. The ANC had a lot of promises to keep, but was faced with a massive shortage of money. To maintain international confidence, Mandela at first kept on the National Party finance minister, but after two years, in 1996, he appointed Trevor Manuel, an ANC man, who held the portfolio till 2009, and earned respect worldwide for his adroit handling of the economy. The rebuilding of the South African economy started under Mandela.

As Mandela departed the stage, the ANC crown prince, Thabo Mbeki, took over the reins of the presidency, taking formal charge of the responsibilities he had already been handling as Mandela's deputy. But where Mandela had Gandhi as a role model, Mbeki was far removed from Gandhi's political heir, Nehru. Mbeki was an intelligent, honest technocrat but arrogant, cold and lacking in generosity. Even with Mandela he showed jealousy and at one stage would not even take his calls. Mandela confided to his friends that he could pick up the phone and talk to any president in the world, with the exception of his own president. Sometimes he had to wait six months to see Mbeki. Mbeki ran an efficient administration, and South Africa prospered under his presidency. The programme of home ownership, and the supply of electricity, water and sanitation for the black population started after 1994 continued to show good results. The economy grew at a rate which reached 5 per cent; health and education for the black population was substantially improved; and the Black Economic Empowerment (BEE) programme opened up new business opportunities for black entrepreneurs, creating a new crop of black millionaires, and even a few black billionaires, who were particularly well connected to the ANC power elite.

The BEE programme sought to address the almost total white ownership of business capital in South Africa. Inspired by the example of the National Party which had promoted Afrikaner ownership at an earlier stage of South Africa's history at the expense of English-speaking whites, the ANC economic team was impressed with the Malaysian model. Mahathir Mohamad's policies for increasing the 'bumiputra' (son of the soil' in Malay) share of national wealth were carefully studied and followed. The BEE programme built up black businessmen who were given minority stakes in large white companies and who needed the support of the ANC government. The programme enriched businessmen with strong connections to those in power, and many sitting ANC members of parliament became directors of established companies. The dollar billionaires that were created by the BEE programme included Patrice Motsebe, who made the *Forbes* list of richest billionaires, and Saki Makozoma, a Mbeki confidante; Cyril Ramaphosa, the former ANC general secretary, who lost out in his power struggle with Mbeki, retired from politics and became a businessman, rising within a few years to billionaire status. Tony Sexwale, the charismatic former freedom fighter who had been premier of the important Gauteng province, also became a billionaire within ten years of his entering the world of business; his political career was sidelined when he was outmanouevred by Mbeki; his qualifications for a business career were a study of guerrilla tactics in Moscow, thirteen years of imprisonment in Robben Island, and the title of 'South Africa's sexiest politician'. He had met and fallen in love with his white wife, Judy, a legal clerk, when he was on death row. But by the time Mbeki's tenure drew to a close, a rising new generation demanded changes and entry to the closed elitist circle of wealth.

While the scramble for wealth absorbed the ANC politicians, the minority parties were allowed to criticize the government. The National Party, whose main ideology had been apartheid, started to atrophy, and first joined the Democratic Party in opposition, and then later disbanded with many of its cadres moving into the ANC. The support for the Democratic Party (DP) of Helen Suzman grew and it now became the main opposition to the ANC under the more aggressive leadership of Tony Leon, who, despite being white, was vehement in his criticism of the ruling party, exposing scandals, and attacking ANC policies on AIDS, BEE and Zimbabwe. The DP felt more under pressure under the Mbeki government as members of the ruling party argued that whites should not be involved in politics, and pressure was put on blacks who considered joining the DP. The easy relationships of the Mandela era were being replaced by harsher politics. Mandela too had often been irritated by Leon's provocations and referred to his party as a 'Mickey Mouse organization', leading Leon to retort that Mandela ran a 'goofy' government. When Leon was hospitalized for heart surgery, Mandela paid him a surprise visit announcing his arrival by calling out, 'Hello Mickey Mouse, this is Goofy. Can I come in?' But democracy endured and flourished with a free press, leading Reporters without Borders, the worldwide press freedom index, to place South Africa at twenty-first place, ahead of the UK (twenty-seventh) and the US (thirty-first).

The biggest failures of Mbeki's government were in controlling AIDS and crime. By 2004 it was estimated that one in four young women in their early twenties were infected with HIV. Rape became so widespread that one report commented that the average South African girl can expect to be violated twice in her lifetime. The murder rate escalated; in 2007 statistics showed 19,000 murders and 50,000 cases of rape. The reputation of the police, already low, plummeted further. South Africa was compared with East European countries that experienced the mafia era during the transition from hard communist government to democracy.

Though Mbeki's economic management was successful, his politics was a failure, leading to his defeat in the ANC elections of 2007, forcing his resignation as president in 2008 and demonstrating dramatically the strength of inner-party democracy within the ANC. Mbeki focused all his energy on governing, on successfully managing the administration of a nation in transition. He had neither time nor inclination for people or for politicking. Over the eight years of his presidency, he alienated too many of the ANC power brokers, but with deputy president Zuma's removal from power due to corruption and rape cases, his position seemed unassailable.

The corruption case looked particularly damaging. Zuma's friend and financial supporter Schabir Shaik had already been sentenced to fifteen years imprisonment for his role in a controversial $5 billion arms deal where he had represented the French company Thomson. Shaik was known to have provided money to Zuma over the years for living expenses and Zuma was known to be in debt to Shaik. Common gossip acknowledged that Zuma had used his influence to support Shaik's business, but the question was still asked: had Zuma been used by Shaik, or was he personally guilty of corruption? The rape case became a joke—Zuma admitted to sex with the HIV-positive woman, but claimed that she was willing; as a 'mitigating circumstance' he mentioned that he had showered after sex to lower the chances of infection! But remarkably, Zuma emerged unscathed from all these accusations to beat

Mbeki for the ANC crown, and on 9 May 2009 Zuma was sworn in as president.

Jacob Zuma was very different from Mbeki. Mbeki had a master's degree in economics from Sussex University in England; Zuma learned to read and write only as an adult in prison. Where Mbeki related through intellect, Zuma related through charm and with his history ranging from resistance to exile and Robben Island prison, he had wide acceptance within the party. Where Mbeki would dazzle an audience with a brilliant policy statement, Zuma would swivel his hips in a Zulu dance step as he burst out into his favourite song from the days of resistance, 'Mshini wami' (Bring me my machine gun). But Zuma had more to bank on than party antipathy to Mbeki. Zuma was Zulu, the largest tribe in South Africa. The ANC had been dominated by Xhosas, the second largest tribe, who due to their better education, had led the freedom struggle. Oliver Tambo, Nelson Mandela and Thabo Mbeki were all Xhosas; now it was the turn of the Zulu. With Zuma in the presidency, it seemed that constitutional immunity would frustrate a third attempt to prosecute Zuma for the corruption case, and he would join Berlusconi of Italy and Zardari of Pakistan in avoiding prosecution by dint of holding the highest office in the land.

17

Iran: Ayatollahs in Command

*I have been chosen by God to perform a task. My visions are
miracles that saved the country.*

   —Shah of Iran to Oriana Fallaci, Italian journalist

*You miserable wretch, isn't it time for you to think and reflect a
little, to ponder where all this is leading you.*

   —Ayatollah Khomeini, referring to the
   Shah in a public speech

The last prime minister of Iran elected under Western
parliamentary democracy was Mohammad Mosaddegh, who
nationalized the Iranian oil industry controlled by the Anglo-
Iranian Oil Company. He was removed in a CIA-orchestrated
coup that brought back the Shah, a dictatorial monarch who

maintained control through his brutal security force SAVAK. After a long rule the Shah was toppled by the remarkable Ayatollah Khomeini and his Islamic revolution. Khomeini is one of a handful of revolutionary figures who have left an indelible imprint on history in the twentieth century. But whereas Ataturk had established the rule of modernizers imbued with Western values in Turkey, and Chairman Mao had established the rule of the Communist Party in China, and Mandela the rule of the blacks in South Africa, Ayatollah Khomeini with his philosophy of Welayat-e-Faqih established the rule of the clergy under the Supreme Leader in his new Islamic Republic. With superhuman will power and determination Khomeini battled the forces that opposed his revolution—the leftists and modernists who contended for power after the Shah's ouster, Saddam Hussein's army which invaded Iran, and America which moved to isolate Iran after the hostage crisis, when militant Islamist students captured the US embassy in Tehran and took fifty-two hostages for 444 days.

Khomeini established a regime in which president and parliament were elected by adult franchise, but in which the political system was dominated by the revolutionary key institutions of Supreme Leader, the Council of Guardians, the Assembly of Experts and the Expediency Council. The Supreme Leader is the most powerful figure in the government. Chosen by the Assembly of Experts, a body of eighty-six clerics, he is head of the armed forces, appoints the heads of the judiciary, the state broadcast media, the Revolutionary Guard and also has de facto control over appointments to key ministries. Khomeini was the first Supreme Leader till his death on 3 June 1989. The Council of Guardians consists of six clergymen appointed by the Supreme Leader, and six civil law experts, appointed by the head of the judiciary (who is himself appointed by the Supreme Leader), and approves or vetoes candidates for parliament or presidency, a power that was blatantly used in banning about 2,500 reformist candidates including eighty sitting members of parliament before the 2004 elections. The Expediency Council mediates in disputes between parliament and the Council of Guardians, and since 2005 also supervises all branches of the government as advisor and delegate of the Supreme Leader. Both the Assembly of Experts and the Expediency Council are headed by former president Akbar Hashemi Rafsanjani. Khomeini also created and empowered the Revolutionary Guard, first as an alternative force whose loyalty could be relied upon to protect the regime against possible counter revolution or coup attempts by the army of the exiled Shah, and then as a key instrument of the regime's control. Khomeini's study of Plato's philosophy of 'rule by a philosopher-king', elaborated in *The Republic*, perhaps inspired his 'Rule of the Jurist Supreme Leader', now firmly rooted in the Islamic Republic. However, from the onset it has met strong opposition from reputed Islamic scholars, both within Iran by Grand Ayatollahs Shariatmadari and Montazeri and dissident Ayatollah Borojerdi, and outside Iran by the revered Ayatollah Sistani in Iraq.

Khomeini was assisted by his key followers: Ayatollahs Ali Khamenei, Montazeri, Beheshti, Shariatmadari and Rafsanjani. Beheshti was head of Iran's judicial system and was one of

Khomeini's closest aides, playing a crucial role as chairman of the Council of Revolution and leader with Rafsanjani of the Islamic Republic Party. He was killed when a bomb destroyed the party's headquarters in Tehran. At the time of the revolution, Shariatmadari was the most senior Ayatollah in Qom. As far back as 1963, under the regime of the Shah, he had saved Khomeini's life by recognizing him as a Grand Ayatollah, thus saving him from execution. But Shariatmadari was critical of Khomeini's doctrine of Welayat-e-Faqih saying that it was neither compatible with Islam nor represented the will of the Irani people, and he was placed under house arrest and later accused of conspiracy to overthrow the Islamic Republic. Though widely believed to be innocent, his family was arrested and tortured leading to his confession and request for forgiveness on television; he remained officially discredited till his death in 1986.

On 19 December 2009, the media announced the death of Ayatollah Hossein Ali Montazeri, a founding father of the Islamic Republic who had crafted the new constitution and the judicial system; but when he died, Montazeri was better known as the spiritual patron of the opposition movement in Iran. Khomeini had appointed Montazeri as his designated successor and had started transferring powers to him in 1980; by 1983 all government offices hung a picture of Montazeri next to the mandatory picture of the Supreme Leader. But Montazeri's criticism of Khomeini's policies led to a fallout as he spoke out for people's rights and justice condemning the growing number of post-war executions by the regime: 'People in the world are getting the idea that our business in Iran is just murdering people.' Before his death Khomeini denounced Montazeri, removing him from his position as designated heir, and stripping him of his title of Grand Ayatollah. Montazeri was later placed under house arrest and acquired fame as a dissident. He was outspoken and critical of Ahmadinejad's nuclear policy, saying, 'One has to deal with the enemy with wisdom, not provoke it . . . His provocation only creates problems for the country.' His comment on inflation under Ahmadinejad was that a country cannot be run on 'slogans'.

Montazeri's fall from grace paved the way for Khamenei's rise to power. The constitution was changed to remove the requirement that the Supreme Leader be a Marja, the highest rank of spiritual leader, allowing Khamenei who had only been a mid-ranking Hojatoleslam before Montazeri's removal to become the new Supreme Leader. Khamenei and Rafsanjani inherited power from Khomeini with Rafsanjani becoming president and Khamenei becoming the Supreme Leader.

The post-Khomeini decade under Khamenei and Rafsanjani saw consolidation and economic stabilization, but there was a long way to go to recover the massive losses of the eight-year war with Iraq. Rafsanjani, a powerful president, was a conservative pragmatist described as 'economically liberal, politically authoritarian, and philosophically traditional'. Despite the corruption and crony capitalism that pervaded, he restored some efficiency in the administration, but his presidency was marred by suppression of civic freedoms, arbitrary arrests, press censorship, torture and summary executions. His lack of respect for democracy was best seen in his remark, 'When the Shah gave us freedoms we drove him

out of the country. We won't make that mistake ourselves.'
Rafsanjani grew rich and was accused of corruption. His family
is believed to control one of Iran's biggest engineering firms, a
Daewoo automobile assembly plant, and Iran's best private
airline, though the Rafsanjanis deny ownership. Family
members control Iran's largest copper mine, the TV network,
the pistachio business and the Tehran metro construction
business, and street gossip talks of billions of dollars stashed
away overseas. The youngest son Yaser owns a thirty-acre stud
farm in the super fashionable Lavasan neighbourhood of north
Tehran estimated to be worth over $100 million.

One easy road to quick wealth was the foreign trade system
while the rial value plummeted. Privileged insiders with the
right connections obtained import licences which, in effect,
allowed them to buy dollars at the rate of 1,750 rials and resell
them at the market rate of 8,000. One such lucky importer was
Asadollah Asgaroladi, whose brother Habibollah as Commerce
Minister was responsible for handing out trade licences.
Asadollah's fortune is estimated at $400 million. But the largest
commercial institutions were the 'Bonyads', the foundations
that were controlled by the clergy, the largest of which had
assets of $10 to $15 billion. These served as giant cash boxes to
pay off the supporters of the mullahs and as cash cows for their
managers. In one of the numerous corruption scandals
businessman Naser Tabasi was arrested and charged with fraud,
but with his powerful father Ayatollah Tabasi looking over his
shoulder, he was acquitted on the grounds that he did not
know he was breaking the law. Billions of dollars a year moved
to Dubai as the new elite plundered an economy that controlled

9 per cent of the world's oil and 15 per cent of its natural gas, while the income of the average Irani fell to levels below the time of the Shah.

Khamenei was elected president in 1981 after the assassination of President Mohammad Ali Rajai. He himself survived an assassination attempt which left him permanently injured, losing the use of his arm. He met the strength of the street with the strength of the state and thousands were killed and executed. His critics were arrested and often beaten by vigilantes. Even his younger brother Hadi was brutally beaten by the Basij, Iran's paramilitary volunteer militia, after criticizing Khamenei in a sermon. In 1989 he was elected Supreme Leader. As Supreme Leader Khamenei remains aloof from day-to-day politics, gives no press interviews, does not meet representatives of Western powers, nor does he travel overseas. His power has grown since the end of Rafsanjani's presidency, and his network of control covers the military, the Revolutionary Guard, the clerics and the bonyads. With Ahmadinejad subservient, Khamenei now has undisputed domination of the machinery of government. Over his twenty years as Supreme Leader he has blocked Rafsanjani's overtures to America, Khatami's aspirations for democracy, and Ahmadinejad's aggressive confrontationist policies.

By the mid-1990s the revolution had settled down, with the anarchy of the Iraq war and the post-revolutionary violence receding into past memory, and the revolutionary clerics now firmly established as the new elite monopolizing power and money. But dissent was growing. The mood was captured by Montazeri's statement, 'There is a great distance between what was promised and what we have achieved.' The influence of the dissidents grew with the growing influence of the philosopher Abdolkarim Soroush, the journalist Akbar Ganji, and the human rights lawyer and Nobel Prize winner Shirin Ebadi. People wanted change, democracy, the rule of law, liberalization and women's rights. The Reformist movement was born, unplanned and spontaneous, and Mohammad Khatami with his surprise victory in the 1997 presidential elections emerged as its new leader, securing massive support from women and youth in an unusually high voter turnout of 80 per cent. Reformist candidates also swept the local body and parliamentary elections that followed. But the conservative diehards were not willing to concede. They may have lost the presidency and the parliament, but they still had the Supreme Leader, the Guardianship Council, the judiciary and the strong Revolutionary Guards. Instead of allowing democracy and the rule of law, they counter-attacked both constitutionally and in the street.

Saeed Hajjarian, the main reformist strategist, was attacked in an assassination attempt that left him paralysed; the convicted assailant was reported to be a member of the Basij. Imprisonment, exile, death sentences and assassinations of notable reformists followed. Press censorship and closure of newspapers, state organized violence and intimidation of protestors, and veto of parliament by the Guardian Council were the establishment weapons of counter-attack. Though Khatami was re-elected in 2001 for a second term, his weakness was evident and he was seen as a loser. In 2004 the Guardian Council disqualified about 2,500 reformist candidates, breaking the back of the reformist movement as the hard-liners swept back to victory in local body and parliamentary elections. The democratic counter-revolution was over.

The defeat of the reformists left a vacuum as the 2005 presidential elections approached. The wily former president Rafsanjani re-entered the fray, this time as the rational democrat. Against him was the new face of Ahmadinejad, the unknown dark horse who emerged on the scene as the champion of the poor. Where Rafsanjani's wealth and love of luxury, his gilded furniture and expensive carpets were well known, Ahmadinejad had a simple and frugal lifestyle. Where Rafsanjani offered rationalism and moderation in government, Ahmadinejad proudly acclaimed his love for the people: 'I take pride in being the Irani nation's little servant and street sweeper.' Rafsanjani appealed to the middle class and the cities; Ahmadinejad appealed to the rural poor. But Ahmadinejad had a hidden ace up his sleeve. The unqualified support of the hundreds of thousands of members of the Basij and the powerful Revolutionary Guard, whose leader circulated the guidelines of the Supreme Leader—a simple lifestyle and modest campaign funds—which clearly signalled that Ahmadinejad was the preferred candidate. It was a David over Goliath victory as the humble professor of traffic engineering took the presidency and the defeated plutocrat, once the most powerful man in Iran, left the centrestage.

The new president brought with him a new set of problems. His readiness to confront the world, and his defiant nuclear strategy took Iran to the brink of war with America as he proudly repeated, 'Nuclear energy is our legitimate right.' His spiritual advisor was Ayatollah Taqi Mesbah-Yazdi, a hard-liner who stated, 'Some people imagine that violence has no place in Islam . . . violence is at the heart of Islam' and made no secret of his disdain for democracy. The new president was inspired by religion and believed firmly that he was the agent of the Mahdi, the Hidden Imam. When he spoke before the United Nations, he felt a divine halo-like light surround him, and on his return told the Ayatollahs about his experience. Ahmadinejad's visionary experiences seemed to leave the Shia clergy of Qom cold. Ayatollah Amoli responded quite dryly, simply remarking that he hoped that the president would focus on implementing his electoral promises. Revolutionary fervour rose, and with it rose state-sponsored violence and repression. Under Ahmadinejad, Iran experienced its own 'cultural revolution'. His vision was clear—no democracy, no economics. Purges removed technocrats and replaced them with Islamist loyalists as the 'fat cats' of the Rafsanjani and Khatami periods fell to accusations of corruption and ideological deviation. Purges also hit the reformists with their vision of democracy. Media was gagged by censorship, and students crushed by Basij militiamen.

Principles of economics were brushed aside as Ahmadinejad announced, 'I pray to God that I will never know about economics.' The president's economics were simple—take the oil money and spend it on the poor. At first it seemed to work, as rising oil prices took Iran's oil bonanza income up to $50 billion. But however fast the money came, Ahmadinejad spent it faster; within the first two years of his presidency he spent over $78 billion on his populist handouts to the poor. If current revenues were insufficient, there was always the reserve oil fund. The president showered largesse on the provinces with spontaneous generosity winning him the adoration of the rural poor. He also firmed up the affections of the Revolutionary Guards by passing them $10 billion in contracts, bypassing the tender process.

The spending spree combined with a low interest-rate policy raised the inflation level and soon met its blowback with rising prices and unemployment. Minimum wages were raised, but what good were rising wages to those whose very jobs were threatened by a deteriorating economy? In 2007 petrol rationing raised the price of fuel from the subsidized ten cents per litre to a new black-market price of $4 a litre. The bravado of the president won admiration in the region, but slowly increased the hardships of daily life for the middle classes and the poor in Iran, and many wondered whether it was time for an end of Iran's 'cultural revolution'.

Presidential elections in Iran had long been a barometer of democracy. Khamenei and Rafsanjani were elected without serious challenge at a time when the anarchy and war that followed the revolution made liberal democracy impossible. But the election of Khatami was a serious upset to the establishment. Though he was a member of the clergy, his victory represented a challenge of the reformists to the ruling conservatives and the eight years of his presidency imposed a hard struggle on the establishment to root out the spreading reformist ideology with its emphasis on democracy and the rule of law. As they restored their monopoly of control, they resolved never to risk such a challenge again.

Ahmadinejad's victory against Rafsanjani looked at first like another surprise upset, but soon it was suspected that he was supported by the Supreme Leader who preferred the subservient rising star to sharing power with his old partner, the powerful and wily Rafsanjani. The role of the Revolutionary Guards and the Basij was questioned, and allegations of rigging were in the air. The losers wondered at the sudden rise of Ahmadinejad's votes in the week between the first and second round from five million to seventeen million; a mysterious six million votes seemed to dance between the candidates, sometimes supporting one, sometimes another. In South Khorasan 298,000 votes were placed in ballot boxes by 270,000 eligible voters. But Rafsanjani was a beaten man, unwilling to continue the fight.

Protests of rigging were louder in the 2009 presidential election which announced Ahmadinejad's second victory with 63 per cent of the votes as against Mousavi's 34 per cent; even Grand Ayatollah Montazeri said that 'no one in their right mind can believe' the official results giving the incumbent a landslide victory. Massive protests took to the streets only to be attacked by the Basij militia, and finally the protests were quashed. But the credibility of those at the top was damaged. The street reality of arbitrary arrests, intimidation, beatings and torture, the complaints of discrimination by ethnic minorities, Kurds, Arabs, Baluchis and Azeris, and the clampdown on political activists and the press were in stark contradiction to the guarantees of Iran's Bill of Rights of equality of all before law, freedom of thought, religion, opinion and speech, and security from arbitrary arrest with fast and fair access to justice.

Democracy in the Islamic Republic is more visible in the laws of its constitution than in the streets of Tehran.

18

Thailand: The King, Thaksin and General Prem

Don't underestimate the people.
Let them decide.

—Thaksin Shinawatra

The year 2009 saw street demonstrations in Iran; the same year Thailand saw demonstrations on the streets too. In Iran democracy battled theocracy; in Thailand democracy battled the monarchy. Where Iran had its Supreme Leader with his special constitutional powers, his Guardian Council, the judiciary and his Revolutionary Guards, Thailand had its king with his special constitutional powers, his Privy Council, the judiciary and his army. With similar populations and living standards, both countries had also implemented successful population control programmes. Both Ahmadinejad and Thaksin Shinawatra were populists with strong rural support. The difference was that Ahmadinejad gave unquestioning allegiance to his Supreme Leader whereas Prime Minister Thaksin seemed to threaten his king; this difference kept Ahmadinejad in power, but moved Thaksin out of power into exile, as democracy lost out in both countries.

Thai politics over the last thirty years has been dominated by three remarkable figures: King Bhumipol, General Prem Tinsulanonda and Dr Thaksin Shinawatra. The period of absolute monarchy came to an end with the 1932 military coup. For the next forty-one years Thailand alternated between short periods of parliamentary rule and longer periods of military rule. King Bhumipol ascended the throne after his brother King Ananda died in mysterious circumstances of a gunshot wound to the head in 1946. He is the world's longest serving head of state, and has ruled through more than fifteen coups, sixteen constitutions and twenty-seven prime ministers. Initially powerless under the military dictator Plaek Phibun, he started to consolidate his position in the 1960s when General Sarit Dhanarajata, with whom he had a strong and close relationship, executed his successful coup endorsed by the king. With wisdom, patience and character he rebuilt the authority of the monarchy as a loved and revered king, and also facilitated the transition to democracy in 1973.

After General Sarit, the king found a champion in General Prem, who served him first as the prime minister in the 1980s and then as a privy councillor. Prem has been a loyal disciplinarian who has been the most important aide to the king over the last thirty years, and has been the éminence grise of Thai politics with an influence that can be compared with Rafsanjani in Iran, or even Talleyrand under Napoleon in post-revolutionary France. He emphasizes a moralist approach to politics. But Prem has grown older as Thaksin has grown stronger.

Dr Thaksin emerged first in business as a telecom billionaire and then as the most powerful prime minister in Thailand's history, the first to see out a full term. His 'Thaksinomics' set of economic policies is credited with the strong revival of the economy after the Asian economic crisis. His brilliant, enterprising but controversial style revolutionized politics in Thailand, and though now living in exile he remains the most popular politician whose importance cannot be ignored.

Thaksin's rise was meteoric. In 1994 he established a GSM phone network, entered politics and became foreign minister; he became deputy prime minister in 1995 and again in 1997 after the Asian financial crash and the currency collapse. A year later he formed the Thai Rak Thai party, and in two years more, swept the elections and came to power over the ruling Democrat party. In 2005 he won a second mandate with an overwhelming 75 per cent majority. Thaksin won on a populist manifesto focusing on the rural poor with his moratorium on farmer's debt, million-baht village development fund and thirty-baht per visit universal health care scheme. He combined a more appealing manifesto with better marketing, better media deployment and massive use of money. Big money backed him as the poor man enthusiastically voted for him. Once in power, he built up his networks with an energy and skill that made him unstoppable, spreading his tentacles into the army, the police, the bureaucracy and big business. His charisma and appeal grew with his successful handling of the economy, and his popular campaigns against drugs and corruption. His opponents lost hope as they feared that Thaksin was forever.

The base of Thaksin's fortune was telecommunications. His wealth was a result of his business genius, his ability to create opportunity out of the crisis of the baht devaluation and the use of political power to expand his business empire. At the start of the 1990s when telecommunication concessions were being given out, Shin Corp, Thaksin's company, received seven out of the twenty-one concessions, more than any other company, without any process of competitive bidding. The head of the Telecommunications Organization of Thailand (TOT), Shin Corp's benefactor, later joined the company as executive vice-chairman. The growth of the telecommunication companies through the 1990s was heavily dependent on influencing the Ministry of Communications, and involved the ruthless use of money and power, both of which Thaksin had in plenty. Even before he became prime minister, Thaksin held the portfolio of foreign minister, and was twice appointed deputy prime minister. The growth of Shin Corp's business into Indochina and Burma was promoted by his term as foreign minister, and the period when Thaksin became deputy prime minister is recognized as a period of 'telecommunications politics'.

Till the time of the 1997 Asian financial crisis and the massive baht devaluation, Thai telecom was dominated by the 'Big 4' telecom companies, all of which had huge foreign currency debts. Shortly before the July devaluation, Thaksin hedged nearly 70 per cent of his group's foreign currency exposure leading to criticism that he had been tipped off by Finance Minister Thanong who was his close friend and later joined the Shin Corp business, further fuelling speculation of collusion. Subsequent parliamentary debates also levied the accusation that news of the impending devaluation had been leaked to Thaksin.

Unfortunately for the king, no one tipped off the palace, and the Crown Property Bureau lost much of its wealth: Siam Cement was left with losses of $1.9 billion and a debt of $4 billion, and Siam Commercial Bank held almost $5 billion in non-performing loans. While the other telecom giants struggled with their post-devaluation financial problems, Shin Corp emerged as the clear leader both economically and politically due to Thaksin's profitable handling of the baht crash. The period of Thaksin's prime ministership was marked by the expansion of the Shin Corp business and the growth of his family wealth. His official trips supported his business expansions in India, China and Burma as his profits grew.

The Shinawatra family was of Sino-Thai origin. As in other Southeast Asian countries, the Chinese community had acquired substantial economic power. In Thailand the community had integrated with the native Thais through intermarriage and change of name, and had also acquired substantial political power. By the 1990s Thai prime ministers who had partial Chinese ancestry included Anand Panyarachun, Chuan Leekpai, Banharn Silpa-archa and Chavalit Yongchaiyudh. By 2001 as many as 90 per cent of Thai MPs had some Chinese ancestry. Both Thaksin's stints as deputy prime minister were under Sino-Thai prime ministers. His meteoric rise may have been promoted by his membership of the elite ethnic club of a very rich and powerful network. It is interesting that the Thai Rak Thai (TRT) party ('Thais love Thais') which swept Thaksin to power was formed by a politician whose great-great-great-grandfather was a Hakka Chinese immigrant from Guangdong. The Chinese in Thailand, although just 10 per cent of the population, control the country's largest banks and conglomerates. All of Thailand's billionaires including the huge Charoen Pokphand Group are ethnic Chinese. They dominate finance, commerce and most of the industrial sector; they also dominate the political scene. Unlike other Southeast Asian countries Thailand has little anti-Chinese sentiment and this ethnic group has been absorbed into the mainstream by cultural assimilation, the suppression of the Chinese language, intermarriage and the taking of Thai names. The one character trait that has endured is the desire and the ability to make money.

The promotion of personal wealth and power by the use and even misuse of official position was common practice in Thai politics, government and even military. This resulted in 'network politics' in which elite groups looked after each other's private interests often at the expense of policy and the people. People in power grew rich. The problem was that Thaksin, with his outstanding efficiency, grew richer than everyone else; this resulted in envy. The emergence of billionaire politicians was not unique to Thailand; Iran had its Rafsanjani, and in India and Pakistan political leaders grew amazingly rich with invisible income streams. The political system was riddled with pervasive corruption, vote buying and even the criminalization of politics, covert partnerships between politicians and mafia dons who controlled drugs, sex rackets, smuggling and other criminal activities. Cleaning up corruption was a regular justification of military coups. Thaksin was involved in an assets declaration case where it was charged that he had failed to correctly declare his assets when deputy prime minister which could result in a five-year ban on holding public office. His fortuitous windfall of profits in the baht devaluation had already raised criticism, and it was common knowledge that his rise in wealth had kept pace with his rise to power. But Thaksin was too popular, too powerful and too smart to be tripped up, and shortly after becoming prime minister he was cleared by the court in the assets case.

After the 2006 coup, the military junta attacked, freezing Thaksin's assets on charges of 'policy corruption'—that he had supported the profits of companies owned by his family by non-transparent policies. This was followed by conflict of interest charges over the purchase of four pieces of land by his wife from the Financial Institutions Development Fund while he was prime minister; these were followed by tax evasion charges on his wife. Thaksin alleged political victimization and moved into self-imposed exile to Dubai where he remains despite winning the elections and making his sister prime minister.

Thaksinomics was Thaksin's new set of economic policies. Though recognizing the importance of exports, he was reluctant to rely solely on export-driven growth with an over-excessive dependence on exports at a time when the Chinese were pricing out others and their exports were taking over the markets. Thaksin emphasized growth of domestic consumption, and a Keynesian approach to stimulate the economy.

His opponents criticized these policies as gimmickry and undid most of his policies after the coup that removed him, but the numbers clearly show that the economy strengthened under Thaksin. The GDP grew from 4.9 trillion baht in 2001 to 7.1 trillion baht in 2006. Thailand paid its debts to the IMF two years ahead of schedule. Incomes in the poor north-east region grew by 40 per cent while nationwide poverty was halved. The stock exchange outperformed other markets in the region, budget deficits were converted into budget surpluses, public sector debt fell and foreign exchange reserves doubled, reaching $64 billion in 2006. Thaksinomics was a success—it could not be explained away by the coincidence of the Asian financial crisis before his prime ministership and the world economic crash after he was removed from power and those who argued that Thaksin was just 'lucky' to fall between.

Though Thaksin had total electoral dominance, the ever-cautious leader also built up strong personal networks of support in big business, the media, the police and the military, recognizing that electoral victory was not sufficient guarantee of retaining power in Thai politics. In this he relied on his own family. His wife was the largest financial donor to the TRT party, and he positioned his sister in the party leadership, his cousin Chaisit as commander-in-chief of the army, and his brother-in-law Priewphan as deputy police chief. He also made full use of his friends and former classmates who may not have been outstanding students or officers but always managed plum promotions. But Thaksin's network overshadowed and eroded General Prem's older network, and in an army of 1,400 generals, favour given to the chosen few led to resentment of the many that were ignored. He had also made an enemy of the still powerful General Prem, who as head of the Privy Council had the ear of the king and used his access to turn the king against the prime minister. Furthermore, the palace was not happy with Thaksin's hard-line repression of the Muslims in the southern border provinces who posed a threat to the legitimacy of the Thai state. Prem warned the army that they owed their allegiance to the king, not to the government, and despite the massive majority victory of the TRT taking 374 out of 500 seats, anti-Thaksin protests hit the streets. When the Shinawatra family sold their Shin Corp shareholding to a foreign company, Temasek Holdings of Singapore, in January 2006 for $1.88 billion, the protests escalated calling for Thaksin's resignation.

The prime minister held a second election in April, which was widely boycotted, again ensuring his majority, but his opposition refused to accept the results and continued street protests. In May the Constitutional Court invalidated the elections and another election was announced for October, but before it could be held, the military took over in a coup, while Thaksin was in New York for the UN summit. The coup announcement stated:

> We have seized power. The constitution, the Senate, the House of Representatives, the Cabinet and the Constitutional Court have all been dissolved. The caretaker prime minister (Thaksin) has caused an unprecedented rift in society, widespread corruption, nepotism, and interfered in independent agencies, crippling them so that they cannot function . . . Thus the Council needed to seize power to control the situation, to restore normalcy and to create unity as soon as possible.

The December 2007 elections again saw a Thaksin victory, this time through the People's Power Party (PPP) that had replaced his TRT party, banned for violating electoral laws. The PPP candidate, Samak Sundarajev, became prime minister but he, too, was banned by the constitutional court—for 'conflict of interest' when he was paid a couple of hundred dollars for appearing in a TV cooking show for it was judged that he could not work for a private company while holding the post of prime minister.

The amateur cook was replaced by Thaksin's brother-in-law, Somchai Wongsawat, but he too was removed and banned from politics when the PPP was dissolved by the court for electoral fraud. Every election had resulted in a Thaksin victory, and it was recognized that another election would only reconfirm the position. In August 2008 Thaksin and his wife flew out to London. In September a second warrant for his arrest was issued; and in October he was sentenced in absentia to two years imprisonment. Thaksin had put his faith in democracy and elections. He was clearly unaware of the Arab proverb that 'The shortest way to prison is to win elections.'

In an attempt to destroy Thaksin, he was prosecuted, hounded into exile, his assets confiscated, and his political parties twice disbanded. But Thaksin proved indestructible.

In the July 2011 general elections the voters gave a massive mandate to the beautiful and charismatic Yingluck Shinawatra who led the Pheu Thai party (PT) to secure 265 out of 500 seats. Abhisit Vejjajiva conceded defeat and Yingluck became Thailand's first female prime minister, joining the elite group of twenty women, wives and daughters related to former leaders who have become prominent political figures in the country.

Yingluck is the sister of Thaksin who masterminded and bankrolled the election campaign from his villa in Dubai. Once again, Thaksin had shown that he could not be beaten in an election, winning for the fourth time since 2001 in defiance of his opponents in the establishment who repeatedly nullified his victories using the army or the courts.

Thaksin continues to live in Dubai—for the time being. But his sister is able to draw on his experience and advice by regular phone calls and Skype conversations. He influenced the selection of the cabinet, and plays an important, if unofficial, part in the policies and strategies of government. Meanwhile Yingluck is 'exploring every avenue to bring him back'. Majority demand wants Thaksin's return, and counters criticism of Thaksin's godfather role: 'Everyone already knows that Thaksin pulls the strings. It's okay because that's what the people want.' Thaksin is eager to return, but will not make a rash move and plays a waiting game, saying he will go back if he is 'part of the solution rather than part of the problem'.

19

India: The World's Biggest Democracy

Corruption and hypocrisy ought not to be the inevitable product of democracy, as they undoubtedly are today.

—Mahatma Gandhi

On 26 December 2009 the *Hindustan Times* carried the story of Ruchika, a pretty fourteen-year-old school girl with a passion for tennis. In 1990 she was called into the office of the inspector general of police S.P.S. Rathore, the president of the Haryana Lawn Tennis Association, who then molested her. She was traumatized and filed a statement before the director general of police.

That should have been enough to finish off Rathore's career. Instead it finished off Ruchika—and eventually nearly finished off her family. Rathore responded by threatening her father that if the complaint was not withdrawn, he would destroy the family. He registered false cases of theft against Ruchika's brother Ashu, who was tortured, beaten and paraded around the neighbourhood like a caged animal. When he was released in December 1993, he had another shock waiting for him. Ruchika had committed suicide. When Ruchika's father tried to get justice for his dead daughter, he was threatened and driven out of his home. He spent several years in hiding from Rathore's vengeance. But with courage and determination the family kept the case alive. In December 2009, nearly two decades after the incident, a court finally held found Rathore guilty. He was sentenced to six months imprisonment with a fine of $20 and walked out of the courtroom smirking.

This is a story, one of thousands, of democracy in India. Ruchika was one of the thousands of Indians who commit suicide every year due to stress caused by family conflict, domestic violence, academic failure, unfulfilled romantic ideals, alcohol, rape, injustice and most of all severe financial strain. In southern India, the nation's information technology hub, about 50,000 people commit suicide each year and one in three suicides are committed by young people. Kerala, Karnataka, Tamil Nadu, Andhra Pradesh and Puducherry showed the highest number of suicides. In April 2009 newspaper headlines announced: '1,500 farmers commit mass suicide in India.' Falling water levels in Chhattisgarh led to crop failure and debt, leaving farmers with only one way out of their misery. For these wretched victims, democracy was just not working.

India's democracy has failed in tackling poverty, conflict and corruption in India. Despite its successful rate of growth of the economy, life for the 300 million at the bottom has remained desperate. The 2011 Global Hunger Index (GHI) recognizes India not just as a country with a serious malnutrition problem, but also as one of the three countries (out of eighty-one reviewed) where the GHI actually increased. Unemployment is an additional burden for the poor. Hunger-related deaths increase even as India's food exports rise; India has never before enjoyed such huge food exports. About 300 million of India's population is illiterate, and even those who are counted as literate pass through schools without textbooks, lavatories or running water, filling the ranks of the 400 million unemployed or unemployable. The Nobel Prize-winning economist Amartya Sen has commented: 'An illiterate population has no use for democratic rights.' Conflict has spanned religion (Hindu–Muslim, Hindu–Sikh and even Hindu–Christian); race, leading to the politics of region and language in the south and the north-east (Assam, Punjab, Tamil Nadu and Andhra Pradesh); caste, with the struggle of the Dalits and OBCs (Other Backwards Classes); and class struggle, with the ongoing Naxalite violence. Corruption keeps India high on the Transparency International list of corrupt nations, and an estimated $5 billion are spent on bribes to the bureaucracy and to politicians, though, admittedly, in 2008 India at eighty-fifth place performed much better than Pakistan at 134th and Bangladesh at 147th.

Only once did India move to dilute or discard the democratic process. On 12 June 1975 the Allahabad High Court found Indira Gandhi guilty of misuse of the government machinery for her election campaign and disqualified her. On 26 June

President Fakhruddin Ali Ahmed, on Indira's 'advice', declared a state of emergency with suspension of civil liberties and rule by decree. Indira's twenty-one-month Emergency was endorsed by respected figures such as Vinoba Bhave, Mother Teresa, industrialist J.R.D. Tata and journalist Khushwant Singh; but Amnesty International condemned the arrest and imprisonment of 140,000 people over the twenty-one months. Indira's son, Sanjay, won notoriety by his harsh programmes of compulsory vasectomy and brutal eviction of slum dwellers in Delhi. The economy, however, seemed to improve as a result of the boost given by the new discipline imposed by the Emergency, and saw growth of agricultural production and manufactures; exports and foreign currency reserves increased; Hindu–Muslim riots ceased; the efficiency of the government improved. But the people of India were enraged, and in March 1977 when the Emergency was removed, they voted against Indira and the Congress leading to her humiliating defeat as both she and Sanjay lost their own seats. Indira's catchy election slogan, 'garibi hatao' (get rid of poverty), was trumped by Jayaprakash Narayan's reply, 'Indira hatao, desh bachao' (get rid of Indira, save the country)! The voters did get rid of Indira, and no further challenge to the principle of democracy was mounted in the country.

Though democracy has failed in tackling many of India's problems, it has nevertheless made considerable contribution to the difficult evolution of this huge but poor nation. Elections have been generally free and fair, despite breach of the rules by many individual candidates. The press and media have been free; the rule of law and an independent judiciary have endured at the higher levels; and most importantly, removal of unpopular regimes and peaceful successions have been facilitated. The culture of democracy has taken root, and the power of the vote is now understood by the electorate. Since 1991 India has shown that democracy and development can be compatible.

Over the last sixty years politics in India has changed. The politicians have changed, the issues have changed, and the parties have changed. In the years following independence, freedom fighters, lawyers, idealists and intellectuals moved out of British prisons into Parliament. Many of today's politicians have criminal records and have made politics one more racket for them to plunder. In the 2009 general elections, 24 per cent of the Lok Sabha members were alleged to have criminal records. Gangsters in politics enjoy the snail's pace of Indian litigation which in most cases will see them die of old age before they can be convicted.

Along with the ugly face of crime that fills the corridors of power we find beautiful film stars, who with their public following and electability, are sought after by political parties. Some have attained serious power, such as M.G. Ramachandran, who served as chief minister of Tamil Nadu from 1977 till his death in 1987, and was followed by his leading lady Jayalalitha. N.T. Rama Rao, a distinguished actor and film producer, served three terms as chief minister of Andhra Pradesh. Several other movie stars also had stints in the Parliament from time to time including the Bachchans (husband and wife representing different parties in the house), Dharmendra, Jayaprada, Shabana

Azmi, Vinod Khanna, Shatrughan Sinha, Sanjay Dutt, Smriti Irani, Govinda, Chiranjeevi—the list goes on. So far beauty queens have not been as successful in politics in India as they have been in Venezuela, where the six-feet Miss Universe Irena Sáez, the successful mayor of Caracas, lost out to Chavez for president. Or in Berlusconi's Italy with his bevy of actresses and beauty queens, including a model who once posed topless and went on to become Minister for Equal Opportunities. Even in the US where governor of Alaska, Sarah Palin, a former beauty queen, strives to be America's future leader.

The party scene had also changed. For the first fifty years the Indian National Congress dominated; but as the memories of the heroes of independence faded and disillusionment grew with the actual achievements of post-Independence politics, voters looked for new inspiration. The Bharatiya Janata Party (BJP) with its Hindutva ideology rose to the challenge. With its campaign led by L.K. Advani in 1989 for a temple dedicated to Lord Ram at the site of the Babri Masjid it drew a large number of voters disillusioned with the Congress and with each successive election increased its strength. Meanwhile regional parties also grew, becoming leading players in many of the states. The two main national parties, Congress and BJP, sought alliances with regional parties to firm up their majorities at the centre as coalition government replaced single-party rule. The coalition partners committed their support in exchange for profitable ministries, and corruption increased.

In the post-Independence years nationalism was the ideology of the victorious Congress, and Nehru's decades of struggle inspired confidence as he committed his energies to building a new India. Under Indira, public support for the party weakened, and 'special events' were required to bring back the vote—the defeat of Pakistan and the creation of Bangladesh saw a revival, and sympathy votes followed the assassinations of both Indira and Rajiv. Nationalism was increasingly challenged by a growing Hindutva ideology. At the regional level parties were formed around religion, race, caste and class, which provided the new ideologies. Within the parties themselves inner-party democracy was replaced by the cult of the supreme leader. Voters were offered the choice of a coalition government led by the BJP and its pro-Hindu allies, or a coalition led by the modernist Nehru dynasty.

Three remarkable foreign women have made India their home. Mother Teresa, the Nobel Prize winner who started life as an Albanian from Macedon but settled in India to care of 'the hungry, the naked, the homeless, the crippled, the blind, the lepers, all those people who feel unwanted, unloved, uncared for throughout society'; Annie Besant, born in England, who served as president of the Indian National Congress before Partition; and Sonia Gandhi, the Italian-born wife of Rajiv Gandhi, the president of the Congress today, and the most powerful figure in current Indian politics.

Sonia joined politics in 1998, quickly rising to the position of the president of the party. Starting in opposition she has led the party through two electoral victories, after which she retained political leadership but passed control of the administration and the economy to Manmohan Singh, her selected candidate for prime minister. Sonia separated party leadership from government, a pattern that China had followed for some time.

Sonia's choice, Manmohan Singh, is from the minority Sikh community and is a highly respected economist, who as finance minister presided over economic reforms that ended the notorious Licence Raj system. He is the only Indian prime minister never to have been elected to the Lok Sabha, and his selection shows Sonia's emphasis of economics over politics. Despite the recent corruption scandals and accusations of policy paralysis, the economy has generally prospered and Sonia has given a new lease of life to the Nehru dynasty paving the way for the succession of her son Rahul Gandhi.

Democratic India is a success when compared to her less democratic neighbours, Pakistan and Bangladesh. She has surpassed them in per capita income, literacy, observance of political and human rights and economic growth; but she is somewhat of a failure when compared with the other Asian giant, China, which has outperformed India in economic growth, quality of life, literacy and military power. The Chinese government, according to the Transparency International corruption index, is less corrupt than India's; and China's military is perhaps stronger, as evidenced from the one war the two countries fought (in 1962) in which China defeated India. India has so far failed in containing corruption, conflict and population growth—the three most dangerous obstacles to development.

Has democracy succeeded in India? It depends on which way you look—at China, at Pakistan, or at the hundreds of millions of wretched Indians living in a degrading poverty that denies them dignity and a decent life.

~

The most successful stories of economic growth in the twentieth century, China, Korea, Singapore and Taiwan, indicate that democracy is not a precondition for growth—in fact, it may even hamper fast growth. Nevertheless, America and the World Bank pressurize developing nations to conform to a semblance of democracy, which emphasizes elections, but turns a blind eye to vote-rigging, corruption and a total disregard for the rule of law. Though America itself did not adopt full adult franchise till 1965, when the blacks were finally allowed to vote in the southern states. It was only well into the twentieth century that the developed nations granted all adults the right to vote, regardless of property ownership, educational qualifications, gender and race. Australia adopted full adult franchise in 1962, Portugal in 1970, Switzerland in 1971, and Spain in 1977 after the death of General Franco. Most developing nations have adopted adult franchise at a much lower stage of their development than the developed nations of the West. Critics of the bad practices of Third World democracies forget that the first democracies of the West were no less flawed—with widespread illegal electoral practices, corruption and fraud. Public offices were sold to the highest bidder, who then proceeded to treat his office as his private property and income source. The 'spoils system' was not restricted to the US, but was also prevalent in Europe, where many offices were almost hereditary.

Democracy, to be successful in poor countries, requires more than just elections. It requires a commitment to the rule of law, an educated public, effective institutions, and sincere leaders. Since these are lacking in most countries, democracy more often than not disappoints us. The common alternative is capture of the state by crooks and sinners—very much worse than ineffective democracy. There are also the rare but exciting success stories of nations where good authoritarian leaders have given their people food before freedom, and where justice, values and discipline have been more important than the vote in increasing the national economic pie rather than bargaining and fighting over how to divide it. Unfortunately, saints are few and far between.

Section Five

SUPERPOWERS DO MATTER

THE ROLE OF THE UNITED STATES

All political power comes from the barrel of a gun.

—Chairman Mao

Americans always try to do the right thing, after they've tried everything else.

—Winston Churchill

In 1776 the Americans signed the Declaration of Independence. Over the next 200 years they moved from colony to empire with a skilled and ruthless use of guns and money. Guns wrested the land from the original inhabitants, the American

Indians, and also won the Mexican territories in the southwest. Money secured the Louisiana Purchase in 1803, as 828,800 square miles of territory were bought from France at the price of $15 million; Napoleon explained his reason for the selling: 'I have given England a maritime rival who sooner or later will humble her pride.' The Louisiana Purchase was followed by the Alaska Purchase in 1867 when the US paid Russia $7.2 million for 586,412 square miles, an equivalent of 1.9 cents per acre. Having secured the territories of North America, she then turned her attention to the world.

The US has repeatedly waged war and conducted military interventions in countries around the world; the list of such countries where its military has intervened with the use of force include China, the Philippines, Korea, Iran, Guatemala, Costa Rica, the Middle East, Indonesia, Haiti, Iraq, USSR, Vietnam, Cambodia, Laos, Thailand, Ecuador, Congo/Zaire, Brazil, Peru, the Dominican Republic, Cuba, Ghana, Chile, Bolivia, Angola, Nicaragua, Yemen, Chad, Libya, Panama, Afghanistan, Somalia, Yugoslavia and Venezuela. President Barack Obama has tried to explain this with his controversial comment: 'Whether we like it or not we remain a dominant military superpower, and when conflicts break out, one way or another, we get pulled into them.'

William Blum's *Rogue State* describes the US global interventions, the assassinations and attempted assassinations carried out by the CIA, the wars, the bombings of over twenty-eight countries, the US use of weapons of mass destruction including depleted uranium, cluster bombs and chemical weapons and the use of torture. Blum describes the CIA's involvement with torture, as the agency.

- Encouraged its clients in the Third World to use torture;
- Pointed out people to be tortured in Guantanamo, Abu Ghraib and Bagram;

- Supplied torture equipment;
- Conducted classes in torture;
- Distributed torture manuals—'how to' books;
- Observed and evaluated torture as it took place.

Blum also describes how the CIA helped send Nelson Mandela to prison, quoting Paul Eckel, a senior CIA operative: 'We have turned Mandela over to the South African security branch. We gave them every detail, what he would be wearing, the time of day, just where he would be. They picked him up. It was one of our greatest coups.' In a hard-hitting response to the numerous literature on so-called 'Rogue States', Blum contends that there is only one rogue state: America.

To support its empire America maintains a military establishment of 1.5 million troops, with a defence expenditure that is not just the largest in the world, but larger than the next ten countries put together. US military expenditure is close to half of the world's military expenditure, and in 2012 the total defence-related expenditure was in excess of $1 trillion. America also maintains numerous military bases around the world. US propaganda says the US is 'saving the world', and has portrayed America as the 'good guy' in its wars including the Cold War and the War against Terrorism, but the reality is more ominous; the Pentagon Planning Guide for 1994–99 is more blunt: 'America must prevent other states from challenging our leadership or seeking to overturn the established political and economic order . . . We must maintain the mechanisms for deterring potential competitors from even aspiring to a larger regional or global role.' America has no hesitation in initiating wars to protect its global hegemony or to promote US economic interests, particularly oil and the role of the dollar as the world's reserve currency.

In response to 9/11 President Bush launched the war against Afghanistan; this was followed by his war against Iraq which offended many. How many countries does America propose to invade? The answer was given by General Wesley Clark, NATO's former Supreme Allied Commander Europe, who exposed the Department of Defence's plan to 'take out' seven countries: Iraq was to be followed by Syria, Lebanon, Libya, Somalia, Sudan and Iran—all having predominantly Muslim populations. Condemning the Bush administration, he said, 'They don't deserve to be in office. They want war with a billion Muslims.' Subsequent to General Clark's exposure, a book was published with the title *Where to Invade Next* in which the list of countries to be taken out dropped Lebanon, Somalia and Libya and substituted them with Pakistan, Uzbekistan, Venezuela and North Korea.

Countries promote the standard of living of their people in terms of production, savings and growth. Empires are different—they promote the lifestyle of their citizens by taking the wealth of other nations. To do this, they use military muscle and maintain armies that are able to dominate other countries, who must either pay tribute or face destruction. The recent financial crisis that rocked America has raised the question: is this the collapse of the American empire? The answer is: probably not. The economy may have collapsed but the US army remains the strongest military force in the world, too powerful for any or all to challenge. As long as the US is able to continue taking the wealth of other nations, she will be able to emerge from the pit into which she has fallen, despite her twin deficits of budgets and trade, despite her debt, both domestic and international, which make her the world's greatest debtor nation. The army is the key to the revival of the American economy.

But surely America does not demand tribute; nor does it like Rome or Genghis Khan invade countries to seize their gold and enslave their people. How then can it be called a predator nation that preys on others? One American politician who has tried to answer that question is Ron Paul, the Texas congressman who has served eleven terms, and has twice tried to run for president. Ron Paul has focused on the role of the dollar. After the end of the Second World War, the dollar replaced the British pound as the pre-eminent world reserve currency. The dollar was backed by gold, priced at $35 per ounce.

In 1971 Nixon closed the gold window, after which the new system kept the dollar as the world's reserve currency, but with no restrictions and no convertibility into gold. The US was free to print as many dollars as served its own interest. From here on whenever America wanted to buy more goods from the world, it simply printed more money. Then the US authorities struck a deal with OPEC to price oil in US dollars exclusively for all worldwide transactions; in return the US promised to protect the various oil-rich kingdoms in the Middle East against the threat of invasion or domestic coup. This had the effect of 'backing' the dollar with oil, giving it further strength and increasing the international demand for the dollar.

Trade deficits were no problem, since the imports that America required were paid for by a never-ending supply of dollars fresh off the printing press; the surpluses of the major exporting nations like the UAE and China were in turn loaned to America at minimum interest rates. Budget deficits too were financed by low-interest loans from the surplus countries, China, Japan, and the oil-rich nations. Cheap money from overseas kept interest rates within America low, and low interest rates led to rising property prices as the bubble grew. American consumers borrowed against their homes, dipping into the never-ending stream of money. Everyone felt rich; working and saving was no longer necessary in the new economy. Meanwhile debt grew as Americans and America borrowed more and consumed more. Factories closed and unemployment grew as both production and jobs moved overseas.

It is an unbelievable benefit for the US to be able to import valuable goods and export depreciating dollars. If this system were workable long term, American citizens would never have to work again. The licence to create money out of thin air allows the bills to be paid through price inflation. But Ron Paul of Texas warns in his speech before the US House of Representatives on 15 February 2006:

> The artificial demand for our dollar, along with our military might, places us in the unique position to 'rule' the world without productive work or savings, and without limits on consumer spending or deficits. The problem is, it can't last. The time will come when our dollars, due to their depreciation, will be received less enthusiastically or even be rejected by foreign countries. That could force us to pay for living beyond our means and our production. That shift in sentiment has already started, but the worst [is] yet to come.

The unbalanced international economic system has endured for two reasons. First, because the trade- and dollar-surplus countries from Southeast Asia and the oil-rich countries are beneficiaries of the status quo and are happy to keep it going; the depreciating dollar is a small price to pay for the prosperity and growth that they enjoy through the system. Second, because the dollar has strong 'backing'—no longer gold but the US military! The military backing for the dollar ensures that dollar domination continues. Those countries that try to defy or resist are quickly taught a lesson and brought back into line. It is no coincidence that Iraq was attacked months after Saddam announced Euro oil sales, or that Chavez was removed by a coup endorsed by the CIA, months after his move to sell Venezuelan oil for Euros—to everyone's surprise Chavez made a quick comeback. As Paul warns, 'Using force to compel people to accept money without real value can only work in the short term; it ultimately leads to economic dislocation.'

To enjoy the fruits of empire America needs a compliant world. Rather than wage war on everybody, America uses three institutions to maintain an international economic system in its best interests: the IMF, the World Bank and the WTO. For decades the expertise and sincerity of these institutions was accepted by all; and then along came Joseph Stiglitz, who had served as chairman of the President's Council of Economic Advisors in the Clinton administration and then as senior vice-president and chief economist of the World Bank. When he expressed criticism and dissent regarding World Bank globalization policies, he was sacked. Unfortunately, Stiglitz then went on to receive the Nobel Prize for Economics for his theories, and became too important to ignore.

Stiglitz argued that the West—acting through the IMF and the WTO—has seriously mismanaged the processes of privatization, liberalization and stabilization, and that by following its advice many Third World countries and former communist states became actually worse off than they were before. The failure of these policies was not due to 'wrong economics' but because their real objective was not the welfare of the poor countries but the promotion of Western interests, Western companies and Western financial institutions. Stiglitz criticized the 'one-size-fits-all' approach of the multilateral institutions, with their four-step programme of privatization, capital market liberalization, market-based pricing and free trade.

The outrageous privatization in Russia that gave birth to the oligarchs, described as 'the Sale of the Century', saw assets worth billions disposed off for mere millions, leaving Russia and the Russian people bankrupt. By contrast, China refused to follow the IMF guidelines for privatization, and emerged as the success story of the century.

Capital market liberalization was equally disastrous and was exposed in the Asian financial crisis as countries such as Indonesia who followed IMF advice floundered, and Malaysia, under the leadership of Dr Mahathir, who rejected the IMF advice, recovered from the exodus of speculative 'hot money' and the currency attacks of George Soros, the New York currency speculator.

Market-based pricing that removed subsidies on food, water and cooking gas resulted in riots—what Stiglitz called 'the IMF riot'—as IMF elimination of subsidies for food and fuel in Indonesia exploded into street protests; Bolivia faced riots over water prices, and Ecuador over the rise in cooking gas prices.

Free trade under the WTO rules fared no better as protestors led the 'Battle in Seattle'. Stiglitz compared the WTO opening of world markets with the Opium Wars in China (1840s and 1850s) when British gunships forced the reluctant Chinese administration to allow the import of British opium to balance the trade deficit caused by export of tea to England. WTO rules looked after Western interests, opening doors for their exports, but barricading Western markets against Third World agriculture. Subsidies in agriculture in the US, Europe and Japan remained firmly in place. TRIPS and TRIMS supported Western intellectual property rights and Western finance and capital, but the WTO turned a blind eye to the service areas where the developing world could score if allowed entry into the rich Western countries.

China and Russia provided the clearest proof of the failure of the IMF policies, as Stiglitz points out in the first chapter of his book *Globalization and Its Discontents*:

> The contrast between Russia's transition, as engineered by the international economic institutions, and that of China, designed by itself, could not be greater: while in 1990 China's gross domestic product (GDP) was 60 per cent of that in Russia, by the end of the decade the numbers had been reversed. While Russia saw an unprecedented rise in poverty, China saw an unprecedented decrease.

The IMF had become a part of the countries' problem rather than part of the solution. Stiglitz concluded: 'A half century after its founding, it is clear that the IMF has failed in its mission ... Once a country was in crisis, IMF funds and programs not only failed to stabilize the situation but in many cases actually made matters worse, especially for the poor.' Meanwhile, the American empire looked forward to the American century. The American way of life rested securely on the two pillars of military supremacy and the mighty dollar; American affluence was reinforced by the connivance of the World Bank, the IMF and the WTO. The rich of the world grew richer and the poor poorer.

The US, with its vast consumer demand, was an essential target for any country that sought an export market to promote its economic growth, and those countries who found the US open to their exports flourished. South Korea and

Taiwan were the first of the high-growth nations to build their growth on exports to the US, but soon China was to dwarf all that had gone before. America was also the largest source of finance, with its huge corporations that are the most important investors around the world, and Wall Street, home to international finance, that dominates equity and portfolio investment. Without American money and markets, a developing country was doomed to stagnate. Others—China, Japan and the oil-rich Arabs—had monetary surpluses, but these found their way to the US from where they were recycled. The legend of American financial expertise endured.

And then in 2008 the US financial system went into meltdown as the subprime mortgage crisis shattered confidence in the economy. Economic growth around the world was reined in with worldwide recession. Stock markets crashed; the property bubble burst; the investment banking industry in America was wiped out; government bailouts pumped hundreds of billions of dollars into the economy and major corporations had to be saved from bankruptcy by government intervention. Ordinary Americans lost their homes in bank foreclosures and lost their jobs in the growing unemployment scenario. As America began the long, hard climb to recovery, Americans prepared for their changed relationship with the world, in which financial dependence would require negotiation, not demand, as American influence waned.

Whereas developing nations that had saved surplus reserves were able to realign their economies, substituting domestic consumption for export dependence on America and the West, the poorer countries prepared for tougher times. Exports were hit as consumers in America tightened their belts and reduced their spending. Both the volumes and the prices of exports fell. Foreign investment fell—both portfolio and direct foreign investment. Exchange rates in developing countries fell drastically too—the South African rand lost 35 per cent of its value in one month; the Indian rupee hit a record low; the Pakistani rupee fell from Rs 60 to Rs 95 to a dollar. Interest rates rose, remittances from overseas workers (the Philippines and Ethiopia) declined, and aid expectations were revised downwards. The only relief was the falling price of oil, an important part of the import bill of most poor and developing nations. The future looked bleak. The economic crisis affected developing countries through declining private financial flows, trade, aid and remittances. By the end of 2009 developing countries were estimated to have suffered losses of income of over $750 billion, rising unemployment, poverty and hunger and an additional fifty million people were trapped in absolute poverty.

Yes, superpowers do matter, and for the time being America is the sole superpower. The right relationship with America is crucial for a developing nation. America can break you by war as in Iraq, or by attrition as in Cuba. And America can make you, as she has made Israel. But after the financial crash, things are starting to change as America gets absorbed in sorting out her own problems; her need to take will leave her less able to give. Poor countries that want to grow rich will have to look beyond just the US for money and markets. The rise of China has begun.

America has been loved and hated by the world. Her great presidents have inspired leaders the world over: George Washington, who created a nation and voluntarily relinquished power at the end of his term in office; or Abraham Lincoln, who lived through the Civil War but died at the hands of an assassin, leaving a legacy of a republic that endured even as slavery perished. Her leaders have contributed to the world:

Franklin Delano Roosevelt, who battled both the Great Depression and Hitler's Nazis; John Kennedy, who put the first man on the moon; Richard Nixon, and his historic trip to China; Bill Clinton, who restored the US economy to financial health. Recently America and the world suffered George W. Bush, who has been described by comedian Bill Maher as 'a catastrophe that walks like a man'. Today, as Barack Obama, America's first black president, prepares for election to a second term, he faces disappointment instead of the exuberant expectations of his first elections. In two centuries America rose from a backward colony to the world's superpower. Now, in a changing world, what comes next?

Section Six

GROWING RICH

EIGHT SUCCESS STORIES
AND ONE FAILURE

*Under capitalism man exploits man, under communism
it is just the opposite.*

—John Kenneth Galbraith

*If you don't know where you are going,
any road will take you there.*

—Lewis Carroll

In 1975, on Christmas day, the band struck up their enthusiastic
rendering of the tune *'Those were the days'*, the favourite song
of Dictator Francisco Macias Nguema, in the national stadium
of Equatorial Guinea, as the 150 plotters of the failed coup
were executed. Macias was a hard man, whose reign of terror

for over eleven years destroyed his nation as a third of the population fled to escape the genocide he unleashed. His successor Obiang Nguema, who seized power in 1979, executed Macias and has ruled ever since. Obiang, a classic African dictator reputed to be more concerned with luxury properties and fancy cars in the French Riviera than with the problems of his people, survived 'The Wonga Coup'—the attempted takeover of his small but oil-rich country by a group of English mercenaries allegedly financed by Sir Mark Thatcher and Eli Calil, a friend and advisor to novelist Jeffrey Archer. The incident also provided the inspiration for the Frederick Forsyth thriller *The Dogs of War*. The mercenaries hired to carry out the coup were led by old Etonian Simon Mann, a former Special Air Service officer, who was caught and thrown into prison with threats that he would be sodomized and then skinned alive, to the great consternation of his wife. When interviewed, Mann, with his considerable experience of danger, merely commented, 'You go tiger shooting, but you don't expect the tiger to win.'

Equatorial Guinea is the champion of the world's growth economies—the unchallengeable league champion that leaves China and India as mere 'also rans'. Over the decade 1997–2007, China struggled to achieve a 15 per cent average annual percentage increase in real GDP whereas Equatorial Guinea averaged 66 per cent, with a per capita income that is the highest in Africa and surpasses that of several European countries. The secret of their success is oil—over 400,000 barrels a day and reserves of 1.77 billion barrels, for a population of less than a million citizens. The country has one of the twenty highest per capita incomes, which according to the CIA Factbook was $36,000 in 2009 (slightly higher than Great Britain); it also has one of the highest rates of corruption in the world; terror, torture and poverty afflict its people. The dictator maintains personal bank accounts in the Riggs Bank in Washington, which at one time held deposits in excess of $700 million for him, much of which arrived as cash wrapped in plastic and stuffed in suitcases. Riggs Bank paid $25 million in fines for money laundering. Equatorial Guinea is living proof that there is more to life than just economic growth.

This section looks at eight countries that have succeeded in developing their economies without oil, through hard work, sacrifice and single-minded determination, and compares them with one country that has so far failed. The success stories described are China, Korea, Singapore, Malaysia, India, Dubai, Israel and Botswana; the failure is Pakistan. The list includes big, middle-sized and small nations, both capitalist and communist, dictatorships and democracies, countries rich in natural resources and countries with none, even two states created to provide a home for their religions—a homeland for Jews and a nation state for Muslims. Though so diverse, the eight successful countries did have a few common characteristics:

- Dedicated leaders
- Political stability
- Good governance, good institutions and good policies
- Education, skills and discipline
- Exports
- Investment capital to fuel growth
- Constructive population control policies
- Determination to succeed

They also recognized and tried to avoid the traps of conflict, corruption and hostility with a superpower, the US. On the other hand, Pakistan has lacked real determination to succeed, has lacked dedicated leaders, political stability, good governance, good institutions and good policies, has a poorly educated, unskilled and undisciplined workforce, has not created a successful export base for its economy, and has not been able to attract foreign investment. Pakistan is high on the list of most corrupt countries, is drowning in conflict, both internal and external, and has experienced sweet and sour periods in her relationship with America. So although the tools of pure economics, fiscal and monetary policy, savings, credit allocation and investment do play an undeniable part in the development process, it is politics and human behaviour that seem to be the key to economic growth. Success requires determined leadership that is concerned about growth of national wealth rather than growth of personal Swiss bank accounts; leadership with a long and stable rule to implement good governance, build good institutions and promote good policies; leadership that improves the education, skills and discipline of the people to increase exports of its manufactured goods while attracting foreign investment to finance growth till self-sufficiency with a high level of savings is achieved.

Per capita	GDP (dollars)
■ UAE	50,070
■ Singapore	36,540
■ Israel	26,260
■ South Korea	17,080
■ Malaysia	7,030
■ Botswana	6,800
■ China	3,740
■ India	1,190
■ Pakistan	960

Although India's per capita income is not significantly greater than Pakistan's, India's economy is seen to be in an upward spiral with its high-tech IT services export boom, whereas Pakistan's stalled economy with its recent IMF bailout and Taliban security problems is seen to be in a downward spiral. Pakistan's unsustainable deficits, budgetary and trade, and a foreign debt that is 24 per cent of the GDP and 157 per cent of the total exports means that even if her people are not much poorer than India's, her government is effectively bankrupt and living on hand-outs.

STABILITY

A long period of stable government was common to the economic growth of all the eight successful countries:

- China's unchallenged domination of the Communist Party for sixty years since independence, and its legendary leaders, Mao, Zhao and Deng.
- South Korea's economic take-off in the nineteen-year period of Park Chung-hee.
- Singapore's political continuity under the control of Lee Kuan Yew from independence till today.
- Malaysia's New Economic Policy successes in the twenty-two-year rule of Dr Mahathir.
- India's first thirty years of Congress party rule and the leadership of Gandhi and Nehru established the stable democracy that endured through subsequent changes in government thereafter.
- Dubai's monarchy and the rule of the al Maktoum—no political distractions.
- Israel's first three decades of Labour Party government

establishing the ruling class that has dominated through the subsequent democratic changes.

- Botswana's long and uninterrupted rule of the Botswana Democratic Party (BDP) since its independence under the clean leadership that has led to growth.

All these countries have been able to implement the long-term vision of determined leaders. On the other hand, Pakistan has suffered instability under alternating civilian and military regimes, policy reversals as governments are replaced in quick succession, and a short-term national vision that looks at the future one month at a time. The level of Pakistan's instability is highlighted by its break-up into the two states of Pakistan and Bangladesh within twenty-five years of Jinnah's creation of an independent country.

EDUCATION

All the successful countries have almost universal adult literacy, well above 90 per cent. They also continue to spend more on education—above 4 per cent of GDP; Botswana has the highest expenditure level of 8.1 per cent of GDP. The exception is India with adult literacy of only 66 per cent, and a low yearly expenditure of 3.2 per cent, but India does have excellent institutions for higher education: the IITs and IIMs. But once again, Pakistan is at the bottom of the list, with adult literacy of 54 per cent and a low level of yearly expenditure of 2.9 per cent.

All the successful countries have recognized the importance of higher education in the information economy which has surpassed the industrial economy as the fastest growth sector. It is scientific and technical excellence that has made them leaders in the knowledge economy of twenty-first century globalization.

EXPORTS

The key to growth is export; countries that wish to prosper must have something to sell to other countries, whether goods, services, money or military might. The successful countries have had strong exports; countries that have not created exports have not been able to succeed.

Exports as a percentage of GDP (2011 figures)

- Singapore   221 per cent
- Malaysia   96 per cent
- UAE   87 per cent
- Korea   50 per cent
- Israel   35 per cent
- Botswana   28 per cent
- China   27 per cent
- India   20 per cent
- Pakistan   13 per cent

CAPITAL

Without money, vision is reduced to mere dreams. All these countries were not rich when they started on the road to development, but they all had to find money to get development started. Initially, poverty made it difficult to generate savings for the investment that was required, but they all found their own ways of raising finance.

South Korea found its answer in Japan, both in the model for inspiration and in the initial start-up finance. Neither country looked to foreign capital but created their own method of squeezing savings from domestic sources into private sector companies which provided the engine for growth: in Japan the Zaibatsu, in Korea the Chaebol. In both countries debt rather than equity provided the money. In Korea's case even the initial start-up money was raised from reparations from Japan. Once the take-off started, high savings kicked in.

Singapore, which had no natural resource base and no local industrial elite, courted multinational companies, offering them the best place to set up their business in the Far East. The multinationals increased exports and created the savings that the highly efficient government turned into the engine for wealth.

Malaysia had the advantage of natural resource—oil, tin, rubber and palm oil which provided the money for the start-up; but aggressive industrialization policies learned from Singapore also brought in foreign capital, both multinationals and portfolio investment, that made the Malaysian stock market one of the developing world's most successful.

China certainly lured in investment from the multinationals, and also maintained a high level of savings, but her special advantage lay in the huge wealth of the overseas Chinese community which provided the major share of foreign investment, boosting the eastern coastal area. The trade surplus that developed combined with huge foreign capital inflow made China a capital surplus country.

The UAE, with its massive oil wealth, had no shortage of capital. But Dubai, which was by no means oil rich, developed its own way of raising the capital required to fuel her exceptional ambitions—from super-rich Abu Dhabi, from DFI, from the 're-export trade', and from a massive property play built on the money of foreign buyers. The pinnacle of Dubai's imagination is seen in Palm Island where sand from the all-encompassing desert was thrown into the sea to form fantasy islands which were resold at a profit to foreign buyers wanting a sun, sea and sand home.

Israel again had no shortage of capital. War reparations from a defeated Germany combined with a generous money flow from the wealthy international Jewish diaspora providing the start-up; this was soon joined by massive financial support from the US. Israeli brain power and skills used this capital to build the highly successful Israeli growth story.

Botswana's start-up capital came principally from diamonds—it has been the world's largest producer of gem-quality diamonds—but her success in maintaining one of the fastest growth rates in the world was the result of her exceptionally good governance with good policies, wise use of revenues from diamonds, and lack of corruption.

India for most of its history has been perennially short of capital and lacked the level of savings required to fuel her take-off. But her unique road to growth was based on IT and offshoring, services which were not dependent on expensive national infrastructure or heavy investment in industrial assets. The key 'capital' was Nehru's legacy of the English language and the technical expertise spearheaded by the IITs, the Indian Institutes of Technology. The English-speaking techies developed an important position in California's Silicon Valley, and provided the network, skills, and when required, the capital to fuel the growth of this sector.

Pakistan has not been too successful in raising the money it needs to build its economy. Instability, weak institutions and flawed governance deter foreign investment. Pakistan's economic history warns would-be investors to be careful of lurking dangers. The hopes of the Ayub Khan-period investors were dashed in Bhutto's nationalizations and 'socialist' policies that followed; Nawaz Sharif's Islamic Bomb and the resulting sanctions led to the collapse of the economy again; Benazir's independent power plants brought in foreign investment, but the hostile attack of the Nawaz government that replaced the PPP made investors regret their decision to have entered Pakistan; and the money that poured in to support Pakistan in the war against the USSR soon created a Frankenstein offering a solution worse than the original problem. Where successful economies have seen a flood of foreign investments and savings, in Pakistan the flood has gone the other way with flight of capital, as Pakistanis move their money out to secure offshore havens.

POPULATION

Excessive population or too little population can hold back economic growth. America, Canada and Australia used immigration to build economic growth. The declining workforce in Japan is an important factor in the long stagnation of the Japanese economy.

India's huge population has been a heavy burden and a major cause of its poverty problem. Though India has made a little progress in dealing with the population growth rate, it has not been overly successful. Sanjay Gandhi's aggressive sterilization campaign was an important factor in his mother Indira's electoral defeat. The economy is unable to support the growing number of poor and destitute Indians—homeless, jobless, sick and hungry.

China, on the other hand, with a population even larger than India's, has been highly successful in population control. After starting with Mao's belief of 'the more the merrier', China started to recognize the danger of excessive population, and moved to the 'two-child policy'; this later tightened into 'the one-child policy', in which material incentive combined with peer pressure ensured population control.

Israel has successfully used immigration and an open-door

policy for all Jews to swell the population numbers and boost economic growth. The surge in immigration in the 1990s, when almost a million Jews arrived from Russia and the former USSR, not only increased Israel's population but also enhanced the number of skilled and highly educated technicians who have played an important part in Israel's subsequent hi-tech growth.

Whereas China had used incentives to reduce the population, the UAE, particularly Abu Dhabi with its huge oil wealth, encouraged its citizens to have bigger families. Dubai, lacking oil wealth, followed a growth pattern dependent on the influx of an expat population who came in to buy property and second homes. The property boom became a speculative bubble that took over the economy till it finally burst in 2009. Dubai has cancelled much of its next phase of planned development, but still has a huge stock of new properties that require buyers. With Europe in recession, new buyers could only come from India, Pakistan, Iran and Russia but Abu Dhabi, Dubai's financer of the last resort, is reluctant to see 'excessive' growth of the expat community. Dubai is an economy that needs population growth if it is to survive.

Botswana does not have a problem of overpopulation. Its 1.8 million people occupy 582,000 sq. km of land—a greater area than Japan and Bangladesh together, with their combined population of 275 million. But with its huge AIDS problem and with some 30 per cent of its people HIV-positive, Botswana may soon have a problem of too few people. High and rising labour cost are forcing Korean companies to relocate production, particularly to China. North Korea, with its ailing economy and a per capita income less than a tenth of that in the South, offers a large culturally homogeneous pool of labour. The politics of population is an important factor in spurring the reunification of Korea.

Pakistan's population in 1947 at the time of independence was thirty-one million. Since then Pakistan has split into two nations—Pakistan and Bangladesh. If Pakistan had not split into two, it would have the world's third largest population of over 325 million, behind only China and India. Pakistan today has a population of 180 million, and it is still growing. Pakistan's overpopulation results in growth of poverty, illiteracy, unemployment; it also results in growth of instability and domestic terrorism. Pakistan seems unable or unwilling to seriously address the population issue, unlike its Islamic neighbour Iran which has been effective in its control of the population.

20

Singapore:
No Corruption,
No Democracy

Lee is like a banana—yellow skin, white underneath.

—Zhao En-lai

Two families that have dominated the politics of their countries in Southeast Asia have been the Kims in North Korea and the Lees in Singapore. The Kims, father and son, have been a disaster for North Korea, whereas Lee Kuan Yew and his son have created the greatest success story of the developing world. Singapore was born with no advantages, a country of poverty and unemployment with no natural resource wealth; even land and drinking water were in short supply. Per capita income was only $427 in 1960; by 2012 it had exceeded $36,000.

Singapore is a shining example of good governance and great leadership. Singapore was the achievement of Lee Kuan Yew.

In 1959 Lee won leadership by just one vote from Ong Eng Guan. Having won power Lee was not willing to let it go. In the half century since his People's Action Party took power till today, Singapore has had only three prime ministers; Lee himself, who held office for thirty-one years; his second-in-command Goh Keng Swee, who had been with him since college and took over when Lee retired; and Lee's son B.G. Lee who followed Goh. Even after retiring, Lee held the posts of first 'Senior Minister' and then 'Minister Mentor' to help his friend and then his son to keep the ship of state on the right path. There has certainly been political stability and continuity with consistent leadership.

Lee was not a believer in the virtues of democracy, and his statements have been unambiguous in this regard: 'With a few exceptions, democracy has not brought good government to developing countries.' In 1965 he aggressively argued his beliefs, 'What does all this free society mean? Does it mean that politicians are free to loot and plunder, that people are free to be hungry and ill-fed and ill-educated?' Though Singapore has all the trappings of democracy, in reality it is a single-party authoritarian state. Though there have been no extra-judicial killings, Singapore has had the highest rate of executions per capita in the world—twice that of Saudi Arabia—and has been notorious for its lack of press freedom.

Lee also had strong views about the destructive effect of corruption, and he was determined to give Singapore clean government. His relentless war on corruption lead at least one accused, Teh Cheang Wan, to commit suicide. Lee was convinced that corruption was the enemy of efficiency, and that development could not take place under a corrupt government. To keep his executives, both politicians and bureaucrats, away from temptation, he rewarded them with extremely high salaries; a junior minister in Singapore earns an income higher than the president of the US, and the top level salaries run into millions of dollars. In addition, bonuses linked to the performance of the economy or particular institutions make public sector employment as attractive as the private sector and ensure that top quality people are retained. Lee wanted quality people; he respected merit, and was clearly in agreement with Aristotle on the importance of 'good men' in nation building. His team of politicians, technocrats and bureaucrats were all talented, very well educated, highly motivated and very well paid; it was this team that achieved the miracle of Singapore Inc.

From the time he took control, Lee's priority was the economy; he was determined to eradicate poverty and create wealth. The situation required innovation, 'We had to create a new kind of economy, try new methods. We had to be different.' Not ideology, but pragmatism guided him as he confessed, 'We were not enamoured by theories.' In defeating the Singapore communists and bringing in the US multinationals he was capitalist; in building the state-owned corporations that dominate the Singapore economy he was socialist; but above all, he was a pragmatist.

The first problems were the shortage of jobs and the shortage of housing. Lee addressed them both by forming the Housing

Development Board (HDB). The board set about building the housing and in the process created the jobs required by the unemployed. The institution was successful and led to the state-dominated housing sector which today houses 85 per cent of the population. The HDB showed that public sector companies and institutions could be every bit as efficient as the private sector.

Whereas the Japanese miracle had used private-sector conglomerates, the Zaibatsu and the Keiretsu, as the vehicles of growth, and South Korea had created the Chaebol, Lee was not prepared to base Singapore's growth on homegrown companies: 'Had we waited for our traders to learn to be industrialists we would have starved.' Instead, he turned to multinational corporations, particularly from the US, whose MNCs he saw not as spawns of Satan, but as doors of opportunity for Singapore. Lee's readiness to give the multinationals open access to Singapore's economy was a revolutionary step at a time when conventional wisdom, as expressed in Japan's development model, preferred to protect homegrown industries. The second leg in Lee's corporate strategy was the promotion of state-owned companies. The HDB was joined by Singapore Airlines, SingTel, the Port and Airport authorities, and holding companies led by Temasek Holdings. The value of state-owned commercial enterprises grew to a fifth of the Singapore stock market, and most of these showed an exceptional quality of management that would make them world leaders.

Lee also defied the conventional wisdom of the time by ignoring import substitution and basing his industrial strategy totally on export orientation. Admittedly, the small size of Singapore's domestic economy made this an easy decision; but Lee by making a virtue out of necessity created an export-based economy that is unparalleled anywhere in the world. Singapore's exports in 2011 as a percentage of GDP are a whopping 221 per cent, the highest in the world.

Economic theory recognizes the importance of savings to generate growth. Nowhere was theory put into practice as aggressively as in Singapore which through the 1990s took gross domestic savings above 50 per cent; even in 2004 the savings rate was 45 per cent. The mandatory savings programme which applied to all Singapore workers was conducted through the Central Provident Fund (CPF), which professionally managed the money with Singapore's reliable level of bureaucratic competence and integrity. These savings, in turn, contributed to the country's exceptional quality of infrastructure.

To attract foreign multinationals and FDI, with its expatriate managers and regular flow of visitors, Singapore focused on quality of life. After flying in on Singapore Airlines, the world's best airline, the visitor flowed through Changi Airport, the world's best airport, through the beautiful garden-lined approach to the city centre, where fabulous hotels awaited. The roads were free from traffic jams due to Singapore's road policies that deterred the use of private cars and encouraged the use of a clean and efficient public transport system. Cars were expensive to buy, requiring the purchase through auction of a permit to buy one, and expensive to drive due to the road poll tax system that made busy times and busy roads prohibitive. All interactions with government were speedy, efficient and totally free of corruption. The city offered a great lifestyle with restaurants, shopping, housing, a high level of services and the widespread use of the English language. The streets were safe; law and order prevailed. Foreign companies were happy to come to Singapore, particularly since the government did its best to make business prosper.

A key part of Singapore's compact with multinationals was its labour force, which initially offered disciplined and cheap labour, but later as wages rose replaced cheap labour with a quality, highly educated workforce. Lee's government style was highly intrusive in its demand for discipline, dictating hairstyle, dress and even controlling personal habits such as smoking and chewing gum. Singapore was disparagingly called 'the nanny state' and was considered an authoritarian police state. But as maverick as this seemed, it worked as Lee pushed his formula—savings, sacrifice, education—pressing his people to defer present enjoyment for future gain.

To be effective Lee needed a top-quality team; the team, in turn, needed top-quality institutions in order to implement their policies. Singapore developed institutions of the highest quality worthy of the capability and dedication of the leaders— world-class champions. The Economic Development Board (EDB) provided the engine of Singapore's economic miracle; the Jurong Industrial Estate, the Housing Development Board, the Central Provident Fund, the Port of Singapore Authority, the Monetary Authority of Singapore (MAS), SPRING, A*STAR, all set examples in excellence. The state-owned commercial institutions were of the same outstanding calibre—

the airlines, the airport, SingTel, Temasek holdings and the numerous other corporations. The educational institutions also vied to be world class, with linkages to INSEAD, Johns Hopkins, Wharton and MIT. Whereas such institutions in other developing countries remained bureaucratic non-events, Singapore's institutions set an example to follow.

While Lee provided the leadership, his lieutenant Goh, the technocrat, provided the economic expertise, ensuring the discipline necessary for a sound economy. Singapore maintained a stable currency, labour peace, high levels of savings and investment, a balanced budget, low tax rates and low interest rates. Its industrial policy focused on efficiency of productivity and prudent control of government spending ensured minimum waste. The standards of governance earned Singapore the title of 'A first world oasis in a Third World region.'

Singapore's success did not come easy but was the result of struggle, skill and strategy. Starting from a difficult beginning of poverty with few, if any, weapons for the struggle, Lee was open minded in his search for solutions, even attempting a merger with Malaysia, but reversing out of the union within two years when it didn't seem to work. In the early years, foreign investors were shy, earning the Jurong Estate the nickname of 'Goh's folly' as it lay empty. The communist threat had to be dealt with to ensure stability, and numerous recessions in the economy had to be tackled. In 1963 growth went negative, reaching minus 4 per cent in 1964; in 1968 Britain's closure of her military base rocked the economy; recession hit again in 1985, and again in 1998 after the East Asian financial crisis; and once more in 2001. Throughout it all, economic

performance topped the PAP agenda, and skilful handling kept
the economy on track, working its way out of trouble even as
Lee explored and developed new opportunities. Though many
of the economic decisions were successful, there were also
some mistakes. The Graduate Mother Scheme which gave
preference to the children of mothers with a university degree
in primary school placement over the lesser-educated, some
attempts on wage policy and population policy, and the merger
with Malaysia were flawed decisions. The Singapore Industrial
Park in Suzhou, China, was launched as a $30 billion scheme,
but was quickly reduced in size and scope as problems in
implementation emerged. But the agile leadership was always
quick to reverse out of bad moves, never committed to its
mistakes.

This readiness to change policy as the objective realities
changed has converted Singapore from a low-wage economy
to a high-wage, knowledge-based economy with new emphasis
on hi-tech, finance, biomedicine, health care and
pharmaceuticals and overseas investment. As new transparency
laws lower the appeal of Switzerland as a banking haven for
private funds, Singapore is building itself up as a new centre
for private banking, with proximity, reliability and its Chinese
character to attract the region's growing wealth. Medical
tourism is another new industry with promising growth
prospects; and Singapore's commitment to the future
knowledge-based economy is evidenced in its civic
requirement that all homes must have broadband access. To
keep its tourist industry abreast of the times, Singapore is
shedding its Victorian image and promoting not only an exciting

nightlife but also two new casinos. Even in education, Singapore has shown its opportunistic approach—for decades the effort was to promote English-language education to enable integration with the world economy, but now with the rise of China, Singapore's education system is increasing its emphasis on Chinese.

Singapore is a small city-state the size of Manhattan, and is running out of space; it has increased land availability by reclaiming about 3,000 acres, and has also created the $23 billion Jurong Island by bringing in sand from Indonesia and dumping it in the sea; but more significantly, Singapore is expanding its economic empire overseas, as the ISCs—the International Singapore Companies—search for expansion opportunities. With less need for accumulation, Singapore is now increasing distribution; this includes privatization. But Singapore's privatization is not about getting rid of rotten state corporations that are losing money. With efficient management and good profitability, Singapore's privatization is about sharing the wealth, as shares are released to the public through stock market offerings with management remaining unaffected.

Singapore offers developing countries an example to follow. Deng Xiaoping of China found his inspiration there, and started his reform programme with a visit to Lee in Singapore to understand its formula for success. It is not too late for other floundering nations to also learn from Singapore.

21

South Korea: General Park and the Chaebols

The person who thinks a job is possible is the one who is going to get it done.

—Chung Ju Yung, founder of Hyundai

An old fox looks homeward when he is about to die.
—Kim Woo Choong, founder of Daewoo, returning home
to imprisonment and death after six years in exile

If any country deserves the title of 'champion of development', it is South Korea. Starting with the weakest base after being divided into two countries, North and South, and bereft of natural resource wealth, its per capita income grew by 15,000 per cent in the period 1965–2007. This growth rate was twice that of Taiwan, three times that of Singapore, four times that of

Japan, seven times that of China and twenty times that of India! Its per capita income grew from $87 in 1962 to $20,000 in 2009; its GDP over the same period grew from $2.3 billion to $970 billion; its exports were a mere $200,000 in 1962; by 2011 they had exceeded $360 billion, almost 40 per cent of the GDP. The number of cars in South Korea grew from 30,000 in 1962 to tens of millions today.

Syngman Rhee, the first president, attained office after forty-one years of exile, seven years of imprisonment and seven months of vicious torture which resulted in burnt arms and mashed fingers. Park Chung Hee, considered the father of Korea's development, lost his wife in a failed assassination attempt, and was himself later assassinated. President Chun Doo-hwan was sentenced to death; he was given amnesty and after apologizing to the nation on television and offering to surrender $24 million, he went into seclusion in a Buddhist monastery as an act of repentance. President Roh Tae-woo who followed Chun was sentenced to twenty-two years imprisonment for corruption, but was later granted amnesty. The next president, Kim Young-sam, won on an anti-corruption platform but saw his own son imprisoned for corruption under his regime. Kim Dae-jung, considered the father of democracy in Korea, who reached the presidency after a long struggle in which he was twice sentenced to death and once kidnapped from a Tokyo hotel, also waged war on corruption, but was let down by his three sons who were all found guilty of fraud. The two Kims were succeeded by Roh Moo-hyun in 2003. Roh was embarrassed by the corruption of his brother, other members of his family and his secretary. He apologized to the nation: 'I have lost my moral cause . . . You should abandon me.' Roh committed suicide, jumping off a cliff. Suicide seemed to appeal to the Korean sense of honour; other prominent suicides included a former prime ministerial aide, a mayor, a provincial governor, son of the founder and chairman of the Hyundai group Chung Mong-hun, and a senior Daewoo executive. Life was not easy for those at the top; it was very difficult for those at the bottom. South Korea undoubtedly succeeded in growing, but at what price?

The three most important causes of growth in South Korea were:

- The role of America
- The role of President Park
- The role of the Chaebols

America's prime concern in the region was the containment of communism, and for this reason the US was determined to promote the capitalist South against the communist North. America provided substantial financial aid to South Korea, which in the early days ran to over 50 per cent of the national budget. America also opened its markets to its ally, allowing the export boom to take off, and promoted South Korea's first agricultural land reforms. These reforms played an important part in eliminating the absentee landlord class and increasing productivity. Land reforms boosted the two successful economies of South Korea and Taiwan, whereas the less effective land reforms in the Philippines left that country as a laggard in the race for economic growth. Concern over the potential appeal of communism led America to push aggressive land reforms; in the decade following 1945 landholdings in South Korea were drastically reduced and self-cultivation became the dominant form of agriculture. The large Korean landlords were not in a position to resist these reforms since they had lost influence due to their collaboration with the Japanese.

In 1961, a military general, Park Chung Hee, took power in a coup. Park was withdrawn and shy, austere and intense; he ruled for nineteen years, combining astounding economic success with intense political repression. He had no time for democracy, maintaining that the vote was meaningless to people suffering from starvation and despair and believing that legitimacy lay in delivering on the economy. Park was obsessed with economic growth, and it remained his priority till his death. In nineteen years Park converted a wretched hopeless country into a strong modern state by creating his own 'Korea Inc.—the Miracle of the Han'.

After the coup Park started to tighten up the country; he arrested the important businessmen and marched them through the streets with dunce caps and placards which proclaimed 'I am a corrupt swine.' But before things could deteriorate further, the Samsung chairman persuaded Park that he could better serve the economy by using the capabilities of the businessmen, and a deal was done to cement the new government–business–finance partnership that was to characterize the Korean model. This deal gave the big conglomerates, known as 'the Chaebol', their pivotal role in the economy. Whereas Singapore had based its growth strategy on multinational corporations and state-owned corporations, and Taiwan's economy was dominated by small- and medium-sized companies with a few larger state-owned corporations, the vehicle of Japanese growth was the large conglomerates known first as Zaibatsu, and then as Keiretsu. This Japanese model influenced Park, whose prime vehicle for growth became the Chaebol. Park's inspiration was Japan's modernization strategy from the Meiji Restoration to the MITI model of development, with its emphasis on partnership between government and business.

Park was as concerned as America about containing communism, due to his face-off with his strong northern twin supported by Mao's China. He wanted to build a 'rich country, strong army'. His strong army was a key to his relationship with the US, as he sent 300,000 Korean soldiers to fight in Vietnam; this not only secured American markets and financial support, but also resulted in substantial exports to Vietnam to support the war effort; at its peak, Vietnam absorbed 94 per cent of South Korea's steel exports.

In 1961 Park nationalized banks. His state control of credit was to be a powerful lever to manage the Chaebols. Credit allocation at cheap interest rates that were frequently negative ensured that the big conglomerates followed his direction and cooperated in his relentless drive to industrialize. Credit allocation also ensured the steady flow of political contributions that were necessary to maintain stable control. Park's strategy for growth used debt, rather than equity, as the main source of finance, and foreign investment was not overly important to Korean growth. In one year alone—1993—China attracted more Foreign Direct Investment (FDI) than South Korea in forty years. The Chaebols' balance sheets were burdened with massive debts, and South Korea by the time of Park's death was the world's third biggest debtor nation.

Park built up an efficient bureaucracy based on merit and a relatively high level of education. His Economic Planning Board showed competence in providing direction and policies for accelerated growth, as Korean industry progressed from the manufacture of wigs to the building of ships. Park wanted heavy industry and prioritized six sectors: steel, non-ferrous metals, chemicals, shipbuilding, machinery and electronics, which grew at a fantastic pace. The Economic Planning Board (EPB) followed the Ministry of International Trade and Industry (MITI) style of 'picking winners' and supporting them with finance, tariff protection, tax benefits and cheap foreign currency to ensure their profitability. The EPB developed a system of multiple exchange rates and subsidized credit to support the new industries in Park's 'Big Push' heavy industrialization programme. After initially focusing on import substitution Park made exports the centre of Korea's industrialization drive; export industry was supported by protection, subsidy and devaluation of the currency to enable it to compete internationally. The struggling new companies of yesterday, such as Hyundai, Samsung and LG, have become the world's market leaders of today.

Park's philosophy was 'growth first, distribution later'; this meant high productivity but low wages; consumption was held down while the level of savings was raised from 2 per cent up to 35 per cent of the GDP. Trade unions and industrial action were outlawed. Inflation was comparatively high, increasing the disparity between the rich and the poor. With lack of transparency in the corporate sector discouraging equity investment, property was favoured by investors and speculators; land prices rose by 180 times in the fifteen years between 1964 and 1979, with 5 per cent of households owning 65 per cent of private land.

In the beginning capital was shy, but war reparations from Japan allowed Park to start his investment drive. The Pohang Iron and Steel Company (POSCO) started in 1973 with production of one million tons; by 1981 POSCO production had increased to 8.5 million and was providing the steel for Korea's growing automobile manufacture and shipbuilding industries. Though the World Bank discouraged the project, advising that 'it is a premature proposition without economic feasibility', Park went ahead defying all advice, thus making POSCO one of the larger and more efficient steel producers in the world. The expressway linking Seoul to Pusan was another important infrastructure project of Park's, and it was built in record time at a cost that was only 40 per cent of the original budget by Park's favourite, Chun Ju Yung, the chairman of Hyundai.

Park created the Chaebols, the massive conglomerates that were the vehicle for South Korea's growth. The Chaebols dominated the economy more completely than even the Keiretsu of Japan, and by the 1980s the combined sales of the top thirty Chaebols equalled 87 per cent of the Gross National Product (GNP). By 1997 the top five companies—Hyundai, Samsung, LG, Daewoo and Sunkyong—were producing 50 per cent of the GNP of South Korea, and the top 300 Chaebols were accounting for 90 per cent of the economy. These groups were family owned and family managed; there was no transparency and they were opportunistic risk takers who took on huge debts. The individual debt of each of the larger Chaebols was larger than that of a medium-sized developing country. Samsung's debt in 1998 at $23 billion matched the debt of Venezuela; and the sixteen largest Chaebols had a combined debt of $192 billion. The one important restriction that Park did impose on them was the prohibition on ownership control of banks—unlike the Japanese conglomerates that were built around a group bank which provided their finance. Money lay with the government, and credit allocation was the tool to keep the Chaebol obedient to Park's strategies. Park demanded growth; and nation building rather than profit or shareholder value was the objective. The Chaebol pursued market share, and when sales reached $279 billion, profit was a mere $6.7 billion. The Chaebols were not highly profitable, but by taking on more and more debt, they grew at an astonishing pace. Credit was allotted on political rather than commercial considerations, and more important than balance sheets was connectivity—who's in favour and who's not. Favour was earned on the basis of growth, exports and contributions of money to those in power; those who did not understand this would pay the price, as did the Samhak distillery which was forced into bankruptcy under the Park and General Chun governments by a credit squeeze by government-controlled banks when it made the mistake of backing Kim Dae-jung in the 1971 elections. A similar fate met the Kukje Group, which went bankrupt for backing the opposition to President Chun. The financial crisis of 1997 also led to empty coffers of overleveraged Chaebols, bringing down the Hanbo and Halla groups, and shattering the myth that they were 'too big to fail'.

The most dramatic ruin was the collapse of the giant Daewoo group, founded by the dynamic Kim Woo Choong in 1967 with a capital of $10,000. Kim grew at an amazing pace, initially because of his close relationship with Park, but then because of his unstoppable energy. By the mid-1990s the Daewoo empire covered cars, ships, electronics, trucks, telecom equipment, machinery, stockbroking, hotels, highway construction, a tyre factory in Sudan, railways in Iran, $10 billion worth of construction in Libya, automobile plants in Iran, Vietnam, India, Poland and Uzbekistan, which due to the massive Daewoo presence, earned the nickname of 'Daewooistan'! Kim built this massive empire in thirty years; he seemed unstoppable, but was ultimately stopped by the 1997 Asian financial crisis. By 1998, when Daewoo was facing an acute cash crunch, Kim collapsed and was rushed into hospital for emergency brain surgery. Still recovering from the surgery, he flew to Hanoi to meet President Kim Dae-jung for assistance in raising new loans. The meeting took place in the Hanoi Daewoo hotel, but the president refused to help. His message to Kim Woo Choong was short but severe: 'It would be better if you left the nation.' Kim left and vanished for six years, remaining incommunicado as he moved from Eastern Europe to Sudan, seeking sanctuaries. After six years, he returned, ready for the inevitable jail sentence that awaited him. Journalists surrounded him asking why he had returned; Kim replied quoting a Korean proverb: 'An old fox looks homeward when he is about to die.' He was sentenced to ten years' imprisonment and a fine of $23 billion. He apologized for having been a burden to his nation. A year later, President Roh pardoned him. At the time of its collapse, Daewoo employed 320,000 people and had sales equal to 10 per cent of the Korean economy; it went down with a debt of $75 billion, one of the world's biggest corporate failures.

The leading Chaebol was Hyundai covering cars, trucks, ships, semiconductors, electronics, heavy equipment, shipping lines, department stores, construction, cement, fund management and brokerage. Its founder chairman Chung Ju Yung was known as 'King Chairman', but he started as a poor boy with only primary school education. Chung's ability to multitask led to simultaneous development of diverse businesses; even as he built the expressway, sleeping in the back of an old jeep, he was building up his ship-building company. Within ten years of starting, Hyundai was the largest ship-builder in the world. Chung was a legend in his time, and remained a power in the land till his death. But after his death tragedy struck his family as feuding brothers divided the empire; death took two brothers who committed suicide, while a car accident killed a third.

The Park model was continued by President Chun, who ruled through the 1980s, maintaining policy consistency for three decades, during which South Korea grew from poverty to affluence. Though Park is remembered as a hero dedicated to the development of the Korean economy, Chun earned a reputation as a villain. Park's single-minded dedication to development was seen in 1974, when a bullet aimed at him during a speech hit his wife who was rushed to hospital. Park

simply said, 'Ladies and gentlemen, I will continue my speech.'
Hours later his wife died of her wounds. Chun is remembered
for the Kwangju massacre, corruption and his final repentance
in a Buddhist monastery.

Even after his second term as president, Park was determined
not to retire. He wanted to remain president for life. His ruthless
repression of opposition was characterized by arrests, torture
and murder. Finally Park was assassinated by Kim Chaegyu,
the Korean Central Intelligence Agency chief, in a restaurant.
The story goes that Park was berating Kim for leniency in
dealing with protesting dissidents, saying he should have shot
a few; Kim replied that he would have had to shoot 3,000, to
which Park retorted, 'I would have shot 30,000.' After Park's
death, the constitution was amended; to ensure that no dictator
could again seize control, future presidents were restricted to
one term.

The South Korean economy continued its successful growth
led by exports through the Chaebols till it was hit by the
1997–98 Asian financial crisis, when debt problems and a
collapsing won led to a 7 per cent contraction. Foreign funds
flowed out, Chaebols were threatened with bankruptcy,
unemployment grew and reserves evaporated. An IMF bailout
of $57 billion imposed harsh conditionality including the
restructuring of the Chaebols by massive reduction of debt-
equity ratios. The Korean people rallied to the situation, selling
wedding rings and other gold possessions to pay the
International Monetary Fund (IMF). By 2000 the economy
was again showing growth rates of 9 per cent, and by 2003 the
recovery was complete with reserves above $140 billion and

exports booming. The recovery effort once more showed the special determination of the South Koreans.

Today, South Korea is a high-income economy, the fourth largest in Asia and the fifteenth largest in the world. It has a highly skilled and motivated workforce, with the world's highest scientific literacy. It also has the smallest gap between the rich and the poor in high-income Asian economies. It is relatively corruption free, placed fortieth on the Transparency International list of 180 nations. Its economic success showed many of the characteristics common to the other successful growth economies—determination, leadership, vision, exports, savings and investment, good institutions, high quality human resources, emphasis on education, stability and policy consistency, and a healthy relationship with a superpower, the US. Though South Korea avoided war, it used its confrontation with North Korea and its dispatch of troops to Vietnam to secure its alliance with the US.

Despite the high-level corruption scandals that hit later presidents—Chun, the two Rohs and the two Kims—South Korea has been relatively free of corruption compared with other Asian and African countries. Park attacked corruption and nepotism and his personal life was above reproach in this regard—his Spartan noodle lunches at the Blue House, the official residence of the South Korean head of state, emphasized his personal austerity. Huge political donations did fall under the control of the political leaders, but these remained part of 'the system' and did not end up in the pockets of the leaders. It has been argued that what corruption did exist was not predatory but more in the nature of sharing the benefits of

policy-induced special profits. The one-term presidencies left
outgoing presidents vulnerable to attack by their successors,
resulting in high-profile scandals; but their prosecution shows
that corruption was not passively accepted, as in most corrupt
countries where accountability is rare.

22

China: A Cat That Catches the Mice

Revolution is not a dinner party; it cannot be advanced softly, gradually, carefully, considerately, respectfully, politely, plainly and modestly.

—Mao Zedong

Poverty is not socialism. To grow rich is glorious.

—Deng

Once in a century a Mao is born; once in a century a Deng is born; in China they shared an era and a struggle to change a destitute nation into the greatest success story of modern times. Over fifty years the Chinese, a fifth of the world's people, have been propelled from poverty to hope, from hope to achievement. China had exceptional leaders. The two titans were Mao, the revolutionary who created modern China, and Deng, the godfather of the Chinese economy. But there were other remarkable men—men of stature, commitment and ability who played their part in the epic of modern China. There was the sophisticated Zhao En-lai, considered one of the world's greatest statesmen; Liu Shaoqi, the head of state who almost eclipsed Mao before his terrible fall; Chen Yun the economist; the great marshals Zhu De, Lin Biao and Peng Dehuai; the reformers Hu Yaobang, Zhao Ziyang and Zhu Rongji; and 'the Immortals', the influential elders who survived 'the Long March' and 'the cultural revolution'. If we are to look for the one factor that was most crucial in creating the Chinese miracle, it would undoubtedly be the quality of leadership.

Mao's victory in 1949 was a peasants' revolution; many of the leaders, the party and the army (People's Liberation Army) had come from homes without running water or electricity, but they were determined to build a modern China. Communism was their guiding inspiration and Mao moved fast to take the land from traditional landlords and distribute it to the peasants. By 1952, 42 per cent of all arable land had been redistributed; within a decade the land was to be taken back from the peasants and bundled into communes. Twenty years later Deng took the land back from the communes and returned it to the peasants. Policies were not consistent—these were revolutionary times.

The successful growth of the USSR economy under Stalin provided the Chinese with a model to follow; it worked, and the 'Big Push' industrialization of Mao's economy achieved excellent growth. The command economy ignored the market, and was characterized by low consumption and high levels of investment, with prices fixed by the state. Idealism replaced material incentives in order to motivate the people. By 1956 Mao and the Chinese leadership had grown arrogant in their success and Mao launched his 'Great Leap Forward' to catch up with the economies of the rich developed nations.

Mao had assembled a high-calibre team, who had been tested and polished through their experience of struggle. Zhao En-lai was his committed lieutenant, but the emerging second in command was Liu Shaoqi, seen as the heir apparent to Mao. The key economist was Chen Yun, whose influence over economic policy was to endure for forty years. But if Mao had a favourite, it was Deng Xiaoping, the rising star who was no great theorist but could be relied on to get things done. In 1957 Mao pointed Deng out to Khrushchev, saying, 'Don't underestimate that little fellow. He destroyed an army of one million of Chiang's best troops.' By 1956, the top four leaders in China were Mao, Liu, Zhao and Deng.

The Great Leap Forward (GLF), launched in 1958, was Mao's greatest mistake, and resulted in famine that led to starvation and the death of perhaps thirty million people. The GLF attempted to accelerate the pace of growth of the economy through intensity of effort, an economic crusade. Initially it seemed to work. It produced a frenzy of economic struggle with campaigns of 'the backyard furnaces' and 'war' to wipe out vermin, flies and even for a while sparrows. It attempted the impossible, and when it started to fail, cover-up lies from the bureaucrats hid the facts from the leaders. A record grain harvest of 200 million tons was misreported as 375 million tons; government grain procurement increased, based on the exaggerated false figures, and the peasants were left with starvation and famine. Key culprits for the disaster were the communes, which failed to deliver the results expected of them, and the ideological fervour which replaced monetary incentives as a source of motivation.

Before the GLF, Mao was regarded as a demigod who could do no wrong; after the GLF Mao was close to losing control. He agreed to step aside, agreed not to interfere and agreed to allow the 'capitalist roaders' Liu and Deng to mend the economy. Chen, who had stepped out when the GLF started, was brought back to guide economic policy. But matters came to a head at Lushan when the Politburo met to review the situation. The straight-talking old general Peng Dehuai, the defence minister, criticized the GLF and Mao's leadership that was bringing the country into disaster. Mao was already unhappy with Peng, under whose command in Korea Mao's son Anying had died. Their animosity exploded as Peng shouted at Mao, 'In Yunan you fucked my mother for forty days. Now I have been fucking your mother for only eighteen days and you want to call a halt.' The brotherhood of the Long March was over; the days of collective leadership were over; the day of one-man rule had begun. Mao waited many years for his revenge as Peng dropped from sight. In 1966 Peng was arrested, tortured and beaten by teams of Red Guards. He was beaten till his internal organs were crushed and his spine splintered. He died in 1974 after 130 interrogation sessions. The old general never gave up, defiant to the end, 'You can shoot me. I fear nothing.'

Very quickly (between 1961 and 1965), the experts mended the economy and swung it back to growth by 1966. The fast recovery did not come as a surprise. The leadership was committed and honest, the institutions of the party, the PLA and the government machinery were disciplined and reliable. Material incentives were revived, the revolutionary fervour was cut back, more moderate policies were put into place, and the workers who had been diverted to overambitious industrial efforts returned to farming. Within a few years China was back on its growth track. Liu and Deng were moving to centrestage as Mao was falling into eclipse.

Despite the spectacular recovery, Mao was not happy with the way things were going—the emphasis on material incentives, the downgrading of ideology, and the growing bureaucratization and corruption of the elite. He did not want China to follow the example of the USSR, where the elite had taken control of the party and the government and were abusing their power for the private benefit of a small clique of the privileged. He fumed in rage against the embezzlers, grafters and degenerates who were subverting his revolution. He also resented being ignored as if he were a 'dead emperor'.

As a consequence, in 1966 Mao launched 'the Great Proletarian cultural revolution'. He unleashed the masses against the elite. At its vanguard were hysterical youth, the Red Guards, who tore down the establishment and replaced it with chaos. Mao used their passion against his political opponents, but he was not the only one to do so. For the most part, the Red Guards were independent demons of revolution who acted on impulse in mercurial response to unplanned stimuli. Mao was certainly not to blame for all their excesses. Nowhere was this exposed as clearly as in the sad death of Dr Nelson Fu, the seventy-two-year-old physician who had saved Mao's life in 1934 when critically ill. More recently Fu had also treated Lin Biao for drug addiction, and Lin Biao felt vulnerable to Fu's knowledge of the details of his addiction. Fu was arrested, paraded through the streets, beaten and reviled. Fu wrote to Mao: 'I saved your life. That at least I did right. Now I hope you will save my life.' Mao wrote his comment: 'This man holds no power, and has committed no serious crime. It seems he should be protected.' Fu, however, was not protected. Three days later he was thrown into a solitary cell, handcuffed, kicked and beaten till his ribs were crushed. Fifteen days later his guards opened his cell to find his body stiff and cold on the cement floor. Mao was helpless to save the life of the doctor to whom he owed the debt of his own life. Fu was one of the 34,000 people killed in the cultural revolution, the oldest of which was an eighty-year-old grandmother, the youngest a thirty-eight-day-old baby. Official figures record 729,500 people had been persecuted.

Whilst the GLF fiasco enabled Liu Shaoqi to overshadow Mao, the cultural revolution destroyed Liu. The sophisticated Liu and his elegant wife were picked up by the Red Guards. Liu was beaten and died in captivity; his wife was humiliated, her hair shaved as she was forced to dress as a prostitute and was then thrown into prison. Liu's mother-in-law, his eldest and second son all lost their lives in the revolution; his wife survived after years in prison.

Today, the cultural revolution is considered one of Mao's

greatest disasters. At the time, the revolution ousted 70 per cent of the central committee, and cut down the powerful bureaucracy to one-sixth of its former size; but those who came to office during the revolution were removed after Mao's death; those who succeeded Mao were themselves victims of the revolution. Nevertheless, Mao considered it to be one of his two greatest achievements, the other being the defeat of Chiang Kai-shek and the Japanese. The revolution battled corruption and the elitist bureaucracy and left a legacy of social justice and populism with an anti-authoritarian culture through its encouragement of mass participation and decentralization, and rectification campaigns against those in authority. Mao's strong views against corruption, which he believed wasted valuable resources and eroded government legitimacy, ensured minimum corruption in China during his lifetime. He made the price of corruption so high that it just was not worth it.

Unlike the economic disaster of the GLF, the cultural revolution, after the initial setback of the first years of chaos, was a period of economic growth. Marked by lower central control, lower consumption and higher production, the upward trend of the economy resumed. Although meagre agricultural growth was positive and industrial growth was rapid, Mao has been criticized for his economics, but his supporters contend that industrial growth under Mao was higher than industrial growth under Deng—13 per cent from 1953 to 1977, as against 12.4 per cent from 1978 to 1995. If we include the massive industrial growth between 1949 and 1953, Mao's achievement looks even better.

During the revolution the education of the elite received a

setback, but the children of poor peasants benefitted. During the so-called 'lost decade' (1965–76) elementary school enrolment rose from 116 million to 150 million, and middle school enrolment rose from nine million to sixty-seven million. Health care for the poor was also promoted as the barefoot doctors brought basic medicine to the masses.

Finally Mao was compelled to call in the PLA to control the Red Guards and restore order. With Liu gone, Mao's new heir was the enigmatic Marshal Lin Biao; but suddenly he was accused of planning a coup and the assassination of Mao. Lin tried to flee and died when his plane crashed. Now Mao again had total control, and he passed the day-to-day management of the government to Zhao En-lai.

Mao had always understood the importance of superpowers; despite huge provocation he had in the early days always accommodated the interests of the USSR. The most dramatic example of this was in 1936, when Zang Xueliang, the 'Young Marshal' of Manchuria, captured Chiang Kai-shek and offered him to Mao as a prisoner. At last Mao could execute and be rid of his arch enemy, but under extreme pressure from Stalin, Mao freed him—an act that would change the history of China and Taiwan. Now there was only one superpower, America. Despite the long enmity with the US, both in the pre-revolutionary days and in the Korean war, despite US sanctions and CIA-attempted assassinations, Mao knew that he needed it. Ever the pragmatist, he was ready to bow down to necessity. In 1972 Nixon came to China and shook Mao's hand. A new era had begun.

Mao and Zhao were now two old men approaching death.

Who was to look after China when they were gone? Zhao persuaded Mao to bring back Deng, and without a ripple Deng returned to the centre of the power circle. But he had to contend with Mao's wife, Jiang Qing, her wild ambitions and her Gang of Four. Mao had long lost hope or trust in her, saying, 'She has a sharp mouth and a sharp tongue and she will always make trouble. A week after I die people will kill her.' But Deng, as always, moved too fast, disturbing Mao who saw 'Left opportunism' on one side with Jiang's Gang of Four, and the 'right deviation' of the capitalist-roader Deng on the other. Deng was sidelined as Mao moved yet another new 'successor' into position, Hua Guofeng. The year 1976 saw the death of Zhao En-lai, Marshal Zhu De and Mao Zedong. With Mao dead, Hua moved quickly to arrest Jiang and her gang. Hua was a dedicated follower of Mao, and offered his solution for China in his philosophy of the 'Two Whatevers': 'We will resolutely uphold whatever policy decisions Chairman Mao made, and unswervingly follow whatever instructions Chairman Mao gave.' But the day of the chairman was over.

Deng offered his alternative for the future, rejecting part of Mao's legacy, while accepting other parts, with his conclusion that Mao was seven parts good and three parts bad. Deng offered economic solutions, and put together an alliance of the PLA, the elders, reformers and provincial leaders. Deng's strength came from the support of Marshal Ye and his generals. Mao had shown that power comes from the barrel of a gun, a lesson not forgotten by Deng, who, within two years of Mao's death, gained complete control.

Deng was determined to improve the living standards of the

Chinese people. His slogan, 'To get rich is glorious', was a revolutionary departure from the Maoist egalitarian approach that extolled collective socialism rather than self-enrichment. He was convinced that the Chinese people valued economic growth more than political liberty. His struggle for reform had two phases; Phase 1 (1978–88) was 'Reform without losers', Phase 2 (1993 onwards), 'Reform with losers'. In-between came Tiananmen and the three-year conservative ascendancy under Chen Yun that rolled back Deng's reforms.

Deng first moved against the problem of a sky-rocketing population curve. He initiated the 'one child policy'. Incentives and deterrents were put into place to ensure that families complied; to the monetary incentives was added social pressure. Deng believed a good policy was only useful if it was implemented. He was good at implementing. The one-child policy quickly brought the population problem under control.

The next step was to increase agricultural production. Mao's commune system was not a success. During the GLF famine, the two worst hit provinces were Anhui and Sichuan. To deal with the problems of these badly hit provinces, Deng sent two of his trusted reformers. Wan Li had proved his capabilities as an administrator, and was also Deng's bridge partner; he was moved to Anhui. Zhao Ziyang was a well-educated bureaucrat who had suffered in the cultural revolution but had established his credentials when he was restored. Zhao was moved to Sichuan. Recognizing the weaknesses of the communes which offered no motivation to the peasants, no reward for hard work, Zhao and Wan allowed families to take small pieces of land, to farm as they wished, under contract.

The first harvest showed the result—a remarkable surge in crops. Zhao and Wan were heroes, and a verse was sung praising them: 'If you want wheat, go to Zhao Ziyang; if you want rice go to Wan Li.' The Household Responsibility System (HRS) was born. Between 1979 and 1982 the central government watched other areas copy Anhui and Sichuan, neither saying yes nor saying no. Deng moved with caution, he believed in 'crossing the river by feeling the stones'. In 1982 the central government formally sanctioned the HRS; within six months 75 per cent of rural China implemented the new system, and by 1983, the system had spread to 98 per cent of farm households. The reforms also increased the price at which the government purchased plan quotas of grain, and allowed the above quota output to be sold freely. The reforms lead to rapid and massive gains in agricultural output, grain, meat, cotton and other crops. Between 1978 and 1985, per capita incomes in rural China multiplied by three; between 1978 and 2000 the value of rural output, in monetary terms, increased seventeen times. The famines had been replaced by food surpluses. The peasants had discovered that 'to grow rich is glorious'.

The peasants now had surplus income, but little to spend it on. Local governments encouraged the development of regional industrialization to meet the demand through collectively owned firms known as Town and Village Enterprises (TVE). The rural industrialization programme had started in the GLF, but now they were developed with a vengeance. They grew at an average yearly rate of 30 per cent to a third of total industrial output; by 1995 twenty-three million TVE employed 129 million people. The TVE supplied the strong demand for consumer goods, but even more importantly they provided jobs, which the capital-intensive heavy industries could not. The Chinese economy needed nine million new jobs a year.

Singapore provided the inspiration for Deng's most important reform strategy. When he visited the island, Deng was impressed with Lee Kuan Yew's successful use of multinationals and FDI to boost export-oriented industrialization. Learning from Singapore's success, Deng launched the first four Special Economic Zones (SEZs), three in Guangdong province next to Hong Kong, and one in the Fujian province across the sea from Taiwan. The location was brilliant, and pulled in overseas Chinese investors from the rich Hong Kong and Taiwan business communities. The success of the first SEZ led to further waves of expansion and more free zone areas that fuelled the massive growth of FDI and exports, as the foreign investors brought capital, technology, know-how and market penetration. Every effort was made to attract foreign capital with tax incentives, easy procedures, availability of land, power and labour. Deng's message was unambiguous: 'Foreign entrepreneurs invest here to make a profit, so we should ensure that they make more profit from investment in China than anywhere else.'

The purpose of the SEZ was to promote FDI inflow and export of manufactures to the world. In 1978, when Deng took control, exports amounted to $10 billion; by 2010 they had grown to $1,200 billion annually and Chinese exports had changed the world. Most impacted was the US where consumers celebrated lower prices by a huge shopping spree, with Wal-Mart, as the gateway to America, becoming the biggest company in the world, overtaking most nations to become China's fourth largest trading partner. By 2005 China had received $500 billion in foreign investment, an amount unmatched by any other country. More than half the FDI came from Hong Kong, which invested $259 billion in 254,000 new projects. Four-fifths of the FDI came from the Chinese diaspora. But the SEZ programme also gave rise to corruption, smuggling and a decay in morality which provoked hostile reaction from the conservative block led by Chen Yun who opposed Deng's reform programme.

Deng changed China with his reforms. The Household Responsibility System revolutionized agricultural production; the Town and Village Enterprises gave a boost to consumer industry; the Special Economic Zones created the massive exports and foreign investment that were the hallmarks of China's growth; but most important of all, Deng's simple slogan—'To grow rich is glorious'—introduced a total revolution in thinking, as it dethroned Marxism and Maoism, and changed forever the core beliefs of the Chinese people.

The reforms also had a social cost—a surge in corruption, graft, smuggling and prostitution. They also eroded communist ideology and the morality of party members and officials. The reforms were also fuelling inflation, which rose to 30 per cent. Many were not happy with the way things were progressing. Chen Yun, the stern old economist, emerged as the leader of the opposition to reform. The conservatives had been brought up on a belief in communism; with his SEZ Deng seemed to be diving headlong into capitalism. Deng defended his SEZs saying they were for foreign investors only. Chen countered,

'Foreign capitalists are still capitalists.' The powerful elders who had empowered Deng now supported Chen against Deng's reforms. The first target was Hu Yaobang, the general secretary of the Communist Party, Deng's leading 'reformer'.

Hu was a bit eccentric and had launched a campaign against the use of chopsticks, recommending their replacement with cutlery; he also served escargots at his dinners. Hu lacked tact, and paid little respect to Mao Zedong; when asked which of Mao's policies could contribute the most to China's modernization, he is reported to have answered, 'I think, none.' Because of his idiosyncrasies Hu made for an easy target. Deng was unable to protect his man, and sacrificed him. He replaced him with Zhao Ziyang, the creative reformer who had earned his spurs in Sichuan with the introduction of the HRS. Zhao was the rising star in Chinese politics, a very capable economic administrator although inexperienced in the realpolitik of the Politburo. Zhao neither understood the ideological base of Chen's power, nor appreciated the deep bonds of a lifetime that linked Deng and the conservative elders. Zhao's adversary was Premier Li Peng, the son of a prominent party martyr who had been brought up by Zhao En-lai. Li was a 'princeling' with strong credentials and an even stronger network of relationships with the party elite.

The showdown came in 1989 at Tiananmen. The key issues for the students were democracy, corruption and inflation; the elders wanted quick, harsh action; Deng wanted a crackdown; Zhao wanted dialogue. The powerful old men who had faced the rage of the masses in the cultural revolution did not want to repeat the experience. Deng, himself a victim of the Red

Guards, had seen his brother 'suicided', his son crippled for life, his home ravaged, his family attacked, and his career purged in those years of chaos. As the infighting between Premier Li and General Secretary Zhao escalated, Deng removed Zhao and brought in the PLA to disperse the students. Zhao was placed under arrest, where he remained for sixteen years till his death in 2005. Control of the economy passed to Li Peng and Chen Yun's conservatives, whose priority was to deal with inflation, corruption and graft. In the three years that followed Tiananmen, Chen rolled back Deng's reforms as Deng was sidelined; his eclipse after Tiananmen resembled Mao's eclipse after the failure of the Great Leap. Like Mao, he had to prepare for his comeback.

Deng made his comeback in 1992 announcing his return in his famous Southern Tour. Deng's return was the result of his 'grand compromise', in which he assembled an alliance of the PLA, the provincial leaders and the reformers. The PLA agreed to support Deng's reforms in return for his promise to fund the modernization programme of the army; the southern provinces had grown rich under Deng's reforms and agreed to provide revenue to a financially weak centre in exchange for a greater role in economic decisions. The centre agreed to finance the PLA modernization with the revenue it secured from the provinces. The timing was perfect. The elders were shaken by the collapse of communism in Europe and the USSR, and not in a mood to resist the demands of the PLA. The PLA was firm; the elders would have to compromise with the reformers. Deng had always understood, 'During an interregnum military power becomes decisive.' Never too enamoured with democracy, he wrote, 'Historical experience shows that to consolidate a political regime one must use the means of dictatorship.' Deng also understood the power of money. His reform programme offered something for everybody, particularly wealth for the provincial leadership and modernization for the army. Deng snatched back control from Chen Yun, the Standing Committee and the Politburo. The PLA was the key.

Deng had lost two of his reformers, Hu and Zhao; he now brought in a third, a tough brash administrator from Shanghai named Zhu Rongji, who had done an exceptional job with his development of Shanghai. Deng respected Zhu's understanding of economics and his effectiveness as an administrator. Zhu managed the second phase of the reforms, 'Reform with Losers'. The accelerated transition that China had experienced during the first phase of reform had thrown up a new set of problems— revenue shortfall in Beijing, inefficient State Owned Enterprises (SOE), bad loans and bankrupt banks, inflation, unemployment, income inequality and ballooning corruption. Important milestones were the takeover of Hong Kong and China's entry to the WTO. These were the tasks that fell to Zhu.

Zhu was a man in a hurry, and often felt frustrated by the system and even by Jiang, his cautious boss whose priority was balancing the politics rather than accelerating economic reform. But he performed. His important tax reform made Beijing the major shareholder in tax revenues enabling the centre to make good its promises to fund the PLA modernization, and also to assist poor provinces which had been left behind as some areas grew rich first. Beijing was no longer dependent on the provinces.

The State Owned Enterprises (SOEs) were at the heart of the socialist economy. When Deng took control in 1978, the SOEs produced 77 per cent of China's industrial output; by 1993, when Deng started his second phase of reform, SOE production had fallen to 33 per cent, as TVE and foreign enterprise in the SEZs grew in importance. But the SOEs were still a serious drain on the economy. Having lost their monopolies, they had become unprofitable, and made good their cash flow deficits from increased bank borrowing, which they had little intention to repay. By 1994 their debt–equity ratios were above 200 per cent (comparable to Japan and Thailand, but not as high as the Korean Chaebols). Old-style managers were unconcerned with efficiency or profits. State-owned banks kept the zombie firms afloat as they burned cash and accumulated debt.

Russia's strategy for its SOEs was shock therapy and a fire-sale privatization programme that was called 'the sale of the century', as it passed the crown jewels to the new oligarchs at throwaway prices. China adopted a gradualist approach, merging the best of capitalism and socialism in its 'socialism with Chinese characteristics'. The Russian transition was a disaster; the Chinese an extraordinary success.

The first step in SOE reforms was the empowerment of management. The interference of the party bureaucracy was reduced, and managers were encouraged to make the decisions. Financial incentives were put into place to motivate the managers who now focused on profitability. The second step was privatization, through a strategy of 'grasping the big, letting go of the small' as smaller units were sold off, mostly to their

managers. Over a decade the number of SOEs were reduced
from 120,000 to 31,000. The largest firms were placed under
the control of the State Asset Supervision and Administration
Commission (SASAC), most of which were in the sectors of
petroleum, metals, electricity, military equipment and telecom.
Improved governance increased the efficiency of the remaining
corporatized state sector.

In 1993 Transparency International had branded China as
one of the world's most corrupt nations. In 1996 Jiang launched
a ruthless campaign against corruption, with a thousand
executions in that year alone. Executions of those convicted of
corruption increased to 3,000 annually as this vice was reined
in. By 2009 China was placed seventy-ninth among the 180 TI
countries' list. In a society in transition, where religion and
ideology have been replaced by naked materialism, it is difficult
to eradicate corruption and racketeering. China, however, has
maintained a steady crusade and has been quite effective in
controlling and deterring those who are tempted to stray.

Unrestrained lending by the four state-owned banks to the
SOE had created a mountain of non-performing loans, bad
debts which could not be repaid. By 1999 these non-performing
loans amounted to 25 per cent of the GDP; the banking system
was bankrupt. SOEs continued to borrow to meet the
requirements of their haemorrhaging cash flow. Spiralling
credit growth also escalated inflation. Zhu tightened credit
policy and raised interest rates, but many bankers just ignored
him; after all, they were government banks lending to
government companies—surely there was nothing wrong in
that. They underestimated Zhu's determination; he imprisoned

several bankers, and even executed one! After that the bankers fell into line, and Zhu's banking reforms started to have effect. Commercially based lending replaced politically influenced lending, the first step in the modernization of the Chinese banking system. Monetary control subdued inflation, which was raging at 35 per cent in 1993–94, but was tamed by 1995. Devaluation boosted exports, which were able to cash in on China's entry into the WTO. In the first quarter after the removal of textile quotas, China's garment exports to the US grew by 1,000 per cent.

Unemployment increased due to release of surplus farm labour and downsizing of the SOEs, which shed forty-one million workers, and the TVEs half that amount. Jobs needed to be found quickly for over eighty million people. The booming coastal cities provided jobs in construction and the fast growing SEZs needed industrial labour for the new projects. In less than a quarter century, Shanghai built over 4,000 skyscrapers, twice the number existing in Manhattan. In Shenzhen, construction teams were completing three floors a day. Fabulous new airports and roads were changing the face of China. A massive migration of 100–150 million floating workers moved from the depressed rural areas in the north and west to the south and east. There may have been dislocation, but at least jobs were found. The disparity between rural and urban wages grew, the gap between rich China and the poorer regions widened.

China's exports pounded on, year after year. By 2010 they had overtaken the US and were second only to Germany. Her massive surpluses and reserves had made her a major creditor nation on whose support the US had become dependent. Her products dominated and reached the homes of the world's consumers. China's production of mobile phones, televisions and laptop computers reached three-quarters of total world production; 90 per cent of the furniture in American homes came from China. Chinese garments clothed the world, rich and poor alike—even the poor who wanted to look rich, with their brand copies, their imitation Chanel handbags. China's Geely Car Corporation came out with their $35,000 copy of the Rolls-Royce Phantom. Chinese buying lifted world commodity prices, boosting copper, aluminum, zinc, steel and most significantly, oil. Chinese economic power changed the balance of power in international relations. How had this happened, so quickly and on such a scale?

Despite its unique combination of size and transition from communism, the factors that caused the Chinese growth were no different from the other successful growth economies. Committed and determined leadership, political stability, population control, good policies delivered by sound institutions (the Communist Party, the bureaucracy and the PLA), education and a disciplined workforce, savings, foreign investment and most important of all—exports, exports, exports.

Deng emphasized that poverty is not socialism, and almost half a billion people had been freed from poverty. China had changed. Whatever worked was labelled 'socialism with Chinese characteristics', even if it was pure and simple capitalism. Did it matter? Deng answered: 'It doesn't matter if a cat is black or white, as long as it catches mice.'

23

Dubai: Hoping for a Comeback

If a person lands in Dubai, he will take a taxi, buy a packet of cigarettes, have a meal, and we will all benefit.

—Sheikh Rashid

To the world Dubai symbolizes glamour and extravaganza—with its award winning Emirates Airlines, the magnificent Dubai airport, perfect highways, ultra luxurious hotels, the world's tallest building, the world's biggest mall, and finally the Palm Islands spreading their fronds into the calm blue sea. In less than half a century a small, dusty desert town was converted into the world's playground, the commercial centre of the Middle East, a bustling metropolis. Dubai lacked natural resources, and had very little oil, but it did have the advantage of two extraordinary rulers—Sheikh Rashid and his son Sheikh Mohammed.

Dubai is one of the seven emirates that together make up the United Arab Emirates, a country created in 1971 through the determination of Sheikh Zayed of Abu Dhabi, a leader loved and remembered as the Father of the Nation, and respected the world over as perhaps the most generous man in history. Abu Dhabi, populated by a few thousand tribesmen in 1950, discovered massive oil deposits, making it the richest little country in the world with the largest sovereign wealth fund of $1 trillion and the highest income per capita for its citizens on the planet. Over the last two hundred years Abu Dhabi moved from extreme poverty to unbelievable wealth. Political instability, assassinations and coups were replaced by peace, stability and progress. This was the legacy of Sheikh Zayed bin Sultan al Nahyan, the last great tribal chief.

Dubai, like Singapore, is a city-state with little natural advantage that has through the quality of its governance outperformed other countries. Both were blessed with exceptional leadership—Lee Kuan Yew in Singapore, and Sheikh Rashid in Dubai, followed by his equally talented son Sheikh Mohammed; both have experienced a long period of stability; both have successfully attracted foreign direct investment; both have built up huge exports; both have built up impressive infrastructure, particularly ports and airports; both have award-winning airlines; both have reclaimed the sea with man-made islands; both have championed state-owned corporations; both have state-led housing sectors; both have mastered the art of governance and clamped down on corruption. And, finally, both have autocratic rulers who have little respect or time for democracy.

The first demonstration of the Maktoum Sheikh's economic philosophy was in 1900. In response to Iran raising taxes on merchants, Dubai slashed the 5 per cent customs duty and made Dubai a free port. The result was an exodus of experienced Irani businessmen to Dubai, where they were welcomed and given every incentive to relocate. The Irani connection endured and Dubai remains home to a large community of Iranian descent. Dubai is Iran's largest trading partner, and billions of dollars flow from Iran to Dubai annually. With 300 flights to Iran weekly, the relationship is crucial to the economies of both countries, and the Dubai trade has helped Iran overcome much of the burden of economic sanctions imposed by the US.

Sheikh Rashid took this philosophy to the extreme—laissez faire, business friendly, fast decision-making, tremendous risk-taking, incentivization and an openness to international markets that would put today's globalization to shame. By 2010 95 per cent of Dubai's population comprised foreign expatriates living and working in Dubai; local Emiratis comprised 100,000 out of a population of two million, a level unmatched anywhere in the world. The foreigners brought skills, capital and contacts which have played an indispensable part in Dubai's phenomenal growth. Dubai's message to foreigners has always been, 'You are welcome. We will do all we can to make your business profitable and your life pleasant. We guarantee you freedom from taxes, freedom from bureaucratic interference and freedom of religion. Government will be honest, efficient and secure. What's good for business is good for Dubai.' The Maktoum Sheikhs have drawn their inspiration from sources as diverse as modern Singapore and Cordoba in its heyday under Muslim rule. Tolerance and open-mindedness are important Dubai traits; even Jews are welcome to do business, as is evidenced by the Atlantis Hotel, the Levant jewellery group, and the growing diamond business in Dubai.

Sheikh Rashid's first major moves were to increase Dubai's connectivity to the region and the outside world. Starting with the investment in dredging the creek to increase shipping and trade, he then made and immediately expanded the new Port Rashid; this was followed by the new Dubai international airport; next came the Jebel Ali port and the Jebel Ali Free Zone. These infrastructure developments opened up Dubai for business with the world. All were huge gambles, involving massive investment with no visible demand, but Sheikh Rashid believed that if you create supply, demand will follow. The Sheikh was an astute risk taker with nerves of steel, ready to take long positions that would terrify any normal man. Even Sheikh Mohammed was unnerved by the huge gamble on Jebel Ali port, and tried to dissuade his father from taking the plunge; but Sheikh Rashid patiently explained to his son, 'I'm building this port now, because there will come a time when you won't be able to afford it.' The Jebel Ali port is the world's largest man-made harbour, and has played a valuable role in Dubai's growth story. The lessons learnt by the young Sheikh Mohammed at the side of his father have influenced his rule, and he has over the years emerged as a risktaker comparable to Sheikh Rashid. The continuity provided by father and son has ensured that the new projects could soar to heights that defied the imagination.

Sheikh Rashid's vision for Dubai was clear. Dubai would be
the trade centre for the region, serving the needs of not just
Iran but also the Indian subcontinent, which supported a
quarter of the world's population. Although Dubai neither
produced goods for export, nor had the internal population to
support significant imports, the emirate could prosper as a 're-
export base' for the region. If the governments of these countries
blocked their own growth with restrictive laws, Dubai would
take the opportunity provided. Sheikh Rashid's priority was
the welfare of Dubai, and he had no qualms in ignoring the
laws of other nations. The export of gold to fill the insatiable
demand of India was not a crime in Dubai, and the trade was
encouraged, creating the first big fortunes of the Dubai business
community. Similarly, the supply to Iran of goods that fell under
US sanctions led to a new generation of fortunes in recent
years.

Sheikh Rashid financed the first infrastructure projects with
debt; when these proved successful, the debt was retired.
Then Dubai found oil, which reached 400,000 barrels per day
at its peak. Although the oil boom was short-lived, oil revenues
enabled the Sheikh to build Port Rashid, the Dry Dock, Dubai
Aluminium, Dugas and Dubai airport. What was amazing was
the scale, the degree of risk, and the level of management
expertise. Port Rashid was conceived with four berths but
completed with thirty-five berths. The Dubai port operating
company grew to become the fourth largest in the world with
operations in twenty-two countries handling 10 per cent of the
world's shipping. Within a few years of the launch of Port
Rashid, construction began on the massive Jebel Ali port, the

world's largest man-made harbour with sixty-six berths in the first phase. This too was a phenomenal success.

Dubai International airport opened for business in 1960. Over a fifty-year period it has grown into the fourth busiest international passenger airport in the world handling over forty million passengers, and the sixth largest cargo airport handling almost two million tonnes. The new Terminal 3, built at a cost of $4.5 billion, is the largest building in the world in terms of floor space. A new airport is being planned for Jebel Ali with a capacity of 120 million passengers, which when completed will be the world's biggest. Dubai has attracted airlines with its 'open skies' policy, and has emerged as the most important Middle East hub. Its duty free shops, by 2009, had become the single biggest airport retail operation in the world.

In 1985 Sheikh Mohammed launched the Emirates Airlines with an investment of $10 million and aircraft leased from PIA. Within nine months the airline was earning profit, which in 2008 had reached $1.5 billion. It is among the handful of top airlines in the world in terms of international passengers flown, cargo carried, efficiency, service and profitability. It is the fastest growing airline in the world and the largest in terms of passenger-kilometres flown, with a fleet utilization of eighteen hours a day.

When Sheikh Mohammed successfully converted Dubai into a major destination for European tourists, package holidays brought in a new stream of customers to fill the ever growing Emirates Airlines capacity. Emirates stole the business from the other airlines in the region, by first introducing Western levels of professionalism to beat the shoddy local competition, and then moving to a level of service and comfort that surpassed the European airlines. Once again, Singapore showed the way; Singapore Airlines had already demonstrated a level of service far superior to anything offered by European and American airlines.

Sheikh Rashid now felt a growing sense of frustration with the Company Law of the United Arab Emirates, which was too restrictive for his liking. Sheikh Rashid had from the beginning been wary of the UAE being dominated by Abu Dhabi, with 88 per cent of the UAE land mass and 90 per cent of its oil, and negotiations between Sheikh Zayed and Sheikh Rashid had in the early days of the federation often skirted brinkmanship. Abu Dhabi wanted to keep the foreigner out; floating on a sea of oil, they needed no one, and didn't want to share their wealth with a host of foreign claimants. Dubai, however, wanted to lure the foreigner in; its economic growth was dependent on 'globalization'. The problem for Dubai lay in the federal law that 'local partners' must retain 51 per cent of all companies doing business in the UAE. This was a big deterrent to foreign investment relocating in Dubai. Sheikh Rashid found a way round the federal law, by forming the Jebel Ali Free Zone, a large area where foreign business could be incorporated and could operate without a local partner, and unfettered by the other restrictions imposed by the UAE Company Law. The Jebel Ali Free Zone waived the UAE 5 per cent import duty, and offered a tax and duty free zone for foreign business. The zone had a slow start, with few takers, but soon picked up speed and by the year 2009 more than 6,400 companies had set up operations. Jebel Ali was the prototype; its success stimulated many more free zones—

Internet City, Media City, the DIFC, Knowledge City, Medical City, Maritime City and others. Dubai had found a way to bypass the Federal Company Law with its restrictive demands for local partners, and could now explode into growth based on the 'Dubai Model'. The crowning success of Dubai's free zone policy was Halliburton moving its headquarters from Texas to Jebel Ali in 2007.

A chunk of Dubai's short-term windfall of oil revenues was invested in the Dubai Dry Dock. Ridiculed as a white elephant, to everyone's surprise it succeeded beyond expectations, proving once again that Sheikh Rashid was no ordinary investor. Commissioned in 1983, in the midst of a recession in shipping, the project was criticized as 'ambition that bordered on folly'. The facility was one of the world's largest, and Dry Dock number 2 was the largest in the world. One year after its commissioning, Iraq and Iran started to target each other's oil tankers; the 'tanker war' led to a huge number of damaged ships. All the damaged tankers limped into Dubai Dry Docks for repairs, resulting in 100 per cent capacity utilization and substantial profits from the first year. Was it just luck, or was it Sheikh Rashid's ability to foresee the future? Everything Sheikh Rashid did was visionary, and everything was criticized at the time.

Unlike his father, who was an astute and wily Bedouin chief, Sheikh Mohammed was a twenty-first century ruler, in much of a hurry. He took his father's innovation and philosophy forward, often refining and improving on the original model. The two most important new initiatives introduced by him were tourism and real estate. No less important was Sheikh

Mohammed's unique management style, with its emphasis on hard work, efficiency and motivation.

When the Iraq–Iran war depressed the Dubai economy in the 1980s, the young Sheikh Mohammed came up with the idea of tourism as a potential new income source. His idea was ridiculed by those who argued that Dubai had nothing to offer tourists other than searing sun, burning sand and humidity. What others saw as Dubai's problems Sheikh Mohammed saw as opportunity, and with obstinate determination he set about developing Dubai tourism. By 2007 tourism had grown to 25 per cent of Dubai's economy, earning $8 billion from seven million tourists, with a target to reach fifteen million tourists by 2015. The Dubai International Airport and the Emirates Airlines were ready to bring in the tourists. The open skies policy added 120 international airlines. Visas were easy and in the case of many countries not even required. The 4,000 hotel rooms grew to 60,000 by 2010, each new hotel more extravagant than the last, creating a new standard in luxury. Winter sun and sandy beaches lured the Western tourist; shopping was the attraction for the Asian tourist; the Russians wanted it all—sun, sea and endless shopping, as boutiques selling fur coats proliferated. The Dubai Shopping Festival, started in 1996, attracted a spending of $1 billion in its first year; by 2009, the thirty-day festival saw over three million visitors spending over $2.5 billion, leading to the creation of a second shopping festival, the Dubai Summer Surprises, to boost the off-season summer months. When the beaches ran out, new beaches were created in the Palm Islands by dumping sand into the sea! Sheikh Mohammed had pulled it off.

Dubai's real estate was Sheikh Mohammed's greatest success. It was also his greatest failure. Till 2008 no one had ever lost money in Dubai property; after 2008 everybody lost. Traditionally, only local citizens could own real estate, and the law of the UAE reinforced that position. In 2002 Sheikh Mohammed passed a decree allowing foreigners to buy freehold property, and the first projects were launched by Emaar and Nakheel, Dubai's master property developers. Glamorous housing projects were launched in Emirates Hills, Meadows and the Jumeirah Palm Islands, which sold out in hours, and quickly commanded premiums. Apartment buildings followed, both massive master projects such as the Jumeirah Beach Residences and individual buildings by private developers. The prices of property went up, up, up. Emaar starting with a capital of $50 million grew to $25 billion in five years, becoming the world's largest developer. The world wondered at the Palm Islands, which 'could be seen from the moon'. Growth was fuelled by investors who bought off-plan, whose money was used to then build the projects. Fortunes were made overnight as investment turned to speculation. The name of the game was 'flipping', where a 10 per cent margin could secure allotment in a new scheme, and resale within a month could generate a 100 per cent return on actual money invested. The speculative portfolios of the young new tycoons ballooned on reinvestment; their spending boosted the profits of shops selling luxury brands, and Toyotas were traded in for Bentleys and Porsches. Sheikh Mohammed's wealth was quoted at $18 billion, making him one of the richest men in the world.

Dubai has always shown a fine disregard for restrictive rules in its quest for growth. It has always turned problems into opportunities, making up for lack of capital with 'OPM— other people's money'. The Dubai Sheikhs have always been ready to innovate, and if necessary, change the rules of the game. They leveraged growth by a combination of debt and money raised from the market, leading to faster growth at higher risk. Dubai has the skill, but it also needs the luck. Success or failure is often determined by events outside one's control. Sheikh Rashid's Dry Dock's fast success was the windfall of the 'Iraq–Iran tanker war', Sheikh Mohammed's property collapse was triggered by the world financial crisis of 2008. Dubai property prices have fallen 50–60 per cent from their peak—perhaps less than the Singapore property crash a decade before, in the Asian financial crisis—but enough to wipe out all the new millionaires, and even some of the old.

Sheikh Mohammed's management style has been an important factor in Dubai's amazing growth. He has personally created and developed the team that has followed his lead and vision. His lieutenants were not part of Dubai's traditional elite; they were modern executives with international exposure, encouraged to take risk, impatient to grow. By taking on massive amounts of debt, they expanded their empires both domestically and overseas. They competed with each other for the ruler's recognition and favour. If Emaar built the tallest building in the world, Nakheel would build one taller. Sheikh Mohammed ran Dubai Inc. as a hands-on CEO. He was a frontline general, visible and accessible, who believed in direct action, admonishing or rewarding performance personally. Two important tools that he relied on were e-governance and feedback. Extensive computerization increased the speed and efficiency of a bureaucracy reasonably free of corruption. To ensure accurate feedback a team of 'mystery shoppers' acted as clients of the administration to test efficiency. To promote good governance, Sheikh Mohammed established the Dubai School of Governance in partnership with Harvard University's John F. Kennedy School of Government and the Lee Kuan Yew School of Public Policy. To develop leadership he established the Mohammed bin Rashid Centre for Leadership Development (MBRCLD). Thus, the importance of good governance was recognized and emphasized.

The 2007–08 crash stunned Dubai and its leadership. Heads rolled. Those who had accumulated the $80 billion debt for their expansion programme were the first to suffer. Mohammed al-Gergawi, Sultan bin Sulayem and Mohammed Alabbar were dropped from the board of Dubai's main holding company, the Investment Corporation of Dubai. Sultan bin Sulayem was also removed from the chair of Nakheel. The next day the governor of the Dubai International Financial Centre (DIFC), Omar bin Sulaiman, was removed. The whizkids were out; their replacements, Mohammed al-Shaibani, Ahmed Humaid al-Tayer and Ali Rashid Ahmed Lootah, were conservative bankers who would bring a different approach to the cash flow crisis. Royals Sheikh Ahmed and Crown Prince Sheikh Hamdan took on more responsibility. Traditional business leaders moved to centrestage as the gunslinger technicians moved out. Dubai approached lenders for a moratorium and restructuring of debt, and turned to Abu Dhabi as financier of last resort.

Abu Dhabi came up with cash to support Dubai in its time of trouble. Apart from a few hiccups, Dubai dealt with the cash flow crisis well. Dubai's population had fallen by 9 per cent in 2009, but the 5 per cent contraction of the economy experienced in 2009 was reduced to 0.4 per cent in 2010. Trade, services and tourism have been stabilized, but the important property sector, which had become the largest part of the Dubai economy, is still not out of the woods. The problem is that demand for property in Dubai is dependent on an influx of foreigners, which contradicts the policy of the UAE to contain growth of the foreign population. Local sentiment is also growing against expats, while jobs and opportunities for locals are few and far between. Though rich locals are concerned about the revival of the property market, the average Emirati is more concerned about employment.

Over three million students study at foreign campuses, and America, England and Australia, the English-speaking countries, host a good number of these. Hosting foreign students is a $100 billion business. Students from Asia make up the largest share of foreign students and the expenditure is an average of $50,000 per student annually. Dubai could prove a magnet for students from the region and for those seeking a Western education in a Muslim environment closer home. Dubai has targeted educational tourism, which may well be an important part of the solution to the property crisis. The demand for quality education of an international standard is strong in Pakistan, where instability has disrupted local education, and in Iran, where those wanting an English-language education are unable to get it.

Dubai has weathered the crash. The panic is over, the economy has stabilized. But the days of Dubai's 'gold rush' with its overnight fortunes are over for the time being. Nevertheless, Dubai remains an outstanding example of what can be achieved in a very short time by a determined and capable leader.

24

Israel: Successful Socialism, Successful Capitalism

Let me tell you something we Israelis have against Moses. He took us forty years through the desert in order to bring us to the one spot in the Middle East that has no oil.

—Golda Meir

If Moses thought the Israelis could do without oil, he was right. The Israelis have built up a successful economy which can be compared with any in Europe, and has a per capita income higher than oil-rich Saudi Arabia. Jews are a competitive and successful group the world over; though only 0.2 per cent of the world's population, they comprise a disproportionate number of billionaires ranging from American tycoons to Russian oligarchs. They have produced 54 per cent of the world's chess champions, 27 per cent of the Nobel physics laureates and 31 per cent of the medicine laureates. In America, 37 per cent of Academy Award-winning directors, 38 per cent of leading philanthropists, 51 per cent of non-fiction Pulitzer Prize winners have been Jews. They have also dominated world crime from Bugsy Siegel and Meyer Lansky of the early days of the American mafia to the Russian mafia of today whose most prominent Jewish and Israeli dons include Semion Mogilevich, 'The Brainy Don', and Sergei Mikhailov, boss of the top crime family, the Solntsenskaya Bratva. Many have made Israel their base and have invested an estimated $20 billion in the haven of Israel. A State Department crime expert, Jonathon Winer, has said, 'There is not a major Russian organized crime figure who we are tracking who does not also carry an Israeli passport.'

The principles of the economic success of the Israelis are much the same as those used by other successful developing nations—political stability, honest and committed leadership, education and skilled manpower, investment capital, exports and superpower support. Where Israel was different was in her fifty years of conflict with her neighbours. But despite six wars, two intifadas, terrorism and economic boycott, Israel did succeed. Between 1950 and 2010 her population grew from 1.3 million to 7 million, her GDP from $4 billion to $195 billion, and her per capita income from $3,100 to $31,000.

The economy of Israel went through four distinct phases:

Successful socialism   —   1947–73
The lost decade   —   1973–85

The stabilization plan   —   1985
Successful capitalism   —   1990–2010

The period of successful socialism enjoyed political stability during the power monopoly of the Labour Party, similar to the quasi-democracies of Singapore, Malaysia, Botswana, and even India during its first decades of Congress party rule. A competent leadership committed itself to nation building. The early leaders, Ben-Gurion, Golda Meir and Shimon Peres, were honest and dedicated. In the first decades the kibbutz agricultural communities combined socialism with Zionism, and the Histadrut Labour Union-dominated industry became Israel's largest industrialist, employing 25 per cent of the workforce. Socialism was the chosen road, and it worked as the growth rate averaged about 10 per cent for the first twenty years. The leaders aspired to European levels of economy, which was understandable, since most of them were of European origin, and the Ashkenazim, the European Israelis, became an elite majority, with the Sephardim (Mizrahi), the Asian and the African minority as second-class citizens; at the bottom of the heap were the Palestinians who remained in Israel, victims of discrimination. The Palestinian refugees, who left or were driven out, were never to be allowed to return, for fear that if their citizenship was restored, they would constitute a majority and take Israel back from the Jews.

Investment capital, essential for growth, was provided by three sources. In the 1950s the rich Jewish diaspora provided 59 per cent of foreign funding, German reparations to Holocaust victims, amounting to $850 million, provided 29 per cent, and the US government provided 12 per cent. Superpower support was provided by America, who over the next fifty years backed Israel with ever increasing levels of money, ensuring that she received the highest aid per capita in the world, and political support both in matters of defence and in the United Nations.

The Ashkenazim, the European Jews, well educated and imbued with national fervour, showed their innovation in developing agriculture in their barren desert land. They met their water shortage with a new drip irrigation system which was later exported to other water-starved nations. Applied science led to improved crops and to the production of agricultural machinery which added to the growing list of exports. Solar energy systems were installed in every house. Small- and medium-sized industry grew, led by textile and clothing; fruit processing followed. Successful export requires not just the ability to produce, but also the ability to penetrate rich markets. In this Israel's efforts were boosted by the support of the network of the Jewish diaspora which was well entrenched in trade in Europe and America. This network was further reinforced by the friends of Israel throughout the West. Traditional skills such as diamond-cutting linked Israel to the Jewish-dominated diamond industry in Amsterdam and New York, and diamonds soon became an important export. Visiting Jews promoted tourism.

Conflict and the wars in 1956 and 1967 actually benefited Israel's economy. The 1956 Suez War was orchestrated with France and England who wanted an excuse to attack Nasser in Egypt, and Israel was rewarded for her role. Shimon Peres negotiated very favourable terms for armaments from France, who became her most important supplier till de Gaulle terminated the relationship. The Six-day War in 1967 resulted in a fast victory. Israel captured the Sinai Peninsula, the Gaza strip, the Golden Heights, the West Bank and East Jerusalem. The legacy of the war has shaped the conflict into what is today. Between 1968 and 1970 the economy grew at an annual rate of 12 per cent. The war economy promoted the development of Israel's own arms industry which soon found export markets, and Israel became the fifth largest exporter of arms in the world. The technical requirements of the military industrial complex promoted Israel's hi-tech capabilities, perhaps the most important factor in her economic success.

But the Yom Kippur War in 1973 re-established the principle that war and conflict are disastrous for the economy, as it heralded the 'Lost Decade' with its downward spiral till 1985, when the Stabilization Plan put a brake on the collapse. In the 1970s defence expenditure rose above 25 per cent of the GNP, increasing the burden on the economy. Whereas the earlier wars were fought outside Israeli territory and did not cause much damage to morale or infrastructure, the Second Intifada, starting in 2000, with its suicide bombers, took the battle into Israel. In 2001 its cost to the economy was estimated at $2.6 billion. The imperative for peace grew. The benefits of conflict in the early years, and the subsequent burden after the Lost Decade, clarified the principle—war is fine if it leads to a quick victory, but a long period of expensive conflict is best avoided.

The Lost Decade (1973–85), born of the Yom Kippur War and the oil embargo with its two oil shocks, was characterized by deficits, debt, defence spending and double digit inflation.

The combination of soaring oil prices and defence expenditure rising above 30 per cent of the GNP brought growth down from its heights of 10 per cent to an average of 3 per cent. Double-digit inflation grew into triple-digit hyperinflation, reaching 400 per cent a year by 1984. Efficiency fell. The socialist economy stalled, as people commented, 'The only way to make a small fortune in Israel is to come here with a large one.'

In September 1984, Shimon Peres became prime minister and pushed for a stabilization plan to bring the economy back on track. The legendary patriarch who has lived through half a century of leadership had already proved his worth by building the special relationship with France in securing arms for the Israeli Defence Force (IDF) and for his role in the Israeli nuclear programme. In 1976 he was the key figure behind the dramatic 'Raid in Entebbe'. Starting as a 'hawk' strategizing the 1956 Sinai campaign, he matured as a 'dove', negotiating the signing of the 'Declaration of Principles' with the PLO for which he won the 1994 Nobel Peace Prize together with Rabin and Arafat. He secured the Treaty of Peace with Jordan and created the Peres Centre for Peace. He has held key government posts, twice as prime minister, three times as foreign minister, twice as defence minister and finally as the ninth president of Israel. Never a popular favourite, he nonetheless managed repeated turns in office due to Israel's own particular type of democracy in which the two main opponents, Labour and Likud, regularly shared power in coalition government.

After 1985 the stabilization plan brought inflation down from 400 per cent to 16 per cent. Sound economic policies put the economy back on track as government spending and deficits were controlled; the deficit was brought down from 15 per cent to 1 per cent. Price controls and devaluation followed, and the Bank of Israel's ability to print money to cover government deficits was curbed. The private sector was encouraged, and the powerful Histadrut labour union which had begun to dominate politics was tamed. The foundation of the new economy was laid. The plan has become a model for other countries facing similar economic crises.

After 1990 almost a million highly educated Russian immigrants arrived; they added further impetus to the hi-tech sector of the economy. Israel now had more scientists per capita than any other country in the world. The private sector grew as the worker's economy diminished; Histadrut employment fell from 25 per cent to 2 per cent of the workforce. The hi-tech sector increased its share in Israel's exports. Growth averaged 6 per cent for six years. In 1996 the growth rate declined as traditional industry contracted; the textile sector, unable to meet competition from China, diminished, leaving increased unemployment in its wake. But within a few years, restructuring led to recovery of the economy, spurred by the US hi-tech boom. The bursting of the US bubble brought recession to an Israel dependent on hi-tech exports, but by 2004 this was reversed by the Israeli Recovery Plan which saw the economy boom between 2004 and 2007 with rising exports and FDI. The growth rate averaged 5 per cent till 2008—the year of the sub-prime financial crisis in the US.

The move from socialism to capitalism in the economy also brought about changes in society as idealism was replaced by self-interest. The rich grew richer and the poor grew poorer; disparity increased, and poverty, which had extended to 8 per cent of the population in the 1950s and 1960s, grew to encompass 20 per cent of the population—the highest rate for any developed country.

The quality of leaders plunged as news headlines revealed corruption at the highest levels and gory sex scandals. In 2006 fifteen legislators were investigated, indicted or convicted for corruption. Ariel Sharon, who had been forced to resign as defence minister for his personal responsibility in the Sabra and Shatila massacres, but had made it back to the prime ministership, was implicated in corruption scandals, to which his son, a member of parliament, pleaded guilty and was sentenced to nine months imprisonment. Sharon fell into a coma, leading an analyst to comment that his ill-health had saved him from also being indicted.

Sharon was succeeded by Ehud Olmert, who also had to resign from prime ministership due to corruption charges. The chief-of-staff, Lt Gen Dan Halutz, sold his stock portfolio, in a classic case of insider trading, hours after Hezbollah kidnapped two Israeli soldiers, triggering the Lebanon War. The chairman of the Knesset Foreign and Military Affairs Committee was indicted for fraud and perjury. The Minister of Justice Haim Ramon was forced to resign after being put on trial for pushing his tongue into the mouth of a female soldier. President Ezer Weizman resigned after revelations that he had received 'gifts' of $450,000 from a French businessman. President Moshe Katsav pleaded guilty in a plea bargain, when accused of sexual harassment and rape. The complainant filed a statement, 'The president would sit there at his desk every morning and take out his penis and stroke it and then ask me to sit beside him and touch it.' Times had changed.

Each country has its own engine of growth. In China it has been industry; in Dubai property; in Israel, where necessity has been the mother of invention, it is innovation. Starting with a high level of education, the skills of the Israelis have been further enhanced by compulsory military conscription with its practical applications and networking relationships in the IDF Science Corps. It is no coincidence that three of the most successful developing countries—Singapore, South Korea and Israel—have all had compulsory military conscription. In the 1990s the large numbers of Russian immigrants added to the science and technology pool. The combination of science and entrepreneurship made Israel into a world leader, with the highest number of scientists per capita and its incredible originality, dynamism and entrepreneurship. In the new capitalist economy the Israeli hi-tech sector exploded on the global scene. All the big names established important facilities—Microsoft, Cisco, Intel, Motorola, IBM, HP, Nortel, Mitsubishi, Deutsche Telecom, and Ericsson. But no less important were the home-grown companies—Amdocs, the leader in telecommunications billing software, Checkpoint with its firewall expertise, Given Imaging with its encapsulated miniature medical cameras, NDS with its digital TV technology solutions, Scitex with its computer graphic technologies, and Teva, a world leader in generic drugs. Israeli technology has become a major player in the fields of telecom, medicine, computers and agriculture.

In the telecom sector Israel has been a world-class innovator in mobile phone technology, voicemail, SMS, transmission of pictures, chat facility and fibre-optics. Its companies have installed satellite stations in Kazakhstan and Uzbekistan and have installed phone networks in Hungary, Poland, India and Ghana. Customers for its services range from Deutsche Telecom to the Chinese National Telephone Corporation.

Almost half of Israel's start-up companies are in the fields of medical and life sciences, which cover medical devices, bio-electronics, diagnostics and smart drugs. Israel's new medical technologies have drawn heavily on the electronic and optical sectors in thermal imaging, remote sensing and lasers. The miniature disposable video camera developed by Given Imaging has replaced the conventional invasive endoscopy technique in which a flexible tube is inserted via the rectum; the new technology merely requires the swallowing of a capsule which takes up to 50,000 images while on its journey through the body—no pain, no discomfort, no hospitalization. A non-invasive surgery technique has been developed by Insightec in which sound waves blast tumours rendering surgery with a knife obsolete. Israeli doctors conducted the first NOA coronary stent system, with the angioplasty procedure of opening a clogged coronary artery with a balloon and inserting a stent. An Israeli professor discovered that Bti is lethal to mosquitoes and black flies, a discovery that has helped in preventing river blindness in eleven African countries, and malaria in the Yangtze region of China.

In computing, Israeli ingenuity is to be found everywhere— from Intel's Pentium MMX and Centrino technology in your computer to the micro-processors that control all the Mercedes-Benz onboard computer systems. Intel employs 5,000 people in Israel and generates exports of over $2 billion a year. Israel's Checkpoint Software Technologies is the global leader in virtual private networks (VPN) and firewall, whose clients include 97 per cent of the Fortune Top 100 companies, and Amdocs, the world leader in billing software, is one of the largest employers in Israel.

One story that sums up the essence of Israeli innovation is that of Mirabilis. Three unemployed computer geeks set up the company to develop an instant messaging service that would allow Internet users to know if friends were online and permit them to communicate with each other. They named their idea ICQ (I seek you). In the first year they acquired a subscriber base of one million users; in the second year they sold ICQ to AOL for $500 million; by the fifth year more than 200 million people were using ICQ! The three geeks decided to celebrate their success; one bought a small dishwasher, the second repaired his motorcycle, and the third bought himself some new T-shirts, an unusual spending spree for new tycoons!

The most important lessons for developing nations lie in Israeli agriculture. Netafim's drip irrigation system remains the key for farming in countries short of water and has been used all over the world to conserve scarce water resources and increase yields. But this is only the first of Israel's many innovations in agriculture. Israeli cows on an average have the world's highest yield in milk; Israeli hens are also champions, laying an average of 280 eggs per bird. Saline desert water has been used to breed fish, and Israeli innovations in fish breeding have resulted in two tons of fish per quarter-acre pond, ten times the normal level. Today Israel exports more than $3 billion worth of agricultural products and technologies annually. Some of the unique products exported defy the imagination— tiny spiders that prey on the mites that feed on strawberries are exported to California; billions of bumblebees, wasps, mites and bugs are exported yearly to Europe, the US and the Far East to pollinate or prey, increasing and improving crop yields. The leader in this strange technology is Bio-Bee Biological Systems which surely must be the only company in the world with its own mass-rearing facility for sterilized male fruit-flies, which are released to mate with females preventing a growth of the fly population!

25

Botswana's Diamonds: A Blessing, Not a Curse

Diamonds are a girl's best friend.
    —Marilyn Monroe in *Gentlemen Prefer Blondes*

Over 400 years ago, the English philosopher Sir Francis Bacon had warned that when a man marries for the second time, it is the triumph of hope over experience. Richard Burton married Elizabeth Taylor for the second time in Botswana; the marriage did not last. The marriage of Seretse Khama, the black African chief who studied law at Balliol College, Oxford, to Ruth Williams, a white insurance clerk in London, not only did last, but led to the creation of Botswana, Africa's miracle economy.

It was certainly 'a marriage of inconvenience' that disturbed everyone. Ruth's father was not happy; Seretse's uncle, the acting chief, was wild with rage; the vicar who was to marry them lost his nerve; the bishop refused to marry them without the consent of the British government; apartheid South Africa and Rhodesia would not accept the marriage; the British were opposed to it too. But Seretse, like Othello, 'loved not wisely, but too well', and in the face of all opposition married Ruth at Kensington Registry Office on 29 September 1948.

Seretse was forced to remain in England and not allowed to return home for six years. In 1956, after the tribe cabled the queen to ask for the return of their chief, he was allowed home as a private citizen after renouncing the chieftainship. He then founded the Bechuanaland Democratic Party, decisively won the 1965 elections and became the first president of Botswana on its independence. When Seretse took over from the British, Botswana was the second poorest country in the world, with a per capita income of $80; after achieving a growth rate of 9.2 per cent for the three decades between 1966 and 1996, Botswana reached a per capita income of $14,000 by 2008. Seretse remained president till his death in 1980. Ruth died twenty-two years after him; she did not live to see her son Ian become the fourth president of the country in 2009.

The most important factors behind the exceptional performance of Botswana have been political stability and the quality of leadership. In its half-century since independence, only one party, the BDP, and only four presidents, have ruled. The three presidents that followed Seretse have all prepared for the job by serving as vice-presidents.

Seretse Khama, the founding president, combined intelligence with integrity. When diamonds were discovered in Botswana a year after independence by DeBeers, Seretse built a relationship of trust with the mining giant. The joint venture company was called Debswana and initially Botswana had a 15 per cent share in the operation, but over five years this was negotiated up to a 50:50 partnership. Where most Third World dictators would have used the opportunity to become billionaires themselves, Seretse made sure that the fruits of renegotiation went solely to Botswana and its people. His handling of the DeBeers relationship was to be the single-most important contribution to the prosperity and growth of Botswana. Seretse established the rule of law in his country, and a government free of corruption. With the proud claim that Botswana has a zero tolerance of corruption, the country has maintained not just the cleanest government in Africa, but one of the cleanest in the world, surpassing many European countries. The wealth from diamonds was invested in education, health and infrastructure, but with expenditures prudently kept below income, savings and reserves accumulated. Debswana is the largest producer of gem-quality diamonds in the world with an annual production of thirty-three million carats; diamonds account for over a third of export earnings and half of the government's revenues.

Seretse's second-in-command and secretary general of the BDP was Ketumile Masire, a nationalist politician who played a key role in making his country a model of economic development. When Seretse became president in 1966, Masire became his vice-president, also holding portfolios of finance and development planning. In 1980, on the death of Seretse, he took over the office of president, which he held till his retirement in 1998, peacefully passing power to his successor.

As finance minister, vice-president and president for a cumulative period of more than thirty years, Masire is recognized as the main architect of Botswana's economy which showed one of the highest growth rates in the world and for three decades outpaced the Asian Tigers. He was the 1989 Laureate of the Africa Prize for Leadership for the Sustainable End of Hunger.

Botswana's third president was Festus Mogae, an economist with degrees from Oxford University and Sussex, who joined the civil services and worked his way up to the post of finance minister and vice-president. After six years as vice-president he succeeded President Masire on his retirement. He was honoured for his 'exemplary leadership' in making Botswana a 'model' of democracy and good government by the French president Nicholas Sarkozy who awarded him the Grand Cross of the Legion d'honneur. He received several other international awards including the prestigious Mo Ibrahim Prize of $5 million and $200,000 annually for life, the largest such award in the world. In his speech at the award ceremony, Festus stated, 'We have proved that natural resources in Africa can be a blessing and not a curse.' Festus Mogae served as president for ten years in which his priority was to tackle poverty, unemployment and AIDS. He was succeeded by Ian Khama, the son of Seretse Khama.

Diamonds do not guarantee prosperity, as Sierra Leone, a country destroyed by the combination of diamonds, conflict and corruption, has demonstrated. In Botswana good leaders secured the maximum income from the diamond mines, and spent the proceeds wisely on education, health and infrastructure, always taking care to keep expenditure below income so that national reserves accumulated. In the years when prices for diamonds fell, Botswana held back from selling and built up a stock pile which they later exchanged when prices recovered for shares in DeBeers; today Botswana owns 15 per cent of DeBeers.

Wise national policies and good economic management played a key part in Botswana's growth. Inflation was kept under control, and on the rare occasions when it threatened disruption, it was curtailed by tight control of money supply. Though corruption was kept firmly in check, cases did occur, as in the mismanagement of tenders for educational materials, and corruption in land transactions. But firm action was taken and in 1992 the vice-president and the minister of local government were forced to resign. Accountability provided a vivid contrast to other developing countries. Botswana became a favourite with the IMF and the World Bank.

Botswana also wisely managed and developed the traditional sectors of the economy. Many families owned cattle, and the national herd comprised 2–3 million heads. As early as 1967 the Botswana Meat Commission (BMC) was established to handle the slaughter and marketing of beef; the Commission was given a monopoly over exports, and expanded to include transport, cold storage and insurance. Special trade agreements with Europe ensured a market and favourable prices. But the beef industry also had its problems; world price fluctuation and foot-and-mouth disease had to be battled. In 2003 exports fell to $30 million, declining by 50 per cent from $63 million in 1998. The government moved to support the cattle farmers,

and BMC increased its purchase price by 40 per cent as
incentive for raising cattle. Plans were also considered to end
the BMC monopoly over exports. In 2005 the Botswana Cattle
Producers Association was formed to give farmers a stronger
voice in industry policy formulation.

Tourism was another well-managed sector. The government
policy of 'promoting tourism, protecting wildlife' resulted in
revenues of over $300 million by the year 2000. No visas were
required for visitors from the UK, the US or the European
Union (EU). The Kalahari Game Reserve spread over 52,000
sq. km is the second biggest in the world, and the Chobe
National Park has the largest herd of free-ranging elephants.
Thus the tourism industry became an important provider of
employment.

There was no manufacturing capacity in 1966 at the time of
independence. The Botswana Development Corporation
(BDC) was formed to promote industry. By 1995 there were
630 medium to large manufacturing companies, half owned by
locals, half by foreigners, producing textiles, beverages,
chemicals, metals, plastic and electrical equipment. The soda
ash industry grew in the south, and the auto industry, led by
Hyundai and the Swedish Motor Corp., started to produce
cars and trucks for the regional market, particularly South
Africa. Despite the small size of the Botswana domestic market,
investors were able to access the countries covered by the
Southern Africa Customs Union (SACU). Though industry
could not compete with the revenues from diamond mining, it
provided employment to a much greater number.

The emphasis on education developed skilled administrators,

and Botswana's bureaucrats were recognized as the best in Africa. The literacy rate of women, at 82 per cent, was even higher than that of men, and many women took jobs at the highest level—a Botswana woman is one of the governors at the World Bank; another has been appointed to the International Court of Justice at the Hague; the governor of the Bank of Botswana is a woman, as are two female high court judges.

Until the end of apartheid, South Africa posed a special problem. Botswana is a landlocked country and is heavily dependent on South Africa as a channel for imports and exports. Botswana is also a member of the Southern African Customs Union (SACU), the world's oldest customs union, which had been dominated by South Africa till its renegotiation in 2001. Botswana opposed South Africa's racist policies till the end of apartheid, and often suffered for this. In 1980 South Africa imposed sanctions on Botswana, disrupting beef exports by withdrawing refrigerated rail carriages and withholding oil deliveries; South Africa worked to destabilize the region and conducted military incursions into Botswana. But relations became cordial after Mandela took over.

Botswana has a high level of disparity which has increased poverty and unemployment, but the biggest problem is AIDS. The disease infects one in three adults, one of the highest levels in the world. This is not only lowering life expectancy, but also debilitating the workforce and destroying families. But Botswana's remarkable response to AIDS has won acclaim, with one of the most comprehensive and effective HIV treatment programmes in Africa, providing free, life-saving drugs to almost all of its citizens who need them.

Like all countries, Botswana had to deal with both opportunity and disaster. But her formula for success and for her amazing growth has been quite simple—committed leadership that does not tolerate corruption, prioritizes education and human skills, spends less than it earns, and uses its resources wisely.

26

Malaysia Does It 'My Way'

I did it my way.

—Frank Sinatra and
Mahathir Mohamad

Over fifty years following its independence Malaysia's economy grew at a rate of over 6 per cent annually, propelling the once poor nation into affluence. By 2011 Malaysia had a GDP of $193 billion and a GDP per capita of $7,030.

The Federation of Malaysia was formed in 1963 by joining Malaya with Singapore, Sarawak and Sabah. Within two years Singapore seceded and the truncated Malaysia battled communist insurgency, confrontation with Indonesia, and Philippine claims to Sabah. Despite this inauspicious beginning, Malaysia has grown into a successful, stable, industrialized nation. Two factors created the Malaysian success story: natural resources and Dr Mahathir Mohamad.

Malaysia was the largest producer of tin, rubber and palm oil in the world. With 59 per cent of the country forested, timber exports have become substantial. Malaysia is oil rich—ranking twenty-fourth in terms of world oil reserves and thirteenth for gas. With its strong resource base, Malaysia had a clear advantage over resource-starved Singapore, South Korea and Israel. But with its divided population of Malays (53 per cent), Chinese (26 per cent), indigenous (11 per cent) and Indians (7 per cent), Malaysia seemed ripe for conflict; and in 1969 riots between the Malay and the Chinese erupted causing death and destruction. But despite being divided by race, religion and language, Malaysia's leaders have succeeded in creating harmony that other resource-rich countries such as Angola, Sierra Leone and Nigeria have failed to achieve.

Dr Mahathir was not your everyday kind of politician. Born a commoner in a country whose traditional leaders were from the aristocracy, he was a straight-talking and passionate man, determined to make Malaysia a frontrunner in Asia. In 1969 the impatient young Mahathir fell out with Tunku Abdul Rahman, the powerful first prime minister, leading to his expulsion from the dominant ruling party, the UMNO. He wrote his book *The Malay Dilemma*, which, despite being banned, became an influential political treatise, and within a decade he was back, becoming prime minister in 1981. Mahathir ruled for twenty-two years, finally retiring in 2003 after transforming the country from a colonial backwater into one of the most developed and prosperous nations in Asia. Under

Mahathir Malaysia's GDP increased from $27 billion to $95 billion, exports increased from $13 billion to $108 billion, and poverty was eradicated; Mahathir brought together the Chinese, the Malay and the Indians and retired leaving a legacy of stability and affluence.

Mahathir was no diplomat. He had a way with words that didn't always win him friends. His critics argue that under his leadership growth was no more impressive than under his three predecessors, and point to South Korea which was poorer than Malaysia in 1981, but had raced ahead by 2003. Mahathir may have been Malaysia's greatest leader, but there is no denying that the leaders he followed were also great men who played a valuable part in building Malaysia. Tunku, the first prime minister, known as the 'Father of Independence', created the federation. The second prime minister, Tun Abdul Razak, launched the New Economic Policy (NEP) which became the platform of Malaysia's development, earning for him the title of 'Father of Development'. The third prime minister, Tun Hussein Onn, earned the title of 'Father of Unity' for his promotion of unity through policies rectifying economic imbalances. These policies, particularly the NEP and the removal of economic discrepancies between the Chinese and the Malays, provided the base for Mahathir's policies that followed.

The Malays and the Chinese shared the same land but lived apart, like water and oil sharing the same pond. When the Indian immigrants arrived, they formed the third separate community. The Chinese lived in the cities, the Malays in the countryside; the Chinese dominated business, the Malays farmed the land, and the Indians worked in the plantations or in the professions. In 1971 ethnic Malays and indigenous people, known as the 'Bumiputras' (sons of the soil), comprised almost 60 per cent of the population but held less than 3 per cent of the nation's wealth. But though the Bumiputras suffered poverty, they controlled political power through a platform based on two pillars—the Barisan Nasional (BN) and the NEP.

The BN has never lost an election, and has remained in power since it was formed. It is a super-party, or confederation of political parties that includes several smaller parties with a more focused appeal. The key components of the BN are the United Malays National Organization (UMNO), the Malaysian Chinese Association (MCA) and the Malaysian Indian Congress (MIC). Individuals join the participating parties rather than the BN, and joint candidates are fielded, ensuring electoral dominance. Power is shared by the ethnic groups, with the UMNO representing the Bumiputra in control. Fair sharing of power and opportunity is the key to unity and stability.

The NEP was the race-based affirmative action programme introduced after the race riots in 1969. Even before the introduction of the NEP, Article 153 of the constitution gave special rights to the Malays and differences on this issue led to Singapore's secession from the federation. The NEP targeted the increase of the Bumiputra share of the economy 'from 2.4 per cent to 30 per cent'; this included education and employment quotas, contracts, and reserved shares in corporate equities. The NEP continued for two decades and formally ended in 1990, but its philosophy and policies continued.

The NEP is important but controversial. It has provided a model to communities in other countries who demand a greater share—the South African post-apartheid BEE (Black Economic Empowerment) programme was based on the NEP. The debate continues as to whether Malaysia's economic growth was as a result of—or in spite of—the NEP policies. Mahathir and the UMNO leadership point to the numbers, and there is no denying that these are impressive and show considerable economic growth; they also argue that the precondition to this growth was the political stability that resulted from these policies. They expound 'the expanding pie theory'—that the Bumiputra share of the economic pie would increase without reducing the size of the non-Bumiputra slices of the pie. Their critics maintain that growth was due to external factors and not the NEP which led to cronyism, corruption and an attitude of entitlement that held Malaysia back as Singapore, South Korea, Hong Kong and Taiwan raced ahead. They argue that a system that condemns non-Malays to being second-class citizens has resulted in a brain drain at a great loss to the nation. The debate is merely academic; realpolitik has its own imperatives. As Mahathir had recognized, the UMNO and the Malay majority was the only road to power. If he did not satisfy Malay aspirations, there was no part he could play in building Malaysia.

On becoming prime minister in 1981 Mahathir engaged in three battles to consolidate his power, the first to cut the power of the sultans, the second to defeat his rivals in the UMNO, and the third to tame the judiciary.

The nine sultans of the states that form the federation elect the Agung, or king, through a rotation process. The royals also exercised important constitutional power at the federal level; royal consent was required for legislation, and the Agung had a degree of discretionary power in the appointment of the prime minister and the declaration of a state of emergency. The problem came to a head in 1983 with the election of the new Agung; both candidates were considered too independent-minded. The Sultan of Johor had been an impetuous young man who had been removed as heir by his father and only reinstated when his father was dying twenty years later. He was now rumoured to threaten that when he was king he would declare a state of emergency and throw out all the politicians with the aid of the army.

Mahathir decided to move first and pre-empt possible problems; he moved the Constitution Amendment Bill of 1983 to curtail the powers of the rulers. The Agung withheld consent and the crisis led to open confrontation between the government and the rulers. Mahathir held a series of mass rallies in which he criticized the extravagant lifestyles and the unbecoming personal conduct of the rulers. Opinion was divided; some supported the rulers, some Mahathir. Finally a compromise offered by Mahathir was accepted and the amendment passed. Mahathir celebrated with a mass rally in which he stated, 'The feudal system is over.'

The army chief resigned and an army shake-up saw 500 other dismissals, strengthening rumours of possible conspiracies. Ten years later, following an attack on a school hockey coach by the Sultan of Johor, a further amendment was passed that curbed the personal immunity of the rulers and also their power to grant royal pardons.

The economic downturn in 1985 led to rising discontent even within the ruling party. Two important UMNO leaders—Musa, the former deputy prime minister, and Razaleigh, the former finance minister—turned against Mahathir and split the party into two factions. Mahathir was criticized for his grandiose projects and the corruption of his system of crony capitalism. As the two groups readied for the party elections they were labelled 'Team A' and 'Team B'. Both were evenly matched and several prominent party leaders including Abdullah Ahmad Badawi, one of the three party vice-presidents, joined Team B. The vacuum created by dissenting leaders threw up new faces, the most prominent being Anwar Ibrahim. Mahathir pressurized his opponents with tax cases and bank loan withdrawals; he also held UMNO assets and the advantage of dispensing patronage. Mahathir was re-elected president, scoring 761 votes against Razaleigh's 718; he also kept control of the supreme council, and won two of the three vice-presidency seats, losing the third to Badawi.

Mahathir had won the elections, but the battle was not over. Team B cried foul and initiated litigation to contest the election on grounds of irregularities; the court declared the UMNO an illegal organization and froze the substantial party assets. Both groups registered new parties; Mahathir secured the name 'UMNO Baru', and Team B became 'Semangat 46'. Mahathir's UMNO defeated Semangat in the 1990 and 1995 elections and in 1996 Mahathir persuaded Razaleigh and his party members to come back into the fold of the UMNO, restoring unity and re-establishing UMNO's dominant position in the politics of Malaysia. In a twist of irony, Mahathir later destroyed Anwar

Ibrahim, his staunchest supporter in this struggle, who was imprisoned on charges of sodomy and abuse of power, and on his retirement Mahathir passed on power to Badawi, a Team B member, who succeeded him as prime minister.

One casualty of the UMNO war was the judiciary. A legacy of British colonialism, the judiciary was independent and respected. Within a month of their decision declaring UMNO illegal, a new legislation was passed to cut down the powers of the judges. This was followed by the suspension of the 'Lord President', the senior judge, for 'gross misbehavior and misconduct', and a tribunal headed by a school friend of Mahathir was constituted to adjudicate. The Supreme Court passed a restraining order to stop the tribunal, resulting in the suspension of five Supreme Court judges for 'gross misbehaviour'. The retired Lord President of the Federal Court, Suffian Hashim, commented that 'Salleh was dismissed simply because he was a man of absolute integrity, whereas the prime minister only wants judges in whom he has confidence.' From then on, the judiciary lost its independence and became subservient to the executive. Ten years later, the role of the judiciary in the Anwar Ibrahim trial for sodomy became a scandal, and even a senior government official described them as a 'bunch of bloody idiots' explaining, 'Of course we want them to favour us, but not to the point where it's so embarrassing'!

Even as democracy grew weaker under Mahathir, the economy grew stronger. In the first phase, lasting from 1981 to 1985, state intervention promoted heavy industrialization and the 'Look East' policy took inspiration from Japan and South

Korea. When falling prices of Malaysia's commodity exports put a strain on the economy, Razaleigh, the finance minister, countered with increased public spending. In 1984, as recession threatened, Razaleigh was replaced by Daim Zainudin, a close friend of Mahathir, who reversed direction with expenditure cuts, opening of the economy and privatization. Under Daim the economy grew, as did his personal wealth. He was replaced by Anwar, on his resignation in 1991, and he in turn replaced Anwar when he was sacked in 1998. The period from the 1985 recession till the 1997 Asian financial crisis saw a high growth rate averaging 8 per cent as Malaysia moved to affluence. This was Malaysia's golden decade.

Excellent physical infrastructure and a business-friendly environment attracted foreign investment. A rising yen combined with a devalued ringgit persuaded industry to relocate to Malaysia, where labour was cheap. Industrial exports grew, particularly in electronics and ICT products; Malaysia emerged as one of the world's largest exporters of semiconductors. The inflow of FDI was supported by a high internal savings rate. Investment in education and technology improved skills and the quality of human resources—30 per cent of university students were sent overseas for advanced education. The colonial legacy of the rule of law and good administration by an efficient civil service inspired confidence, and sound macroeconomic policies protected the economy against inflation, excessive debts or foreign exchange crises. Good management made the most of the strong natural resource wealth. Through it all, the NEP ensured political stability.

In 1997 the tornado of the financial crisis hit Malaysia. The 8 per cent growth rate was replaced by a massive contraction of the economy to minus 8 per cent. The ringgit lost a third of its value; the stock market more than half. The Western financial establishment blamed 'Mahathir's crony capitalism'. Mahathir, in turn, blamed George Soros and the Wall Street speculators. Though Malaysia's debt levels were reasonably low, large amounts of portfolio investments had been attracted to the booming Kuala Lumpur stock market. This hot money ran for the exits creating a currency crisis. Unlike the other affected countries that turned to the IMF for help, Mahathir's approach was, 'I don't like your policies, and I don't want your money.' Like Frank Sinatra, he preferred to do it 'My way'. Relying on currency controls rather than the IMF formulas of higher interest rates and tight money supply, he followed China's policies rather than those of Washington's. Malaysia recovered faster than its neighbours and by 1999 was again recording robust growth.

When Mahathir took on the IMF and Wall Street, he was opposed by his finance minister, Anwar Ibrahim. At this time of crisis, Mahathir was in no mood to tolerate opposition or conspiracy. Anwar was brought down with charges of sodomy and abuse of power, and replaced by the proven and reliable Daim Zainuddin, back in his old job. Mahathir defied orthodoxy that advocated IMF conditionalities. Instead, he pushed public spending and large budget deficits to stimulate the economy. It seemed to work.

Mahathir loved big projects. His North–South Highway, Multimedia Super Corridor, Port of Tanjung Pelepas, the massive Kuala Lumpur International Airport and the Petronas Towers, once the world's tallest building, changed the face of Malaysia. Many fortunes were made by those close to the UMNO as the economy surged. By 2007 there were 48,000 dollar millionaires in Malaysia—over twice as many as China. New Bumiputra billionaires included 'proxies' who fronted for the UMNO party interests. But despite decades of NEP policy, the top ten, with a combined wealth of $30 billion, were still dominated by the Chinese. The two richest—Robert Kuok, a Chinese tycoon, and Ananda Krishnan, an Indian— were together worth close to $20 billion. Ananda's son chose to live in a forest as a Buddhist monk rather than enjoy his father's fortune!

Mahathir himself was not seduced by the desire for personal wealth and was proud of his relative poverty on retirement, when compared with other presidents in the region, or even with some of his own deputies. He did not want to start a dynasty and advised his sons, 'Choose one or the other, business or politics.' His sons chose business. Mirzan went into transport, Mokhzani into health care and Mukhriz into fibre-optics and tourism. It is generally accepted that though their strong connections certainly helped, their success was the result of hard work and competence and not the result of graft, gifts or special monopoly licences.

Though many of Mahathir's initiatives succeeded, some failed. Billions were lost in Perjawa Steel and in the collapse of the Bumiputra Malaysian Finance in Hong Kong. The state also suffered huge losses speculating in tin and currency. Heavy state subsidies to various sectors of the economy also required and consumed substantial funds. All this, successes and failures alike, was made possible by the oil and gas giant Petroliam Nasional Berhad or Petronas.

Few outside Malaysia have heard of Hassan Marican, the unsung hero of the Malaysian boom, who transformed Petronas from a Malaysian company to a global success story. By 2007 Petronas was the eighth most profitable company in the world, outperforming well-known giants such as Microsoft, Toyota and Berkshire Hathaway. Even today in 2012, despite Malaysia's declining oil reserves, Petronas with profits of $21.9 billion beats world giants such as Ford Motor, Bank of China, J.P. Morgan Chase, AIG, HSBC, Walmart, GE, Samsung, Citigroup, Nestlé, and the famed Berkshire Hathaway, and contributes almost half the federal government revenue of Malaysia. Since its inception in 1974 Petronas has contributed over half a trillion ringgits to the government.

Marican is an accountant who after joining Petronas imposed strict financial discipline, leading by example and setting high standards of teamwork, integrity and professionalism. Petronas' performance stands in stark contrast to Pertamina, Indonesia's state oil company—in 2002 Pertamina made a profit of $697 million on a turnover of $23.7 billion, whereas Petronas with a lower turnover of $21.4 billion made a profit of $4 billion. Over the years, Petronas has expanded its activities to exploration and liquidification of gas, together with downstream projects in refining, marketing, petrochemicals and shipping; it has expanded to thirty-five countries including Iran, Sudan, South Africa and China and today, a substantial part of its revenues come from non-traditional activity. In 2010,

Marican was retired. Mahathir expressed concern, 'From what I see is that some of the top politicians have been making a mess of our economy. If you want them to make a mess of Petronas, then I think they should become the top executive or chairman of Petronas.'

Sarawak has been an important area for oil and gas. Situated in Borneo adjacent to Brunei, it covers a land mass equal to almost 40 per cent of Malaysia, an area as large as Bangladesh, but with a population of less than 2.5 million. Sarawak was home to the White Rajas, a strange dynasty founded by an Englishman, James Brooke, that lasted a hundred years while he and successors from his family ruled. The dynasty ended when the Japanese invaded Sarawak in the Second World War, and the family ceded sovereignty to the British Crown. Today's 'Rajah' is Taib Mahmud, Sarawak's strongman, who has held power for twenty-six years after removing his uncle. There are allegations that Taib has built a large fortune through corruption.

In 2003 Mahathir retired, passing power to Abdullah Badawi. In the 2004 general elections, Badawi secured a landslide victory which gave him the confidence to assert his independence from his former leader. He declared an end to the economic legacy and grandiose projects of his predecessor, and arrested several Mahathir-era cronies for corruption. But by his second term, his popularity had waned, as many in his own party joined the opposition in calling him to resign. Rumours were voiced of abuse of power involving the business activities of his brother and his son, including a scandal involving one of his son's companies producing nuclear components for Libya. Mahathir, dramatic as ever, announced he was quitting the party having lost confidence in Badawi, and said he would only rejoin once Badawi stepped down; he expressed regret in picking Badawi as his successor.

Badawi was succeeded by his deputy Najib Razak. Najib was the son of the country's second prime minister and the nephew of the third; educated in England he had an economics degree from Nottingham University. But Najib came with the baggage of scandal from his time as defence minister, when Malaysia had spent $1.2 billion on the purchase of submarines from the French company Armaris, a subsidiary of DCN that was also involved in the submarine kickbacks scandal in Pakistan. Najib's close friend, Razak Baginda, was paid commissions worth $150 million through a company formed in the name of his wife, it was claimed. The matter was further complicated by the fact that the interpreter in the negotiations, a beautiful Mongolian model named Altantuya, was reputed to be Baginda's lover. When jilted, Altantuya tried to blackmail Baginda for a sum of $500,000. She was shot dead in the jungle outside Kuala Lumpur and then her body was blown up to prevent identification. The two men convicted for the murder were former bodyguards of Najib from his days as defence minister.

Najib's ascendancy to the prime ministership came at a bad time. The ruling party was weakened by the results of the 2008 general elections, and the world financial crisis dealt him a second blow, killing the growth of Malaysia's economy. Exports fell, as did the prices of Malaysia's export commodities; FDI was halved. But Najib has moved firmly to restore growth.

Undeterred by growing budget deficits, his government implemented a large stimulus package to prime the economy and reduce unemployment. The 30 per cent requirement for Bumiputra equity was removed. The government also cut subsidies on fuel and sugar, and raised the price of electricity and petrol. Subsidies were placing a heavy burden on the budget, and this was highlighted in a strong statement by Idris Jala, the head of the government's Performance and Management Delivery Service: 'Malaysia will go bust in nine years if it does not slash subsidies and cut government expenditure to curb spiralling debt.' Anwar opposed the subsidy cuts, saying they would hurt low-income groups and urged instead that cutting waste and leakage would be more effective in reducing the 7 per cent budget deficit. Najib responded that even after the cuts, prices for fuel and sugar in Malaysia would still be the lowest in the region due to the subsidies of $2.44 billion that remained. The issue of subsidies is likely to play a key part in the 2013 elections in which a short-term pandering to the vote will carry greater weight than long-term abstract economic interests. By 2012 the economy had moved out of recession with a growth rate of close to 5 per cent.

Under twenty-two years of Mahathir's rule the economy has taken off and there is no going back. The infrastructure is in place, the education levels are high, the attitude of government is pro-business, and the resource base is strong. Mahathir's legacy has secured Malaysia's place among nations that have succeeded.

Yes, Mahathir was helped by Malaysia's strong resource base, but he was also handicapped by ethnic division waiting to explode, and by the lack of education of a majority of Malays. His formula for success used the same tools as other successful economies—stability, exports, attracting foreign investment, education, industrialization, bold economic policies focused on stimulating growth, and most important of all, sincere, capable and committed leadership.

27

India: A Story of Accidents

The forces in a capitalist society, if left unchecked, tend to make the rich richer and the poor poorer.

—Jawaharlal Nehru

A nation is empowered by its people. A people are empowered by their capabilities. People's capabilities are created by investments in their education.

—Manmohan Singh

The year 2004 marked Sonia Gandhi's triumph as she installed Manmohan Singh as the new prime minister. In 2004 India's growth rate hit 8.3 per cent and the participants in the new economy celebrated. It was also the year that Akku Yadav, a gangster, murderer and rapist, was hacked to death by two

hundred poor Dalit women in the Nagpur district court. For
fifteen years Akku had terrorized the slum residents of
Kasturba Nagar dominating them by rape and murder. He had
tortured one woman, Asho Bhagat, in front of her daughter;
after cutting off her breasts he killed her slicing her body into
pieces in the street. Complaints to the police were met with
ridicule; the police were in his pocket. On 6 August the slum
dwellers rose up and tore down Akku's house. The police took
him in for protective custody and a date was fixed in court for
his bail hearing. On 13 August two hundred women whom he
had victimized, robbed and raped attended the hearing. Akku,
unrepentant, taunted them and hell broke loose as the women
attacked him with their kitchen knives. He was stabbed and
hacked to death; as revenge for his cutting off Asho's breasts
they hacked off his penis with a vegetable knife. Retired
Mumbai High Court judge Bhau Vahane congratulated the
women: 'In the circumstances they underwent, they were left
with no alternative but to finish Akku. The women repeatedly
pleaded with the police for their security but the police failed
to protect them.'

There are two Indias. One is the success story of economic
reforms, IT and outsourcing, of Manmohan Singh and Sonia
Gandhi, the Ambanis and Azim Premji. The other is the
tragedy of the hundreds of millions of poverty-stricken Indians
who live without opportunity, without justice and without
hope as they have done for centuries.

India is today an economic success story. After a long and
slow start between 1947 and 1991, India changed track and
moved to high growth after the 1991 liberalization. The early

socialist policies of the Nehru and Indira governments were not as fruitful as the communist economies under Stalin and Mao in Russia and China. The economy was stifled under the Licence Raj which imposed regulation, protectionism, public ownership and isolation under a corrupt bureaucracy. Foreign capital was suspect and not welcome. Instead of exports India pursued import substitution, blind to the reality that poor domestic markets could not compete with rich international markets in generating wealth. India substituted state planning for enterprise, unaware that people create wealth, not governments. India had yet to learn that good economic policies promote growth by simply rewarding the hard work and enterprise of individuals. The result was chronic foreign exchange shortages and a bankrupt government unable to provide services and infrastructure, or meet its financial obligations to its international creditors.

The first forty years were dominated by Nehru and his daughter Indira. The economy grew at 4 per cent under Nehru, up from the 1 per cent growth rate during British rule. Indira however was a disaster; her policies resulted in India's worst period of economic stagnation. The situation improved under her son Rajiv, who took the first steps in opening up the economy, though within a few years fiscal and current account deficits led India to the brink of bankruptcy. In 1991, Prime Minister Narasimha Rao brought in Manmohan Singh, a non-political economist, as finance minister of India. Singh moved confidently to change the Indian economy through his reform programme, creating the success story of modern India, a trend that continued under the Atal Behari Vajpayee government that followed. When Sonia won the elections in 2004, she elevated Manmohan Singh to the office of prime minister.

The reforms of 1991 triggered twenty years of successful growth. In 1991 India sold gold to boost its depleted foreign exchange reserves. In 2009 India flush with reserves bought back 200 tonnes from the IMF. The numbers show the extent of the economic turnaround over the fifteen years between 1991 and 2007: annual inflow of FDI grew from $100 million to $19.5 billion; portfolio investment from $6 million to $7 billion; remittances from Indian overseas workers grew from $2 billion to $28 billion; trade as a proportion of GDP grew from 16 per cent to 49 per cent. In 1991 India had a total of 5.1 million telephones; in 2006 India added 5.2 million telephones a month! By 2009 an estimated 300 million destitute Indians had escaped extreme poverty.

The reforms moved Indian economic policy from socialism to capitalism. State sector monopolies such as telecom and electric power generation were opened to the private sector; privatization replaced nationalization. The reforms ended the policies of isolation; foreign capital was welcomed and Coca-Cola, which had exited India in 1977 when the Foreign Exchange Regulation Act (FERA) demanded disclosure of their secret formula and a dilution of the US stake, returned. The solution to India's economic stagnation that had defied the country's leaders for almost half a century proved unexpectedly simple—private sector capitalism and globalization based on exports and foreign capital. It took the confidence of Manmohan Singh to unlock the riddle.

The Nehru–Gandhi dynasty has dominated Indian politics

since independence. After Nehru, Indira, Rajiv and Sonia, the family is preparing for the fifth chapter of its rule as Rahul, Nehru's great grandson, moves towards the centrestage. But surprisingly it is Sonia, the Italian-born wife of Rajiv, who has made the greatest contribution to the Indian economy. Though she was initially reluctant to enter the political arena after the assassinations of her mother-in-law and her husband, she finally stepped forward to revive the fortunes of the Congress party and quickly grew from apprentice to maestro. She won her first two battles, taking control of the party and beating Vajpayee in the elections; but then her opponents and rivals raised a third obstacle, her Italian origin, arguing that it was unseemly for India to choose a 'foreigner' as prime minister over a billion Indians. Sonia confounded her critics by announcing that she was not a candidate for prime ministership, and then adroitly manoeuvred to install her preferred candidate Manmohan Singh, an economist with no political base.

Later, when faced with the office for profit controversy over her simultaneous positions as MP and chairman of the National Advisory Council, she again showed her confidence and lack of personal ambition when she resigned from both positions, saying, 'I have done this because I think it is the right thing to do.' Her resignation despite her lack of guilt or wrongdoing further elevated her stature. Sonia has given Manmohan Singh the authority to build the economy, but it has always been politics under control. Coalitions must be protected and public sentiment acknowledged. She learnt an important lesson from the fall of the Vajpayee government despite its successful economic performance. She continued the family tradition of bowing to the popular will, so aptly put by Indira Gandhi: 'There exists no politician in India daring enough to attempt to explain to the masses that cows can be eaten.'

In 2006 when General Musharraf and Manmohan Singh met, it was a strange union. The Pakistani president had been born in India and the Indian prime minister in Pakistan. Manmohan Singh's father owned a dried-fruit shop near Islamabad. His dedication to his studies led him through a series of scholarships and awards to a doctorate at Cambridge University. Singh's economic expertise is universally acclaimed. Modest, humble, incorruptible and without political ambition, he admitted, 'I am a politician by accident.' On his journey to the prime ministership he never won an election to the Lok Sabha, the lower house of Parliament. The Sonia–Singh partnership has built up a strong and capable economic team that includes Montek Singh Ahluwalia, a Rhodes scholar who was also president of the Oxford Union and is currently the vice-chairman of the Planning Commission, and P. Chidambaram, a lawyer with an MBA from the Harvard Business School.

The quality of leadership has been the most important factor in India's economic surge. India has inspired exceptional people to exceptional achievements, even in the harsh world of business. The two most famous business houses in India are Tata and Ambani, both located in Mumbai, India's business capital, famous for its stock market and film industry. Despite controlling empires of comparable size, they are very different. Tatas are old business aristocracy; Ambanis are the new rich.

Tatas have given most of their wealth to the Tata charitable trusts; Mukesh Ambani takes pride in being the richest individual in India, and aspires to top the international *Forbes* list of billionaires. Ratan Tata, the chairman of the Tata group, lives in a simple bachelor flat in Mumbai; Mukesh Ambani's house 'Antilla' is the most expensive private home in the world, rumoured to have cost well over a billion dollars with 37,000 square meters of built-up area and rising to a height of 173 m. Reputed to be bigger than the palace of Versailles and serviced by a staff of six hundred servants, it has been described as 'obscenely lavish' and stands in naked contradiction to Manmohan Singh's advice to 'eschew conspicuous consumption'. It stands in Mumbai, the city of slums.

The Tata group employs 350,000 people in eighty countries and its companies cover steel, hotels, automobiles, power generation, telecom, IT and numerous other businesses. It has been headed by five chairmen in 142 years. The chairman, Ratan Tata, who is due to retire in December 2012, is a shy loner who does not drink or smoke, whose loves include dogs, books and speed. His predecessor, J.R.D. Tata, was the great man of Indian industry; he took the Tata group from Rs 620 million in 1938 to Rs 100 billion in 1991. A man of the highest ethical standards, he never allowed the group he controlled to indulge in bribery or underhand behaviour, and stated, 'I never had any interest in making money. None of my decisions were influenced by whether it would bring me money or wealth.' When J.R.D. died, the Indian parliament adjourned in his memory as a sign of respect. The Tata group has expanded its traditional manufacturing base in India, and has developed the

Nano, the world's cheapest car, but it has also made bold strides into the new economy with Tata Consultancy Services, India's leading IT company, and also into the exploding telecom sector. In 2008 Tata expanded beyond Internet and mobile telecom by acquiring VSNL, the government submarine cable company; Tata now owns 232,000 km of submarine cable making it a leading global provider linking 200 countries. Over the last few years, overseas acquisitions such as Corus Steel and Jaguar and Range Rover automobiles have given the group a more visible international profile. The Tata group of companies have flourished under Ratan's chairmanship and between 1991 and 2010 have shown growth in the number of employees from 119,209 to 320,258; growth in revenues from Rs 30,920 to Rs 293,562 crore ($65 billion); growth in profits from Rs 2,627 to Rs 10,867 crore ($2.4 billion); and growth in market capitalization from Rs 26,172 to Rs 367,145 crore ($81 billion).

Dhirubhai Ambani, the founder of the Reliance group of companies, was born the son of a village school teacher, and as a young boy earned his first money selling potato fries at a village fair. Moving on to Aden in Yemen, he started as a petrol pump attendant, and returned to India in 1957 with Rs 500 in his pocket. He started his business in Mumbai with a capital of $350, and lived with his family in a small one-bedroom apartment. He took his company public in 1977. In the twenty-five years till his death in 2002, his Reliance group's turnover and profit multiplied 1,000 times. In 2010 the group turnover stood at $45 billion and profit at $3.6 billion, with activities covering oil and gas, petrochemicals, retail, polymers, polyesters, chemicals, textiles and telecommunications. Today, the Ambanis are the second richest family in the world, second only to the Waltons of Wal-Mart.

Dhirubhai was a risk-taker with the ability to take, even create opportunity. In the difficult days of Licence Raj, he was able to manipulate and control the politicians and bureaucrats who were essential to getting things done. He was the first Indian businessman to recognize the unlimited growth opportunity in tapping the equity market, and started the 'equity cult'. More than 58,000 investors subscribed to the Reliance IPO in 1977, and the number grew to over three million shareholders. One in every four investors in the Indian stock market is a Reliance shareholder, making it one of the world's most widely held stocks. To accommodate the multitude of shareholders, annual meetings were held in sports stadiums. Despite the scandals and controversies that surrounded his business activities, Dhirubhai made good his claim that he had always made money for his shareholders. The importance of the Reliance group has been highlighted by an Indian journalist who wrote in 2002, 'The Reliance group accounts for 3 per cent of India's GDP, 5 per cent of its exports, 10 per cent of the government's indirect tax revenues, 15 per cent of the weight of the sensitive index of the Bombay Stock Exchange and 30 per cent of the total profits of all the private companies in the country put together.'

Information Technology (IT) in India, along with exports of Chinese manufactures, has been one of the two most important phenomena in shaping the twenty-first century world economy. If Ratan Tata is an 'accidental' tycoon and Manmohan Singh an 'accidental politician', the greatest of India's 'accidents' is the Indian IT industry, born of a series of coincidences with unintended consequences. Nehru has been criticized for his unproductive economic policies which led to the Licence Raj and the 'Hindu rate of growth', but two of his policies were to prove visionary and key to future success. Nehru's emphasis on the importance of technical education led to the creation of the Indian Institutes of Technology (IIT) modelled on America's MIT. He also believed in the importance of the English language to India, and spread its usage particularly in the institutions of higher learning. These policies resulted in a profusion of capable, English-speaking engineers, 200,000 of whom found their way to Silicon Valley in the 1970s and 1980s. One in four graduates of the IITs moved to America; a third of the engineers in Silicon Valley are Indians, 40 per cent of start-ups in the US are by Indian entrepreneurs and one in every fourteen firms has an Indian chief executive. These expatriates play a crucial role in the promotion of the Indian IT industry by providing know-how, capital and networking.

The dot-com bubble led to massive overinvestment in long-distance communications. The bubble burst leaving a world criss-crossed by fibre-optic cables but no users; cost of communication crashed, with prices of long-distance phone calls falling to 5 per cent of their former levels, and data became practically free. As the end of the millenium approached, computer users the world over panicked fearing that all computers would crash at the dawn of the new year. America and Europe searched desperately for cheap manpower to handle the simple but massive volume of work needed to protect their data. India was the only source of supply, and the Indian IT industry took off. Software, outsourcing and call centres boomed. The economy moved from traditional manufacturing to services. Tata Consultancy Services (TCS), Infosys, Wipro and Bharti Airtel replaced older manufacturing companies on the list of India's ten biggest companies.

Azim Premji of Wipro became, after Ambani, India's second richest man with a personal wealth of $17 billion. Wipro stands for 'Western India Pine Refined Oil', the name of the company during its early years when it was a producer of cooking oils and fats. On taking over the business from his father, Azim moved the company into IT, turning the $2 million company into one of the world's most important IT companies with 112,925 employees, revenues of $6 billion and billion-dollar profits. *Business Week* magazine has recognized Premji as one of the 'world's greatest entrepreneurs' responsible for Wipro emerging as one of the world's fastest growing companies. India's second richest man, in stark contrast to the richest, has a modest lifestyle, driving a Toyota Corolla car, flying economy class, and living in company guest houses rather than luxury hotels.

The Indian IT industry includes call centres, back-office operations, loan enquiries, credit card work, bank transactions, invoicing, collections, accounting, customer care, human resource and payment services, medical transcription, insurance claims and general bulk processing. By 2009 the IT industry was employing 2.3 million people with revenues of $50 billion from outsourcing. The success of the industry has produced a political backlash in the US. India is blamed for job losses in

America, and the state of Ohio has even banned off-shoring. One example of the speed of growth is the outsourcing of US tax returns to Indian companies. In 2003, 25,000 US tax returns were prepared in India; this grew to 100,000 in 2004 and 400,000 in 2005—a growth of 1,600 per cent in three years. The Indian advantage of language, education and cost when combined with fast and cheap communication defied competition. Today, more than a quarter of Fortune 500 companies have back-up operations in India; the list includes GE, Citibank, British Airways, American Express, HSBC, IBM and AT&T. India has emerged as the back office to the world and as skills grow, it is steadily moving up the value chain.

Weak infrastructure, byzantine red tape and scarcity of bank finance were impediments to the growth of industry in India. But the new IT sector lived in a rarified world which did not need roads, ports or the massive power requirements of industry; its interaction with the government bureaucracy was minimal; it was not dependent on bank finance. By 2005, the top four software companies in India generated $6 billion in revenues, 170,000 jobs and $40 billion investor wealth without borrowing a single cent or rupee from the banking system. The industry existed outside the system, so its growth was unrestricted by the deficiencies of the Indian economy.

The economic reforms opened up telecom and electricity, traditional government monopolies, to the private sector. The telecom reforms succeeded, the electricity reforms failed. By 2006 India had a total installed generation capacity of 128,000 MW; in 2006 alone China created additional capacity of more than 100,000 MW. By 2010 India's per capita electric consumption was hardly a third of China's, and a mere 2 per cent of Qatar's, who topped the world electricity consumption tables. Two-thirds of India's power generation was thermal, just under a third hydro; of the thermal 80 per cent was coal and less than 2 per cent was from oil, the most expensive thermal fuel. Under the prevailing system, transmission and distribution were state subjects. After 1975 the Central government was allowed to generate electricity, and the 1991 reforms allowed the private sector to enter. Independent private power producers were required to sign long-term Power Purchase Agreements (PPAs) with the State Electricity Boards (SEBs) for the take-off of their production. The SEBs were financially bankrupt, so the PPAs signed by them were not suitable collaterals for bank lending. Foreign investors were scared off by the Enron fiasco over the massive private power generation project at Dabhol. SEB bankruptcy was a result of inefficiency and theft. They were overstaffed with low plant load factor and riddled with corruption. 'Line losses', which included transmission losses and theft, or non-payment of bills, were as high as 40 per cent of the total electric generation. To keep their voters happy, politicians kept electricity prices low, or even free—after the 2004 elections Andhra Pradesh, Maharashtra, Punjab and Tamil Nadu gave free electricity to farmers.

Although India's economy is booming, it has not solved the problems of the 60 per cent of the workforce engaged in agriculture, which remains mired in poverty due to low productivity, illiteracy and lack of bank credit. The Green

Revolution in the 1960s and 1970s ended famine in India, and led to self-sufficiency in cereals. India is the largest producer of milk and fruit in the world and the second largest producer of wheat, rice, sugar and cotton, but yields per acre are still only half that of high-yield countries. Illiteracy and the sad state of the public education system, with its decrepit schools and absentee teachers, hold back improvement in farming techniques. The antiquated and ineffective land records, a holdover from the past, prevents land use as collateral for bank credit, and has led to the strong comment from Azim Premji: 'We must overhaul our land laws. Some 90 per cent of land in India is subject to legal disputes over ownership.'

As rich India grows richer, poor India stands still. But the new confidence and the change in attitude of leaders both in government and in the private sector is likely to bring solutions to those parts of the economy that still lag behind, giving a second boost to future growth.

28

Pakistan: Failed or Failing?

Democracy is the best revenge.

—Asif Ali Zardari

The top ten failed states in the Failed States Index of 2010 include seven disastrous African nations and two countries devastated by war. These nine unhappy countries are Somalia, Zimbabwe, Sudan, Chad, the Democratic Republic of the Congo, Iraq, Afghanistan, the Central African Republic and Guinea. The last country that completes the list is Pakistan. In 2005 Pakistan was praised as Asia's second fastest growing economy. In just five years Pakistan had moved from success story to failed state.

Pakistan is a conflict-ridden nation that has earned the title of 'the most dangerous country in the world'. According to

Transparency International corruption in Pakistan reached an all-time high in 2010. Economic collapse necessitated an IMF bailout programme. Two major disasters have devastated the nation: the earthquake in 2005 in which 80,000 people were killed, and the floods in 2010 which hit fourteen million people. The population grows too fast, and poverty grows even faster. Despite a bankrupt economy, a dysfunctional political system, a breakdown of law, order and security and devastating floods, its politicians boast of Pakistan's democracy.

Has democracy been successful in Pakistan? Economic growth under Pakistan's political regimes has been lower than under its military rulers:

- The 1960s under Field Marshal Ayub Khan saw a growth rate of 6.8 per cent.
- The 1970s under Zulfiqar Ali Bhutto saw a growth rate of 4.5 per cent.
- The 1980s under General Zia saw a growth rate of 6.5 per cent.
- The 1990s under Benazir and Nawaz saw a growth rate of 4.8 per cent.
- The years 2000–07 under General Musharraf saw a growth rate of 7.5 per cent.

Without a doubt, special international factors have contributed to the economic ups and downs that Pakistan has experienced. The Pak-American partnership in the Afghan War against the USSR resulted in important US financial support to General Zia's government; the American sanctions after Nawaz Sharif's nuclear test blast brought the economy to its knees, resulting in the freezing of foreign currency accounts; General Musharraf's economy was boosted by American support after 9/11, when he responded positively to the US ultimatum, 'You are either with us or against us' and the American threat to bomb Pakistan 'back to the stone age'. But despite better economic performance, the generals have failed in acquiring long-term legitimacy. Promising clean government and concern for the nation, they have enjoyed initial honeymoon periods followed by subsequent rejection. The last president, General Musharraf, made a series of mistakes which once again sullied the legitimacy of military rule. Starting with the Provisional Constitutional Order (PCO) and his dismissal and house arrest of a hundred judges who refused to take the oath and swear allegiance, and ending with his National Reconciliation Ordinance (NRO), which gave amnesty and rehabilitation to 8,041 beneficiaries guilty of corruption, including the incoming president and prime minister, he seemed blind to the sensitivities of the Pakistani people as he moved from his referendum to his re-election; the final straw was his sacking of Chief Justice Iftikhar Chaudhry, and when the Supreme Court restored him to the bench, he declared an 'Emergency', suspended the constitution and once again sacked the chief justice. Musharraf tried to explain his position in his autobiography *In the Line of Fire*, but the people had had enough of Musharraf, and rejected him and his supporters in the 2007 elections.

Pakistan's economy stagnated through the 1990s decade, but under Musharraf came back on track. During the period 2000–07, the economy grew at an average of 7 per cent, making

Pakistan one of the four fastest growing economies in Asia. In 2005 headlines announced: 'The world's second fastest growing economy after China is no longer India. It's Pakistan.' Even the Pakistan People's Party (PPP) government that followed lauded the performance of Musharraf's economy in a memorandum submitted to the IMF: 'Pakistan's economy witnessed a major economic transformation in the last decade.' The country's real GDP increased from $60 billion to $162 billion, with per capita income rising from under $500 to almost $960 in the last ten years. The new PPP government took over in 2008 and the economy collapsed, the stock market nose-dived, capital flight set in, foreign exchange reserves plummeted, the rupee lost one-third of its value and the country was forced to return to the IMF for a bailout package. In September 2010 the Asian Development Bank (ADB) declared that there was no money left for running the federal government. Within two years, the Zardari government had taken 'the world's second fastest growing economy' down into the 2010 Top 10 list of Foreign Policy's annual Failed States Index. How did this happen? How did this happen so fast?

Pakistan's recent economic collapse has resulted from bad economics, bad politics, instability, conflict and, finally, floods. Life has become unlivable for most Pakistanis. The poor are plagued by rising prices and unemployment; a burgeoning population throws ever more young men into a job market that has no jobs for them; prices of essentials have risen to a level where deprivation and starvation are the only option. Over the last four years, the price of basic foodstuffs such as sugar, flour, tea and vegetables has increased by 200–300 per cent.

Poverty, as defined by those living on less than a dollar a day, affects seventy million Pakistanis, and if we include those living on less than $2 a day the number rises to 120 million. Desperate young men, uneducated and lacking skills that could qualify them for employment, have limited options—to join their local political mafia, to enlist in the Jihadist armies, to search for jobs in the oil-rich countries of the Middle East, or turn to crime. Organized crime is now rampant in Pakistan, including drug-trafficking, money-laundering and kidnapping; 19,943 kidnapping cases were recorded in 2008, and this does not include many ransoms that were privately and confidentially settled. The middle class is hit by inflation, corruption and the inadequacies of the legal system. Those with money have moved whatever they could from the profitable real estate and share markets of the Musharraf era into dollars or dirhams to sit out the bad times as the rupee depreciates. Their children have already taken Canadian or some other second nationality as insurance for the future.

The twin deficits of budget and trade highlight the fundamental weakness of the Pakistani economy. Pakistan's low tax revenues are hardly 9 per cent of GDP due to a combination of widespread tax evasion and a low tax base in which direct taxation covers a mere two million taxpayers. This small revenue base is just not enough to finance the essential expenditures. The combination of debt servicing (4.4 per cent), defence expenditures (2.6 per cent), subsidies (1.6 per cent) and pensions (0.5 per cent) totals 9.1 per cent of GDP, an amount slightly more than total tax revenues. The general operating expenses of the federal government require borrowings to cover their cost which amounts to another 2.9 per cent of the GDP. Losses of state-owned enterprises (SOEs) amount to Rs 245 billion, approximately $3 billion. The finance available, insufficient to cover essential expenditures to start with, is then wasted through corruption, incompetence and mismanagement, so that budgetary deficits grow even if social services do not, leaving a vacuum in health, education, infrastructure, security, administration and an ineffective system of law and order.

Pakistan's exports just can't keep up with her imports. *The Economist* magazine shows 2011 trade figures as 'Exports—$17.6 billion. Imports—$34.7 billion'. This has resulted in a persistent current account deficit leading to a series of crises where the erosion of foreign exchange reserves repeatedly threatens default to international creditors. In the last fifty years the rupee has depreciated against the dollar from Rs 4.7 to Rs 95. Pakistan's exports have been dominated by one industry—textiles and garments have provided 70 per cent of the exports—but the industry has faced problems since the introduction of the Multi-Fibre Agreement in 2004. This ended the quota system under which a country would only be allowed to export to the US under its quota, and opened up competition in textile exports. Rising world oil prices have led to increase in the import bill. The gap between foreign exchange earned and foreign exchange spent has been met by support from the international community in the form of aid and loans, by FDI, and by the remittances of expatriate Pakistani labour. Whenever the level of international aid and loans or the quantum of FDI falls, Pakistan faces another financial crisis.

Pakistan's demand for foreign currency and the Pakistan government's hunger for money to spend have led to mounting national debt. Between 2004 and 2010 foreign debt has increased from $35 billion to $57 billion. Domestic debt was even higher, taking Pakistan's total public debt above Rs 10 trillion by the end of 2010, up from Rs 6 trillion in 2008. The fiscal deficit necessitated financial discipline in the government, but this was ignored by the Zardari-led PPP, which instead rushed headlong into further deficit. Debt and bankruptcy clouded Pakistan's prospects.

Although the collapse of the economy was caused by the corruption, incompetence and mismanagement of the Asif Ali Zardari government which came to power, the seeds of the crisis were also partially sown in the last years of Musharraf, when inflation and national debt started to rise. The textile industry's problems had been exacerbated by the power crisis which led to price increase and blackouts. Rather than attack the fundamental problem of the trade deficit, Musharraf used the $10 billion US aid package to finance his dollar needs. He also successfully attracted FDI and portfolio investment into the stock market which for the first four years of the century was hailed as the top performing stock market in the world. The combination of aid, loans and strong FDI enabled him to postpone the day of reckoning. The policies of his prime minister, Shaukat Aziz, a banker from Citibank, promoted consumer loans, consumer spending and telecommunications, and satisfied the wealthy and the middle class, but failed to reach the poor, who were plagued by rising prices and unemployment. M. Ziauddin, a prominent journalist, commented, 'The rich have become very rich since 9/11, and the middle class is better off, but not the mass of Pakistanis.' The new Zardari government was hit by an immediate crisis of confidence, its own mini-Asian financial crisis, as foreign portfolio investment exited. Pakistanis, flush with money from booming property and stock markets, also moved their funds out. The flight of capital precipitated crisis and collapse. Lacking the credibility to draw funds from the world, Zardari turned to the IMF for a bailout.

The IMF money came with the usual conditionalities. The government had no qualms at squeezing the public and moved quickly to eliminate subsidies, and to raise the costs of electricity and petrol, but was either helpless or less keen to spread the tax net to the agricultural sector and displease the large landowners who filled parliament; they were also not eager to cut down government spending, which would hurt their own vested interests. The budget deficit and the level of government debt remained unacceptably high; the government was not willing to bind itself with the limitations of prudent financial management. The top two finance officials of the government resigned—the State Bank governor, Salim Raza, for personal reasons and the finance minister, Shaukat Tareen, for business reasons. As the retiring finance minister left to raise equity for his 'Silk Bank', the incoming finance minister, Hafis Shaikh, took leave of absence from the 'New Silk Route', the investment fund in which he was a partner, as he returned to Pakistan to take over his portfolio.

The flood brought disaster destroying roads, schools, hospitals and an estimated two million homes. The cotton crop was badly affected, losing perhaps two million bales of the expected harvest of fourteen million bales. Up to 20 per cent of the nation's farmland was inundated. Prime Minister Gilani announced losses of $43 billion; the Carnegie Endowment, a respected American think tank, replied: 'These are overstatements, as the immediate damage and long-term effects will be much less.' In their view the government was exaggerating the damage in order to get more money from the international community. Donors were reluctant to put money in the hands of the government for fear that it would be siphoned off. Later the government gave a much reduced estimate of flood damage at $9.7 billion. The credibility of the government was further eroded by stories of the prime minister's Harrods shopping spree, and the president's flying visit to his château in France. The final embarrassment was the exposure of stage-set flood relief camps set up to provide bogus picture opportunities for the prime minister without putting him to the trouble of actually having to visit those whose lives had been torn apart by the flood. Even as the image of the ruling politicians was tarnished by their behaviour during the calamity, respect for the army increased as they battled to save life and property.

Pakistan's assets are its people, its land, the Indus River and its large expatriate community working overseas. But the growth of population and illiteracy are fast turning this large uneducated mass into a real liability. Productivity of agricultural land remains low, due to lack of skills, infrastructure and inputs. The mighty Indus is sometimes dry, sometimes in flood; water is wasted, and its use uncontrolled as Pakistan's great irrigation system falls into disrepair. One bright spot is remittances of overseas workers which have crossed $8 billion and are now the greatest source of Forex earnings after textiles, but rich overseas Pakistanis have not provided the investment or network support that has played such an important part in the Chinese and Indian growth stories. Without dramatic and fast reform there seems little likelihood of reversing this downward spiral.

Conflict and corruption have been the principle cause of the economic debacle; but Pakistan's own version of democracy has definitely not helped. Investment will remain shy for as long as the war against the Taliban destabilizes the North West Frontier, suicide bombers and kidnappers threaten civilians throughout Pakistan and insurgency rages in Baluchistan. In addition, a predatory government that preys on business rather than supports it has frightened away new investors.

General Musharraf on taking power moved quickly against corrupt politicians, but soon moved from accountability to manipulation. The corrupt would be protected if they joined Musharraf. These tactics were exposed in a startling interview given to *Dawn* newspaper by Lt Gen (retd) Muhammad Aziz Khan, the former Chief of General Staff, who had served as chairman of the National Accountability Bureau (NAB) under Musharraf and had resigned in protest against his policies. According to Gen. Aziz the entire anti-corruption process was sacrificed to expediency as pressures from the presidency ensured that cases did not proceed against the 'big names'; 'I was told repeatedly not to create problems and not to destabilize the government. [The president and his team] gave a strange logic that corruption and economic development go hand-in-hand.' He quoted a former NAB chairman sent to persuade him, 'If you stop corruption, there will be no development. If ministers and politicians are not given personal benefits in contracts, why would they pursue development schemes? They have to be given personal incentives . . . contracts to their sons and kin.' (*Dawn*, 6 December 2009). General Aziz said that he was repeatedly asked by President Musharraf to close down cases against the Chaudhrys, the leaders of the ruling party. He also put Malik Riaz Hussain, a land developer, whose phenomenal rise made him a contender for the title of Pakistan's richest man, on the Exit Control List to prevent his escaping investigation. But the president insisted that Malik Riaz be removed from the list. He quoted Musharraf's demand: 'As president of Pakistan I give my personal guarantee that he would not run away. Isn't a personal guarantee of the president of Pakistan sufficient to satisfy you?' General Aziz claimed that Prime Minister Shaukat Aziz and his economic team were all responsible for corruption and wrongdoings in the oil pricing, and that the prime minister had also frustrated his inquiries into telecom, banking and the stock market due to his personal interest in these sectors.

Pakistan has sunk deeper into poverty, but its leaders have grown phenomenally rich. Wikipedia, the free Internet encyclopedia, has come out with a list of Pakistanis by net worth, according to which Asif Zardari is the second richest Pakistani with assets stated as $1.8 billion at that time; Nawaz Sharif with $1.4 billion is included as the fourth richest in the list. The Wikipedia site also has a column for 'Sources of Income and Wealth' and shows the source of Zardari's wealth as 'Government Positions'. Another Internet site, 'Factfile', has a detailed entry under the title 'Pakistan's richest—comparing 2008 to 2009', according to which Zardari's wealth has risen from $1.8 billion to $4 billion over the year while he has been in power. David Usborne in his article of 19 May 2010, published in *The Independent*, puts Zardari at eighth place in the list of the world's richest leaders, with his billion-dollar fortune being four times that of the Queen of England and five times that of the ruler of Kuwait.

Democracy in Pakistan disregards the rule of law. Laws in Pakistan, particularly during periods of 'democratic' governments, exist to protect the powerful and punish the poor. The police act as a personal mafia for the rulers, judges are often in the control of politicians, and the bureaucrats follow their own interests and those of their masters rather than the rules of the land and the welfare of Pakistanis. As a result public morality has diminished as fast as the wealth of the rulers has grown. Elections are decided in the countryside where the bulk of the voters live. The rural vote is dominated by the larger landowners. Most of those elected to parliament have focused more on their role as 'dons' in parties that themselves lack any democratic structure, rather than as lawmakers; parliaments have been reduced to rubber stamps. Pakistan is perhaps the only country in the world where a political party can be inherited through a will!

Strangely, the strongest voice for democracy in Pakistan has been the urban middle class. They have spearheaded the struggle for democracy and have achieved two notable successes—a strong media and an independent chief justice whom they kept in office despite Musharraf and Zardari's efforts to get rid of him. Though the urban 'civil society' has played an important part in moulding opinion and in protesting against tyranny, they have not played too relevant a part in elections, in which they can be safely ignored by major electoral parties. An example of this is the inability of Imran Khan, perhaps the most popular individual politician in Pakistan, to score any significant electoral success for his party. To win elections to the assemblies requires money, a traditional feudal hold and mafia politics. Elections are not won by law-abiding citizens—most MPs enter Parliament by spending more than the law permits on their election campaigns, and then misuse their office to refill their depleted bank accounts. The urban middle class feels impotent in the electoral process, and many do not even bother to vote. They are disparagingly referred to as 'drawing room politicians' by the mainstream leaders who find their over-democratic views inconvenient. Repeatedly, this urban middle class, after winning the struggle for democracy, has grown disillusioned with its harvest, and has welcomed military intervention to clean up the mess.

Population growth must be reduced to a reasonable level, and education recognized as a priority. Improving the quality of Pakistan's manpower is essential if productivity is to grow, whether agricultural or in industry or in services. Whereas religion has obstructed family planning in Pakistan, Iran, her Muslim neighbour, has been a model of success. Ayatollah Khomeini's family planning programme brought population growth down from a high of 3.2 per cent in 1986 to a low of 1.2 per cent in 2001, proving that birth control can succeed in an Islamic republic.

Tax reform and restructuring of the government's foreign debt, including write-offs, are short-term solutions to the crisis economy; privatization of badly managed public sector enterprises can save the annual losses which are costing the exchequer $3 billion annually. But the real take off of the economy can only be achieved by massive increase of exports and FDI, and by a qualitative improvement of manpower through education. Till the energy crisis is resolved the thrust of export growth can only be in services and agriculture. India has shown the way in services, particularly IT, and Israel has shown how much can be done in the agricultural sector when knowledge is used to defeat natural handicaps. Perhaps Pakistan's strong community of doctors in the US can develop Pakistan as a back-room for medical IT support.

Conflict and corruption have frightened away both FDI and portfolio investment and even a large amount of the savings of Pakistanis. This flight of capital can only be reversed if stability, security and clean government are re-established. Building a nation requires large amounts of money which must be attracted from private sector sources, both Pakistani and foreign; Pakistan must promote policies that make investment profitable in Pakistan. Instead of seeing business as an adversary to prey on, Pakistani leaders should follow the advice of Daim Zainuddin, Mahathir's finance minister: 'The government, after all, is an indirect shareholder in all your companies. If you make more money, government revenues will increase. Government wants to see business profitable because it has 28 per cent stake in the profits through income tax.'

Agriculture offers the greatest opportunity for fast economic recovery if infrastructure, inputs, water and know-how are properly addressed. The advantages in this sector are a high productivity increase to investment ratio, a high employment to investment ratio, a ready market for agricultural exports in the Middle East, and large tracts of underutilized farmland with ready availability of labour. Pakistan desperately needs another Green Revolution. The bill for extensive land reforms introduced by the Muttahida Qaumi Movement in parliament will shake up the political status quo, whether for the better or the worse.

Today, Pakistanis suffer an acute electricity crisis, with blackouts and exorbitant electric bills. Shortage of generation constrains manufacturing and increases the costs of production, handicapping Pakistan's important textile exports. In 1994, when Benazir opened up private power, Pakistan's private power policies were lauded the world over as a successful model to follow. By 1997 Pakistan was surplus in generation, but the opportunity to export power to India was lost due to wrong policy decisions. Benazir started with oil-based power plants to meet the immediate power shortfall, but recognized that the long-term solution lay in hydel power. Agreements were signed with foreign companies for substantial new hydel capacity.

A change in government led to a reversal of policy as Nawaz Sharif attacked the private power industry. His friend Saif ur Rehman, the NAB boss, started arrests of private power chiefs

and extorted confessions from them that they had bribed
Zardari, but later these confessions were retracted as having
been made under duress. The new chief minister of the NWFP,
where the newly sanctioned hydel plants were located,
cancelled ongoing developments, such as B.C. Hydro's
Malakand project, for reasons of his own, and awarded the
licence to new developers. Developers hit by cancellation of
their projects took losses of millions of dollars; they left never
to return, and no new hydel projects were developed in the
private sector. In Musharraf's time new private power was
ignored, but the rental power concept was started by his
powerful crony capitalists working closely with the new chief
of the government's power monopoly. The Zardari government
expanded rental power despite the outcry over exorbitant
pricing till finally the scandal of rental power resulted in
Supreme Court intervention. Since Pakistan's power
generation includes a substantial hydel component, it is
surprising that the electricity price charged by WAPDA, the
government's power distribution monopoly, is so high. The
answer lies in theft—up to 25 per cent 'line losses' from
WAPDA's grid, and in the high government taxes on oil, the
fuel for Pakistan's thermal plants. Development of hydel power
is the only solution to Pakistan's electricity crisis.

Pakistanis have shown their ability to excel even on the
world stage. Pakistan has produced some exceptional people:
Jinnah, the founder of Pakistan; Abdul Salam, the Nobel Prize-
winning physicist; Faiz Ahmad Faiz, the poet who was
awarded the Lenin Peace prize; Chaudhry Zafrullah Khan,
the judge of the International Court at the Hague; Agha Hasan

Abedi, the creator of the BCCI bank; and Dr Qadeer Khan, the father of Pakistan's bomb. Pakistan's world-class sportsmen include the Khan family who dominated world squash for a decade; Imran Khan who led the champion Pakistani cricket team; and Zia Mahmood recognized as perhaps the greatest bridge player of all time. Can Pakistan produce the quality of leadership required to lift the country out of failure?

Jinnah, the founder of Pakistan, a man of high integrity and intelligence, was not looking to create a fundamentalist state. A lawyer himself, he strongly believed in the rule of law. Unfortunately, he died shortly after achieving independence, and had little impact on what followed. Had he lived, he would have been shattered by the recent assassination of Governor Salman Taseer at the hands of his own bodyguards. The assassin when arrested stated that he had killed Taseer for trying to change the blasphemy laws; in court he was garlanded by 2,000 lawyers who all signed on to defend him, and later a procession of hundreds of thousands of activists was taken out by religious leaders in his support. Is this the face of the new Pakistan?

Conclusion

Leaders Make the Difference

Be not afraid of greatness. Some are born great, some achieve greatness, and some have greatness thrust upon them.

—William Shakespeare

We shall heal our wounds, collect our dead and continue fighting.

—Mao Zedong

Emphasis on rights divides men, emphasis on duties unites them.

—Mahatma Gandhi

- Robert Mugabe presided over a billion per cent inflation rather than resign as president of Zimbabwe, valuing his personal power more than the welfare of his people.
- Islam Karimov, president of Uzbekistan, boiled two 'terrorists' alive to demonstrate his authority.
- Obiang Nguema of Equatorial Guinea did not believe in transparency—he declared oil revenues a state secret.

- Hosni Mubarak of Egypt ruled through a thirty-year-old emergency law.
- Daniel Arap Moi, president of Kenya, banned food imports from neighbouring Uganda because he wanted food prices in his country to rise to earn windfall profits for a friend.
- Gurbanguly Berdimuhamedov, the dentist who became president of Turkmenistan, renamed the months of the year after himself and his family.
- Lieutenant Yahya Jammeh, the Gambian dictator, liked titles and demanded the appellation 'His Excellency Sheikh Professor Alhaj Dr Yahya Abdul Aziz Jemus Junkung Jammeh'. He has vowed to rule for forty years and has claimed to have discovered the cure for AIDS; he also believes that by looking into a man's eyes he can predict the exact date of his death.
- General Abacha of Nigeria organized a multi-party election in which each of the five contesting parties put up Abacha as its candidate; but before he could fight his election against himself, he died due to an overdose of Burantashi (a native virility drug similar to Viagra) after an orgy with prostitutes.

These are but a few examples of bad leaders who have made a mess of their countries.

Mao, Mandela, Gandhi, Ho Chi Minh and Deng are five of the century's greatest leaders who spent their lives fighting oppressive systems of government. They are revolutionaries who dismantled the past and created the future. Lee Kuan Yew, Mahathir and Manmohan Singh are the administrators whose management built up their nations and their economies. Successful nations are the achievement of these founders and these managers. But there were also other types of leaders whose influence was significant; the military leaders who built nations, Ataturk, Nasser and General Park of South Korea; the guerrilla leaders Che and Osama; the Shia leaders Ayatollah Khomeini and Ayatollah Sistani; and the long list of exceptional Chinese leaders from Zhao En-lai to the collective leadership of today's Politbureau Standing Committee (PBSC). These were men moved by ideals and principles, dedicated to the welfare of their countries, uninterested in wealth or possessions. Though they controlled the lives of millions, some were unable to control their own children. Mao and Mandela were unable to control their wives whose wild political ambitions and follies were an embarrassment and a source of torment to them. Nevertheless, they controlled the destinies of their nations and the course of history, changing things for the better.

Mao unified China, achieved an impressive rate of growth, restructured the health and education systems, improved living standards and fought America to a standstill in Korea. Unlike Stalin he ruled by consensus. His over-enthusiasm was shattered by the failure of the Great Leap Forward, after which he withdrew from day-to-day running of the party. His return through the cultural revolution battled corruption and the entrenched bureaucratic elites, and avoided the example of the Soviet system in which the party elites had 'converted their function of serving the masses into the privilege of dominating them'. But the cultural revolution went too far, destroying more than it created. Mao's achievements were tarnished by his serious mistakes, but nevertheless his contribution to China was overwhelming. He died the most revered leader of the century, influencing the thinking of not just China but the world. His *Little Red Book* was the most widely read book in the world, with five billion copies in print. His impact on world history is unparalleled.

Mandela's twenty-seven years in prison has made him a hero to a world that shudders at the thought of his 7 feet by 7 feet cell in Robben Island. He modestly says he was not naturally brave but had to learn to be so. His favourite quote from Shakespeare is: 'Cowards die many times before their death.' But his greatness encompasses more than his courage and perseverance in the face of impossible odds. His decision to start a dialogue with the authorities while still a prisoner, without clearance from the ANC high command, showed a readiness to take risks and acute political skills. Over the years between his release and his securing agreement to elections on the basis of one man one vote, he steered through the political minefield of white resistance to black rule, violent hostility with Buthelezi's Zulus, rivals within the ANC and racist extremism of both whites and blacks, ready to destroy the edifice he was slowly building. During this period he demonstrated his exceptional skills both as a political strategist and as a negotiator. Finally, after taking power through the elections, he rose to even greater heights with his race reconciliation and creation of the rainbow nation, thereby ensuring that white money and skills did not desert his new South Africa.

George Washington retired from office after two terms; Mandela retired after one, bowing out with humility and grace: 'Many of my colleagues are head and shoulders above me in almost every respect. Rather than being an asset, I'm more of a decoration.' He was inspired by Lincoln and like him included some of his fiercest rivals into his first cabinet. Like Lincoln he asked, 'Am I not destroying my enemies when I make them my friends?' Mandela was indifferent to almost all material possessions and was intolerant of injustice. His twenty-seven years in prison taught him self-control, discipline and deep sympathy for human frailty. He entered prison as a hot-headed young man; he emerged mature and slow in making decisions: 'Don't hurry, think, analyse, then act.' He learned to manoeuvre through the frustrations of ANC democracy, commenting, 'We are a democratic organization. I sometimes come to the NEC with an idea and they disagree with me and overrule me. And I obey them even when they are wrong! That is democracy!'

Ho Chi Minh, the frail leader of Vietnam with a will of steel, explained to his American enemy: 'You can kill ten of my men for every one I kill of yours. But even at those odds, you will lose and I will win.' Uncle Ho defeated France, Japan and America in long and bloody wars; over his life he worked as cleaner, waiter, cook's helper, poet, guerrilla fighter, president, statesman and leader; he was fluent in English, Chinese, French, German and Russian other than his native Vietnamese; Uncle Ho was one of history's greatest heroes. He struggled for and achieved the impossible—the defeat of the US and the reunification of Vietnam. After his death, Saigon, the capital of South Vietnam, was renamed 'Ho Chi Minh City' in his honour.

Deng Xiaoping successfully outmanoeuvred Mao's declared successor and took control of China despite never becoming head of state, head of government, or head of the party. Having survived three purges of the party, he unleashed the greatest explosion of productivity and economic growth in history. His uncanny political skills, dogged commitment to economic reform, and sheer good fortune propelled his vast country to prosperity and power. His style was pragmatic and cautious. He opened the economy and legitimized the pursuit of wealth, but denied democracy and maintained party control, creating the key features of the new China. When he died in 1997 he requested his corneas be donated to an eye bank, his body be dissected for medical research and his ashes cast into the sea.

Mahatma Gandhi, the 'naked little fakir', took on and defeated the British Empire, on which the sun never set, with his strategy of non-violent struggle and his experiments with truth. He inspired leaders from Martin Luther King to Mandela with his philosophy which was often more spiritual than political. Ho Chi Minh praised him, saying, 'I and others may be revolutionaries but we are disciples of Mahatma Gandhi directly or indirectly, nothing more, nothing less.' Einstein commented, 'Generations to come will scarce believe that such a one as this walked the earth in flesh and blood.' Gandhi advised would be leaders, 'For a man who would conquer the world, the first step is conquering himself.'

Nasser, Ataturk, Jinnah and Sukarno were four great Muslim leaders. Gamal Abdel Nasser led the Egyptian Revolution, nationalized the Suez Canal, built the High Dam at Aswan, achieved a glorious victory against Great Britain, France and

Israel in the Suez War, suffered a shameful defeat in the Six-day War against Israel, resigned all offices, withdrew his resignations due to massive public demand, and died on 28 September 1970. Five million Egyptians walked with his dead body in a spontaneous outpouring of grief. The heart of Egypt stopped.

After the defeat of the Ottoman Empire at the end of the First World War, the fearless and brilliant general Mustafa Kemal Ataturk was victorious against the Allied forces and secured the independence of the modern state of Turkey. He ended the Sultanate and the Caliphate, and led Turkey to modernization and Westernization; he inspired a generation of secular modernists including Reza Shah of Iran and Jinnah of Pakistan.

Mohammad Ali Jinnah's biographer wrote: 'Few individuals significantly alter the course of history. Fewer still alter the map of the world. Hardly anyone can be credited with creating a nation state. Mohammad Ali Jinnah did all three.' In creating Pakistan, a separate nation, a separate state, Jinnah single-handedly stood against the might of the Congress party and the British. His approach was brilliant but practical, 'We have to deal not with angels but with men, with passions, prejudices, personal idiosyncrasies, innumerable cross currents of motives, of desire, hope, fear and hate.'

Sukarno fought the Dutch, achieved the independence of Indonesia, created a unified nation by holding together 3,000 islands inhabited by people speaking numerous languages, and split by ideologies of nationalism, socialism and Islam. He, together with Nehru, Tito, Nkrumah and Nasser, started the

Non-aligned movement which by 1995 had grown to 113 members and included Mandela, Castro and Arafat. He defined his objective as building a new world, 'Build it solid, strong and sane. Build that world in which all nations exist in peace and brotherhood, fit for the dreams and ideals of humanity.' Flamboyant, charismatic, Sukarno was a great communicator, an orator who could set fire to his audience's hearts. He spoke Javanese, Balinese, Indonesian, Dutch, German, English, French, Arabic and Japanese. He was ousted in a very bloody coup by General Suharto, who was supported by the West, despite the fact that his rise to power was facilitated by the massacre of 800,000 Indonesians and he is recognized as the most corrupt ruler of the twentieth century.

Whereas there is unanimity on the need for great leaders, there is no unanimity on how best to get them. Today's leaders come from the institutions of monarchy, democracy, military and the party. All have produced good leaders, all have produced bad leaders. In the UAE Sheikh Zayed and the Maktoum sheikhs Rashid and Mohammed have played an important role in building their nation. In Botswana Seretse Khama was a royal who took back his right to rule through electoral politics. In India Sonia Gandhi emerged through the democratic process and has presided over India's greatest economic growth. South Korea's General Park was a military leader, as were Ataturk and Nasser in Turkey and Egypt. China has shown that the Communist Party can provide great leadership. Lee Kuan Yew of Singapore and Mahathir Mohamad of Malaysia were elected leaders who had little love for democracy and yet led their nations to success.

Successful economies have been built on the partnerships of power players and economic administrators—Sonia and Manmohan Singh, Lee Kuan Yew and Goh Keng Swee, Mahathir and Daim Zainudin. Deng used his economic experts, the reformers Hu Yaobang and Zhao Ziyang, though he had to discard them both under pressure from the conservatives and party elders. He later imposed Zhu Rongji on a somewhat reluctant Jiang Zemin; even today the current Hu-Wen administration reconfirms the leadership partnership principle. In each case the role of the economic administrator has been crucial, but it has always been politics in control.

Despite the experience of poor countries, America aggressively promotes democracy as their solution. The conviction of the West in the superiority of democracy is surprising in the face of China's outstanding success with its own alternative system. Even Russia has done far better under Putin than under Yeltsin with his Washington Consensus policies. Lula was scathing in his criticism of Western confidence with his remark, 'The economic crisis was caused by the irrational behaviour of white people with blue eyes, who seemed to know everything, and have now shown that they don't know anything.' Developing nations look at America's failures and China's success and start to question the doctrines of the West. Elections in America are as capable of throwing up a Bush as a Clinton. The Chinese system, on the other hand, gives birth to the Politbureau Standing Committee, all suited, vetted and prepared for leadership over a twenty-year apprenticeship monitored by the Party Organization Department, which is more professional in its selection process than even the best of American companies such as GE and GM. The Department prepares dossiers over decades on all senior cadres and evaluates their performance in all their previous jobs. Their subordinates and superiors over the years are interviewed, and the qualities, skills and attitudes recorded. It is a merit system that takes into account their ability, luck and personal networks including their connections with powerful patrons. The system knows too well the strengths and weaknesses of its candidates and minimizes the chance of a wrong selection. In terms of pure results, the Chinese system has outperformed the American in producing superior leadership. Is this the achievement of the Communist Party? Or is this the result of wisdom gleaned over centuries from the teaching of sages such as Lao Tzu, Sun Tzu and Confucius? Or finally, is this just luck, recognized by Napoleon as the most important factor of success with his demand, 'I do not want a good general, I want a lucky one'? But even Napoleon kept a well thumbed copy of Sun Tzu's *Art of War* with him on his campaigns.

But perhaps the ups and downs of nations are just accidents in time, and we who suffer them mere pawns in the cycle of life. In the words of the great Persian poet Omar Khayyam:

> 'Tis all a chequer-board of nights and days,
> Where destiny with men for pieces plays,
> Hither and thither moves, and mates, and slays,
> And one by one back in the closet lays.'

A Note on Sources

Writing this book involved three stages. The first stage included fifty years of experience and general reading on economics, politics and current affairs which focused me on the question 'why some countries grow rich and others don't'. The second stage was 1-2 years of specific reading as a preparation for the book. The third stage involved converting a theory into reality—facts about people and places—and required a detailed research of newspapers, magazines archives and more books. This was made a lot easier by the Internet which enabled me to locate the thousands of reliable sources that were needed as illustrations. The section on corruption was particularly sensitive, since many of those mentioned are still alive, and some still in power. I have avoided expressing my opinion on these and have instead quoted people and sources which are undisputed. Throughout I have taken care not to infringe the legal rights of those I have written about. The result has been a book that is not just a theory, but a vivid tour through the actual world we live in.

Bibliography

Ali, Akhtar. *The Political Economy of Pakistan: An Agenda for Reforms*, Royal Book Company, 1996.

Ali, Tariq. *The Duel: Pakistan on the Flight Path of American Power*, Simon & Schuster, 2008.

Allawi, Ali A. *The Crisis of Islamic Civilization*, Yale University Press, 2009.

Allawi, Ali A. *The Occupation of Iraq: Winning the War, Losing the Peace*, Yale University Press, 2007.

Adair, John. *Inspiring Leadership: Learning from Great Leaders*, Thorogood Publishing Ltd, 2002.

Backman, Michael. *Asian Eclipse: Exposing the Dark Side of Business in Asia*, John Wiley & Sons, 2001.

Backman, Michael. *Asia Future Shock: Business Crisis and Opportunity in the Coming Years*, Palgrave-Macmillan, 2008.

Backman, Michael. *The Asian Insider: Unconventional Wisdom for Asian Business*, Palgrave-Macmillan, 2006.

Backman, Michael. *Inside Knowledge: Streetwise in Asia*, Palgrave-Macmillan, 2005.

Bar-Zohar, Michael. *Shimon Peres: The Biography*. Random House, 2007.

Bhutto, Benazir. *Reconciliation: Islam, Democracy and the West*, Simon & Schuster, 2008.

Blum, William. *Rogue State: A Guide to the World's Only Superpower*, Zed Books, 2006.

Bolton, Giles. *Aid and Other Dirty Business: An Insider Reveals How Good Intentions Have Failed the World's Poor*, Ebury Press, 2007.

Brahm, Laurence J. *Zhu Rongji & the Transformation of Modern China*, John Wiley & Sons, 2002.

Breen, Michael. *The Koreans: Who They Are, What They Want, Where Their Future Lies*, Thomas Dunne Books, 1998.

Bergsten, C. Fred, Gill, Bates, Lardy, Nicholas R. and Mitchell, Derek, Center for Strategic and International Studies and the Institute for International Economics. *China: The Balance Sheet: What the World Needs to Know Now About the Emerging Superpower*, PublicAffairs, 2006.

Chang, Gordon. *The Coming Collapse of China*, Arrow Books, 2002.

Chua, Amy. *World on Fire: How Exporting Free Market Democracy Breeds Ethnic Hatred and Global Instability*, Anchor Books, 2004.

Cockburn, Patrick. *The Occupation: War and Resistance in Iraq*, Verso Books, 2006.

Collier, Paul. *The Bottom Billion: Why the Poorest Countries Are Failing and What Can Be Done About It*, Oxford University Press, 2008.

Collier, Paul. *Wars, Guns, and Votes: Democracy in Dangerous Places*, HarperCollins Publishers, 2009.

Cohen, Stephen S. and DeLong, J. Bradford. *The End of Influence: What Happens When Other Countries Have the Money*, Basic Books, 2010.

Cole, Juan. *Engaging the Muslim World*, Palgrave-Macmillan, 2009.

Coughlin, Con. *Khomeini's Ghost: The Definitive Account of Ayatollah Khomeini's Islamic Revolution and Its Enduring Legacy*, Macmillan, 2009.

Cumings, Bruce. *Korea's Place in the Sun: A Modern History*, W.W. Norton & Co., 2005.

Davidson, Christopher M. *Abu Dhabi: Oil and Beyond*, Hurst & Co., 2009.
———.*Dubai: The Vulnerability of Success*, Hurst & Co., 2008.

Davis, Helen & Douglas. *Israel in the World: Changing Lives through Innovation*, Weidenfeld & Nicolson, 2005.

DeSoto, Hernando. *The Mystery of Capital: Why Capitalism Triumphs in the West and Fails Everywhere Else*, Basic Books, 2000.

Engardio, Pete, ed. *Chindia: How China and India are Revolutionizing Global Business*, McGraw-Hill, 2007.

Evans, Richard J. *Deng Xiaoping and the Making of Modern China*, Hamish Hamilton, Penguin Books, 1993.

Economist, The. *The Economist Pocket World in Figures 2010*, Profile Books, 2009.

Feigon, Lee. *Mao: A Reinterpretation*, Ivan R. Dee, 2002.

Felshtinsky, Yuri and Pribylovsky, Vladimir. *The Age of Assassins: The Rise and Rise of Vladimir Putin*, Gibson Square Books, 2008.

Fisk, Robert. *The Great War for Civilisation: The Conquest of the Middle East*, Fourth Estate, Penguin Books, 2005.

Fisman, Raymond and Miguel, Edward. *Economic Gangsters: Corruption, Violence, and the Poverty of Nations*, Princeton University Press, 2008.

Freeland, Chrystia. *Sale of the Century: The Inside Story of the Second Russian Revolution*, Abacus, 2000.

Friedman, Edward and Gilley, Bruce. *Asia's Giants: Comparing China and India*, Palgrave-Macmillan, 2005.

Friedman, Thomas L. *The World Is Flat: The Globalized World in the Twenty-first Century*, Penguin Books, 2006.

Wenqian, Gao. *Zhou Enlai: The Last Perfect Revolutionary*, PublicAffairs, 2007.

Ghani, Ashraf and Lockhart, Clare. *Fixing Failed States: A Framework for Rebuilding a Fractured World*, Oxford University Press, 2008.

Goldman, Marshall I. *Petrostate: Putin, Power, and the New Russia*, Oxford University Press, 2008.

Guha, Ramachandra. *India After Gandhi: The History of the World's Largest Democracy*, Macmillan, 2007.

Chang, Ha-Joon. *Bad Samaritans: The Guilty Secrets of Rich Nations & the Threat to Global Prosperity*, Random House Business Books, 2008.

————.*The East Asian Development Experience: The Miracle, the Crisis and the Future*, Zed Books, 2006.

————.*Kicking Away the Ladder: Development Strategy in Historical Perspective*, Anthem Press, 2003.

————.23 Things They Don't Tell You about Capitalism, Allen Lane, Penguin Books, 2010.

Halperin, Morton H., Siegle, Joseph T. and Weinstein, Michael M. The Democracy Advantage: How Democracies Promote Prosperity and Peace, Routledge, 2005.

Hawksley, Humphrey. Democracy Kills: What's So Good about Having the Vote?, Macmillan, 2009.

Hoffman, David E. The Oligarchs: Wealth and Power in the New Russia, PublicAffairs, 2002.

Hoffman, W. John and Enright, Michael. China into the Future: Making Sense of the World's Most Dynamic Economy, John Wiley & Sons, 2008.

Hussain, Zahid. Frontline Pakistan: The Struggle with Militant Islam, Columbia University Press 2007.

Jalan, Bimal. India's Politics: A View from the Backbench, Penguin Viking, 2007.

Jomo, K.S., ed. Southeast Asian Paper Tigers? From Miracle to Debacle and Beyond, RoutledgeCurzon, 2003.

Kaplan, Robert D. Surrender or Starve: Travels in Ethiopia, Sudan, Somalia, and Eritrea, Vintage Books, 1988.

Karmin, Craig. Biography of the Dollar: How the Mighty Buck Conquered the World and Why It's under Siege, Crown Business, 2008.

Keane, John. The Life and Death of Democracy, Simon & Schuster, 2009.

Khanna, Parag. The Second World: How Emerging Powers Are Redefining Global Competition in the Twenty-first Century, Random House, 2008.

Kidwai, Rasheed. Sonia: A Biography, Penguin Viking, 2003.

Klare, Michael T. Resource Wars: The New Landscape of Global Conflict, Owl Books, 2001.

Klein, Naomi. The Shock Doctrine: The Rise of Disaster Capitalism, Penguin Books, 2008.

Krane, Jim. Dubai: The Story of the World's Fastest City, Atlantic Books, 2009.

Krugman, Paul R. The Return of Depression Economics and the Crisis of 2008, W.W. Norton & Co., 2009.

Byeong-cheon, Lee. *Development Dictatorship and the Park Chung-Hee Era*, Changbi Publishers, 2003.

Leith, J. Clark. *Why Botswana Prospered*, McGill-Queen's University Press, 2005.

Lucas, Edward. *The New Cold War: How the Kremlin Menaces Both Russia and the West*, Bloomsbury, 2009.

Mohamad, Mahathir bin. *The Malay Dilemma*, Times Books, 1970.

Mahbubani, Kishore. *The New Asian Hemisphere: The Irresistible Shift of Global Power to the East*, PublicAffairs, 2008.

Malik, Iftikhar. *Pakistan: Democracy, Terrorism, and the Building of a Nation*, Olive Branch Press, 2010.

Marti, Michael E. *China and the Legacy of Deng Xiaoping: From Communist Revolution to Capitalist Evolution*, Brassey's Inc., 2002.

McCargo, Duncan and Pathmanand, Ukrist. *The Thaksinization of Thailand*, NIAS Press, 2005.

McPherson, James M. *Abraham Lincoln*, Oxford University Press, 2009.

Milne, R.S. and Mauzy, Diane K. *Malaysian Politics under Mahathir*, Routledge, 1999.

———.*Singapore Politics under the People's Action Party*, Routledge, 2002.

McGregor, Richard. *The Party: The Secret World of China's Communist Rulers*, Allen Lane, Penguin Books, 2010.

Meredith, Martin. *Mandela: A Biography*, Simon & Schuster, 2010.

———.*The State of Africa: A History of Fifty Years of Independence*, Free Press, 2005.

Meredith, Robyn. *The Elephant and the Dragon: The Rise of India and China and What It Means for All of Us*, W.W. Norton & Co., 2007.

Milam, William B. *Bangladesh and Pakistan: Flirting with Failure in South Asia*, Hurst Publishers, 2009.

Miller, T. Christian. *Blood Money: Wasted Billions, Lost Lives, and Corporate Greed in Iraq*, Back Bay Books, 2006.

Münchau, Wolfgang. *The Meltdown Years: The Unfolding of the Global Economic Crisis*, McGraw Hill, 2010.

Naji, Kasra. *Ahmadinejad: The Secret History of Iran's Radical Leader*, I.B. Tauris, 2008.

Naughton, Barry J. *The Chinese Economy: Transitions and Growth*, The MIT Press, 2007.

Nilekani, Nandan. *Imagining India: Ideas for a New Century*, Allen Lane, Penguin Books, 2009.

Nitzan, Jonathon and Bichler, Shimshon. *The Global Political Economy of Israel*, Pluto Press, 2002.

Pan, Philip P. *Out of Mao's Shadow: The Struggle for the Soul of a New China*, Simon & Schuster, 2008.

Panagariya, Arvind. *India: The Emerging Giant*, Oxford University Press, 2008.

Peerenboom, Randall. *China Modernizes: Threat to the West or Model for the Rest?*, Oxford University Press, 2007.

Perry, Alex. *Falling off the Edge: Globalization, World Peace and Other Lies*, Macmillan, 2008.

Paul, Ron. *End the Fed*, Grand Central Publishing, 2009.

Rajadhyaksha, Niranjan. *The Rise of India: Its Transformation from Poverty to Prosperity*, John Wiley & Sons, 2007.

Rashid, Ahmed. *Descent into Chaos: The World's Most Unstable Region and the Threat to Global Security*, Allen Lane, Penguin Books, 2008.

————.*Taliban: Islam, Oil and the New Great Game in Central Asia*, I.B. Tauris, 2009.

Remnick, David. *Resurrection: The Struggle for a New Russia*, Vintage Books, 1998.

Richter, Frank-Jürgen and Nguyen, Thang D. *The Malaysian Journey: Progress in Diversity*, Times Editions, 2004.

Risen, James. *State of War: The Secret History of the CIA and the Bush Administration*, Free Press, 2006.

Rodrik, Dani. *One Economics, Many Recipes*, Princeton University Press, 2007.

Russell, Alec. *After Mandela: The Battle for the Soul of South Africa*, Hutchinson, 2009.

Sachs, Jeffrey D. *Common Wealth: Economics for a Crowded Planet*, Penguin Books, 2008.

Salisbury, Harrison E. *The New Emperors: Mao and Deng: A Dual Biography*, HarperCollins Publishers, 1992.

Sampler, Jeffrey and Eigner, Saeb. *Sand to Silicon: Going Global: Rapid Growth Lessons from Dubai*, Motivate Publishing, 2008.

Sanyal, Sanjeev. *The Indian Renaissance: India's Rise After a Thousand Years of Decline*, World Scientific Publishing, 2008.

Schuman, Michael. *The Miracle: The Epic Story of Asia's Quest for Wealth*, Harper Business, HarperCollins Publishers, 2009.

Senor, Dan and Singer, Saul. *Start-up Nation: The Story of Israel's Economic Miracle*, Twelve, 2009.

Shenkar, Oded. *The Chinese Century: The Rising Chinese Economy and Its Impact on the Global Economy, the Balance of Power, and Your Job*, Wharton School Publishing, 2006.

Shevtsova, Lilia. *Putin's Russia*, Carnegie Endowment for International Peace, 2003.

Shinawatra, Thaksin. *Tackling Poverty*, AIT Publishing, 2009.

Shirk, Susan L. *China: Fragile Superpower*, Oxford University Press, 2007.

Silber, Laura and Little, Allan. *Yugoslavia: Death of a Nation*, Penguin Books, 1995.

Singh, Patwant. *The Second Partition: Fault-Lines in India's Democracy*, Picus Books, 2007.

Smick, David M. *The World Is Curved: Hidden Dangers to the Global Economy*, Portfolio, Penguin Books, 2008.

Smith, David. *Growling Tiger, Roaring Dragon: India, China and the New World Order*, Douglas & McIntyre, 2007.

Sperry, Paul. *Crude Politics: How Bush's Oil Cronies Hijacked the War on Terrorism*, WND Books, 2003.

Stiglitz, Joseph. *Globalization and Its Discontents*, Allen Lane, Penguin Books, 2002.

————.*Making Globalization Work*, Allen Lane, Penguin Books, 2006.

Studwell, Joe. *The China Dream: The Elusive Quest for the Greatest Untapped Market on Earth*, Profile Books Ltd, 2002.

Taheri, Amir. *The Persian Night: Iran under the Khomeinist Revolution*, Encounter Books, 2009.

Vietor, Richard H.K. *How Countries Compete: Strategy, Structure, and Government in the Global Economy*. Harvard Business School Press, 2007.

Vietor H.K., Richard and Kennedy, Robert E. *Globalization and Growth: Case Studies in National Economic Strategies*, Harcourt College Publishers, 2001.

Wood, Ellen Meiksins. *Empire of Capital*, Verso Books, 2003.

Wright, Robin. *Dreams and Shadows: The Future of the Middle East*, Penguin Books, 2008.

Wrong, Michela. *I Didn't Do It for You: How the World Betrayed a Small African Nation*, Harper Perennial, HarperCollins Publishers, 2005.

Zakaria, Fareed. *The Post-American World: And the Rise of the Rest*, Allen Lane, Penguin Books, 2008.

Ziyang, Zhao. *Prisoner of the State: The Secret Journal of Chinese Premier Zhao Ziyang*, Simon & Schuster, 2009.

Websites Accessed

SECTION ONE: CONFLICT

1. NORTH AFRICA, EGYPT AND ALGERIA

http://en.wikipedia.org/wiki/Muslim_Brotherhood
www.mideast.org
www.alkhharitah.com/NewsDetails.aspx?NID=3052
http://en.wikipedia.org/wiki/Sayyid_Qutb
http://www.guardian.co.uk/world/2001/nov/01/
afghanistan.terrorism3
http://www.martinfrost.ws/htmlfiles/jan2009/egypt-frightening-
future.html
http://en.wikipedia.org/wiki/Algeria
http://en.wikipedia.org/wiki/Armed_Islamic_Group_of_Algeria
http://en.wikipedia.org/wiki/Abdelaziz_Bouteflika

2. LIBERIA AND SIERRA LEONE: LORDS OF WAR

http://www.bbc.co.uk/news/world-africa-14094194
http://news.bbc.co.uk/2/mobile/africa/2963086.stm.
http://en.wikipedia.org/wiki/Sierra_Leone_Civil_War
http://en.wikipedia.org/wiki/Revolutionary_United_Front
http://en.wikipedia.org/wiki/First_Liberian_Civil_War
http://en.wikipedia.org/wiki/West_Side_Boys

http://en.wikipedia.org/wiki/Samuel_Doe
http://en.wikipedia.org/wiki/Liberia
http://en.wikipedia.org/wiki/Sierra_Leone
http://topics.nytimes.com/top/reference/timestopics/people/t/
charles_taylor/index.html
http://www.bbc.co.uk/news/world-africa-13729504
http://iconicphotos.wordpress.com/2009/07/03/the-torture-of-
samuel-doe/
www.peacewomen.org/news/Sierra Leone/july04/warcourt.html

3. ANGOLA: OIL VERSUS DIAMONDS

http://en.wikipedia.org/wiki/Angola
http://en.wikipedia.org/wiki/Jonas_Savimbi
www.traveldocs.com/ao/economy.htm
www.eisa.org.za/WEP/angrecovery2.htm
http://www.globalwitness.org/media_library_detail.php/227/en/

4. ETHIOPIA AND ERITREA: A VERY LONG WAR

http://www.bbc.co.uk/news/world-africa-13349078

5. ISRAEL: HERO OR VILLAIN?

http://www.mideastweb.org/nutshell.htm
http://www.mideastweb.org/timeline.htm
http://www.independent.co.uk/news/world/middle-east/the-big-
question-what-are-israeli-settlements-and-why-are-they-coming-under-
pressure-1692515.html
http://en.wikipedia.org/wiki/Israeli_settlements
http://en.wikipedia.org/wiki/Proposals_for_a_Palestinian_state
http://news.bbc.co.uk/2/hi/middle_east/8099757.stm
www.adampletts.com/gallery http://israelipalestinian.procon.org/
view.resource.php?resourceID=000632
http://www.mideastweb.org/timeline.htm
http://www.ifamericansknew.org/history/
http://www.globalresearch.ca/the-us-and-israel-the-hypocrisy-of-un-
security-council-resolutions/2867

http://www.voanews.com/english/2009-09-08-
voa42.cfm?renderforprint=1
http://mydd.com/2009/5/2/us-arms-sales-to-the-middle-east-soar
http://www.lovearth.net/therealcostofussupportforisrael.htm

6. IRAQ: SADDAM'S THREE WARS

http://en.wikipedia.org/wiki/1991_uprisings_in_Iraq
http://en.wikipedia.org/wiki/Depleted_uranium
http://en.wikipedia.org/wiki/Iran-Iraq_War
http://en.wikipedia.org/wiki/US_support_for_Iraq_during_the_Iran-
Iraq_war
http://en.wikipedia.org/wiki/Timeline_of_the_Gulf_War
http://www.historyguy.com/GulfWar.html%20Persian% 20Gulf%
20War%201990-1#.UKjS9uRvCIU
http://www.themodernreligion.com/ugly/unholy.html
http://www.ccnr.org/bertell_book.html
http://rense.com/general64/du.htm
http://www.iranchamber.com/history/articles/arming_iraq.php

7. THE YUGOSLAV WARS: EUROPE'S OWN HORROR STORY

http://en.wikipedia.org/wiki/Slobodan_Milosevic
http://en.wikipedia.org/wiki/Yugoslav_Wars
http://en.wikipedia.org/wiki/Srebrenica_massacre
http://www.absoluteastronomy.com/topics/Yugoslav_wars
http://usproxy.bbc.com/2/hi/europe/605266.stm
http://www.guardian.co.uk/world/2000/jan/16/balkans3
http://www.telegraph.co.uk/news/worldnews/africaandindianocean/
1370864/Yugoslavia-milked-of-millions-by-Milosevic.html
http://www.rferl.org/content/article/1099033.html

8. SOUTH ASIA: A NUCLEAR CONFLICT ZONE

http://news.bbc.co.uk/2/hi/south_asia/8046577.stm
http://en.wikipedia.org/wiki/Death_of_Zia-ul-Haq
http://www.jkalternativeviewpoint.com/statenews.php?link=6018

http://www.csmonitor.com/2003/0508/p01s02-wosc.html
http://www.washingtonpost.com/wp-dyn/content/article/2009/04/22/AR2009042200863.html
http://dawn.com/provinces/
www.rediff.com/news/2008/jan/30spec.htm
http://www.dailytimes.com.pk/default.asp?page=story_21-1-2005_pg7_11 http://reddiarypk.wordpress.com/2009/08/13/pakistans-baloch/ http://www.crisisgroup.org/en/regions/asia/south-asia/pakistan/B069-pakistan-the-forgotten-conflict-in-balochistan.aspx
www.india-defence.com/reports/1073
http://en.wikipedia.org/wiki/Balochistan,_Pakistan
http://en.wikipedia.org/wiki/Sino-Indian_relations
http://en.wikipedia.org/wiki/Indo-Pakistani_wars_and_conflicts
http://en.wikipedia.org/wiki/Naxalite
http://en.wikipedia.org/wiki/Northeast_India
http://en.wikipedia.org/wiki/Religious_violence_in_India
http://en.wikipedia.org/wiki/Anti-Christian_violence_in_India
http://en.wikipedia.org/wiki/Sri_Lankan_Civil_War
http://en.wikipedia.org/wiki/Insurgency_in_North-East_India
http://www.aljazeera.com/focus/indiaelections/2009/04/200941365558852919.html
www.globalsecurity.org/military/world/war/seven-sisters.htm
http://www.infoplease.com/encyclopedia/world/assam.html
http://www.zimbio.com/Bhutan/articles/508/Assam+independence+shows+Cracks+India+Isha
http://en.wikipedia.org/wiki/United_Liberation_Front_of_Asom
http://articles.timesofindia.indiatimes.com/2009-10-11/india/28102116_1_maoists-jharkhand-special-auxiliary-police
http://news.bbc.co.uk/hi/english/static/in_depth/south_asia/2002/india_pakistan/timeline/default.stm
http://en.wikipedia.org/wiki/Timeline_of_the_Kashmir_conflict
http://www.mcclatchydc.com/2009/10/11/76954/terrorist-attack-in-pakistan-shows.html)
www.nuclearfiles.org/menu/key-issues/nuclear-weapons/history/post-cold-war/ind

http://uk.reuters.com/article/2006/11/21/uk-india-china-border-idUKDEL19894620061121
http://www.globalsecurity.org/military/world/war/india-china_conflicts.htm
http://www.nytimes.com/2009/09/04/world/asia/04chinaindia.html?pagewanted=all
http://www.c3sindia.org/strategicissues/913
http://www.globalsecurity.org/military/world/war/indo-prc_1962.htm

SECTION TWO: CORRUPTION

9. CORRUPTION IN IRAQ: SADDAM, AMERICA
    AND DEMOCRACY

http://www.meforum.org/716/iraq-and-the-importance-of-the-uns-oil-for-food
http://www.foxnews.com/story/0,2933,132609,00.html
http://en.wikipedia.org/wiki/Oil-for-Food_Programme
www.freerepublic.com/focus/f-news/1068890/posts
http://en.wikipedia.org/wiki/George_Galloway
http://www.thehighroad.org/archive/index.php/t-70476.html&s=9f5bb49d97d40b42a3b7594253df9548&
http://www.guardian.co.uk/world/2005/feb/08/usa.iraq
http://www.theamericanconservative.com/articles/money-for-nothing/
http://www.theamericanconservative.com/articles/2005/10/
http://www.time.com/time/magazine/article/0,9171,733760,00.html
http://www.washingtonpost.com/wp-dyn/content/article/2006/02/12/AR2006021200732.html
www.rezkowatch.blogspot.com
http://www.thenation.com/blog/156346/secret-report-corruption-norm-within-iraqi-government#
http://www.independent.co.uk/news/world/middle-east/how-bribery-became-a-way-of-life-in-iraq-1722466.html

http://en.wikipedia.org/wiki/Dale_Stoffel
http://en.wikipedia.org/wiki/Radhi_Hamza_al-Radhi
http://www.cbsnews.com/8301-18560_162-4009328.html
http://www.nytimes.com/2009/05/03/world/middleeast/
03iraq.html?_r=0

10. RUSSIA: THE KREMLIN, THE OLIGARCHS AND THE MAFIA

http://www.law.nyu.edu
http://robertamsterdam.com/2008/10/comparative_corruption_of_
russia_and_china/
http://www.opendemocracy.net/author/zygmunt-dzieciolowski
http://www.nytimes.com/2005/08/13/international/europe/
13russia.html?pagewanted=all
www.cdi.org/russia/johnson/2008-30-22.cfm
http://en.wikipedia.org/wiki/Privatization_in_Russia
http://www.seoprofiler.com/analyze/
freedomliberationmovement.com
http://news.bbc.co.uk/2/hi/europe/787475.stm
http://www.nytimes.com/1999/03/24/world/yeltsin-s-inner-circle-
under-investigation-for-corruption.html.
http://www.guardian.co.uk/world/1999/aug/26/russia.philipwillan
http://www.rollingstone.com/politics/blogs/national-affairs/death-of-
a-drunk-boris-yeltsin-dead-at-76-20070423
http://the-spark.net/csart264.html
http://www.theotherrussia.org/2007/07/28/kasparov-on-the-putin-
mafia/
http://www.democraticunderground.com/discuss/
duboard.php?az=view_all&address=102x1646942
http://www.nybooks.com/articles/archives/2008/may/15/the-truth-
about-putin-and-medvedev/?pagination=false
http://www.justicefornorthcaucasus.com/jfnc_message_boards/
human_rights.php?entry_id=1246119315&title=finrosforum%3A-
report%3A-corruption-taints-courts-in-russia
http://ireport.cnn.com/docs/DOC-220247

http://www.guardian.co.uk/world/2007/dec/21/russia.topstories3
http://en.wikipedia.org/wiki/Igor_Sechin
http://larussophobe.wordpress.com/2009/05/30/gazprom-on-its-knees/
www.gasandoil.com
http://www.forbes.com/forbes/2006/0724/094_print.html

11. SAINTS AND SINNERS IN AFRICA

http://www.nigerianmuse.com/20090713053327zg/sections/general-articles/of-looters-leaders-and-the-efcc-list/
http://traceaid.com
www.washingtonpost.com/wp-srv/inatl/longterm/nigeria/stories/corrupt060998.htm
http://news.bbc.co.uk/2/hi/business/2043403.stm
www.davidajao.com/blog/2008/01/16/scandals-rock-obasanjos-family/ www.thenation.com/doc/20090720/caplan/print http://elendureports.com/index.php?option=com_content&task=view&id=342&Itemid=1
http://elendureports.com/index.php?option=com_content&task=view&id=124&Itemid=29
http://en.wikipedia.org/wiki/Nuhu_Ribadu
www.unodc.org/unodc/en/frontpage/nigerias-corruption-busters.html
www.nigerianmuse.com/20080503081802zg/nigeriawatch/officialfraud/Nigeria_cor
http://allafrica.com/stories/printable/200905080949.html
www.washingtonpost.com/wp-dyn/content/article/2009/05/22/AR2009052202025_p
http://allafrica.com/stories/printable/20070918019.html
http://allafrica.com/stories/200709180019.html
www.nationsencyclopedia.com/economies/Africa/Congo-Democratic-Republic-of-T
http://news.bbc.co.uk/2/low/africa/1050310.stm

12. SUHARTO: THE TWENTY-BILLION DOLLAR MAN

http://news.bbc.co.uk/2/hi/3567745.stm

http://www.slate.com/articles/news_and_politics/explainer/2004/
03/how_did_suharto_steal_35_billion.html
www.time.com
http://www.highbeam.com/doc/1G1-12233763.html
http://www.insideindonesia.org/weekly-articles/tommys-toys-
trashed
http://en.wikipedia.org/wiki/Timor_Car
http://www.corpwatch.org/article.php?id=14941

13. CHINA GETS TOUGH ON CROOKS

http://www.theepochtimes.com/news/8-2-29/66784.html
http://www.washingtonpost.com/wp-dyn/content/article/2006/02/
14/AR2006021400672.html
http://carnegieendowment.org/2007/11/20/corruption-in-china-how-
bad-is-it/2028
http://www.voanews.com/english/archive/2002-09/a-2002-09-26-
4-Analysts.cfm?renderfo
www.atimes.com/atimes/China/H101Ad01.html
www.realestatejournal.com/regionalnews/20070207-areddy.html
http://shanghailist.com/2006/09/27/hus_in_charge.php
http://www.washingtonpost.com/wp-dyn/content/article/2007/03/
31/AR2007033101124.html
http://www.washingtonpost.com/wp-dyn/content/article/2008/10/
19/AR2008101900658.html
www.asianews.it/view4print.php?1=en&art=13415
www.asiasentinel.com/index2.php?option=com_content&task=
view&id=409&pop
http://chinanewswrap.com/2009/06/15/chinese-netizens-speculate-
on-identity-of-xu-zong
http://english.peopledaily.com.cn/english/200007/31/
print20000731_46885.html
http://en.wikipedia.org/wiki/Chen_Xitong
http://www.carnegieendowment.org/files/pb55_pei_china_
corruption_final.pdf

http://www.nytimes.com/2006/10/22/weekinreview/
22yardley.html?pagewanted=all
http://news.bbc.co.uk/2/hi/asia-pacific/5388054.stm
www.militaryphotos.net/forums/showthread.php?t=158895
www.chinadaily.net/2006-10/18/content_711066.htm
http://courses.wcupa.edu/rbove/eco343/030Compecon/China/
030706graft.txt
http://www.nytimes.com/2006/10/26/world/asia/26iht-corrupt.
3294532.html?pagewanted=all

14. INDIA: EVERYBODY STEALS, NOBODY GETS CAUGHT

http://en.wikipedia.org/wiki/The_Emergency_(India)
http://en.wikipedia.org/wiki/Pamulaparthi_Venkata_Narasimha_Rao
http://en.wikipedia.org/wiki/Bihar
http://en.wikipedia.org/wiki/Lalu_Prasad_Yadav
http://en.wikipedia.org/wiki/Fodder_Scam
http://en.wikipedia.org/wiki/Mayawati
http://en.wikipedia.org/wiki/Mulayam_Singh_Yadav
http://en.wikipedia.org/wiki/Hawala_scandal
http://en.wikipedia.org/wiki/Abdul_Karim_Telgi
http://en.wikipedia.org/wiki/Barak_Missile_scandal
http://en.wikipedia.org/wiki/Babubhai_Khimabhai_Katara
http://en.wikipedia.org/wiki/Corruption_in_India
http://en.wikipedia.org/wiki/Sharad_Pawar
http://en.wikipedia.org/wiki/Cash-for-votes_scandal
http://en.wikipedia.org/wiki/Taj_corridor_case
www.indianetzone.com/2/indian_prime_ministers.htm
www.hindustan.org/forum/showthread.php?t=22
http://indiatoday.in/content_mail.php?option=com_content&name=
print&id=22821
http://www.expressindia.com/latest-news/sukhram-convicted-in-
disproportionate-asset-case/426033/
www.worldlatestnews.com/business-news/petroleum-minister-
makes-money-should

www.stockmarketguide.in/2009/01/huge-scam-in-satyam-computers.html

www.absoluteastronomy.com/topics/Indian_political_scandals

www.absoluteastronomy.com/topics/Jessica_Lal

www.financialexpress.com/printer/news/344093/

http://news.bbc.co.uk/2/low/south_asia/1220044.stm

http://www.washingtonpost.com/wp-dyn/content/article/2008/07/23/AR2008072303390.html

http://www.rediff.com/news/2007/jun/28telgi.htm

www.indianexpress.com/story-print/488090/

www.financialexpress.com/news/mulayam-lashes-out-at-mayawati/309141/

http://www.business-standard.com/india/news/chargesheet-ready-against-mayawati-in-disproportionate-assets-case/00/48/67420/on

www.zoominfo.com/people/Mayawati_Kumari_339775666.aspx

www.countercurrents.org/print.html

http://www.nytimes.com/2000/02/10/world/india-politician-s-jewels-glare-at-her-latest-trial.html

http://news.bbc.co.uk/2/hi/south_asia/4762593.stm

http://www.financialexpress.com/old/ie/daily/19990428/iex28066.html

www.american.com/archive/2009/the-indian-railway-king/article_print

http://www.hindu.com/2005/07/01/stories/2005070103931500.htm

www.bihartimes.com/poverty/S_N_Sinha.html

http://timesofindia.indiatimes.com/home/stoi/Chandraswami-The-good-bad-and-the-ugly/articleshow/1172693124.cms

www.dnaindia.com/dnaprint.asp?newsid=1082262

http://news.bbc.co.uk/onthisday/hi/dates/stories/june/12/newsid_2511000/2511691.stm

SECTION THREE: DEMOCRACY

http://www.carnegieendowment.org/1999/02/26/economic-
institutions-democracy-and-development/3i9
http://www.freedomhouse.org/article/democracy-momentum-
sustained http://ideas.repec.org/p/igi/igierp/302.html

15. ISLAMIC DEMOCRACY

http://www.ijtihad.org/isladem.htm
http://www.meforum.org/1680/can-there-be-an-islamic-democracy
www.meforum.org/1763/are-muslim-countries-less-democratic
http://en.wikipedia.org/wiki/Islam_and_democracy
www.mtholyoke.edu/acad/intrel/rwright.htm
www.howardwfrench.com
www.csmonitor.com/2004/0728/p08s03-cojh.html
www.meforum.org/627/indonesian-democracy-vs-islamist-
fundamentalism
http://en.wikipedia.org/wiki/New_Order_(Indonesia)
www.meforum.org/216/why-turkey-is-the-only-muslim-democracy
http://en.wikipedia.org/wiki/Politics_of_Turkey
http://en.wikipedia.org/wiki/Mustafa_Kemal_Ataturk
www.meforum.org/1893/turkey-and-democracy
www.opendemocracy.net/democracy-turkey/turkey_divided_4593.jsp
www.meforum.org/1672/does-prime-minister-erdogan-accept-turkish-
secularism

SECTION FOUR: FOUR SKETCHES OF DEMOCRACY

16. SOUTH AFRICA: MANDELA AND AFTER

http://en.wikipedia.org/wiki/History_of_South_Africa
www.southafrica.info/about/democracy/polparties.htm
http://www.freedomhouse.org/report/freedom-world/freedom-
world-2009

http://www.npr.org/templates/story/story.php?storyId=91330104
www.duke.edu/~gwc/southafrica_reflection.htm
http://www.time.com/time/world/article/0,8599,1843253,00.html
http://www.bbc.co.uk/news/world-africa-17450447
http://www.nytimes.com/2005/10/26/opinion/26iht-edherbst.html?gwh=D4C98011CDF60319B8F088C5A93775E3
www.andiquote.co.za/authors/Jacob_Zuma.html

17. IRAN: AYATOLLAHS IN COMMAND

http://en.wikipedia.org/wiki/Timeline_of_the_iranian_revolution
 http://en.wikipedia.org/wiki/Ali_Khamenei
http://en.wikipedia.org/wiki/Iranian_Reform_Movement
http://en.wikipedia.org/wiki/Hosein-Ali_Montazeri
http://en.wikipedia.org/wiki/Mohammad_Beheshti
http://en.wikipedia.org/wiki/Akbar_Hashemi_Rafsanjani
www.forbes.com/forbes/2003/0721/056_print.html
www.nybooks.com/articles/15523
http://news.bbc.co.uk/2/hi/middle_east/2699541.stm
http://www.freedomhouse.org/report/freedom-world/2009/iran?country=7627&page=22&year=2009
http://www.time.com/time/world/article/0,8599,1905356,00.html
www.counterpunch.org/downing06162009.html
http://dilbertblog.typepad.com/the_dilbert_blog/2007/03/is_irn_as_demo.hmtl www.dailykos.com/story/2009/6/16/743351/-Grand-Ayatollah-Montazeri-confirms
http://iran115.org/
www.mnforsustain.org/iran_model_of_reducing_fertility.htm

18. THAILAND: THE KING, THAKSIN AND GENERAL PREM

http://en.wikipedia.org/wiki/Thaksin_Shinawatra
http://en.wikipedia.org/wiki/Thaksinomics
www.rgemonitor.com/asia-monitor/256415/backgrounder_on_thailands_political_cr
www.thaiwebsites.compolitical-history.asp

http://www.nytimes.com/2009/04/15/world/asia/15bangkok.
html?gwh=41CCF7EEDFC6D602E6FB3C8A0DE3469E
http://khamerlogue.wordpress.com/readings/
www.generalprem.com/love-book.html

19. INDIA: THE WORLD'S BIGGEST DEMOCRACY

http://en.wikipedia.org/wiki/Elections_in_India-
www.hindustantimes.com/StoryPage/Print/491010.aspx
www.indiademocracy.org/article/viewArticle/id1056
www.strategypage.com/militaryforums/72-15943.aspx
http://askmeany.com/2009/03/27/actors-in-politics/
www.goarticles.com/cgi-bin/showa.cgi?C=2285288
www.cato.org/pub_display.php?pub_id=6709
http://www.rediff.com/news/2004/apr/15spec.htm
www.zeenews.com/printstory.aspx?id=522425
http://news.bbc.co.uk/2/hi/south_asia/7914229.stm
www.huffingtonpost.com/2009/04/23/berlusconi-stacks-
parliam_n_190644.html http://us.asiancorrespondent.com/atanu-dey-
blog/2004/04/20/democracy-in-india

SECTION FIVE: SUPERPOWERS DO MATTER

http://killinghope.org/bblum6/assass.htm
http://killinghope.org/bblum6/overthrow.htm
http://killinghope.org/superogue/bomb.htm
http://transnationallawblog.typepad.com/transnational_law_blog/
2009/03/rethinking-the-w www.choike.org/2009/eng/informes/
778.html
www.cato.org/pub_display.php?pub_id=5233
www.dailypaul.com/node/119142
http://en.wikipedia.org/wiki/List_of_countries_by_military_
expenditures www.rense.com/general34/realre.htm
www.armscontrolcerter.org/policy/securityspending/articles/
fy09_dod_request_glob http://blogs.cgdev.org/globaldevelopment/
2008/09/us-financial-crisis-will-mean.php

http://siteresources.worldbank.org/ROMANIAEXTN/Resources/
Oct_31_JustinLin_KDI_remarks.pdf
www.iss.nl/layout/set/print/DevISSues/Articles/The-financial-crisis-
and-developing-c
http://siteresources.worldbank.org/ROMANIAEXTN/Resources/
Oct_31_JustinLin_KDI_remarks.pdf
www.house.gov/paul
http://www.lewrockwell.com/paul/paul303.html
www.globalresearch.ca/PrintArticle.php?articleId=3482
http://en.wikipedia.org/wiki/American_imperialism

SECTION SIX: GROWING RICH

http://www.independent.co.uk/news/world/africa/an-african-
adventure-inside-story-of-the-wonga-coup-794470.html
http://en.wikipedia.org/wiki/Equatorial_Guinea
http://www.bbc.co.uk/news/world-africa-13317174
http://www.irinnews.org/Report/80768/EQUATORIAL-
GUINEA-Poverty-rife-in-Africa-s-Kuwait
http://news.bbc.co.uk/2/hi/africa/3597450.stm

20. SINGAPORE: NO CORRUPTION, NO DEMOCRACY

http://mpra.ub.uni-muenchen.de/4741/
http://en.wikipedia.org/wiki/Politics_of_Singapore

21. SOUTH KOREA: GENERAL PARK AND THE CHAEBOLS

www.mongabay.com/reference/coountry_studies/south-korea/all.html
www.mongabay.com/reference/country_studies/south-korea/all.html
http://countrystudies.us/south-korea/15.htm
http://en.wikipedia.org/wiki/Economy_of_South_Korea
http://en.wikipedia.org/wiki/List_of_Presidents_of_South_Korea
http://en.wikipedia.org/wiki/Roh_Moo-hyun

22. CHINA: A CAT THAT CATCHES THE MICE

http://en.wikipedia.org/wiki/Communist_Party_of_China http://factsanddetails.com/china.php?itemid=79&catid=2
www.newworldencyclopedia.org/entry/Deng_Xiaoping
www.nytimes.com/learning/general/onthisday/bday/0822.html
www.nytimes.com/1995/04/12/obituaries/chen-yun-who-slowed-china-s-shift-to-mar www.guardian.co.uk/news/2007/jan/24/guardianobituaries.obituaries1/print
http://www.nytimes.com/1992/06/23/world/li-xiannian-china-ex-president-and-rural-economist-dies-at-82.html
http://en.wikipedia.org/wiki/Zhu_Rongji
http://www.jamestown.org/programs/chinabrief/single/?tx_ttnews%5Btt_news%5D=4482&tx_ttnews%5BbackPid%5D=197&no_cache=1
http://news.bbc.co.uk/2/hi/asia-pacific/7055718.stm
http://www.thedailybeast.com/newsweek/2002/11/24/china-s-princelings-problem.html
http://www.thedailybeast.com/newsweek/2007/12/22/xi-jinping-china-s-new-boss-and-the-l-word.html
http://chinadigitaltimes.net/2007/03/princeling-takes-key-step-up-power-ladder-jane-macartney/
http://econ.worldbank.org/WBSITE/EXTERNAL/EXDEC/EXTRESEARCH/0,,content www.economicexpert.com/a/Crown:Prince:Party.htm
www.thechinaforum.com/17.html
http://www.nytimes.com/2003/03/19/world/the-former-premier-who-ended-china-s-splendid-isolation.html
www.atimes.com/atimes/printN.html
http://www.brookings.edu/research/papers/2007/11/trade-woo

23. DUBAI: HOPING FOR A COMEBACK

http://www.bloomberg.com/apps/news?pid=newsarchive&sid=a0E6_6cfEeqI
http://dro.dur.ac.uk/793/

24. ISRAEL: SUCCESSFUL SOCIALISM, SUCCESSFUL CAPITALISM

www.israel21c.org/opinion/israel-the-history-of-an-economic-miracle
http://meria.idc.ac.il/journal/2002/issue3/jv6n3a3.html
http://www.jewishvirtuallibrary.org/jsource/isdf/text/Melnick_Mealem1.html
http://countrystudies.us/israel/66.htm
http://en.wikipedia.org/wiki/1985_Israel_Economic_Stabilization_Plan
http://en.wikipedia.org/wiki/Economy_of_Israel
www.biu.ac.il/SOC/besa/books/kanov/chap2.html
www.historama.com
http://edition.cnn.com/2008/BUSINESS/01/10/israel.economy/
http://www.ynetnews.com/articles/0,7340,L-3871593,00.html
www.ahavat-israel.com/eretz/economy.php
http://israelapartheidguide.com/sample/
http://www.politicsforum.org/forum/viewtopic.php?f=32&t=76973
www.iva.co.il/content.asp?pageId=41
http://www.bankisrael.gov.il/en/Research/Periodicals/Pages/01_iser_1.aspx
www.counterpunch.org/avnery09282006.html
http://www.nytimes.com/2010/01/12/opinion/12brooks.html?_r=0&gwh=03B7D50B4E6FC6AF05BF507E603DEEC4

25. BOTSWANA'S DIAMONDS: A BLESSING, NOT A CURSE

http://www.google.co.in/url?sa=t&rct=j&q=&esrc=s&source=web&cd=1&ved=0CB8QFjAA&url=http%3A%2F%2Fpsclasses.ucdavis.edu%2FIRE190%2FDocuments%2FBotswanaFile8.doc&ei=6ECqUKO-C9GxrAedgYHoBA&usg=AFQjCNHFS6rQj9k5Xruok-WzY6LijhYDUQ
www.thuto.org/ubh/bw/skhama.htm Seretse Khama 1921-80
www.innertemple.org.uk
www.deependrajha.com2009/01/botswana
www.bookrags.com/biography
www.state.gov/r/pa/ei/bgn/1830.htm
www.eisa.org.za/WEP/botoverview6.htm

http://myafrica.allafrica.com
http://books.google.co.in/books?id=g25SCDCuYbQC&pg=
PA167&lpg=PA167&dq=Botswana:+Island+of+Hope+(+Jan+
1976+by+Robin+Wright)&source=bl&ots=KEAWiwZVY2&
sig=P32jYGNU8_ZnInSKGO_X8BZQipE&hl=en&sa=
X&ei=SkGqUNmoOoP_rAfj6oH4Dg&sqi=2&ved=0CB0Q6A
EwAA#v=onepage&q=Botswana%3A%20Island%20of%20Hope%20
(%20Jan%201976%20by%20Robin%20Wright)&f=false
https://www.cia.gov/library/publications/the-world-factbook/geos/
bc.html
www.moibrahimfoundation.org
http://www.wto.org/english/forums_e/debates_e/festus_mogae_
popup_e.htm

26. MALAYSIA DOES IT 'MY WAY'

http://en.wikipedia.org/wiki/Mahathir_bin_Mohamad
http://en.wikipedia.org/wiki/Economy_of_Malaysia
http://en.wikipedia.org/wiki/Politics_of_Malaysia
http://en.wikipedia.org/wiki/Petronas
www.wrmea.com/archives/sept03/0309042.html
http://www.hindustantimes.com/news/specials/leadership2006/
ht_091106.shtml
http://online.wsj.com/article/SB10001424052748703569004
575010130947732978.html
http://www.ceri-sciencespo.com/cherlist/camroux/112003.pdf
http://news.bbc.co.uk/2/hi/asia-pacific/2059518.stm
http://news.bbc.co.uk/2/hi/business/521017.stm
http://sophiesworld-sophiesworld.blogspot.com/2007/11/
http://dinmerican.wordpress.com/2010/07/11/malaysias-rapid
http://en.allexperts.com/e/m/ma/mahathir
www.businessweek.com/magazine/content
www.highbeam.com/doc/1G1-110461706.html
www.project-syndicate.org/commentary/stiglitz91/English
www.dapmalaysia.org/all-achive/English/2003/jan03/1ks2031.htm
www.state.gov/r/pa/bgn/2777.htm

http://www.jomoks.org/research/other/rp015.htm
http://en.wikipedia.org/wiki/Abdullah_Ahmad_Badawi
www.referenceforbsiness.com/biography
http://money.cnn.com/magazines/fortune/global500/
http://skorcareer.com.my/blog/top-10-malaysias-richest-people
www.telegraph.co.uk/news/worldnews/asia/malaysia
http://asiasentinel.com/index.php?option=com_content&task=view&id2406&Itemid=178
https://groups.google.com/forum/#!topic/go-press-releases-news—opinion/s3sNNam3THshttp://www.topix.com/forum/world/indonesia/T3UDO1AAM35NTNE3H
http://news.bbc.co.uk/2/hi/asia-pacific/382110.stm
www.illegal-logging.info/item_single.php?it_id=2240&it=news

27. INDIA: A STORY OF ACCIDENTS

http://www.guardian.co.uk/world/2005/sep/16/india.gender
http://en.wikipedia.org/wiki/Economy_of_India
 http://en.wikipedia.org/wiki/Economic_liberalization_in_India
http://en.wikipedia.org/wiki/Reliance_Industries
http://en.wikipedia.org/wiki/Dhirubhai_Ambani
http://en.wikipedia.org/wiki/Azim_Premji
http://en.wikipedia.org/wiki/List_of_states_and_union_territories_of_India_by_population
http://unidow.com/statewise_gdp.html
http://inidpw.com/statewise_gdp.html
http://www.india-seminar.com/2003/521/521%20paranjoy%20guha%20thakurta.htm
http://economictimes.indiatimes.com/articleshowpics/6264312.cms
www.brookings.edu/opinions/2009/0327_india_panagariya.aspx
www.indian-elections.com/dr-manmohan-singh.html
www.brookings.edu/opinions/2009/0526_indi_government_panaga
http://findarticles.com/articles/mi_2242/is_1647_282/ai_100605223
http://blog.mitsomail.com/?p=72
http://business.mapsofindia.com/sectors/export.html

www.brookings.edu/opinions/2008/0218_india_economy
www.indexmundi.com/india/gdp_real_growth_rate.html

28. PAKISTAN: FAILED OR FAILING?

http://connection.ebscohost.com/c/articles/48109185/ihs-global-insight-report-pakistan-country-intelligence
http://afpak.foreignpolicy.com/posts/2010/06/24/is_pakistan_a_failed_state_no
http://news.oneindia.in/2009/12/06/musharrafforced-nab-to-drop-cases-against-his-close-aides.html
http://dawn.com/business/
http://www.riazhaq.com/2010/03/pakistans-economy-review-2008-2010.html
http://southasiainvestor.blogspot.in/2010/09/pakistans-economic-history-101.html
http://www.riazhaq.com/2008/07/shaukat-azizs-economic-legacy.html
http://southasiainvestor.blogspot.in/2008/08/musharrafs-economic-legacy.html
http://www.riazhaq.com/2010/01/incompetence-worse-than-graft-in.html
http://www.thenews.com.pk/Todays-News-13-941-No-money-left-to-run-government
https://www.cia.gov/library/publications/the-world-factbook/geos/pk.html
http://www.guardian.co.uk/news/datablog/2010/oct/26/corruption-index-2010-transparency-international
www.prlog.org/10591939
http://eurasia.foreignpolicy.com/posts/2010/090/08.pakistans-year
http://pakteahouse.wordpress.com/20010/04/09/food-for-future
www.thenews.com.pk/26-08-2010/lahore
http://thenews.jang.com.pk/daily_detail.asp?id=243743
http://www.economist.com/node/16846266
http://www.carnegieendowment.org/2010/09/29/pakistan-after-

floods/blsq http://seattletimes.com/html/nationworld/2012959494-
pakistanflooding22.html
http://www.bbc.co.uk/news/world-south-asia-11060119 http://
www.nytimes.com/2010/09/29/world/asia/29pstan.html?
pagewanted=all&gwh=CA57FA0BBF715C89E3304D6ED7560602
www.thenews.com.pk/29-09-2010/Top-Story/945.htm http://
axisoflogic.com/artman/publish/printer_61268.shtml
http://archives.dawn.com/archives/73737
http://www.nytimes.com/2010/07/19/world/asia/19taxes.html?
pagewanted=all&gwh=17D70699F7888E66019D07B90091C9A0
http://asifalizardari.wordpress.com/report
http://en.wikipedia.org/wiki/List_of_Pakistanis_by_net_worth
www.zohaibhisam.com/tag/zardari-corruption-statistics
http://pakalert.wordpress.com/2009/08/06/assets-of-dictators-and-
politicians www.thelondonppost.net
http://thenews.jang.com.pk/print1.asp?id=223002
http://thenews.jang.com.pk/daily_detail.asp?id=243749
http://thenews.jang.com.pk/top_story_detail.asp?Id=27053
http://pkpolitics.com/discuss/topic/pakistan-debt-is-rising
http://www.project-syndicate.org/commentary/musharraf-s-return-
www.thenews.com.pk/29-09-2010/Top-Story/950.htm
http://www.paksimple.com/electronics/2011/04/16/highlights-of-
pakistan-budget-2010-2011/
www.atimes.com/atimes/South_Asia/JC19Df02.html
http://www.accessmylibrary.com/article-1G1-218111278/edl-
increased-2-3.html

CONCLUSION: LEADERS MAKE THE DIFFERENCE

http://www.nytimes.com/2006/05/02/world/africa/02
zimbabwe.html?pagewanted=all&gwh=1204CFFB   66053F7
B0640381C40AD1BD2
http://www.guardian.co.uk/world/2003/may/26/nickpatonwalsh
www.informationclearinghouse.info/article3943.htm
www.foreignpolicy.com/.../sucking_up_to_dictators
www.pysih.com/2008/06/06/president-yahya-jamneh
http://www.onlinenigeria.com/abacha_last_days.asp

Index

A*STAR, Singapore, 264
Abacha, Sani, 86, 123, 124–26, 383
Abdel-Rahman, Omar, 15
Abdullah Al-Hourani, 93
Abhisit Vejjajiva, 222
Abramov, 104
Abramovich, 104, 118
Abu Al-Abbas, 93
Abu Dhabi, 35, 254, 257, 312–13
Abu Ghraib prison, Iraq, 49, 97, 236
Abubakar, General, 124, 127
accountability, 95–96, 280
Addax (oil trading company of
    London), 125
adult franchise, 232; Iran, 201
adult literacy, 252
Advani, L.K., 78, 149, 229
Aeroflot Russian Airlines, 104, 114
Afewerki, Isaias, 26, 28–29
Afghanistan, 63–65, 66, 86, 169,
    236, 365; guerrilla warfare, 74.
    See also Russia; United States
Afghans, 186
Africa, 2, 4, 11, 18, 21, 26, 29, 31, 68,
    89, 94, 122–34, 147, 169, 180,
    188, 248, 279, 324, 327, 329–
    30, 333. *See also* individual
    countries of Africa; North
    Africa; South Africa

African National Congress (ANC),
    175, 189, 191, 192–99, 385–86
agriculture, 243; Angola, 25; China,
    287, 290–91, 293; Ghana, 132;
    India, 227, 364; Israel, 35, 318,
    324–26; Mali, 180; Pakistan,
    372, 373, 377, 378, 379; South
    Korea, 271; United States,
    subsidies, 243
Agung, 340
Ahluwalia, Montek Singh, 356
Ahmadinejad, 190, 204, 206, 208–
    11, 213
Ahmed, Fakhruddin Ali, 227
AIDS and HIV: Botswana, 133, 333;
    South Africa, 197
AIG, 346
aircraft leasing: Dubai, 306;
    Indonesia, 138
Akali Dal, India, 76
Aksai Chin (Jammu and Kashmir),
    Indo-China dispute over, 72
Al Jazeera, 172
al Qaeda, 14, 46, 47, 63, 65
Alabbar, Mohammed, 312
Albright, Madeleine, 50
Algeria, 13–17, 94; Front Islamique
    du Salat (FIS), 16; National
    Liberation Front (FLN), 15–16;
    oil, conflict and Islam, 15–17

Ali, Mansoor, 61
Allawi, Ayad, 97
All-Russia Automobile Alliance
    (AVVA), 103
Altantuya, 348
Ambani, Dhirubhai, 358–59
Ambani, Mukesh, 157, 357
Ambanis, 352, 356–57, 359
Amdocs, 323, 325
American Express, 362
Amin, Idi, 171
Amnesty International, 38, 227
Amoli, Ayatollah, 209
Anand Panyarachun, 216
Ananda, King, 213
Anglo-Iranian Oil Company, 200
Angola, 4, 123, 236, 336; Movimento
    Popular de Liberacao de Angola
    (MPLA), 24–25; National
    Union for the Total
    Independence of Angola
    (UNITA), 24–25; oil versus
    diamonds, 23–25; war of
    independence against colonial
    regime of the Portuguese, 24
Annan, Kofi, 94, 133, 168
Annan, Kojo, 94
anti-Christian violence, 76
Aondoakaa, Michael Kase, 87
Arab(s), 211; oil embargo, 34; in
    Palestine, 32
Arafat, Yasser, 320, 389
Arcadia (oil trading company of
    London), 125
Archer, Jeffrey, 248
Archipelago, Gulag, 164
Argentina, 164, 168
Ari, grandson of Suharto, 138–39
Aristotle, 170

Arkan, 55–57
Arunachal Pradesh, Indo-China
    dispute over, 72
Asgaroladi, Asadollah, 205
Ashkenazim, 317, 318
Asian Development Bank (ADB),
    164, 368
Asian financial crisis (1997), 139, 181,
    214, 215, 219, 242, 265, 276,
    278, 311, 343, 372
Assange, Julian, 172
assembly elections (2002) Uttar
    Pradesh, 174–75
AT&T, 362
Ataturk, Mustafa Kemal, 171, 182–
    84, 201, 384, 387, 388, 389;
    abolished Sultanate, 183
Attrition War, 33
Australia, 232, 256, 313
Autovaz, 102, 120
Ayub Khan, 74, 171, 255, 366
Azad Kashmir, 73
Azeris, 211
Azhar, Masood, 66
Aziz, Shaukat, 67, 371, 375
Azmi, Shabana, 229

Babangida, General, 124
Babri Masjid demolition, 78, 229
Bachchan, Amitabh and Jaya, 228
Bacon, Francis, 327
Badawi, Abdullah Ahmad, 341,
    347–48
Baghdad Pact (1955), 40
Baginda, Razak, 348
Bagram prison, Afghanistan, 236
Baht devaluation, Thailand, 215–16
Balkanization, 70
Balochs, Baluchistan, 62, 70, 80, 211;

National Party, 70. *See also* Pakistan

Balzac, Honoré de, 47

Bambang, son of Suharto, 138

Bandaranaike, Solomon, 61

Bangkok Bank, 136

Bangkok Criminal Court, 218

Bangkok Metropolitan Bank, 136

Bangladesh, 60, 94, 178, 226, 231, 252, 347; Awami League, 62, 75

Banharn Silpa-archa, 136, 216

Bank Central Asia Group, 137, 138

Bank of China, 346

banking system, China, 298–99; Western, 123

bankruptcy; India, 353;—Indian Railways, 154;— Indian State Electricity Boards, 363; Pakistan, 371; South Africa, 194; South Korea, 275, 278; United States, 244; Yugoslavia, 59

Banna, Hasan al, 14

Barak Missile scandal, 157

Basij, 206, 207, 208, 209, 211

Basra, Riaz, 67

Basu, Jyoti, 77

Battles, Custer, 97

Baturina, Yelena, 112–13

Beheshti, Ayatollah, 202

Belarus gas market, 110

Belarus Liberal Party, 94

Belgrade's Pink Television, 56

Belhadj, Sheikh, 16

Belkovsky, Stanislav, 111, 117, 119

Bells University, 127

Ben-Gurion, 317

Benedict XVI, Pope, 76

Benjedid, 16

Berdimuhamedov, Gurbanguly, 383

Berezovsky, Boris, 102–03, 104, 117

Berkeley Mafia', 181

Berlusconi, Silvio, 160, 199, 229; scandals, 160

Besant, Annie, 230

Bhagat, Asho, 352

Bhandari, Romesh, 151

Bharatiya Janata Party (BJP), 75, 78–79, 229; attacking Muslims in India, 167

Bharti Airtel, 361

Bhatnagar, S.K., 150

Bhave, Vinoba, 227

Bhindrawale, Jarnail Singh, 77

Bhumipol, King, 213

Bhutto, Benazir, 94, 167, 366; assassination, 61

Bhutto, Murtaza, 65

Bhutto, Zulfiqar Ali; death, 61, 64, 178, 255, 366

Bihar, 80, 151, 153, 155–56

Bimantra Group, 138

Bio-Bee Biological Systems, 326

Birendra, King of Nepal, 61

Black Economic Empowerment (BEE), 195–96, 339

black money, 87

black-market: Algeria, 16, Iran, 210; Yugoslavia, 58

Blackwater (American mercenary army), 98

Blood Diamond, 21

Blue Star Operation, 77, 149

Blum, William, 3, 10, 43, 236, 237

Bofors scandal, India, 149–51. *See also* Gandhi, Rajiv

Bolivia, 236; riots over water prices, 242

Bombay Stock Exchange (BSE), 359

Bongo, Omer, 131

Borojerdi, Ayatollah, 202

Bosnia, 52–53; Muslims, 54; Serb forces committed genocide, 54; war (1992–95), 53, 58

Botswana, 132, 133–34, 249, 252–53, 255, 257, 327–34, 389; Bechuanaland Democratic Party (BDP), 328, 329; Cattle Producers Association, 332; Democratic Party (BDP), 252; Development Corporation (BDC), 332; Meat Commission (BMC), 331–32

Boudiaf, Mohamed, 16; assassination, 17; Charter for Peace and Reconciliation, 17

Bouteflika, Abdelaziz, 17

BPPC, Indonesia, 138

brain drain, 11, 88

Branson, Richard, 139

Bratva, Solntsenskaya, 316

Brazil, 236

Brevnov, Boris, 107

bribes, kickbacks illegal use of big money, 85–87, 167, 170; China, 141, 143–46; India, 148, 150–52, 157–58, 226, 357; Iraq, 92, 94; Nigeria, 87, 123–25, 128–29; Pakistan, 380; Russia, 109; Thailand, 175

British/Britain: colonialism, Malaysia, 342; dismantled Italian empire in Africa, 30; invasion of Iraq, 47; mandate of Palestine, 14; rule in India, 353

British Airways, 362

British Banking Association, 126

British Petroleum, 108

Brooke, James, 347

budget deficit: Malaysia, 344, 349; Pakistan, 251, 369–72; Thailand, 219; United States, 238, 239

Bugti, Baramdagh, 70

Bugti, Nawab Akbar, 61; assassination, 70

Buhari, General, 124

Bulgaria, 168; Socialist Party, 94

Bumiputra Malaysian Finance, Hong Kong, 345

Bumiputras (sons of the soil), 186, 195, 338–39, 345, 349

bureaucracy, 169; Algeria, 15; Botswana, 333; China, 142, 159, 283, 285, 287, 297, 300, 362; Dubai, 303, 312; India, 153, 226, 353, 362; Pakistan, 376; Russia, 102, 103; Singapore, 261, 263, 265; South Korea, 273; Thailand, 215

Burton, Richard, 327

Busby, Chris, 43

Bush, George H.W. (Sr.), 129

Bush, George W. (Jr.), 44, 46–47, 238, 246, 390

Buthelezi, 193, 385

CACI International, US contractor, 97

Calil, Eli, 248

Caliphate, 388

Cambodia, 165, 236

Canada, population, 256

capital, 253–56

capital market liberalization, 242

capitalism, 160, 293; India, 173, 354; Iran, 204; Russia, 102, 116

Carfagna, Mara, 160

Carla Del Ponte, 52

Carnegie, Andrew, 162

Carnegie Endowment for
    International Peace, 143, 373

Carroll, Lewis, 247

Carter, Jimmy, 38

cash flow deficits, China, 297

cash for votes scandal, India, 158

cash payment system, 95–96

Castro, Fidel, 389

Cattan, Zaid, 98

Ceca, Svetlana, 55–56

Central African Republic, 123, 365

Central Intelligence Agency (CIA),
    39–40, 65, 109, 129, 130, 175, 181,
    200, 236–37, 241, 288

Chad, 94, 123, 236, 365

Chadha, Win, 150

Chaebols, 253, 262, 268–80. *See also*
    South Korea

Chagoury, Gilbert, 125

Chandra Shekhar, 150–51

Chandraswami, 150–51, 152

Charoen Pokphand Group, 217

Chaudhry, Chief Justice Iftikhar, 367

Chaudhrys, 375

Chavalit Yongchaiyudh, 216

Chavan, Ashok, 158

Chavez, Hugo, 48, 229, 241

Che, Gueuevera, 384

Chechnya, Russia, 105; mafia, 112;
    war, 115

Checkpoint Software Technologies,
    Israel, 325

Chemezov, 120

Chen Liangyu, 144–45

Chen Xitong, 144

Chen Yun, 282, 283, 284, 290, 293–
    94, 295, 296

Cheney, Dick, 45, 47, 96–97

Cheng Kejie, 144, 146

Chernomyrdin, Viktor, 109–11

Chiang Kai-shek, 66, 283, 287–88

Chidambaram, P., 356

Chile, 168, 236

China, 25, 48, 94, 136, 140–46, 168,
    231, 236, 239, 243–44, 248–49,
    251, 253, 254, 256, 257, 267,
    272, 281–300, 344, 346, 353,
    368, 374, 389, 390; Communist
    Party (CCP), 143, 159, 169, 201,
    251, 294, 389, 391;—
    Organization Department, 141;
    conquered Tibet, 72; Cultural
    Revolution, 282, 285, 286–88,
    294, 384; Party Organization
    Department, 390; People's
    Liberation Army (PLA), 282,
    285, 288–89, 295–96; Red
    Guards, 284–86, 288, 294–95;
    takeover of Hong Kong, 296;
    Politburo Standing Committee
    (PBSC), 141, 384, 390

Chinese in Thailand, 217

Chinese National Telephone
    Corporation, 324

Chirac, 93

Chiranjeevi, 229

Christians, 67, 84; reconversion to
    Hinduism, 76

Chuan Leekpai, 216

Chubais, 102, 105, 107–08, 111

Chun Doo-hwan, 269, 275, 277–79

Chung Ju Yung, 268, 274, 277

Chung Mong-hun, 270

Churchill, Winston, 176

Cisco, 323

Citibank, 126, 362, 371

Citigroup, 346
civil wars, 165; Algeria, 17; Angola,
    23, 24, 25; Liberia and Sierra
    Leone, 18, 19–20, 21; Pakistan,
    60, 71; United States, 245
Clark, Wesley, 238
class conflicts, 10; in India, 80, 226,
    230
Clinton, Bill, 57, 160, 241, 246, 390
Coalition Provisional Authority
    (CPA) of US, 95–96
coalitions, India, 154, 159, 229–30,
    355; Israel, 320; Malaysia, 185,
    187
Coca-Cola, India, 354
Cold War, 6, 10, 26, 166, 237
Collier, Paul, 165, 179
commune system, China, 290
communism, 10, 64, 160, 270, 293;
    China, 282; collapse in Europe
    and USSR, 295; communist
    insurgency, Malaysia, 335;
    Russia, 102; computer
    technology, Israel, 323–24, 325
conflict and violence/insurgency, 61,
    236, 249; in Africa, 11; in
    Algeria, 15–17; Egypt, 13–15;
    India, 71–84, 225–26, 231;—
    north-east, 82; Iraq, 91; Israel,
    316, 318–19; Malaysia, 336;
    Middle East, 11; Pakistan,
    internal and external, 62–71,
    178–79, 250, 365, 368, 374;
    Sierra Leone, 330; South Asia,
    11; South Africa, 193; Yugoslavia,
    11; cause of human suffering, 9;
    between nations and within
    nations, 10; over diamonds and
    oil, 23–25

Confucius, 391
Congo Crisis (1961), 30
Congress, 77, 78, 94, 149, 157, 191,
    229–30, 251, 317, 388
corporate sector, South Korea, 274
corruption, 85–89, 164, 249;
    Afghanistan, 86, 148; Africa,
    122–34; Angola, 23–25;
    Bangladesh, 148; Botswana, zero
    tolerance, 329, 330–31; China,
    89, 143, 159, 285, 287, 293–96,
    298, 384; Dubai, 302;
    Equatorial Guinea, 248; Ghana,
    132; India, 89, 140, 147–62, 226,
    232, 353, 363; Indonesia, 86, 135,
    236, 242; Iraq, 47, 86, 89;—
    Saddam Hussein, America and
    democracy, 91–100; Israel, 322;
    Malaysia, 187, 188, 347–48;
    Myanmar, 148; Nepal, 148;
    Nigeria, 86, 87, 123–29, 140;
    Pakistan, 148, 179, 250, 366, 367,
    369–70, 371, 375; Philippines,
    86, 135; Russia, 101–21, 140;
    Sierra Leone, 330; Singapore,
    war on, 260–61; South Africa,
    194; South Korea, 269, 278–80;
    Thailand, 136, 215, 218; Zaire,
    86, 129–31, 236
Costa Rica, 236
Cote d'Ivoire, 123
Cotecna, 94
coups: Bolivia, 170; Equatorial
    Guinea, 247–48; Ghana, 133;
    Liberia, 19; Pakistan, 171;
    Thailand, 218, 221
credit policy, China, 298
crime, inflation and corruption;
    Malaysia, 188; syndicates,
    Russia, 111

crimes against humanity, 52, 54
criminalization of politics; Thailand,
218; Yugoslavia, 59
Croatia, 52–53; war of
independence (1991–95), 53, 57
Croats, 53, 56, 57
crony capitalism, 136
crop failure, India, 225
Crown Property Bureau, Thailand,
216
Cuba, 236, 245
current account deficit: India, 353;
Pakistan, 370; Palestine, 35

Daewoo, 205, 274, 276–77
Dalits and OBCs (Other Backward
Classes) in India, 84, 226
de Clerk, 192
DeBeers, 328, 329, 331
Debswana, 329
debt–equity ratios, China, 297
decentralization, China, 287
defence expenditure; Israel, 320
Delta Prospectors Ltd, Nigeria, 125
democracy, 163–76, 189–90, 249,
251, 252, 302, 317, 390;
Botswana, 330; China, 294, 296;
India, 224–33; Iran, 200–11;
Israel, 320; Malaysia, 188, 342;
Pakistan, 366, 374, 376; no in
Singapore, 259–67; South
Africa, 191–99; South Korea,
269, 271; Thailand, battled the
monarchy, 212–23; Turkey, 184;
Western, 179
Democratic Republic of the Congo.
See Zaire
Deng Xiaoping, 8, 142, 144, 162,
251, 267, 281–85, 287, 289–97,
300, 383, 387, 390

depleted uranium (DU), 43
Derg, 28
Deripaska, 120
Dermawan, Sukma, 187
Desai, Morarji, 149
Desert Storm Operation, 43
Deutsche Telecom, 323, 324
development model, Japan, 262
development, South Korea, 268–69,
277
DFI, 254
Dhanarajata, Sarit, 213
Dharmendra, 229
diamond industry: Botswana, 327–
34; Israel, 33, 35, 315–23; Sierra
Leone, 30–31
dictatorship, China, 296; Liberia, 19
Dindic, Zoran, 52–53
displacement, India, 60; Liberia, 20
Doe, Samuel, 19–20
Dolgoprudnenskaya, 105
domestic market: Botswana, 332;
India, 353
domestic savings, Singapore, 263
Dominican Republic, 236
Domnikov, Igor, 115
dot-com bubble, 360
Dravid Munnetra Kazhagam
(DMK), India, 158–59
drug mafias, drug-trafficking, 87;
Pakistan, 369; Russia, 104
Dubai, 249, 251, 254, 301–14; Dry
Dock, 305, 308, 311; tolerance
and open-mindedness, 302–04
Dubai Aluminium, 305
Dubai International airport, 305,
306, 309
Dubai International Financial
Centre (DIFC), 312

Dubai School of Governance, 312
Dubai Shopping Festival, 309
Dugas, Dubai, 305
Dulles, John Foster, 31
Dutt, Sanjay, 229
Dyakov, Anatoly, 107
Dzhabrailov, Umar, 111–12

Ebadi, Shirin, 207
Eckel, Paul, 237
Economic and Financial Crimes
    Commission (EFCC), Nigeria,
    127–28
economic reforms, China, 296; India,
    166, 173, 352, 354, 362
economic sanctions on Iran, Iraq,
    Libya and Syria, 34
economy, economic performance,
    244, 245, 251, 256; Algeria, 17;
    Botswana, 327, 329–30; China,
    136, 143, 232, 282–85, 287, 289–
    90, 292–97, 300, 387; Dubai,
    309, 313; India, 152, 173, 226,
    227, 231–32, 251, 351–56, 358,
    360–64, 389; Indonesia, 135–36;
    Iran, 210; Iraq, 41; Israel, 257;
    Japan, 256; Liberia, 20;
    Malaysia, 340, 335, 338, 342–5,
    347, 348–49; Pakistan, 250–51,
    255, 365–66, 367–68, 369–
    74;—collapse, 366; Philippines,
    135–36; Russia, 105, 116, 119, 121;
    Singapore, 135, 232, 261–63,
    265; South Africa, 186, 194, 195;
    South Korea, 232, 270, 2171,
    274–75, 277–80; Taiwan, 232,
    270; Thailand, 214, 215, 219;
    USA, 48, 238, 246; USSR, 282
Ecuador, 236; riots over cooking gas
    price rise, 242

education, 249, 252; Botswana, 252,
    329, 334; China, 287–88; Dubai,
    313; India, 360, 362, 364; Israel,
    316; Malaysia, 338, 343, 348–50;
    Pakistan, failure, 71; Singapore,
    267; South Korea, 279
Egypt, 13–17, 389; conflicts, 13–
    15;—external with Israel, 15;
    National Democratic Party, 93;
    Revolution, 387; Six Day War
    against Israel, 33, 319, 388
Einstein, Albert, 161, 387
electoral frauds, 167–68
electoral politics: Botswana, 389;
    India, 149, 230; South Korea,
    expenses, 175; Thailand, 220–22
electoral practices, 174
electricity reforms, India, 362–63
Elena, 114
Elizabeth, Queen, 162
Emaar, 310, 311
Emergency, India, 1975–77, 149,
    227; Pakistan, 367
Emirates Airlines, 306, 309
Enron fiasco, 363
equality before law, 168
Equatorial Guinea, 247–48, 382
equity cult, 359
Erbakan, Necmettin, 184
Erdogan, Recep Tayyip, 184, 185
Ericsson, 323
Eritrea, liberation, 31
Ethiopia, 245; and Eritrea, thirty
    years war, 26
ethnic cleansing, Bosnia, 54, 56
ethnic conflicts, 10; Serbia, 52
ethnic groups: economic
    discrepancies, Malaysia, 338;
    Iran, 211; Pakistan, 62

Eural Transgas, 110, 119
European Union (EU), 38, 166, 180, 185, 332
exchange rates, 245
exports, 6, 7, 239, 240, 243–44, 249; Algeria, 15; Botswana, 253, 329, 331–33; China, 242, 253, 292, 293, 299, 300; Dubai, 302, 305; India, 226, 227, 251, 253, 353, 354, 359; Iraq, 41; Israel, 34, 35, 253, 316, 318–19, 321, 325–26; Liberia, 20; Malaysia, 253, 336–37, 343, 348, 350; Pakistan, 250, 253, 370, 378–79; Russia, 103, 116, 120–21; Singapore, 253, 254, 263; South Korea, 269, 270, 272, 273, 275, 278–79; Thailand, 219
extrajudicial killings, Pakistan, 67
Eyadama, 131

Failed States Index (2010), 365, 368
family politics: Egypt, 174; Lebanon, 174; Syria, 174
famine, China, 283–84, 290, 291
farmers mass suicide, India, 225
Federally Administered Tribal Areas (FATA), Pakistan, 60
Federov, Boris, 110
Fernandes, George, 158
Fimaco scandal, Russia, 114
financial crisis; Malaysia, 344; Pakistan, 370; South Korea, 275; United States, 321
Financial Institutions Development Fund; Thailand, 218
financial management, Pakistan, 372
financial system, United States, 244
fiscal and monetary policy, Pakistan, 250

fiscal deficit, Pakistan, 371
Fisk, Robert, 172
Floods, Pakistan (2010), 366, 368, 372–73
fodder scam, India, 153–54
food programme, Iraq, 100
food surplus, China, 291
Ford Motor, 346
foreign capital, India, 354
foreign debt, Pakistan, 371
foreign direct investment (FDI), foreign investment, 10; China, 272, 292–94; Dubai, 302, 303; India, 354, 362–63; Israel, 321; Malaysia, 343, 348; Pakistan, 255–56, 370, 371–72; Singapore, 263, 292; South Korea, 272
foreign exchange crises, Malaysia, 343
Foreign Exchange Regulation Act (FERA), India, 354
foreign exchange reserves; India, 354; Indonesia, 182; Pakistan, 368, 370; Thailand, 219
forgery and fraud, Russia, 108
Forsyth, Frederick, 248
France, 86, 95
Franco, General, 232
Frankenstein, 62
freedom of religion, Dubai, 303
Friedman, Mikhail, 104

Gaidar, 102, 112
Galbraith, John Kenneth, 247
Al-Galda, Imad, 93
Galespie, April, 42
Galloway, George, 93
Gandhi, Indira, 61, 77, 147, 148–49, 226–27, 230, 256, 353, 355–56; assassination, 61, 77

Gandhi, M.K., 61, 76, 82, 84, 147,
    161, 174, 191–92, 195, 251, 354,
    383; assassination, 61
Gandhi, Rahul, 231, 355
Gandhi, Rajiv, 61, 83, 149–50, 230,
    353, 355; assassination, 83
Gandhi, Sanjay, 76, 149, 227, 256
Gandhi, Sonia, 230–31, 351, 352,
    354–56, 389, 390
Ganji, Akbar, 207
gas and other natural resources, 87,
    249; Baluchistan, 69, 70;
    Botswana, 330; Dubai, lacks,
    301; India, 359;—North East,
    83; Indonesia, 181; Iran, 206;
    Malaysia, 254, 336, 343, 346–
    47; Russia, 103, 109–10, 117–21,
    166; Singapore, lacks, 254, 259;
    South Korea, 268;
    Turkmenistan, 110; Zaire, 130
Gaz, 120
Gaza Strip, 38
Gazfond, Russia, 118
Gazprom Media Holdings, 118
Gazprom, Russia, 93, 109–11, 117–
    19
Gbenga, 127
Gecamines, 130
Geldof, Bob, 28
General Electric (GE), 346, 362, 391
General Motors (GM), 391
Genghis Khan, 239
Georgia, 165
al-Gergawi, Mohammed, 312
Germany, 86, 255
Ghana, 132, 133, 236
Ghanem, Shukri, 93
Ghazi, King of Iraq, 42
Gilani, Yousaf Raza, 373

Giraldi, Philip, 95–96
Girenko, Nikolai, 115
Girhotra, Ruchika, 224–25
Glasnost, 101
Glencore, 125
Global Hunger Index (GHI), 226
globalization, 252, 303, 307, 354
Gobind Singh, Guru, 153
Goh Keng Swee, 260, 265, 390
Golden Temple, Amritsar, India,
    Sikh militants in, 77
Goldovsky, 119
good governance, 1, 2, 7, 168–71,
    249–50; Botswana, 255; Dubai,
    312; Pakistan lacks, 171, 249;
    Singapore, 169, 260
Gorbachev, Mikhail, 101
Govinda, 229
Gowon military regime, Nigeria,
    124
Great Depression, 46, 246
Great Leap Forward, China, 283–
    84, 287, 287, 290, 291, 295, 384
Green Revolution, India, 364
Greenhouse, Bunny, 96
gross domestic product (GDP), 252;
    China, 243, 248, 298; India,
    354; Israel, 316; Malaysia, 337;
    Pakistan, 369–70; South Korea,
    269, 273
gross national product (GNP);
    Israel, 319, 320; South Korea,
    274
Groupe Islamique Armee (GIA), 17
Guangxi Zhuang Autonomous
    Region, 144
Guantanamo, 236
Guatemala, 236
Guinea, 123, 365

Guinea-Bissau, 123
Gujarat genocide, 76, 79
Gul, Hamid, 65
Gulf War (1991), 39, 42–44; role
  of America, 45
Gunvor, 117, 119
Guzinsky, Vladimir, 103, 117
Gwadar port, 70

Habibie, 181
Habibollah, 205
Hadi, brother of Khamenei, 206
Haditha, Mashhour, 93
Hague trial, 57
Haile Selassie, Emperor of Ethiopia,
  26, 27–28, 29
Haiti, 86, 165, 236
Hajjarian, Saeed, 207
Halabja massacre, Iraq, (1988), 41
Halliburton, 87, 96–97, 125
Halperin, 165
Halutz, Dan, 322
Hamdan, Prince Sheikh, 312
Haq, Fazle, 61
Hathaway, Berkshire, 346
Haviv, Ron, 55, 56
Hawala Scandal, India, 158
Hawksley, Humphrey, 164
Herzegovina, 52
Herzl, Theodor, 32
Hezbollah, 34, 322
Hindu militancy and communalism,
  75, 84
Hindu–Muslim tension and violence,
  78, 227
Hinduja brothers, 150
Hiroshima and Nagasaki, 4, 9
Hitler, Adolf, 58, 246
Ho Chi Minh, 383, 386–87

Holbrooke, Richard, 57
Hong Kong, 135, 292, 293, 339
Hopkins, Johns, 265
Household Responsibility System
  (HRS), China, 291, 293, 294
housing, Singapore, 261–64
HP, 323
HSBC, 346, 362
Hu Jintao, 142–43, 145, 296
Hu Yaobang, 282, 294, 390
Hua Guofeng, 289
human rights, 163; Indonesia, 139
Hungarian Interest Party, 94
Huntington, Samuel, 164
Husain, Altaf, 167
Hussain, Malik Riaz, 375
Hu-Wen, 390
Hyderabad, princely states, India, 73
hyperinflation. See inflation
Hyundai, 270, 273–74, 277, 332

IBM, 323, 362
Ibori, James, 128
Ibrahim, Anwar, 187–88, 341–42,
  343–44, 349
Ibrahim, Dawood, 78
Ijaz-ul-Haq, 65
ijma (consensus), 177
ijtihad (interpretation), 177
illegal taxation and protection
  money, India, 80
illiteracy: India, 226, 364; Liberia,
  20; Mali, 179; Pakistan, 179, 258
immigration to enhance population,
  256–57
import substitution: India, 353;
  Singapore, 262; South Korea,
  273
impoverishment, Liberia, 20

incompetence and mismanagement, Pakistan, 370

India, 48, 71–84, 168, 189–90, 217, 248–49, 251, 253, 368; China war, (1962), 60, 71–72, 83; and Pakistan three wars, 60, 71;—(1947–48), 73;—(1965), 71, 73–74;—(1971), 74; a story of accidents, 351–64; world's biggest democracy, 224–33

Indian Airlines hijacking settlement (1999), 66

Indian Institutes of Technology (IITs), 255, 360

Indian Peace Keeping Force (IPKF), 83

Indian Railways, 154–55

Indonesia, 135, 168, 175, 181–82, 267, 388; Islamic democracy, 178, 181–82

industrialization: China, 282, 323; Singapore, 292

industry: Botswana, 332; China, 287, 291–92, 297; India, 356, 357, 360–62; Israel, 317; Malaysia, 254, 336, 342, 343, 350; Singapore, 262, 265; South Korea, 273

inflation, hyperinflation; Botswana, 331; China 293–96; Israel, 320, 321; Malaysia, 343; Pakistan, 69, 71, 369, 371; Russia, 114; South Korea, 273; United States, 240; Yugoslavia, 59; Zaire, 130–31

Information Technology (IT), 352, 359–61, 362

Infosys, 361

infrastructure project, South Korea, 274

Inkombank, Russia, 104

innovation, Israel, 323–26

INSEAD, 265

Intel, 323, 325

Inter-Services Intelligence (ISI), Pakistan, 63–65, 66, 83

intermediaries, 85; Russia, 110, 119

international community, 46, 370, 373

International Court of Justice (ICJ), 37, 54, 333

International Criminal Tribunal, 54

international economic system, 240–41, 243

international markets, 303, 353

International Monetary Fund (IMF), 166, 219, 241–42, 243, 251, 278, 344, 354, 366, 368, 372

International Singapore Companies (ISCs), 267

investment banking industry, United States, 244

investment capital, 249; Israel, 317–18

Iran, 178, 189, 190, 212, 217, 236, 238, 258, 346; Bill of Rights of equality of all before law, 211; Council of Guardians, 167, 201–02, 207, 212; Council of Revolution, 203; Cultural Revolution, 209, 210; Dubai, connection, 303, 305; Expediency Council, 202; –Iraq war (1980–88), 39–42, 204, 309; Islamic Republic Party, 203; Revolutionary Guards, 201, 202, 206, 207, 208, 210–12

Irani, Smriti, 229

Iraq, 86, 131, 236, 238, 241, 365;

Ba'ath Party, 40; Commission on Public Integrity (CPI), 97, 99–100, 129; Defence Ministry scandal, 98; invasion of Kuwait, 42; resistance to American occupation, 50; war declared by United States (Iraq War), 39, 45

Islam, 13, 62, 66, 175, 388; exploitation for partisan politics, 17

Islambuli, Khalid, 14–15

Islamic democracy, 16, 177–88; Pakistan, 178–79

Islamic guerrilla groups, 17

Islamic Revolution, 189, 201

Islamic socialism, 16

Israel, 14, 32–38, 41, 245, 249, 251, 253, 255, 256; Defence Force (IDF), 320; Histadrut Labour Union, 317, 321; Kadima Party, 38; Knesset Foreign and Military Affairs Committee, 322; Labour Party, 251; Lost Decade (1973–85), 33, 317, 319–20; occupied the Sinai Peninsula, East Jerusalem, Gaza Strip, Golan Heights, West Bank, 37, 319; settlements in the West Bank and the Gaza Strip, 54; successful socialism, successful capitalism, 315–26. See also Palestine, Palestinians

Itera, 110, 119

Ivanishvili, 104

Ivanov, Sergey, 115

J.P. Morgan Chase, 346

Jain brothers, 158

Jaish-e-Mohammed (JeM), 66

Jala, Idris, 349

Jammeh, Lieutnant Yahya, 383

Jana Sangh, 75

Janata Party, 149

Japan, 86, 135, 239, 253–54, 274; Liberal Democratic Party (LDP), 175

Jayalalitha, J., 148, 156, 159, 228

Jayaprada, 229

Jebel Ali Free Zone, Dubai, 304, 307

Jebel Ali port, Dubai, 304, 305, 306

Jefferson, Thomas, 172

Jerusalem, 37–38

Jewish, Jews, 178, 249, 257, 315, 318; diaspora in Israel, 255, 317, 318; lobby in United States, 34

Jhangvi, Haq Nawaz, 67

Jharkhand Mukti Morcha (JMM), 151, 152

Jia Qinglin, 144

Jiang Qing, 289, 296, 298

Jiang Zemin, 141–45, 390

jihad, 14, 15, 62, 64, 66

Jinnah, Muhammad Ali, 161, 178, 252, 387–88

John Atta-Mills, 133

Johnson, Prince of Liberia, 20

Jones, Jamie Leigh, 97

Jordan, 168

Judiciary: in China, 169; Malaysia, 186, 339, 342

Junagarh, princely state, 73

Jurong Industrial Estate, 264–65

Jurong Island, 267

justice systems, 168

Kadannikov, Vladimir, 102

Kagnew communications base, Asmara, Ethiopia, 29–31
Kahan committee, 36
Kalahari Game Reserve, Botswana, 332
Kalmadi, Suresh, 148, 158
Kamalism, 184
Karadzic, Radovan, 52
Kargil war, 71, 74. *See also* Pakistan
Karimov, Islam, 382
Karunanidhi, M., 148
Karzai, Hamid, 63
Kashmir issue, 60, 66, 74; Hindu pandits, 79–80; Indo-Pak Conflict, 73–74; princely state, 73. *See also* Pakistan
Katsav, Moshe, 160, 323
Kaunda, Kenneth, 167
KBR, 87, 97, 125
Keeler, Christine, 160
Keiretsu, Japan, 262, 272, 274
Kennedy, Joe, 163
Kennedy, John F., 129, 160, 246
Kennedy, Robert, 160
KGB, 65, 115, 116, 118, 120, 174
Khalid (son of Nasser), 93
Khalistan, 77
Khama, Ian, 330
Khama, Seretse, 8, 327–30, 389
Khamenei, Ayatollah Ali, 202, 204, 206, 210
Khan, A.Q., 64
Khan, Liaquat Ali; assassination, 61
Khan, Lt Gen (retd) Muhammad Aziz, 374–75
Khanna, Vinod, 229
Khashoggi, Adnan, 150
Khatami, Mohammad, 206, 207, 209, 210

Khatloni, Iskandar, 115
Khayyam, Omar, 391
Khodorkovsky, Mikhail, 104, 109, 117
Khomeini, Ayatollah, 40, 189, 200, 201–04, 377, 384
Khrushchev, Nikita, 283
Kia car, 138
kickbacks and fraud, Iraq, 100; Nigeria, 124 killing and kidnapping and torture: Iraq, 99; Pakistan, 369; Zaire, 130
Kims in North Korea, 259, 269, 279
Kim Chaegyu, 278
Kim Dae-jung, 269, 275–76
Kim Woo Choong, 268, 276–77
Kim Young-sam, 269
King, Martin Luther, Jr., 9, 147, 387
Kirkuk oil, 44–45
Klebnikov, Paul, 115
knowledge-based economy, Singapore, 266
Koda, Madhu, 148
Korea, 236, 249, 253; reunification, 257
Kosovar Albanian women, 57
Kosovo, 52, 57; war (1996–99), 53
Kouk, Robert, 345
Kovalchuk, Yuri, 118
Kozlov, Andrei, 115
Krahn tribe, Liberia, 19
Kremlin, 113, 114, 116; Property Management Department, 116
Kripalani, Jivatram B., 149
Krishnan, Ananda, 345
Kuala Lampur International Airport, 345
Kudrin, Oleg, 106
Kukje Group, 275

Kurds, 41, 44, 47, 50, 168, 211;
    Peshmargas, 70
Kwangju massacre, 278
Kyrgyzstan, 168

Lahoud, Emile, 93
Lamborghini Car Company, 138
land reclamation, Indonesia, 138
land reforms, South Korea, 270–71
land speculation, China, 143
Lansky, Meyer, 316
Lao Tzu, 391
Laos, 236
Lashkar-e-Jhangvi (LeJ), 67
Lashkar-e-Taiba (LeT), 66
Lausanne Treaty, 183
law and order, breakdown, Pakistan,
    68
Lebanon, 93, 238; War, 33, 322
Lee Kuan Yew, 5, 161, 189, 251, 259–
    65, 267, 292, 302, 383, 389, 390
Lee, B.G., 260
Leon, Tony, 197
Letizia, Noemi, 160
Lewinsky, Monica, 160
LG, 273, 274
Li Peng, 294–95
Li Ping, 144
liberalization, 241; India, 352
Liberia and Sierra Leone, 18–22;
    Liberia National Patriotic Front
    of Liberia (NPFL), 19
Libya, 93, 123, 236, 238
Licence Raj, India, 152, 173, 231, 353,
    359, 360
life expectancy, Botswana, 333
Lin Biao, 282, 286, 288
Lincoln, Abraham, 245, 386
Line of Control (LoC), 73

literacy, 252; Botswana, 333; India,
    231; South Korea, 279
Litvinenko, Alexander, 116
Liu Jinbao, 140
Liu Shaoqi, 283–86, 288
Liu Zhenhua, 146
Liu Zhihua, 141, 145–46
Live Aid concerts, 28
Livni, Tzipi, 38
loan for shares scheme, Russia, 108
Look East policy, 342
Lootah, Ali Rashid Ahmed, 312
Lord of War, The (movie), 18
Lukoil, Russian company, 93, 108
Lula, 390
Lumumba, Patrice, 30
Luzhkov, Yuri, 103, 111, 112, 113

Mabetex scandal case, 113–14
Macedonian conflict (2001), 53
Madani, Abassi, 16
mafia capitalism, Russia, 160
mafia, Uttar Pradesh, 157
Mahato, Shailendra, 151
Mahdi, the Hidden Imam, 209
Maher, Bill, 246
Mahmud, Taib (v/v), 347
el-Mahroug, Karima, 160
Makozoma, Saki, 196
Malaysia, 6, 7, 8, 94, 136, 175, 249,
    253–54, 265–66, 335–50, 389;
    Barisan National (BN), 187, 188,
    338; Chinese ethnic minority,
    186; Constitution Amendment
    Bill (1983), 340; Indonesia,
    confrontation, 335; Islamic
    democracy, 185–88; Malay and
    Chinese, economic
    discrepancies, 337;—riots, 336;

United Malay National Organization (UNMO), 185, 186, 187, 336, 338, 341–2, 345

Malaysian Chinese Association (MCA), 185, 338

Malaysian Indian Congress (MIC), 186, 338

Malcolm X, 172

Mali, 179–80; Islamic democracy, 179–80

malnutrition, India, 226

Mamiek, 137

Mandela, Nelson, 8, 131, 147, 161, 175, 186, 191–99, 237, 383–87, 389

Manipur, princely state, 81, 82

Mann, Etonian Simon, 248

Manuel, Trevor, 194

Mao Zedong, 3, 8, 65, 80, 142, 162, 201, 235, 251, 256, 272, 281–90, 294–95, 353, 382–85, 387

Maoism, 24, 293

Marcos, Ferdinand, 86, 136, 137, 165–66

Marcos, Imelda, 137, 156

Mariam, Mengistu Haile, 26, 28, 31

Marican, Hassan, 346–47

market-based pricing, 242

Marshal Ye, 289

Marxism, 293

Masire, Ketumile, 329–30

Masud, Baitullah, 68

Masud, Hakimullah, 68

Maude, Lt. Gen. Sir Stanley, 47

Mayawati, 148, 156–57

Mbeki, Judy, 196

Mbeki, Thabo, 195–99

McGrory, Daniel, 116

McMahon Line, 71–72

McMahon, Sir Henry, 71

media censorship, Iran, 209

media function in society, 171–72

medical and life sciences, Israel, 324

medical tourism, Singapore, 266

Medvedev, Dmitry, 109, 117

Megawati (Sukarnoputri), 94, 181

Meiji Restoration, 272

Meir, Golda, 315, 317

Meron, Theodor, 38, 54

Mesbah-Yazdi, Ayatollah Taqi, 209

Microsoft, 323

Middle East, 34–35, 46, 93, 166, 236, 301, 306, 369

Mikhailov, Sergei, 316

military insurgency, Pakistan, 63

military power, China, 295–96; India, 231

Miller, Alexey, 117, 119

Milosevic, Marko, 58

Milosevic, Mira, 52

Milosevic, Slobodan, 51–53, 57–58, 86

Mirzan, 345

mismanagement and corruption. See corruption

MIT, 265

MITI, 272

Mitsubishi, 323

Mladic, Ratko, 52, 54–55

mobile telecommunication: Indonesia, 138; Israel, 324

Mobutu, Sese Seko, 27, 86, 123, 129–31, 166

modernization and Westernization: Turkey, 388

modernization strategy, Japan, 272

Modi, Narendra, 79

Mogae, Festus, 330

Mogilevich, Semion, 104, 110, 316
Mohamad, Mahathir bin, 8, 161, 185–87, 195, 242, 251, 335, 336–37, 339–45, 347–49, 378, 383, 389–90
Mohammad, Maulana Sufi, 177
Mohammed, Sheikh, 301, 302, 304, 306, 308–12, 389
Moi, Daniel Arap, 167, 383
Mojisola, 127
Monetary Authority of Singapore (MAS), 264
money laundering; Equatorial Guinea, 249; Pakistan, 369; Russia, 104, 114–15
Mongolia, 168
Monroe, James, 19
Monroe, Marilyn, 160
Montazeri, Ayatollah Hossein Ali, 202, 203–04, 206, 211
Mosaddegh, Mohammad, 40, 200
Moscow apartment bombings, 116
Moscow telecommunications company, 112
Motorola, 323
Motsebe, Patrice, 196
Mousavi, Mir-Hossein, 190, 211
Mu Suixin, 140
Mubarak, Hosni, 15, 93, 383
Mugabe, Robert, 28, 167, 382
Muhajir refugees from India, 62
Muhammad, Murtala, 124
Mujahedeen, 62
Mukhriz, 345
Multimedia Super Corridor, 344
multinational corporations (MNCs), Singapore, 262, 292; South Korea, 271
Mumbai bomb blasts (1993), 78

Musa, 341
Musharraf, Pervez, 65–67, 167, 171, 176, 356, 366, 367–69, 371, 374–75
Muslim Brotherhood, 14–15
Muslim hostility to Israel, 34
Muslims, 57, 84, 249
Myanmar, 86, 135

Nagas, 82
Najib Razak, 348–49
Nakheel, 310, 311, 312
Napoleon, 172, 214, 236, 391
Narayan, Jayaprakash, 149, 227
Nasrullah, Hassan, 34
Nasser, Gamal Abdel, 13–14, 93, 131, 318, 384, 387–89
National Accountability Bureau (NAB), 374–75
National People's Congress (NPC), 144
National Reconciliation Ordinance (NRO), 179
natural resources. See gas and other natural resources
Nawaz Sharif, 255–56
Naxalite movement, India, 80, 84
NEC, 386
Nehru, Jawaharlal, 8, 82, 147, 174, 195, 230–31, 251, 255, 351, 353–55, 360, 388
Nelson Fu, 286
Nemtsov, Boris, 120, 121
Nestle, 346
Netanyahu, Benjamin, 37–38
network politics, Thailand, 217
Nevzlin, 104
New Economic Policy (NEP), Malaysia, 251, 337, 338, 339, 343

Nguema, Francisco Macias, 247–48
Nguema, Obiang, 131, 248, 382
Nicaragua, 236
Nigeria, 5, 86, 87, 94, 123–29, 336, 383
9/11. *See* United States of America
Nitish Kumar, 155
Nixon, Richard Milhous, 129, 239, 246, 288
Nkrumah, Kwame, 132, 388
no-bid contracts to American companies, Iraq, 95, 96–97
Non-aligned movement (NAM), 389
Norilisk Nickel, a Russian company, 108
Nortel, 323
North Africa, 3, 13–17
North Atlantic Treaty Organization (NATO), 238; bombings of Yugoslavia (1995–96 and 1999), 53
North Korea confrontation, South Korea, 279
North Korea, 48, 86, 238
North West Frontier Province (NWFP), Pakistan, 61, 69, 73, 374, 380
Northern Areas, Pakistan, 73
North–South Highway, 344
Novikov, Sergey, 115
nuclear programme; Israel, 320; Pakistan, 64
nuclear tests blast; Pakistan, 366

Obama, Barack, 37–38, 45, 236, 246
Obasanjo Farms, 127
Obasanjo, General, 124, 125, 127
Obshina, 105
Occupied Palestinian Territory, 37

offshore banking and money laundering, Russia, 114
oil industry, oil resources, 240, 369; Abu Dhabi, 257; Arabs, 244; Equatorial Guinea, 248; Iran, 200, 206; Islamic states, 175; Malaysia, 336, 346; Nigeria, 123–29; Russia, 119–20; Saudi Arabia, 166
oil prices, 34–35, 121, 124, 209, 320, 370, 375
oil revenues: Dubai, 305, 308; Equatorial Guinea, 382; United Arab Emirates, 307
oil shocks, Israel, 320
Oil-for-Food programme (OFF), 92, 94–95
Okulov, Valery, 104
oligarchs and the mafia in Russia, 101–21
Olympic Games, Beijing, 145
Omar, Mullah, 63
one-child policy, China, 256, 290
Ong Eng Guan, 260
Opium Wars, China, 242
Organization of the Petroleum Exporting Countries (OPEC), 25, 48, 239
organized crime: Pakistan, 369; Russia, 110, 119, 316
Osama bin Laden, 15, 46, 65, 384
Ottoman Empire, 182, 388
outsourcing, India, 352, 362

Pakistan, 62–71, 94, 165, 168–69, 170 178–79, 217, 226, 231, 249, 252, 253; relations with America, 250;—pro-US regime, 63;—partnership in Afghan War against USSR, 366; Baloch uprising in the West, 71; cross-border terrorism, 74; Dual Policy, 66; failed or failing state, 365–81; India, three wars, 60, 71, 83;—(1947–48), 73;—(1965), 71, 73–74;—(1971), 74; international factors, 366; Multi-Fibre Agreement, 370; National Reconciliation Ordinance (NRO), 367; partition (1971), 60, 72–73, 258; People's Party (PPP), 368, 371; prisoners of war (POWs), 62; Provisional Constitutional Order (PCO), 367

Palestine, 33, 35, 36, 37–38, 93, 165, 317

Palestine Liberation Organization (PLO), 93, 320

Palestinian Intifadas, 33; Second, 319

Palin, Sarah, 229

Palm Islands, Dubai, 254, 301, 309, 310

paper pulp scandal, India, 151

Park Chung Hee, 175, 251, 269, 271–75, 270, 277–79, 384, 389

Parliament of India, terrorists' attack, 74

partition of Indian subcontinent, 60, 73, 80, 192

Pasha, Mahmoud an-Nukrashi, 14

Pasha, Syed Husain, 177

Pashtuns, 73

Pathak, Lakhubhai, 151, 152

Paul, Ron, 239–41

Pawar, Sharad, 148

Peng Dehuai, 282, 284

per capita income; Botswana, 328;

China, 291; Equatorial Guinea, 248; India, 251; Israel, 33, 315, 316; Pakistan, 251; Singapore, 259; South Korea, 269

Peres Centre for Peace, 320

Perestroika, 101

Peres, Shimon, 32, 317, 319, 320

Perjawa Steel, 345

Perle, Richard, 45

Pertamina, 137

Peru, 168, 236

Petronas (Petroliam Nasional Berhad), 346–47

Phalangist paramilitary forces, 36

Phibun, Plaek, 213

Philippines, 94, 135–37, 165, 168, 236, 245, 270; claims to Sabah, 335

physical infrastructure, Malaysia, 343

Pilger, John, 44, 49, 172

Pinochet, Augusto, 166

Plato, 202

Pohang Iron and Steel Company (POSCO), 274

police, failure, India, 352

policy and pragmatism, 173

Polisario Front and Morocco, Western Sahara War (1975–1991), 30–31

politics, 168; Abu Dhabi, 302; Australia, 256; China, 294, 296; India, 228–31, 351, 354–60, 362–63; Israel, 317; Malaysia, 186, 187, 339, 341, 343; Pakistan, 165, 249, 250, 366; Singapore, 259; Thailand, 213, 214, 217–18, 220

Politkovskaya, Anna, 116

population, 249, 256–58; Botswana,
    257; China, 256, 290; India, 256;
    Israel, 256–57, 315; Pakistan,
    258; politics in North Korea and
    South Korea, 257; Thailand, 213;
    United States, 256
portfolio investment, 244; India,
    254; Malaysia, 354; Pakistan,
    371–72, 378
Portugal, 232
Potanin, Vladimir, 104, 108
Potocari Memorial Cemetery, 54
poverty, 245, 253, 256, 265; India,
    155, 225, 352, 354, 364;
    Botswana, 330, 333; Equatorial
    Guinea, 248; Ethiopia, 29; Iraq,
    47, 91–92, 100; Israel, 322;
    Malaysia, 337, 338, 345; Mali,
    180; Nigeria, 123–24; Pakistan,
    179, 258, 366, 369, 375;
    Philippines, 137; Russia, 102;
    Singapore, 259; Zaire, 130
power crisis: Pakistan, 371
power politics, 34
Power Purchase Agreements
    (PPAs), 363
Prabhakaran, Vellupillai, 83
Prem Tinsulanonda, 213, 220
Premadasa, Ranasinghe, 61
Premji, Azim, 352, 361, 364
press censorship, Iran, 207
price controls and devaluation,
    Israel, 321
price rise; Iran, 210; Pakistan, 368,
    371
private banking: Singapore, 266;
    Switzerland, 87
private sector, 173; Japan, 262; South
    Korea, 253

privatization, 241; India, 354;
    Malaysia, 343; Russia, 105–08,
    111, 120, 159, 242, 247;
    Singapore, 267
Probosutedjo, half-brother of
    Suharto, 138
Profumo, John, 160
property rights and enforceability of
    contracts, 169
protection and extorting money,
    India, 83
proxy war between Saudi Arabia
    and Iran on Pakistani soil, 67
public sector employment,
    Singapore, 261
public transport system, Singapore,
    263
Putin, Vladimir, 93, 103, 111, 113–21,
    172; Washington Consensus
    policies, 390

Qasim, Abd-al Karim, 39–40, 42
Quattrocchi, Ottavio, 150
quota system: India 170; Pakistan,
    370
Qutb, Sayyid, 14; manifesto
    'Milestones', 14

Rabri Devi, 154
racist extremism, South Africa, 385
Radhi al Radhi, 98, 99–100, 129
Radisson Hotel, 111
Rafsanjani, 202–03, 204, 205, 206,
    208, 209–11, 214, 217
Rahman, Sheikh Mujibur, 61, 75
Rahman, Tunku Abdul, 336
Rahman, Ziaur, 61
Raj Narain, 148–49
Raja, Andimuthu, 148, 158–59

Rajai, Mohammad Ali, 206

Ramachandran, M.G., 156, 228

Ramaphosa, Cyril, 196

Ramon, Haim, 322

Rao, N.T. Rama, 228

Rao, P.V. Narasimha, 78, 147, 150–52, 353

Rashid, Maktoum sheikh, 8, 251, 301–05, 307–08, 311, 389

Rashtriya Swayamsevak Sangh (RSS), India 75

Rathore, S.P.S., 224–25

Rawlings, Jerry, 132, 133

Raza, Salim, 372

Razak, Abdul, 337

Razaleigh, 341, 343

Raznatovic, Zeljko, 55

Reagan, Ronald, 129

Red Corridor (Jharkhand, Chhattisgarh, Madhya Pradesh, Bihar, Andhra Pradesh, West Bengal and Orissa), 80

red directors, Russia, 105–08

Red Fort, terrorists' attack, 66

red mafia, Russia, 104, 105

Red Mosque siege, Islamabad, 63

red shirts, 190

Red Star football club, Yugoslavia, 55

reform process: Iran, 207; Russia, 110, 121

regional conflicts, 34

Reliance group, 358–59

religious conflicts, India, 75, 84

religious fundamentalism: Turkey, 184

reserve currency, dollar's role, 6, 48, 237, 239

Ribadu, Nuhu, 127–29

Rice, Condoleezza, 160, 166

rich and poor disparity, South Korea, 273

Rich, Marc, 125

Riggs Bank, Washington, 249

Robben Island, 385; prison, 195, 199, 385

Roh Moo-hyun, 269–70, 279

Roh Tae Woo, 175, 269, 277, 279

Romanian Labour Party, 94

Roosevelt, Franklin Delano, 246

Rossiya Bank, 118

Rosukrenergo, 110, 119

Rove Karl, 45

rule of law, 5, 10, 168, 169, 232; Botswana, 329; India, 75, 79, 228, 233; Iran, 207, 210; ousted in Iraq, 92; Malaysia, 343; Pakistan, 376, 381; South Africa, 192; Zaire, replaced with fear and patronage, 130

Rumailia oil field, Iraq, 42

Rumsfeld, Donald, 45, 49, 97

Russia (USSR), 9, 10, 26, 48, 62, 95, 131, 136, 159, 168, 169, 174, 236, 243, 257, 285, 288, 353, 390; Association for Solidarity, 93; Communist Party, 93, 105, 159; Kremlin, the oligarchs and the mafia, 101–21; support to Ethiopia, 31; largest beneficiary of Saddams largesse, 92–93; Liberal Democratic Party, 93; National Democratic Party, 93; Orthodox Church, 93; Peace and Unity Party, 93; Second October Revolution, 113; war with Afghanistan, 65

Russneft, 93

Sabah, 335

Sabra and Shatila massacres, 36, 322

Sadat, Anwar El, 34; assassination, 14

Saddam Hussein, 32, 39, 62, 201, 241; three wars, 39–50; overthrown by United States, 44

Saeed, Hafiz, 66

Sáez, Irena, 229

Salleh, 342

Samhak distillery, South Korea, 275

Sammarae, Aiham Al, 97–98

Samsung, 271, 273–75, 346

Sankoh, Foday, 20

Santos, Jose Eduardo Dos, 23–24

Sarawak, 335, 347; Japanese invasion, 347

Sarkozy, Nicholas, 330

Saudi Arabia, 64, 94, 121, 166, 175, 260, 315

SAVAK, 40, 164, 201

Savimbi, Jonas Malheiro, 24, 25

science and technology pool, Israel, 323

Scitex, Isreal, 323

Sechin, 118

sectarian killings, the kidnappings, 63

Sen, Amartya, 226

Sephardim (Mizrahi), 317

Serb nationalism 52–53

Sexwale, Tony, 196

Shaalan, Hazem, 98

Shah of Iran, 40, 164, 200–01, 202, 203, 204

Shah, Reza of Iran, 388

Shaibani, Mohammed al-, 312

Shaik, Schabir, 198

Shaikh, Hafis, 372

Shakespeare, William, 382

Shakur, Tupac, 21

Shamir, Yitzhak, 32

Shariatmadarai, Ayatollah, 202, 203

Sharif, Nawaz, 67, 167, 366, 375

Sharif, Shahbaz, 67, 167

Sharon, Ariel, 36, 322

Sharpville massacre, 193

Shastri, Lal Bahadur, 74, 147

Shaw, George Bernard, 163

Shchekochikhin, Yuri, 115

Sheba, 26–27

Sher Shah Suri, 153

Sherpao, Hayat, 61

Shias, 45, 50, 63, 67, 168; Kurd alliance, 50

Shin Corp, Thailand, 215–16, 220

Shiv Sena, 75

shura (consultation), 177

Shvartsman, Oleg, 120

Siam Cement, Thailand, 216

Siam Commercial Bank; Thailand, 216

Sibneft, Russia, 118

Sibur, Russian petrochemical company, 119

Sick massacre, Delhi, 77

Sidanco, 93

Sidanko, the Siberian oil company, 108

Siegel, Bugsy, 316

Siegle, 165

Siemens, 87

Sierra Leone, 330, 336; Revolutionary United Front (RUF), 20

Sigit, son of suharto, 138

Sikhs, 84; nationalism, 76–77, 80

Sikkim, 81; Indo-China dispute over, 72

Sinai, 38

Sinatra, Frank, 344

Sind language riots, 62

Singapore, 169–70, 249, 251, 253, 254, 268, 271, 292, 302, 304, 307, 335–36, 338–39, 389; Central Provident Fund (CPF), 263–64; Economic Development Board (EDB), 264; Graduate Mother Scheme, 266; Housing Development Board (HDB), 261–62, 264; Industrial Park, Suzhou, China, 266; no corruption, no democracy, 259–67; People's Action Army (PAP), 260, 266; Port of Singapore Authority, 264

Singapore Airlines, 262–63

Singh, Ajeya, 151

Singh, Buta, 151, 152

Singh, Charan, 149

Singh, Khushwant, 227

Singh, Manmohan, 76, 77, 80, 152, 158, 230–31, 351, 352–57, 360, 383, 390

Singh, Sweety, 152

Singh, V.P., 150, 151

Singh, Zail, 76

SingTel, 262, 265

Sinha, Shatrughan, 229

Sipah-e-Sahaba (SSP), 67

Sistani, Ayatollah, 161, 202, 384

Skuratov, Yuri, 113–14

Slovakian Communist Party, 94

Slovenia, 53; War (1991), 53

Smith, Adam, 169

social justice and populism, China, 287

socialism, 13, 388; India, 354; Israel, 315–26

Sogaz, Russia, 118

solar energy systems, Israel, 318

Solntsevskaya, 105

Solomon, 26–27

Somalia, 86, 123, 236, 238, 365

Somchai Wongsawat, 221

Song Zuying, 141

Sophonpanich, 136

Soros, George, 242, 344

Soroush, Abdolkarim, 207

South Africa, 24, 169, 186, 189, 192; Customs Union (SACU), 332–3; Democratic Party, 196–97; Inkatha Freedom Party, 193–94; National Party, 193, 194, 195, 196; South Asia, 11, 169; corruption, 147–48, 168; a nuclear conflict zone, 60–84

South Korea, 136, 175, 251, 253–54, 336–37, 339; Economic Planning Board, 273; General Park and the Chaebols, 268–80

Southern Serbia conflict (2000–01), 53

Soyuzneftgaz, 93

Spain, 94, 232

Special Economic Zones (SEZs), China, 292, 293–94

SPRING, Singapore, 264

Srebrenica massacre, 54

St Kitts forgery scandal, 151–52

stability, stabilization, 241, 251–52

Staines, Graham, 76

Stalin, 51, 282, 288, 353

Stambolic, Ivan, 58

Standing Committee of the
Politburo. *See* China; Politburo
Standing Committee (PBSC)
Stanley, Jack, 125
Starovoitova, Galina, 115
State Assessment and
Administration Commission
(SASAC), china, 298
State Owned Enterprises (SOE);
china, 296; Russia, 297;
Singapore, 262; South Korea, 271
state sector monopolies, India, 354
Stevens, Siaka, 21
Stiglitz, Joseph, 241–42, 243
Stoffel, Dale, 99
Storchak, Sergei, 120
Sudan, 86, 94, 123, 238, 346, 365
Sudwikatmono, cousin of suharto,
138
Suez Canal, 13, 387
Suez War, 33, 318, 388
Suharto, General, 135–39, 181, 389,
389
suicide bombers, Pakistan, 67, 374
suicides in India, 225
Sukarno, 181, 387, 388–89
Sulaiman, Omar bin, 312
Sulayem, Sultan bin, 312
Sultan of Brunei, 150
Sultan of Johor, 340
Sultanate, 388
Sun Tzu, 391
Sunkyong, South Korea, 274
Sunnis, 50, 168
superpower politics, 23, 25, 26, 29,
235–46, 249, 279, 288, 316, 318
Surgutneftegaz, a Russian company,
108, 117
Suzman, Helen, 193, 197

Swedish Motor Corp., 332
Switzerland, 86, 94, 232, 266
Syngman Rhee, 269
Syria, 93, 238
Systema, 112–13

Tabasi, Ayatollah, 205
Tabasi, Naser, 205
Taiwan, 136, 268, 292, 339
Taj Corridor scam, 157
Taliban: regime in Afghanistan, 65;
security problems in Pakistan,
62, 63, 65, 68, 71, 80, 178, 251,
374; US war against, 67
Talleyrand, 214
Tambo, Oliver, 199
Tambon syndicate, 105
Tamil insurgency, 83
Tanjung Pelepas Port, Malaysia, 344
Tanzania, 168
Tareen, Shaukat, 372
Taseer, Salman, 61
Tata Consultancy Services (TCS),
358, 361
Tata, J.R.D., 227, 357
Tata, Ratan, 357, 358, 360
Tatas, 356–58
Tatiana, 114
Tatum, Paul, 111
tax evasion: China, 143; Pakistan,
369; Thailand, 218–19; United
States, 125
Tayer, Ahmed Humaid al-, 312
Taylor, Charles, 18–21
Taylor, Elizabeth, 150, 327
Teh Cheang Wan, 261
Tehrik-i-Taliban Pakistan, (TTP),
68
Tejaphaibul, 136

telecom sector: India, reforms, 362; Israel, 324; Thailand, 215

Telgi scam, 157

Temasek Holdings, Singapore, 220, 262, 265

Tepsurgayev, Adam

Teresa, Mother, 161, 227, 230

terrorism and violence; Iraq, 91; Israel, 316; Pakistan, 258

Teva, 324

Thackeray, Bal, 75

Thailand, 94, 136, 168, 189, 190, 236; collapse of governments, 136; the King, Thaksin and General T. Prem, 212–23; People's Power Party (PPP), 221; Pheu Thai Party (PT), 222; Privy Council, 212, 220; Telecommunications Organization of Thailand (TOT), 215; Thai Rak Thai (TRT) party, 214, 217, 220;

Thaksin Shinawatra, 138, 212–23; total electoral dominance, 219

Thaksin, 190

Thanong, 216

Thatcher, Mark, 248

Thomson, French company, 198

Tiananmen Square incident (1989), 142, 290, 294–95

Tibet: conquered by China, 72; Indo-China dispute over, 72

Timchenko, Gennady, 117–18, 119

Timor, 138

Titiek, 137

Tito, Josip Broz, 51, 52, 237, 388

Togo, 168

Tolbert, William, 19

Tommy, son of suharto, 138

Tour, Toumani, 180

tourism industry: Botswana, 332; Dubai, 309; Israel, 318

Town and Village Enterprises (TVE), china, 291, 297

trade deficit, 238; China, 242; Pakistan, 251, 369, 371; United States, 239

trade surplus, China, 254

Transcorp, Nigeria, 127

Transparency International (TI), 25, 86, 87, 120, 125, 147–48, 193, 226, 231, 279, 298, 366; Corruption Perception Indexes, 123, 135, 140, 148, 231

Tripura, princely state, 81, 82

True Whig party, 18

Truth and Reconciliation Commission (TRC), 192

Tun Hussein Onn, 337

Tunku, 336, 337

Turkey, 94, 178, 201, 389; Islamic democracy, 182–85; Justice and Development Party (AKP), 184, 185; Liberal Republican party, 184; Republic People's Party, 184; Shaikh Said Rebellion, 184; War of Independence, 182

Turkmenistan, 86, 383

Tutsis, genocide in Rwanda, 31

Tutu, Archbishop, 192

Tutut, daughter of Suharta, 137

2G spectrum scam, 158

Uganda, 123, 383

Ukraine Social Democratic Party, 93

unemployment, 7; corruption and, 88; in Algeria, 15, 16; Botswana, 330, 333; China, 296, 299; India,

226; in Indonesia, 182; Iran, 210; in Iraq, 100; in Israel, 35, 321; in Liberia, 20; Malaysia, 349; in Pakistan, 179, 258, 368, 371; in Singapore, 259, 262; South Korea, 278; in United States, 240, 244, 245; in Zaire, 130

United Arab Emirates (UAE), 94, 175, 239, 253, 254, 257, 302, 313; Company Law, 307

United Energy Systems (UES), 106, 107

United Kingdom, 86

United Liberation Front of Assam (ULFA), 82–83

United Nations (UN), 20, 29, 30, 36, 37, 42, 54, 55, 57, 73–74, 92, 94, 123, 133, 209, 318; Security Council (UNSC), 94; University, 168

United States of America (USA), 9, 10, 24, 25, 26, 46, 66, 68, 86, 166, 180, 229, 255, 316; aid to Pakistan, 64, 371; China, relations, 288; Corrupt Practices Act, 87; declaration of Independence, 36, 235; economic sanctions on Iran, 303; Eritrea, rights in, 30; Ethiopia, support to, 30; global interventions, 236; and Gulf war, 42–43; and Iran-Iraq war, 39–43; Israel, support to, 34–35; military expenditure, 237; military, inhuman incidents on prisoners of war, 49; Saddam Hussein, support to/supplied chemical weapons to him, 39–42; South Korea, alliance/ financial aid to, 270, 279;

superpower, 235–46; terrorists' attack on World Trade Center (WTC), 10, 15, 35, 47, 65, 74, 178, 186, 238, 367, 372; USSR, proxy war, 62; use of weapons of mass destruction, 236; war Policy, 45; War against Afghanistan, 10, 186, 238; war against Iraq, 10, 48–49, 95, 186, 238; War on Terrorism, 10, 35, 237

untouchables, 100

Uzbekistan, 86, 238, 382

Vahane, Bhau, 352

Vajpayee, Atal Bihari, 79, 147, 149, 353, 355

Vekselberg, 104

Venezuela, 48, 236, 238, 275

Verwoerd, H.F., 193

Vietnam, 94, 236, 272, 279, 386; reunification, 386

Volcker, Paul, 94

vote-rigging, India, 232

VSNL (Videsh Sanchar Nigam Limited), 358

Vukovar hospital massacre, 56

Vukovic, Goran, 55

Vyakhirev, 109, 110

Wahabi group, 66

Wahid, 181

Wal-Mart, 292–93, 346, 359

Wan Li, 290–91

Wang Jianrui, 146

Wang Shouye, 141, 146

war crimes, 52

war economy: Algeria, 17; Israel, 319

War of Independence: Croatia, 53; Israel, 33; Turkey, 182

Washington, George, 245, 386
Weinstein, 165
Weizman, Ezer, 322
Welayat-e-Faqih, 201, 203
Wempel, Joseph, 99
Wen Jiabao, 142
West Bank, 38
West Side Boys (West Side Niggaz), 21
Western Sahara War (1975–1991), 30–31
Wharton, 265
Wikileaks, 172
Wikipedia, 375–76
Williams, Ruth, 327, 328
Wilson, Charlie, 178
Winer, Jonathon, 316
Wipro (Western India Pine Refined Oil), 361
Witanhurst, 112
Wolfowitz, Paul, 45, 160
Wolpert, Stanley, 161
Women, Botswana, 333
World Bank, 128, 160, 164, 166, 232, 241, 243, 274, 331, 333; globalization policies, 241
World Bank, 274, 333
World Economic Forum, 128
World Trade Organization (WTO), 180, 241, 243; China's entry, 296
World War I, 182, 388
World War II, 4, 9–10, 29, 51, 52, 74, 239, 347
Wrong, Michela, 130

Xhosas, 199
Xu Zong-Heng, 146

Yadav, Akku, 351–52
Yadav, Lalu Prasad, 148, 151, 153–55
Yadav, Mulayam Singh, 148
Yahya Khan, General, 75
Yaser, son of Rafsanjani, 205
Yeddyurappa, B.S., 148
'Yellow Water', Chagai, Pakistan, 70
Yeltsin, Boris, 101–02, 104, 107, 109, 111, 113–15, 117, 120–21, 390
Yemen, 94, 236
Yevtushenkov, Vladimir, 112–13
Yingluck Shinawatra, 222
Yom Kippur War (1973), 33, 319, 320
Yudhoyono, Susilo Bambang, 181, 182
Yugoslavia, 165, 236; Left Party, 94; Socialist Party, 94; wars, 4, 51–59; Yugoslav People's Army (JNA), 53
Yukos, a Russian oil company, 93, 109
Yushchenko, Victor, 115
Yushenkov, Sergei, 115
Yutar, Percy, 192

Zaibatsu, 253, 262, 272
Zainudin, Daim, 343–44, 390
Zaire (Congo Democratic Republic), 123, 129–31, 365
al-Zaiydi, Muntadhar, 172
Zakaria, Fareed, 164
Zang Xueliang, 288
Zardari, Asif Ali, 67, 94, 174, 176, 179, 199, 365, 368, 371–72, 375–77, 380

al-Zawahiri, Ayman, 15
Zayed bin Sultan al Nahyan, Sheikh
    of Abu Dhabi, 8, 302, 307, 389
Zeng Quinhong, 145
Zhang Yike, 146
Zhao Ziyang, 282, 290–91, 296, 390
Zheng Ziaoyu, 141
Zhirinovsky, Vladimir, 93
Zhou En-lai, 251, 259, 282–83, 288–
    89, 294, 384
Zhu De, 282, 289, 290
Zhu Rongji, 282, 296, 298–99, 390

Ziauddin, M., 371
Zia-ul-Haq, 64, 171, 178, 366;
    assassination, 61, 65, 178
Zimbabwe, 123, 131, 165, 174, 197,
    365, 382
Zionism, Israel, 14, 32, 317
ZNGG, 106
Zulus, 199, 385
Zuma, Jacob, 198–99